DEVELOPING AND MANAGING HEALTH/FITNESS FACILITIES

Robert W. Patton
University of North Texas

William F. Grantham
Little Rock Athletic Club

Richard F. Gerson
Gerson, Goodson, Inc.

Larry R. Gettman
National Health Enhancement Systems, Inc.

Human Kinetics Books
Champaign, Illinois

Library of Congress Cataloging-in-Publication Data

Developing and managing health/fitness facilities / Robert W. Patton
. . . [et al].
    p.   cm.
  Includes index.
  ISBN 0-87322-203-2
  1. Physical fitness centers--Management.   2. Physical fitness
centers--United States--Management.   3. Health facilities--United
States--Administration.   I. Patton, Robert W.
GV428.5.D47 1989
338.7'616137'097--dc19   88-13428
                                                 CIP

Developmental Editor: Sue Wilmoth, PhD
Production Director: Ernie Noa
Copy Editor: Claire Mount
Assistant Editor: Holly Gilly
Typesetter: Brad Colson
Text Design: Keith Blomberg
Text Layout: Kimberlie Henris
Cover Design: Jack Davis
Printed By: R.R. Donnelly & Sons Company

ISBN: 0-87322-203-2

Printed in the United States of America

10 9 8 7 6 5 4 3 2 1

Human Kinetics Books
A Division of Human Kinetics Publishers, Inc.
Box 5076, Champaign, IL 61820
1-800-DIAL-HKP
1-800-334-3665 (in Illinois)

Contents

Preface

Few would question that there is a fitness boom going on in America. According to a survey released last year by a New York City marketing-consulting firm, Americans spent $17.4 billion pursuing health and fitness. New products are being introduced daily to satisfy consumer demands. New journals and books are hitting the marketplace at record levels. A significant percentage of the adult population is now engaging regularly in planned exercise. Many of these fitness enthusiasts are members of clubs or organizations that have facilities and equipment for participating in a wide variety of fitness and sports activities.

Health/fitness professionals are now being trained through both preservice means, such as colleges and graduate schools, and in-service means, such as on-the-job management training offered by many organizations. A number of texts are available to assist the aspiring professional in the implementation of health/fitness programs in such areas as nutrition, exercise, weight control, substance-abuse control, and stress management. However, very few resources are available to the health/fitness professional with regard to designing, operating, and managing the facilities in which the programming occurs.

Those facility design books that are available are usually technical references for architects or practical references for those interested in public school gymnasium design and construction. None of these has attempted to assist the professional practitioner in planning, designing, and developing health/fitness facilities. Moreover, there is no single resource that is dedicated to managing the health/fitness business in the many settings in which it is found. We have attempted to do all of the above in a single book that can be used both as a college text for professional preparation programs and as a reference book for the practitioner in the health/fitness field. The book is written by individuals with both academic and practical backgrounds who will address the needs of both the aspiring student and the practitioner.

Part I compares the various settings in which health/fitness programs are found. Distinctions in emphasis of generic functions such as promotional, programming, and management activities are portrayed in commercial, corporate, hospital, and community settings. The major distinctions are the target population and the marketing research methods that determine the feasibility of a given program. Once the project is found to be feasible, the program concept is developed further by defining such parameters as membership, facility, program, personnel, and cost-benefit. Finally, the project is presented to the investor(s), owners, or corporate chief executive officers who will pass judgments on the worth of the project proposal.

Part II begins with the selection of appropriate consultants who assist in the planning and design of a new facility, remodeling an existing structure, or selecting a community-based facility as the future site for the programming. The facility planning and construction processes require detailed solutions to many problems. A discussion of these factors and their interactions is presented.

Part III begins with staff selection and development. Details for a generic approach to program planning and development that is appropriate in any setting are provided. The types of equipment to be selected and cost, purpose, space utilization, durability, versatility, safety, appearance, user appeal, and legal liability are discussed. Practical con-

siderations such as maintenance are also discussed. Finally, the marketing process is discussed to complete the gearing-up phase and launch the program on a successful course of action.

Part IV discusses the crucial issues that keep a program fiscally fit and the membership enthusiastically involved. These issues include operations, management, documentation procedures, and financial considerations. This section explains how to run a health/fitness program from a very practical and proven approach. Issues and trends confronting the professional practitioner are also presented to give you some broader perspectives of the health/fitness field.

The appendixes at the end of several of the chapters provide a wealth of resources that should prove helpful in running a program, including information on equipment manufacturers, professional organizations, and periodical publications. These resources should assist you at any stage of facility development.

Acknowledgments

We want to thank everyone who taught us what we know about health/fitness facilities, most notably Thomas Wills for his expertise in space planning. We also wish to thank our graduate students and employees who contributed in many ways to development of the book. Particularly significant were Susie Kania, who was involved throughout as an editorial consultant and assisted in chapter development; and Tony Ezell, Terry Widmer, and Sharon Harding, who contributed to specific chapter development.

Bill Baun, John McCarthy, Bill Day, and Thomas Wills provided significant input and feedback, and Sue Wilmoth at Human Kinetics Publishers provided significant guidance in the development of the book. To you all, we say thanks.

A special thanks is in order to the significant women in our lives who have read manuscripts, suffered unintended neglect, and carried on without us all too often. Thanks Elisa, Robbie, and Sharon for being so special.

About the Authors

ROBERT W. PATTON

Robert W. Patton is a professor of physical education and biology at the University of North Texas in Denton, Texas, where he has been instrumental in developing the health/fitness management graduate program, one of the largest of its kind in the nation. Dr. Patton is an associate editor for three journals, is a Fellow in three professional societies, and has consulted with over 50 agencies in developing health/fitness programs. He is also vice president of Consulting Services of Healthscape, Inc., a company based in Orlando, Florida, that designs, staffs, and manages health/fitness facilities throughout the U.S. He has published numerous articles and is writing his third fitness-related book. Dr. Patton received his bachelor's and master's degrees from the University of Florida and his PhD from Florida State University. He is a fitness enthusiast who has run 30 marathons.

WILLIAM C. GRANTHAM

William C. Grantham recently assumed the responsibilities of manager of the new Little Rock Athletic Club in Little Rock, Arkansas. He was previously director for 12 years of the Aerobics Activity Center in Dallas, Texas, where he supervised all aspects of the 3,000-member health/fitness club. As a member of the Aerobics Center Consultative Division, a group of health/fitness authorities from across the nation, he has counseled more than 20 major clients, including hospital wellness programs and commercial, corporate, and community ventures. He has published a variety of articles in professional and lay journals and has lectured extensively. He holds a BS in physical education from the University of Nebraska and an MS in physical education from North Texas State University. His daily exercise routine combines jogging, weight training, racquetball or volleyball, and cycling. He also enjoys hiking and skiing.

RICHARD F. GERSON

Richard F. Gerson is president of Gerson, Goodson, Inc., a multifaceted professional services marketing, management, and public relations firm. He has published numerous health/fitness-related articles in the professional and popular press, and his fourth book, *Marketing Health/Fitness Services* (Human Kinetics Publishers, Champaign, Illinois), will soon be released. He also leads workshops, seminars, and lectures on the topic of marketing. Dr. Gerson received his PhD from Florida State University in 1978. He and his family include fitness activities as an integral part of their lifestyle.

LARRY R. GETTMAN

Larry R. Gettman is vice president of research and development for National Health Enhancement Systems in Phoenix, Arizona. He specializes in designing health screening assessments, fitness tests, medical exams, health education reports, and health promotion products for hospitals, physicians, health care professionals, and corporations. During the past 20 years, Dr. Gettman has gained professional experience in the clinical, community, corporate, and commercial settings of the health/fitness industry. He has served as director of corporate fitness programs for Mesa Petroleum Co. in Amarillo, Texas, and executive director of the Institute for Aerobics Research in Dallas, Texas. In 1986 he received in Fulbright scholarship to southeast Asia in the field of health and fitness. Dr. Gettman serves on the Preventive and Rehabilitative Exercise Program Committee of the American College of Sports Medicine. He received his BA from Colorado State College, his MS from the University of Illinois, and his PhD from Kent State University. He is active in skiing, racquetball, tennis, cycling, and jogging.

Getting Started

Part I is intended to ease your start in the health/fitness business, especially if you want to develop, build, and manage a fitness facility. The section begins by discussing the various settings in which programs are found, and grouping them into corporate, commercial, clinical, and community environments. This recognition that health/fitness programs occur in a variety of contexts and environments is key. Certain activities, such as promotion, programming, and management tasks, occur regardless of the environment. But other features, such as specific exercise programs, are shaped according to the environment; for example, exercise programs in a cardiac rehabilitation unit would differ greatly from those in an aerobics studio. The program objectives and the user population also influence the manifestation of the program and the facility being developed. This clarification of program objectives and user population becomes critical in *concept development*.

Through concept development, the process of defining the program objectives and user population, you produce a document to be given to decision makers such as chief executive officers in corporations or commercial loan officers in banks. Here, too, the nature of the document takes on a certain orientation depending on the environment of your facility. However, the processes for all environments have many similarities, and we discuss them to help make these start-up considerations less overwhelming.

CHAPTER 1

Differing Needs of Health/Fitness Settings

Perhaps the best way to begin a book on health/fitness facility development and management is to look at the various settings in which these facilities are found and to examine some of the unique features of each. In this chapter, we will examine and contrast the health/fitness facilities in the various settings and illustrate how the different emphases in functional programming areas will influence the type of facility that should be planned and the type of program that should be implemented. We will explore areas that tend to modify programs, such as objectives and participants. In addition, we will provide an overview of the organizational strategies in each setting, as well as a comparison of facilities in the various settings. The settings can be categorized as follows: commercial, corporate, and community. Each of these plays an important role in the growth of the health/fitness movement.

TRENDS IN THE HEALTH/FITNESS MOVEMENT

The magnitude of the health/fitness movement can be illustrated with the following developments. First, according to Steve Tammaro, National Account Executive for Club Industry, Inc., there are over 33,000 health/fitness facilities in the United States delivering various types of programs. A recent survey by the National Heart, Lung, and Blood Institute has indicated that over 31% of the nation's companies with more than 100 employees now provide some form of exercise or wellness program (Tammaro, personal communication, July, 1985). Approximately 90% of these employee programs are scheduled or underwritten by the company, and many of these companies have their own worksite facilities (Patton, Corry, Gettman, & Graf, 1986). Next, there are over 2,000 community YMCA programs and 275 Jewish Community Centers providing health/fitness services to individual, family, and corporate members. There is also a recent trend for governmental agencies to offer health/fitness programs and facilities to employees at local, state, and federal levels. Hospitals are rapidly expanding the concept of health care to include health promotion as well as disease management. In addition, many hospital-based wellness centers are being planned and constructed for future demands. According to a survey of 450 hospital administrators (Jense & Miklovic, 1985), hospitals are experiencing a tremendous growth in health and wellness programs. A summary of the planned increases appears in Figure 1.1. Moreover, the Readex Corporation recently conducted a survey of hospitals and medical centers. Seventy-one percent of the respondents plan to offer a fitness center as part of their health promotion programs (*Athletic Business*, 1987).

In addition, a number of factors in our culture have influenced major trends in facility design and function, including the movement away from a single-purpose club (e.g., racquetball center) to a multipurpose athletic/

fitness/social club (see Figure 1.2), the movement from indoor-only to four-season indoor/outdoor clubs, the movement from an annual dues plus pay-as-you-play pricing system to an initiation fee plus monthly dues system, and the changing role of the health care delivery system.

Despite these general trends and the growth in the number of clubs, no two facilities and programs are exactly alike. Each facility differs according to management philosophy and style, personnel, and so forth. It is possible to distinguish health/

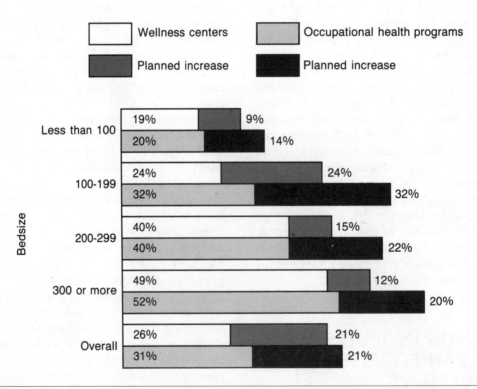

Figure 1.1. Planned increases in occupational health and wellness programs offerings over the next 12 months. *Note.* From "Occupational Health, Wellness Offerings Gaining Popularity Among Employees" by J. Jense and N. Miklovic, 1985, *Modern Healthcare*, Dec., p. 51. Copyright 1985 by *Modern Healthcare*. Reprinted by permission.

fitness facilities according to their particular settings: corporate, commercial, and community. Each of these settings requires distinct program planning and delivery.

Consequently, each program has a unique set of needs to accommodate, including the setting in which the program is placed; the target population being served; and the outside influences such as owner preference, industry trends, and local competition. Few architects and space planners are trained and experienced enough to attend to the subtle differences in the facility needs of a given setting, and few professional preparation programs train personnel adequately for careers in the health/fitness industry. This book is an attempt to help close some of these gaps in knowledge.

FUNCTIONAL PROGRAMMING AREAS

The major functional programming areas fall under the categories of (a) promotion, (b) program, and (c) management. Promotional activities include advertising, marketing, public relations, membership drives, and other activities that create an attractive image for the program. Programming activities include fitness and nutrition testing and prescription, exercise classes, seminars, and workshops. Management activities include supervision, budgeting, office operations, insurance, payroll, scheduling, and maintenance. All three of these generic functions must take place in any health/fitness center.

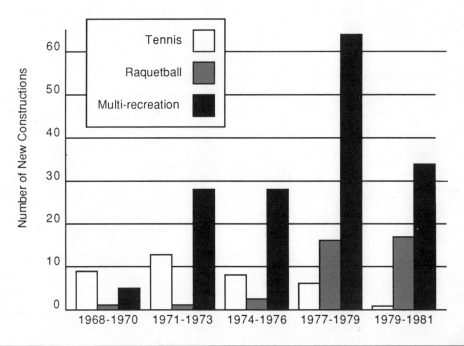

Figure 1.2. New construction of tennis, racquetball, and multirecreation facilities from 1968 to 1981. *Note.* From "Industry Data Survey" by the International Racquet Sports Association, 1984, Brookline, MA: IRSA. Copyright 1984 by International Racquet Sports Association. Reprinted by permission.

However, the relative emphasis of each of these functions will differ according to the diverse settings in which the programs are found.

Corporate Programs

Corporations have not been concerned in the past with external promotion of their programs but have focused their promotional energies on programming for their employees. Corporate programs are characterized by facility- and personnel-intensive features that provide the most effective programming experiences possible for the employees and optimize their adherence to the program. Table 1.1 illustrates the programming emphases of an incidental sample of corporate health/fitness programs during 1987.

Commercial Programs

Commercial health clubs, in contrast, have promoted their facilities by making year-round marketing efforts, launching membership drives, and selling memberships in advance of opening their facilities. These clubs have been criticized in the past for such activities because they have neglected choosing well-trained personnel and quality programming for the members. Fortunately, there is a definite trend toward more program and personnel emphasis in the commercial sector. It seems that new and bright, shiny equipment is no longer a distinguishing factor among commercial clubs—they all have this feature. Quality programs and professionally trained personnel are now necessary to attract the increasingly knowledgeable and demanding health/fitness member. Management activities are the benchmark of the

Table 1.1 Selected Corporate Health/Fitness Program Components[1]

Company	Screening and evaluation	Exercise classes	Nutrition and weight control	Smoking cessation	Stress management	Health education
Campbell Soup	+	+	+	+	+	+
Control data	+	+	+	+	+	+
Forney Engineering	−	+	+	−	−	−
Hudson-Shatz	−	+	−	−	−	−
IBM	+	+	+	+	+	+
Johnson & Johnson	+	+	+	+	−	+
Kimberly-Clark	+	+	+	+	−	+
Mesa Petroleum	+	+	+	+	−	+
Pepsico	+	+	+	+	+	+
Tenneco	+	+	+	+	−	+
Texas Instruments	−	+	−	−	−	+
Xerox	+	+	+	+	+	+

[1]+ = present; − = not present.

commercial setting. These programs must orchestrate the maximizing of revenues and minimizing of expenses at all times to maintain positive cash flow and desirable balance sheets. To accomplish this, management activities must be foremost in the minds of decision makers and action takers, weighing in balance the cost-effectiveness of their decisions and actions.

Community Programs

Community health/fitness program is a catch-all name to describe the remainder of the programs, including hospital-based wellness programs, YMCA programs, governmental programs such as parks and recreation centers, and college and university programs. These programs, as a whole, have tended to emphasize promotion, program, and management with equal weight. For example, the well-established Y programs are based on a formula that works for them. Y administrators have come to recognize that, although marketing is very important, it should never outweigh the importance of the program that

is being delivered. In addition to this, management training is an integral part of personnel development in the Y program.

The community-based hospital wellness program is the newcomer on the block. Wellness, or lifestyle, programs are designed to help businesses keep their employees well by helping to change those lifestyle habits that may increase health risks. Administrators of these programs are quick to model them after the winners, recruiting program directors from all settings to develop a well-balanced health/fitness program based on the corporate setting to accommodate the hospital's own employees; the commercial setting to generate a profit to pay for facility costs; and the community setting, which tends to focus on goodwill and community service.

Trends in Functional Programming Areas

Table 1.2 illustrates both past and present trends in emphasis regarding the promotional, programming, and management functions of the different health/fitness settings.

Table 1.2 Functional Contrasts in Health/Fitness Program Components[1]

Setting	Promotion (advertising, memberships, sales, public relations)	Program (testing, activities, scheduling)	Management (personnel, budgeting, maintenance)
Past:			
Corporate	1	3	2
Community	3	3	2
Commercial	3	1	2
Present:			
Corporate	2	3	3
Community	3	3	2
Commercial	3	2	2

[1]3 = highest emphasis; 1 = lowest emphasis.

These numerical assignments of emphasis are arbitrary and based upon empirical judgments. From the table it is clear that all three elements are important for successful programs to occur. Indeed, if the columns are added together, greater value is given to all of the functions when comparing past ratings with present ratings. Future trends in emphasis may more equally represent the three functional aspects. In the meantime, let us examine the factors that tend to modify programs.

PROGRAM MODIFIERS

Many factors influence and modify the nature and scope of a health/fitness program. The cultural trends of a heightened health consciousness and a general concern for fitness have been a boost to programs. The early baby boomers are now middle-aged, and their growing demands for fitness programs have positioned the industry in a favorable marketing situation. The concern about reducing health care costs and taking more control of one's health has influenced a general trend toward the more frequent offering of alternative programming such as nutrition, weight control, and stress management. The size of the industry itself (i.e., increased number of facilities) has led to program specialization. These are all examples of how cultural changes can influence the direction of program development. Two additional program modifiers are program objectives and target populations.

Program Objectives

The objectives of the program ultimately influence everything that goes on in a health/fitness center. If profit is the main objective,

then every program cost must be weighed in balance against the direct or indirect revenue it will generate. This is the basis of the cost-benefit analysis. For example, if the primary objective of a corporate health/fitness program is increased employee morale, then a set of different influences impinges on the decision-making processes in a program. The following sections discuss the different objectives in the corporate, commercial, and community settings.

Corporate

Because the corporation has a captive audience, its employees, it has opportunities that other facilities do not. For instance, it can supply extra support services beyond simple education and can influence a positive employee attitude by showing an interest through providing the health/fitness programs. Corporations also have access to data about employees that other facilities would not; thus more precise needs assessment, goal setting, and evaluation is possible. Some of the expected primary and secondary objectives of corporate programs are listed in Table 1.3.

Community

Many organizations and agencies serve clients in community-based settings, including voluntary health agencies (American Heart Association, American Cancer Society, YMCA, American Red Cross, etc.), schools, churches, and private social service agencies. In each of these settings, the objectives depend on the expected goals of the particular organization. Table 1.4 lists some of the expected primary and secondary objectives of health/fitness programs in community agencies.

Table 1.3 Objectives of Health/Fitness Programs in the Corporate Sector

Primary objectives (net cash value)	Secondary objectives (nonfinancial benefits)
Reduced illness	Improved morale of workers
Reduced absenteeism	Improved company image
Reduced accidents	Reduced inflation
Reduced health insurance premiums	Reduced turnover of disgruntled employees
Increased productivity, energy, and creativity of workers on a daily basis	Greater ability of employees to cope with new or otherwise stressful situations
Greater continuity of performance: reduced training of new employees to replace ill or deceased employees	Greater ability of employees to manage personal lives with consequent reduction of stress at work
Increased competitiveness of corporation	Increased employer recruitment potential
Increased profit to stockholders	Improved employee interactions

Table 1.4 Expected Outcomes of Community Health/Fitness Programs

Type of agency and programs	Primary objectives	Secondary objectives
Voluntary health organizations (health promotion)	Improve health status of clients; defeat disease	Increase volunteers, private donations, and political influence
Schools (health promotion)	Improve health status of students; fulfill legal requirements; facilitate full development of students	Improve psychological atmosphere of school to make it more conducive to learning; increase attendance; improve funding based on school attendance
Churches	Improve spiritual life	Improve ability to cope; increase membership and church attendance; improve psychological atmosphere of congregation; increase political power; help church members fulfill their religious obligations
Private social service agencies	Improve health status of clients	Increase private donations, volunteers, and attendance at center.

In addition to the previously mentioned community programs, hospital health/fitness centers and wellness programs have identified the need to provide more health education and fitness experiences as part of their delivery system. However, because there are many types of hospitals, their objectives, along with the types of health education and fitness experiences, vary greatly. A list of some primary and secondary objectives for hospital health/fitness programs is given in Table 1.5.

Commercial

Commercial, or for-profit, health/fitness enterprises have been around for many years. Since the 1980s, they have experienced explosive growth that has coincided with the recreation and wellness movement. The obvious primary objective for commercial programs is profit. Other secondary objectives dictate the establishment of quality programs and a well-trained, professional staff. Table 1.6 lists typical objectives for commercial health/fitness centers.

Target Population

The nature of the target population of the program has an immense impact on the direction a program takes in its development and operation. One of the major issues to consider is the size of the target population. A corporate employee fitness program, for example, has a finite number of individuals from which to draw. Due to this finite number, each participant becomes a precious commodity, and failure to involve any one person or to create a positive experience for this individual effectively reduces the population on which program impact can be made. The health/fitness professional in the corporate setting is acutely aware that every

experience must be positive, thus creating a very program-intensive environment.

The nearly infinite population from which commercial fitness centers draw places less of a burden on the health/fitness professional to make a positive first impression (or subsequent impressions, for that matter) on the members. Because the target population normally resides or works within 10 minutes' travel time of the facility, there is almost always someone waiting in the wings to replace a disgruntled member in the commercial setting. In fact, a previously commonplace tactic was to lure a member through payment in advance of an annual fee and a pleasant initial exposure to the facility, then to discourage continued attendance through inattention and ignorance. This tactic provided a larger membership base for any size of facility. Most of today's commercial fitness centers no longer use such marketing tactics and tend to follow the strategies of the other health/fitness settings. This is due to a variety of reasons; however, one major reason might be that the increased density of facilities in a given geographical area effectively reduces the once infinite target population to a more finite number of increasingly intelligent and discriminating consumers.

Community health/fitness facilities have a participant population made up of a diverse group of individuals from the community. The size of the target population depends to a great extent on the size of each facility and its overall objectives. For instance, hospital-based programs will have employee members as well as community members, and this will tend to complicate the direction the program will take in its development and operation.

Organizational Strategies

An important part of each health/fitness facility is its organizational structure, which

Table 1.5 Objectives for Hospital Health/Fitness Centers

Primary	Secondary
Improve compliance of patients with treatment regimens (nonprofit and for-profit, private and public community hospitals)	Create a marketing vehicle to develop goodwill within the community
Gain reasonable profit for services rendered to community and corporate worlds (community and private for-profit hospitals)	Recruit clients for the hospital (inpatient and outpatient)
Render services to the community on a cost-recovery basis (community hospitals)	Provide an entertainment device for ambulatory-care patients
Meet accreditation standards of the joint commission (all hospitals)	Improve the general health of the community as part of hospital's overall role
Provide employee health/fitness programming to reduce hospital costs and increase productivity (all hospitals)	

Table 1.6 Objectives for Commercial Health/Fitness Centers

Primary	Secondary
Obtain reasonable profit on capital invested	Encourage manageable, sustained growth on the client base, staff, and number of outlets
	Increase customer satisfaction
	Provide a safe, supervised exercise environment to reduce legal risks and meet health standards of regulatory agency
	Assure customer satisfaction by providing effective and entertaining health/fitness experiences

obviously differs across the various corporate, commercial, and community settings. Staff structures depend upon the type of organization and the purpose of the program in each particular setting.

Corporate Settings

In the corporate setting, the health/fitness staff is usually organized under the supervision of the personnel, medical, or human resources department. Occasionally, the health/fitness program only answers to the chief executive officer (CEO) or the owner of the company, but this is a rare occurrence. Various organizational strategies are illustrated in Figure 1.3.

The size of the health/fitness staff depends upon the size of the company, the number of expected participants, and the extent of the

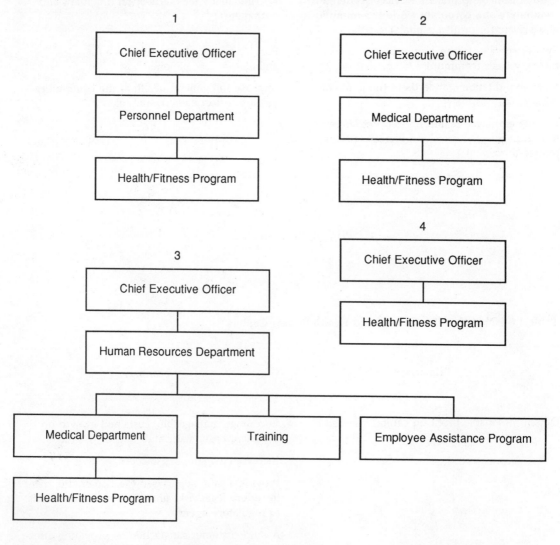

Figure 1.3 Four organization strategies in corporate settings.

company's resources. Many corporations employ their own health/fitness directors, whereas others draw these professionals from outside agencies.

In those corporations with organized health/fitness programs, medical consultation is of prime importance. Some corporations use medical consultants from the community, whereas others have their own medical departments. Two examples of staff organization, one in a corporation with a medical department and one that uses medical consultation, are shown in Figure 1.4.

Community Settings

Health/fitness staff structures in community settings vary, as they do in corporate settings, according to the type of community agency and the purpose of its service. Health/fitness professionals in social service agencies such as the American Cancer Society may include volunteer physicians, psychologists, nurses, nutritionists, administrative specialists, and health educators. Fees for these services are usually nominal.

In other community agencies, such as the YMCA, health/fitness programs are delivered to individuals and corporate organizations for moderate-to-high fees to raise money to support their social services. The health/fitness staff at YMCAs are usually college graduates with degrees in physical education, exercise physiology, or health-related areas.

Hospital health/fitness staff structure will depend upon the scope of each wellness program. For instance, if the program includes employee fitness, there will most likely be a health/fitness director on staff. However, if the program consists of wellness education without the fitness or exercise component, the hospital will probably draw upon nutritionists, physicians, psychologists, and others within the hospital staff.

Commercial Settings

As mentioned previously, a main purpose of commercial facilities is to make a profit, and health/fitness professionals deliver their programs with this goal in mind. Private health/promotion facilities usually have well-qualified physicians, psychologists, nutritionists, exercise specialists, and health educators. These professionals act as paid consultants or part-time staff members who deliver their services to corporations or individuals.

Other commercial settings, such as dance studios and health spas, vary greatly in their size, services, and , consequently, staff structure. Two important changes that have resulted from the rapid expansion and intense competition of the 1980s are hiring trained professionals and implementing quality programs. In the future these factors will determine the success or failure of commercial facilities.

Generic Practitioners' Roles

The following example should illustrate the way in which organizational strategies are determined by program setting. Table 1.7 lists some of the characteristic duties of a health/fitness practitioner (Patton et al., 1986). Compare this list to Table 1.8, which rates the relative importance placed on each role according to program setting. Note, for example, the high emphases placed on management and supervision in the corporate setting compared to their relatively low emphases in community and commercial settings. This comparison underlines the importance of the distinctions among various settings in the health/fitness industry.

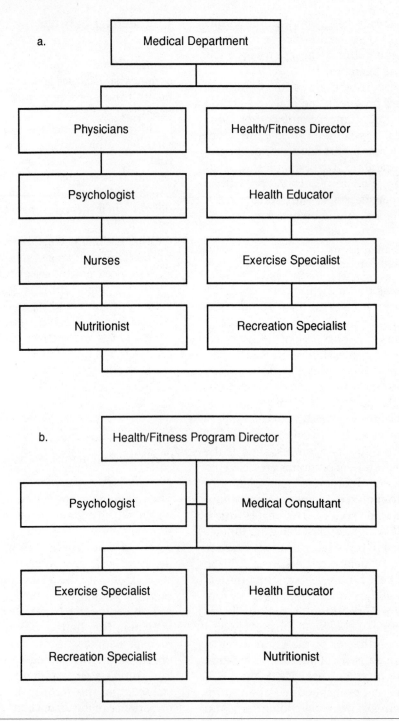

Figure 1.4 Staff organization in: (a) a corporation with a medical department; (b) a corporation that uses medical consultants.

Table 1.7 Some Characteristic Duties of the Health/Fitness Practitioner

Manager
Administer daily operation
Design program activities
Control program
Guide and direct staff
Purchase equipment
Maintain facilities
Regulate budget
Schedule activities
Communicate with staff and participants
cooperate with other departments

Planner
Assess organization needs
Establish goals for program
Design program
Organize resources
Arrange schedule

Supervisor
Hire and dismiss staff
Oversee program and staff
Coordinate staff and program
Motivate staff
Evaluate staff

Educator
Train staff
Instruct participants
Evaluate learning
Develop curricula

Exercise leader
Guide participants
Conduct classes
Use safe techniques
Provide a role model

Motivator
Give impetus to program
Persuade participants
Influence participants
Induce changes in participants
Incite action

Counselor
Advise participants
Suggest changes
Express opinions
Judge effectiveness of actions
Recommend action
Consult with participants

Promoter
Design marketing technique
Encourage participation
Use sales techniques
Advance program advantages

Assessor
Conduct participant tests
Interpret test results
Follow safe procedures

Evaluator
Design program-evaluation procedures
Perform statistical analyses
Interpret results
Analyze program trends
Convey reports to management

Note. From *Implementing Health/Fitness Programs* (p. 74) by R.W. Patton et al., 1986, Champaign, IL: Human Kinetics. Copyright 1986 by Human Kinetics. Reprinted by permission.

Table 1.8 Rank Orders of Practitioner Roles in Health/Fitness Settings[1] by Importance

Role	Corporate	Community	Commercial
Manager	5	3	2
Planner	5	5	4
Supervisor	4	1	1
Educator	4	4	1
Exercise leader	4	5	3
Motivator	5	5	4
Counselor	3	3	2
Promotor	2	4	5
Assessor	2	3	1
Evaluator	2	1	1

[1]5 = highest emphasis; 1 = lowest emphasis.

COMPARISON OF FACILITIES IN DIFFERENT SETTINGS

Finally, it is helpful to compare the facilities and program components of corporate, commercial, and community health/fitness programs and to look at the emphasis given to each in the various settings. Table 1.9 summarizes the facilities offered in the corporate, commercial, and community settings.

SUMMARY

In this chapter, we have introduced the book by defining the settings in which facilities are planned, designed, and operated. This introduction was essential because the setting will determine the specific characteristics and objectives of each facility and its program.

Corporate programs, for example, were found to be very program intensive, whereas commercial programs were more marketing intensive. Community programs tend to emphasize a combination of program, marketing, and management functions. However, evidence has shown that programs are becoming more, rather than less, homogeneous in their nature and makeup. The target populations are the major determinants in this trend toward more similarity. Community and commercial programs are proliferating at such a rate that the market for members is more competitive than ever. Yet, the difference in program objectives, emphasis on profit versus nonprofit, and so forth will continue to assure a distinction in health/fitness delivery systems in the foreseeable future. It therefore behooves the intelligent owner/developer/manager to realize the subtle differences that exist among the various settings if he or she hopes to plan, build, and operate a health/fitness facility successfully.

Table 1.9 Space Allocations in Health/Fitness Settings (square feet/percent of total)[1]

Area	Corporate	Community	Commercial	Clinical; cardiac/ pulmonary
Administration (testing, control, offices)	2,109/5%	1,695/4%	3,095/8%	1,758/5%
Exercise circuits	18,050/49%	16,806/43%	16,419/12%	18,688/49%
Warm-up/cool-down	4,050/11%	3,450/9%	3,895/10%	4,895/13%
Multipurpose rooms	2,461/7%	2,475/6%	1,375/4%	3,403/9%
Locker rooms	6,466/18%	7,087/18%	6,450/17%	4,950/13%
Storage	963/3%	858/2%	1,027/3%	1,631/4%
Laundry	422/1%	450/1%	422/1%	675/2%
Nursery	—	900/2%	774/2%	—
Snack bar	—	675/2%	844/2%	—
Circulation	2,350/6%	4,061/13%	4,458/11%	1,800/5%
Total square feet	36,871	38,421	38,729	37,800

[1]Similar total square footages were adopted for ease of comparison of space use; examples given are very large facilities.

2 Concept Development

Most health/fitness professionals at some time think about running their own program and operating their own facility. The purpose of this chapter is to flesh out the procedures in this process. The first major step is called *concept development*. The concept development for a health/fitness facility is a complicated process that entails different procedures for each of the settings described in chapter 1. Planning for a commercial setting has a large financial element attached to it, whereas planning for a corporate setting often has very important nonfinancial elements. Planning for the clinical setting such as a hospital-based wellness program takes on the corporate nonprofit characteristics with regard to the employee health/fitness aspects, but clearly has profit motivations in the community outreach for wellness programming.

There are, however, some common elements to the planning of any facility or program. The idea stage leads to a statement of goals and is then followed by a data-gathering and analysis stage in which all the relevant information is obtained and analyzed. The data gathering process is followed by decision making about the feasibility of the project. All of these stages interact with each other and can proceed in a circular direction. For example, new information about the target population can create a new programming idea that will better accommodate the

projected members, which might, in turn, alter the goals of the project (Figure 2.1). In this chapter we will discuss the stages of development that should occur in various settings in which facilities and programs will be planned. This concept development program can be adapted to corporate, commercial, or community settings alike.

CONCEPT DEVELOPMENT IN THE CORPORATE SETTING

The idea stage of an employee fitness program may originate anywhere within the corporation; however, the idea must be tested at the

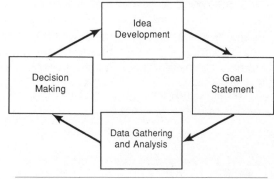

Figure 2.1. Generic concept development stages.

top before anything definitive is to happen. If the CEO initiates the idea to examine the feasibility of an employee health/fitness program, an influential management-level person is given the job of coordinating the concept development. Usually, this person has already made a personal commitment to a healthy and fit lifestyle and thus is a natural for the job. A dynamic fitness enthusiast within the personnel division, employee assistance program, or medical services is a good candidate for such a project coordinator.

Idea Development

The idea development stage necessitates that the project coordinator gathers input from several sources prior to the final formulation of program goals. Although it would be tempting simply to model the program after successful ventures by other corporations, it would likely fail because the success of a program is largely dependent upon the unique needs and interests of the management and employees of a particular setting. Even franchise fitness centers with standardized facilities and procedures have different staff characteristics and membership demands.

Management input is very important in determining the focus of the health/fitness program. The participation of the employees in the projected health/fitness program is governed to a large extent by the level of support provided by line managers. The designated project coordinator should seek input from the managers through personal interviews whenever possible, because resistance to the program due to misconceptions and bias can be addressed at this stage. Because line managers are sensitive to their superiors' positions on issues, it is sometimes impossible to get interviews from all the essential managers within the corporation. Frequently, it becomes necessary to resort to an anonymous questionnaire like the following.

There are many misconceptions about health/fitness and other descriptors such as wellness or health promotion. Care should

---

Questionnaire for Managers

We are gathering input from Corporation XYZ employees to determine the feasibility of offering an employee health/fitness program. Input from the managers is essential if we are to implement properly. Indeed, interest and support from the managers in such a program is essential if an employee wellness program is to be successful. Please give us your opinion on the following questions and return the questionnaire in the attached envelope. Your response will be completely confidential. Thanks in advance for your help.

1. What is your level of interest in the development of an employee health/fitness (wellness, health promotion) program?

_____ Very high _____ High _____ Neutral _____ Low _____ None

2. What type of program services should we try to offer the employees?

_____ None _____ Health screening _____ Exercise _____ Nutrition

_____ Stress management _____ Weight control _____ Safety (CPR)

3. When should the program be offered? During:

_____ Prework hours _____ Work hours _____ Scheduled breaks

_____ After-work hours _____ Mixture of work and nonwork hours

4. Would you participate in a high-quality employee health/fitness program?

_____ Yes _____ No

5. Would you encourage your employees to participate in such a program?

_____ Yes _____ No

---

be taken to clarify the preliminary concept regarding the nature and intent of the program and to reinforce the thought that input from the managers will be used to further define and develop the program concept. This clarifies the purpose and gives some ownership of the program to the line managers. Involvement of the managers at this stage yields good dividends later.

Input from employees is also important in clarifying program concepts. Again, it is important to conduct some initial interviews or develop some focus groups to get a clear picture of the general interests of the employees and to detect any areas of misunderstanding or misconception. It might prove helpful to send out a cover memorandum describing the preliminary nature of the program and the desire to get employee input into the planning of the program. It is always helpful and most would think necessary to get endorsement from the CEO's office to generate support and involvement in the planning process. The following questionnaire illustrates the kind of information you can derive from an interest survey.

Employee Questionnaire

Demographic information:	Age:	Sex:	Children:
_____ Exempt staff	_____ < 20 yr	_____ Male	_____ None
_____ Nonexempt staff	_____ 20-29 yr	_____ Female	_____ 1-2
	_____ 30-39 yr	Marital status:	_____ 3 or more
	_____ 40-49 yr	_____ Single	
	_____ 50-59 yr	_____ Married	
	_____ > 60 yr		

1. Would you be willing to participate in a cost-shared wellness/fitness program?

_____ Yes _____ No

(Cont.)

Employee Questionnaire (Continued)

2. If yes, check the activities that interest you the most.

_____ Health assessment

_____ Health survey _____ Treadmill exercise test _____ Physical examination

_____ Blood pressure screening _____ Other (please list) _____

_____ Exercise

_____ Walking _____ Jogging _____ Cycling _____ Dance/exercise

_____ Strength training _____ Racquetball _____ Tennis _____ Team sports

_____ Other (please list) _____

_____ Nutrition (weight control)

_____ Healthy nutrition classes _____ Weight control classes _____ Other (please

list) _____

_____ Stress management

_____ Time management training _____ Stress reduction techniques
_____ Relaxation training _____ Assertiveness training _____ Other (please list)

_____

_____ Substance-abuse control

_____ Tobacco _____ Alcohol _____ Other (please list) _____

_____ Low back pain management

_____ Prevention (proper lifting techniques) _____ Treatment (exercise therapy)

_____ Other (please list) _____

3. When would you prefer to participate in the program?

_____ Before work _____ Morning _____ Lunch _____ Afternoon

4. Who should be allowed to participate in the program?

_____ Employees only _____ Employees and spouses _____ Employees and family
members

Once the input from the managers and employees is obtained, the project coordinator can begin formulating some generalizations regarding the nature and amount of interest in the health/fitness program. After the data have been examined and some tendencies have emerged, it might be appropriate to seek some external advice and/or consultation, providing such resources are available. Cost-free resources within the community, such as the local YMCA director or the area college physical eduction department chairperson, may provide some direction in formulating the program idea further. There are, in addition, professional consultants available to assist the project coordinator. These consultants will be discussed further in chapter 4. It is very important to seek help at this stage of the concept development. Most often the project coordinator has not had the benefit of experience and education to circumvent potential problems and to be aware of the state of the art in program development. Thus the outside resource is called upon to provide direction to the idea development. However, the outside resource does not have a grasp of the political conditions that must always be dealt with when planning a program. The CEO, for example, may be a jogger, and it would be imprudent not to include jogging activity in the concept development and proposal for the program. Therefore, by working together, the project coordinator and the resource can begin to formulate the tentative program goals.

Goal Statements

The goals are initially developed from the information received from the managers and employees. The managers, especially upper management, usually will be concerned about such issues as reducing health care costs, reducing absenteeism, increasing work productivity, improving employee morale, lowering turnover, and recruiting better employees. These management issues can then be translated into program goal statements for a health/fitness program.

In contrast, the employee issues will probably be more related to health promotion matters such as providing opportunities for exercise, weight control, healthy nutrition, smoking cessation, and healthy back programs as well as reducing work-related stresses. Other issues that frequently concern employees are matters of child care and flex-ible work schedules. These issues can also be addressed and translated into a mission statement or program objectives for the health/fitness program.

The need for a vehicle to galvanize the overall program goals to reflect the concerns of both management and employees should be apparent. The most common way this is accomplished is through the creation of an advisory committee. This committee should comprise members from both management and the work force. Typical composition of such a committee might include individuals from personnel, employee assistance, trade union, medical services, legal services, upper management, safety, and, perhaps, an outside consultant. Any individual with a strong desire to assist could be helpful in developing the program concept. Employee ownership in the health/fitness program is the key to designing a set of goals that best represents all of the factions involved. It should be noted, however, that some management styles make such a committee difficult, or impossible, to function effectively. Be prepared to cope with autocratic processes.

Let's assume that we have a democratic environment and that a functioning committee determined that the most pressing issue for management was the reduction of health care costs and the most pressing employee-related concern was health promotion. The committee, or its designated individuals, could then begin a data-gathering process to more clearly focus the specific means of reducing health care costs and promoting employee health.

Data Gathering

The major goals that have been identified by our fictitious corporation in developing a health/fitness program are reducing health care costs and implementing health promotion strategies. Let's examine the goal to reduce health care costs first. The following data-gathering steps might be used to more clearly determine the specific focus the program might take:

1. Gather records on past health care costs and get central tendencies for the types of health care problems that have been occurring. Then develop projected trends for health care needs.
2. Gather data on current health status through such instruments as health risk appraisals (Patton et al., 1986).
3. Project which intervention strategies would be most cost-beneficial. For example, if a large number of employees are hypertensive and the cost of implementing a high blood pressure screening program through an agency such as the American Heart Association is very low, then such a program would be cost-beneficial. This service is reported to have a cost-benefit ratio of 1:1.6. Thus it would produce a benefit 1.6 times greater than its cost to implement the program. Chapman (1984) has reported the following cost-benefit ratios for selected interventions:

Intervention	Cost:benefit
Stress management	1:5.5
Smoking cessation	1:5.9
Hypertension screening	1:1.6
Medical self-care	1:3.0
General health-promotion	1:2.5

4. Gather data on successful programs already in existence.
5. Determine the feasibility of introducing the identified intervention strategies in the present corporate context. Look at available resources such as volunteer community agencies and contract services, as well as in-house programs being developed.

6. Strategically design a plan for implementing the health/fitness program by staging in the interventions that have the greatest impact on health care costs.

Next, data must also be gathered to delineate the direction the health promotion program should take in its development. Let's suppose that the main interest in health promotion was in the area of exercise. The following steps might be taken to gather data on the exercise aspects:

1. Gather information relative to employee interests. Information obtained from interviews and questionnaires described earlier in this chapter can be used to determine the nature of employee interest regarding exercise. Specifically, it would be important to determine the degree of interest in the various types of exercise such as strength training and cardiovascular training (aerobic dance activities, jogging, swimming, ergometer exercises).
2. Gather data on health status that relate to health problems that can be ameliorated by exercise programs. Several of the health risk appraisal instruments provide data that can yield information of this nature. Also, many company-sponsored medical screening programs exist and would be a resource for this type of information. A company in which a large percentage of the employees are older and more prone to heart disease might benefit from dedicating a large component of the exercise program to cardiovascular programming. Assembly line operations requiring a great deal of lifting and twisting, which produce a large number of lower back injuries, might consider a healthy back exercise program. A work environ-

ment with a large percentage of women in the workforce might want to consider offering prenatal and postpartum exercise classes such as the YMCA's "You and Me, Baby."

3. Project the greatest exercise needs for the program based upon the employees' interests and the medically based exercise needs. Ranking the exercise programs needed for the health/fitness programs will prove helpful when the time comes to make decisions regarding programs, facilities, and personnel.

4. Determine the feasibility of offering various exercise programs relative to contracting outside vendors in off-site facilities, bringing instructors on-site for selected exercise classes, or planning for long-range development of a company-based facility.

5. Gather data on employee participants in other programs.

Decision Making

There are a number of decisions to make as a part of the concept development process in a corporate setting.

- What are the definitive goals for the corporate health/fitness program?
- Will the management accept these goals as valid?
- What kind and amount of corporate resources will be dedicated to the program?
- Will the program be contracted to an off-site vendor such as the YMCA for fitness programs and a management firm to engage in cost-containment procedures to reduce health care?

- Will the program be developed in-house and will professional staff be employed to implement the program?
- Will a facility be constructed or developed for the program?
- What is the timetable for the implementation of the program?

The above list of questions is representative of the types of decisions that must be made before a program can become operational. Each question breeds many others that must be dealt with—all of which take time and expertise. Formulation of the program goals must be weighed in balance with both management and employee needs as well as the political forces that arise between these groups. Special interests of the upper management certainly skew the goal statements. Economic fluctuations and cycles definitely influence the program goals. Unfortunately, a contracting marketplace can ring a death knell for some or even all of the aspects of the health/fitness program, as it is viewed by many as a nonessential service. The project coordinator, the consulting resources, and the advisory team can channel the forces influencing the decision making process into a proposal document that can be used to educate management that health/fitness is, indeed, an essential service and to serve as a guide to action in subsequent implementation of the project. Patton et al. (1986) have an excellent discussion on proposal development and provide supportive data to document cost-benefit as well as cost-effective concerns.

In summary, we have attempted in this section to illustrate the generic model for concept development as it pertains to the corporate setting. Although each corporate setting will have some unique features that dictate a tailor-made approach to accommodate them, a generic model for a proposal has been presented. This generic model can be adapted to other settings as well. Perhaps the hospital-based wellness program, which usually has an employee health/fitness component, is most closely related to the corporate applications. The next section applies the generic model of concept development to the commercial setting, which has distinctly different approaches to the problem.

CONCEPT DEVELOPMENT IN THE COMMERCIAL SETTING

The idea stage in a commercial setting, where the primary motivation is profit, usually originates from some professional who is working for someone else in the health/fitness industry or with an entrepreneur who has a strong personal interest in fitness and wellness. At one time or another most of us have entertained the thought of starting our own business. What usually prevents the follow-through is not understanding how to develop the concept. This section should provide direction to the budding entrepreneur for successful concept development. We will again use the generic model outlined earlier to illustrate its conceptual utility.

Idea Development

The idea stage is usually initiated by the idea maker, who observes that the industry has a gap in the service or in the product lines being offered or that there is a market that is not yet being served. This unmet need observed in the marketplace serves as the spark to ignite the idea development for the new business enterprise. At this point several important questions should be addressed. Is there really a need for this concept? Is there an available market that would support such an idea? Do the trends in the health/fitness field look favorable? Who are the potential customers? Who are the competitors? When should the business begin? How much money will it take to reach a break-even point where revenues equal expenses? Often, there are no answers to these questions, only educated guesses. Yet, these are the kinds of questions that have to be answered before the project can proceed. A business plan must be developed from the idea that was germinated. Goals must be developed and refined. Numbers must be generated either to confirm or to disprove the value of the idea, because banks and other investors have to be sold on the project's merits before they will invest large sums of money.

Each year about 250 major commercial health/fitness facilities and three to four times as many small exercise studios open their doors in the U.S.; unfortunately, about the same number close their doors. More often than not, the reasons for failure in this business can be traced to poor planning: It has been said that a failure to plan is a good plan for failure. Successful start-up health/fitness businesses plan for adequate capitalization—there should be enough money to sustain the operation to a projected break-even point. They also plan good management strategies and hire qualified personnel well in advance of opening to plan adequately for the promotional and programming activities. Little is left to chance; however, a fair amount of luck is needed to be successful even when every detail is planned out to the highest degree.

Those of you who are planning to go into the health/fitness business should realize that there are over 100 different types of facilities. Different settings, sizes, members, management structures, and personnel, as well as facilities and equipment, serve to customize each program. To further complicate the issue, the health/fitness industry is in its infancy when compared to more traditional businesses. Lending institutions evaluate business plans for a new retail clothing or grocery store, or even a manufacturing plant, according to time-tested guidelines. Unfortunately, there are few gold standards available to judge the potential success of a business plan for a new health/fitness enterprise. The best that you can do is to model your efforts after traditional approaches so that lenders can deal with such a plan with greater confidence. You as a prospective borrower can approach the lender with greater assurance of success if you are able to communicate effectively and in a traditional fashion. At any rate, you should have developed a clear idea as to which of the 100 different types of health/fitness businesses you propose to establish, and this should be communicated in writing as concisely as possible in the form of a business plan.

The Business Plan

A carefully prepared business plan is crucial to the success of any new business venture. A properly written business plan is an invaluable tool that provides a rationale for your financial needs, assists in procuring capital, and even helps in recruiting staff. Finally, it is a vehicle that describes the critical path that will be followed to start the business and evaluate its performance. A formal business plan is usually presented to the potential investors or bank representatives in the following outline format:

- Summary and purpose
- Goals and objectives
- Industry analysis
- Market analysis
- Marketing strategies
- Management plan
- Business format

Summary and Purpose

A statement of the summary and purpose should be the culmination of the idea development stage. The summary should be written concisely, with intent to persuade and sell the reader on the merits of the business plan. Often, the summary is all that will be read by a busy bank officer or potential investor. A well-organized summary should take only 5 minutes to read and should provide the necessary information to answer preliminary questions.

The contents of a good summary should give an accurate description of the business and the population it will serve. The focus of the description should be how your project is going to differ from that of the competition. As the health/fitness industry continues to grow and expand, investors are going to be interested in how your concept will differ from existing facilities. Because the health/fitness industry is constantly changing, you must communicate in the summary whether you are going to base the success of a new venture on an already established market or create a new one. An example of creating a new market evolved when aerobic dance, jazzercise, and conditioning exercise classes became popular. Overnight, dance/exercise studios were built to meet the demand. The result was a clear understanding that a new market had been established.

The summary should also include a description of the management team. Emphasis should be placed upon the relevant skills of each key individual and what makes his or her expertise stand above that of the competition. Each health/fitness facility is different in its management approach. Some prefer a separate sales staff with a support staff. Others prefer to combine the sales aspect with the fitness staff. The direction chosen should provide an honest explanation of why your approach will work and what possible deficiencies might hinder its success.

The summary ends with a projected financial statement. The nationwide consulting firm of Arthur Andersen and Company states that financial projections should include not only the first year of operation, but also the next 3 to 5 years. This allows the potential investor or bank officer to quickly view the projected figures and determine if the project is financially worth pursuing.

Remember, the fate of many new business ventures depends on not only a good business plan, but also a well-written summary. Today's venture capitalists and bank officers simply don't have the time to read a detailed business plan. Take the necessary time to think through and summarize each facet of the plan. The end result should be a concise representation of the project you wish to undertake.

Goals and Objectives

The next step associated with writing a business plan (and the next stage of concept development) is to determine exactly what you want the new business to accomplish. This process is achieved by writing objectives and goals. To avoid confusion, it is important to note the distinction between an objective and a goal. Dr. Karl Albrecht (1978) defines *objective* as "any kind of desire and condition, however vaguely or specifically it can be stated." He further states that a *goal* is "any objective which can be stated so specifically and concretely that anyone will know when it has been achieved" (p. 73). Objectives are usually written in general terms, whereas goals are more specific and leave no question as to what will be achieved (see Figures 2.2 and 2.3).

An often overlooked part of writing an objective is determining what is achievable. Is the business or staff capable of achieving what is stated? What is occurring in other similar facilities? Should a conservative or

Figure 2.2. Characteristics of an effective objective statement.

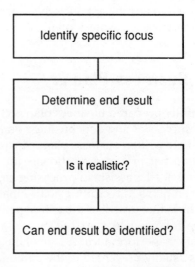

Figure 2.3. Characteristics of an effective goal statement.

optimistic approach be adopted? Clearly, striking a balance between what's practical and what's obtainable is preferable to stretching the capabilities of the facilities and staff. Examples of specific objectives and goals that meet those criteria are outlined in Table 2.1.

Table 2.1 A Contrasting Table of Goals and Objectives

Objectives	Goals
The XYZ Fitness Center will provide efficient and state-of-the-art facilities.	The architect chosen to design the XYZ Fitness Center will have previous experience designing similar facilities.
The XYZ Wellness Center will provide programs that will facilitate lifestyle changes.	The program schedule for the XYZ Wellness Center will include daily exercise classes, private instruction, leagues, and special events.
The staff of the XYZ Corporate Fitness Program will demonstrate leadership and professionalism.	The staff of the XYZ Corporate Fitness Program must have at least 2 years of experience in the fitness field to qualify for employment.
The XYZ Community Center will provide a successful plan for financial management.	The XYZ Community Center will contract with a CPA to provide financial guidance.

Quantifiable goals are preferred, because they provide a measuring capability. For example, a quantifiable goal would be projected numbers of new members per month, annual projected adherence rates, or estimated annual profit. By injecting these figures, the manager develops performance standards that he or she and the staff must strive to accomplish.

The next stage of the concept development is data analysis. However, as part of the business plan for the commercial setting, data must be gathered and information obtained from a variety of contexts. These data and information are then included in the industry analysis and market analysis portions of the business plan.

Industry Analysis

The industry analysis section of a business plan provides a general overview of the health/fitness industry and summarizes its past, present, and future trends. A determination of where the industry has been and what the projections are for the future is important to both management and potential investors. Table 2.2 illustrates the type of information that should be included in a good industry analysis.

Following the industry analysis overview comes an explanation of how your concept will fit into the already established fitness market. A new venture has to fit within an existing concept, or a new concept must be created. The decision to create a new industry is often considered risky. Such a leap requires a large capital investment and extra work to define the area of service. It is easier to fit into a preestablished market by adopting a *niche*, which is a concept innovation that makes your business endeavor different from other existing facilities.

An example of creating a niche in the health/fitness market occurred when hospitals began joint ventures with fitness centers to create wellness centers. Both groups decided

Table 2.2 Trends in the Health/Fitness Industry

Years and settings	1950s	1950-1970	1970s	1980-1985	1985>
Community	• YMCAs • Recreational sports		• YMCA face-lift • Joint ventures	• 80 million Americans exercising regularly	• Tax status • Aging programs
Commercial	• Boxing clubs • Weight-lifting clubs	• Health spa chains • Tennis clubs	• Increase in racquet sports: racquetball clubs • Electronic funds transfer • Aerobic dance	• Move to multi-purpose facilities • Rapid growth • Foreign market entrance • Large chain club acquisitions • Instructor certification • Sales tax on fitness clubs • IDEA • Video business	• Consumer protection legislation • Children's health clubs • Certification • Expansion • Licensure
Corporate	• Phillips Petroleum (recreational program) • National Cash Register (calisthenics on the assembly line)	• 1968 NASA study • Construction of in-house facilities	• Blue Cross/Blue Shield • General Mills • Kimberly Clark • AFB growth	• New professional journals • Small- and medium-sized programs joint venture with other facilities	• Expanded services to include child care, comprehensive wellness programs
Wellness/clinical			• Cooper clinic • Pritikin Center • Cardiac Rehabilitation • Sports Medicine	• DISD study • 50% of all hospitals have community education programs • 450 sports medicine facilities • Americans spend $17.4 billion pursuing health/fitness • Health care exceeds $200 billion	• Expanded wellness movement • Aging programs

to respond to a more sophisticated fitness market that demanded a scientifically sound approach to health and exercise. The American Hospital Association (AHA) reported in 1985 that over 300 hospitals in the United States were involved in joint health promotion programs with clubs.

To provide credibility to this section, it is important to verify the statements. Previous studies on market research should be included to provide a meaningful dimension to the existing and future markets. Historical data and reliable forecasts from industry, professional, and government sources are recommended.

The health/fitness industry has recently begun providing data to include in an industry analysis. To assist in writing this section, a recommended list of professional associations follows:

- Association for Fitness in Business
  310 N. Alabama, Suite A 100
  Indianapolis, IN 46204
- American College of Sports Medicine
  PO Box 1440
  Indianapolis, IN 46206
- American Hospital Association
  840 N. Lakeshore Drive
  Chicago, IL 60611
- American Medical Association
  535 N. Dearborn St.
  Chicago, IL 60610
- International Racquet Sports Association
  112 Cypress
  Brookline, MA 02146
- President's Council on Physical Fitness and Sports
  450 5th Street N.W. #7103
  Washington, DC 20001
- YMCA of the USA
  101 N. Wacker Dr.
  Chicago, IL 60606

Market Analysis

Recently, entrepreneurs, hospital administrators, physicians, businesspersons, and governmental agencies, as well as the armed forces, have entered into the health/fitness market. Because many of these groups have limited personnel resources and expertise in the health/fitness field, consultants are generally hired to perform the feasibility study to determine economic viability of the planned enterprise. Consultants have included fitness specialists, club owners, college professors, and certified public accountants (CPA). Special attention should be paid to choosing a consultant who is experienced in conducting feasibility studies and consulting the resources necessary to provide a good data analysis. (Consultants will be discussed further in chapter 4.)

Because the market data have been limited in the health/fitness industry, the market analysis section of a business plan is studied closely by investors and loan officers. If the statistical data are not present to support the site and scope of the venture, financing is often refused. For this reason, it is essential that the proper time and capital be spent in obtaining as thorough a market study as possible. Figure 2.4 represents the necessary components for a demographic analysis.

Define Target Population. Before attempting to define the target population, you should ask the following questions about the projected facility:

1. Based on the scope of the project, what type of population would be serviced?
2. To meet the financial projections, what would the average member income level need to be?
3. What average age ranges and sex ratios are preferred?

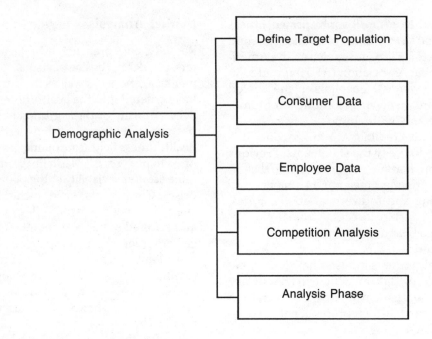

Figure 2.4. Components for a demographic analysis.

These are just examples of questions that should be addressed. By attempting to answer these questions, you create a basis for comparison during the consumer analysis phase. If a developer enters into this phase without population prerequisites, the demographic information received cannot be thoroughly understood. Essentially, you establish a series of hypotheses about the target population that the market research study can test.

Once these questions have been answered, a more exact definition of the target population is required. Typically, a target population is defined by those individuals within 10-15 minutes' travel time of the desired location of the club. As you evaluate various locations, the population characteristics can assist you in deciding on the best site. If a desired location doesn't meet the defined population requirements because of the income base or unsuitable age, sex, or professional/nonprofessional ratios, further demographic research of the

desired location is not necessary. If the target population of the desired location meets the defined population requirements, further demographic analysis is required.

Consumer Data. Because the health/fitness industry is predominantly a service business, it is essential to learn everything possible about the surrounding population. This information provides raw data on which to base decisions and provides guidelines for determining the potential success of the project.

Demographic data can be obtained in various ways. The first method is to obtain an area map by zip code(s) of the particular city of interest. Zip codes provide an excellent means of sectioning a city while establishing a radius distance from proposed facility sites. A commercial facility with no major competition should obtain memberships from about

1% to 2% of the total population within a 7- to 10-mile radius. Some successful clubs have achieved a 5% penetration in favorable locations.

Once this step is completed, the process of data collection begins. Irving Burstiner (1979) stated that "there are basically two categories of information—primary and secondary. Primary information is those facts which are not readily available and which require of the investigator considerable initiative and effort; secondary information will encompass facts which are normally available although they necessitate some searching" (p. 217). The key to both these data sources is to know how and where to locate the information.

It is not uncommon for many small health/ fitness facilities to include only secondary data in their business plans (see Figure 2.5). This process is considered less time-consuming and cheaper, and the information can be easily obtained by the owner or investors. However, an extensive multirecreation complex that requires a large investment often supports the secondary data with primary data. This approach acts as a double-check system that provides added support to both sources.

Secondary data is generally obtained from a variety of sources. Local, state, and federal governments provide the greatest variety. Private sources, such as professional associations and national firms (e.g., A.C. Nielsen Company), provide additional information.

The two generally accepted approaches to collecting primary data are asking people (the survey method) and watching people (the observation method) see Figure 2.6.

The *survey method* is the most widely used for collecting primary data. Surveys are conducted by telephone or mail and through personal interviews.

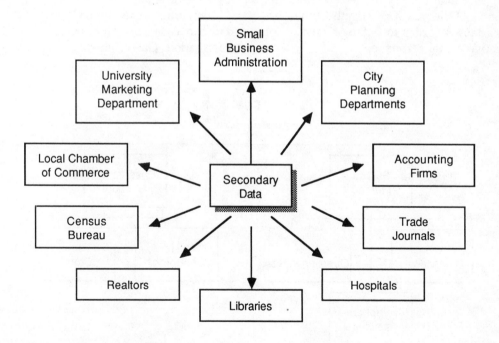

Figure 2.5. Sources of secondary data.

Telephone interviews account for an estimated 55%-60% of all primary marketing research (Kurtz & Boone, 1984, p. 148). The reason for this high percentage is that telephone interviews are the least expensive way to produce the most immediate response. Mail surveys are also inexpensive, but the return on questionnaires is unpredictable. Personal interviews are considered the best way of obtaining detailed information, but they are the most time-consuming and expensive of the three.

The key to a good interview or questionnaire is in its preparation; it requires good thinking and planning. Special consideration should be given to wording, sequencing of questions, ease with which the results can be tabulated, and validity of the questions (Dillman, 1978).

The *observation method* involves observing people's behavior as they react to a question. Examples would include filming people at a shopping mall as they are asked about the opening of the new XYZ Health Club or using a tape recorder to obtain a positive or negative verbal response.

Another form of the observation method is the *focus group*. This group is made up of professionals in the health/fitness field who are brought together to react to a new facility that is about to enter the construction phase.

It should be emphasized that, because this method involves only the observation of people's behavior, it might not always be the most reliable.

Employee Data. Working professionals make up the largest market in the health/ fitness industry. A 1985 market research study (Game Plan, Inc., 1985) reported that the average member of a health/fitness club is between 25 and 44 years of age and has an average income of between $45,000 and $65,000; over half of all members have earned college and/or graduate degrees. Because the working professional represents a major portion of the target population, additional information regarding employee demographics is helpful.

The methods used for collecting consumer data can also be used for obtaining employee information. Gathering secondary data is the

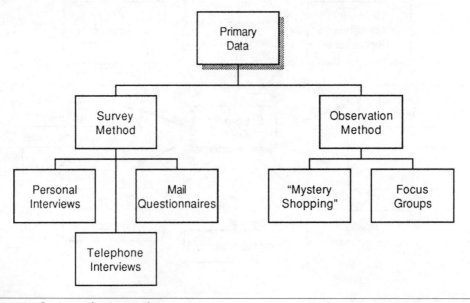

Figure 2.6. Sources of primary data.

preferred method because the majority of information can be obtained through the Census Bureau or local city planning departments.

Basic employment data should consist of a list of the major corporations, where they are located, the total number of employees, and employee growth projections. These data will project the employee-density relationship needed for organizing marketing promotion, membership, and financial projections.

Another area of important information is the journey-to-work data. Once you have obtained the locations of the major corporations, you can use a map to determine where the central business district is located. It's also good to locate major transportation thoroughfares and their distances from the proposed site. Estimated traffic patterns are then established for business and residential areas. You use this information to analyze and determine which direction the growth of the city is heading.

Employee data are a means to understanding the current and projected characteristics of a target population. Understanding these data will help support and add focus to the decision-making process. Figure 2.7 summarizes the data needed for demographic analysis.

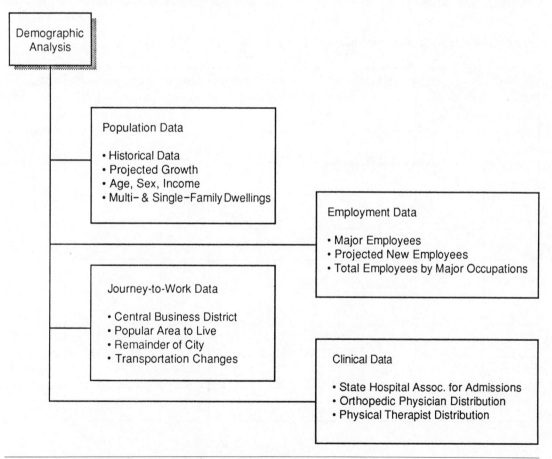

Figure 2.7. Checklist data for demographic analysis.

Competition Analysis. Prior to starting any business, you need to analyze the existing and potential competition in the market. There are three phases to analyzing the competition:

1. Define the various competitors
2. Collect data on similar facilities
3. Conduct a data analysis of competitors

Defining the various competitors and determining their respective locations should be the first steps you take. Include in the list all the following types of facilities:

- Multipurpose fitness centers
- Hospital wellness programs
- Corporate fitness programs
- Tennis/racquetball centers
- Community recreation centers
- Colleges and universities

Once the various markets have been identified, the data collection phase begins. Personal visits, interviews, and phone surveys are considered the best ways to obtain data. Pertinent questions should be based upon location and facility characteristics, membership characteristics (e.g., types, number, fee structure, capacity, and growth rates), and programs/services offered. The following are examples of data collection forms.

Data collection on the competition is followed by data analysis. Prospective investors are particularly interested in seeing what

Competitor analysis form for multipurpose clubs.

Club and location	Club size (square feet)	Club age	Number of members	Member capacity	Member fee	Waiting list	Adherence rate	Hours of operation		
								M-F	Sat	Sun

Competitor analysis form for a multipurpose club (detailed information).

Name and location	Pretesting	Nautilus equip.	Universal equip.	Free-weights	Exercycles	Treadmills	Racquetball	Tennis	Indoor jogging	Outdoor jogging	Swimming pool	Sauna	Restaurant	Exercise class	Massage	Basketball	Pro shop	Volleyball	Professional staff numbers	Member fee	Hours of operation

share of the market you intend to capture. This projection should include not only current estimates, but also projected market growth for 3-5 years. It should also include how you expect to draw customers from the competition. Comment on how your facility will fit into the market, and summarize the strategy to be used to gain your desired share of the market. It is also a good idea to insert a discussion of the competitive factors regarding facilities, staffing, programs, hours of operation, membership fees, and other amenities. In short, you must convince your investor(s) or banker that your facility will be different from and/or better than that of the competition.

Finally, it's important to be realistic at this phase. Many would-be health/fitness owners overestimate their competitive strength and underestimate the strength of the competition. Investors are less likely to back an individual who doesn't have a realistic view of the market and the competition. An alternative might be to present three projections: pessimistic, realistic, and optimistic.

Analysis Phase. Finally, after all the market research data have been gathered, it is time to convert data into information. Data and information are not synonymous terms. David Kurtz and Louis Boone (1984) indicate that data refers to statistics, opinions, facts, or predictions categorized on some basis for storage retrieval. Information is data relevant to the manager in making decisions. This phase provides information to use in making decisions by providing managers, club owners, and directors with the current and future trends of the market, and in identifying market responses to company and competitor actions.

Consumer and demographic analyses should begin by dividing the city population into more manageable segments. This can be accomplished through the use of zip codes, census tracts, or preestablished city codes.

Once this step is completed, color-code radius distances of 5, 10, and 15 minutes' travel time from the proposed site. This process will identify the specific target populations and provide population densities that will aid in membership projections.

Next, gather all secondary and primary data related to population, employment, journey-to-work, and industry demographics. All responses derived from surveys or questionnaires should be totaled and divided against the total number of respondents to determine a percentage ranking. The findings should then be taken and compared to relevant industry standards. Determine if the information that was collected coincides with similar business plans or feasibility studies of other health/fitness centers. Additional credibility is obtained when the data are compared and referenced in the business plan. A list of professional associations that might aid in this comparison was provided in the ''Industry Analysis'' section of this chapter.

Once these data are collected and analyzed, a demographic profile can be established. A demographic profile summarizes the data results, so that specific statements can be made regarding the target population. An example of a demographic profile would be as follows:

1. Of the people surveyed, 85% were between the ages of 25 and 55. This age group distribution is essential because the XYZ Health Club will be an adult-oriented club.
2. Thirty-two percent of the sample population had incomes in excess of $25,000, whereas 36% of this income sample had incomes greater than $35,000. This suggests that the bulk of the sample fell in the middle to upper middle income range, which is the target population for the XYZ Health Club.
3. Sixty-two percent of the population surveyed exercised at least three times

per week. The frequency of exercise is an indication of high utilization—a positive sign for the XYZ Health Club.

4. An overwhelming majority of the respondents preferred to exercise in the late afternoon and early evening. This helps to determine peak usage hours in program planning.

5. Fifty percent of the respondents exercised at home, whereas 30% exercised at privately owned health clubs. These figures demonstrate that the XYZ Health Club must target its marketing to the 50% that exercise at home.

6. Of the respondents surveyed, 51% would be interested in joining a fitness center that offered a variety of exercise facilities. This percentage suggests an initial market that is interested in a multipurpose health/fitness center.

7. Contrary to focus group findings, 63% of the people surveyed did not belong to a health club or country club.

8. The majority of the people surveyed would pay between $25 and $50 a month for membership dues. This figure represents an annual membership range of $300-$600 and is consistent with the assumed income ranges of the respondents (1% of annual gross income).

The data presented in the demographic profile can also be presented through graphs, charts, and tables. Eighty-five percent of all information stored in the brain is stored visually. Often a busy venture capitalist or loan officer would prefer to interpret a bar graph or pie chart than to read paragraphs of information. Various forms of graphic analysis are shown in Figure 2.8.

The specific statements derived from each response will be the key aspects of the market analysis. Essentially, the data interpretation will provide early guidelines for the decision-making stage of concept development. The statements will determine boundaries and specifically establish target groups on which to focus marketing strategies.

It is not uncommon at the end of the market analysis phase to notice that the project does not have the necessary demographic characteristics to be successful. It's best to become aware of this during this phase. A lot of time and money can be saved by facing facts and stopping the project. If, on the one hand, a positive demographic profile cannot be presented in the business plan, then the recommendation is not to attempt financing. If, on the other hand, the demographic profile is positive, several decisions must now be addressed. Noteworthy among these decisions are marketing strategies to be used, membership planning, promotion and advertising plans, and management plans.

Marketing Strategies

In the health/fitness industry, exercise itself must be viewed as a commodity and, as such, should be considered a product that has a cash value associated with it. The techniques for selling exercise as a product are no different from the selling techniques of other businesses.

The key element in selling any product is a well-organized marketing plan. The most common methods have not changed over the years and consist of (a) identifying the target population, (b) investigating all that is necessary for their needs, and (c) trying to satisfy those needs with the right service approach.

The marketing strategies section of a business plan sets the stage for, or summarizes, the detailed marketing plan. Specific guidelines should indicate the marketing direction that will be followed. Equally important is the need to show investors how the ideas presented can actually be turned into profit. The following is a checklist of points that should

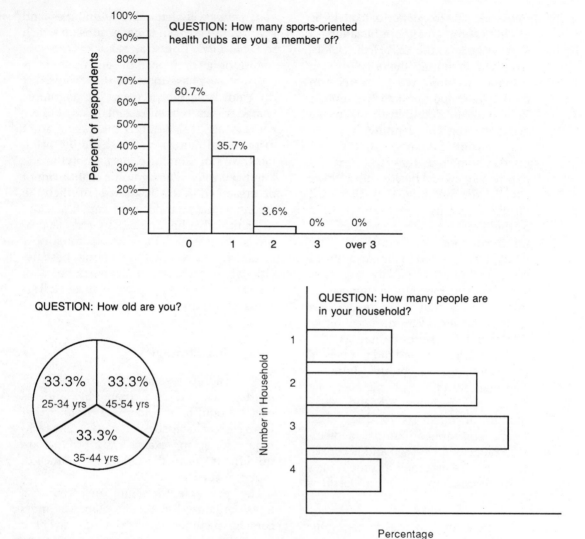

Figure 2.8. Various graphic analyses for a business plan.

be summarized in the marketing strategies section.

- Goals for market penetration
- Strategy and effect on competition
- Membership sales approach
- Membership pricing policy
- Promotion and advertising plan

- Management plan
- Business format
- Personnel

Goals for Market Penetration. As discussed earlier in this chapter, goals should be quantitative, realistic, and consistent with the marketing analysis. A clear understanding of the target population is necessary to prepare marketing goals. After the goals are determined, they become the guidelines from which marketing objectives and plans are derived. They provide direction and serve as standards in evaluating performance. Properly written goals will serve as an action plan to follow as strategies are addressed.

Strategy and Effect on Competition. Once the goals have been established, you must design a plan for marketing strategy to achieve these goals. The plan must choose the most suitable market population and list the steps necessary to attract the attention of consumers and get them interested in the business. In addition, there must be a plan for drawing existing members away from other facilities.

The image of the facility is important. The way people think of your facility is influenced by the way you conduct your business. When potential members come into your fitness facility, their image of the business is influenced by the way they are treated, the cleanliness of the floors, and the quality that is reflected in the service they receive. The Small Business Administration recommends that you make a conscious effort to formulate the image that you want customers to have of your business.

When this list is completed, you can then develop a written strategy to accomplish these goals. Remember, keep this section short. A marketing plan will go into more detail on each topic area.

Membership Sales Approach. The rationale for membership sales is explained during this section. Will a separate sales team be hired to sell memberships? If so, will sales team members be paid a straight salary or an incentive compensation? If a separate sales team is not used, will the fitness instructors be used, and, if so, what incentives will they have? In addition, what will the payment

policies be for membership? Do you prefer to handle cash only, or are various forms of credit available (e.g., credit card or electronic funds transfer)?

Next, will sales quotas be established? These quotas are an important tool for marketing control, because they produce standards against which actual performance can be measured. Without such standards, no comparison can be made. These quotas are also needed for the financial section of the business plan, because they represent the major source of projected income.

The answers to these questions will affect the day-to-day operations of the club. Adequate time must be spent comparing other clubs' sales techniques and deciding which approach fits your club's image. Once these decisions are made the image is difficult to change.

Membership Pricing Policy. A pricing policy that is fair to the customer and to yourself is best. The ideal situation is a pricing structure that covers the operational expenses while providing an acceptable profit margin. Because this area is so important, you might want to seek the advice of an accountant or consultant in establishing these policies. The areas that should be considered for a well-structured pricing policy are as follows:

1. What varieties of memberships will be offered?
   - Individual
   - Family
   - Corporate
   - Senior citizen
   - Cardiac rehabilitation
   - Other
2. What will the payment structure be?
   - Initiation fees
   - Monthly dues
   - Quarterly/biyearly dues
   - Annual dues
   - Other

3. What will the membership fees be?

4. How will payment be accepted?
   - Cash
   - Billing
   - Electronic fund transfer
   - Credit card
   - Other

5. Are there membership restrictions?
   - Age
   - Invitation or referral
   - Sex

The pricing policies must be competitive with those of similar facilities. This information comes from the competitive analysis that was conducted during the marketing data phase. These figures should be a measuring device to make sure the prices are competitive.

Promotional and Advertising Plan. Once you have established the concept, price structure, and sales approach, it is now time to decide how to convince potential members why they should be consumers of your services. The promotion and advertising plan sells the business and builds an early membership base from which to work.

The following are steps to follow in promoting your club:

1. Determine and state the areas that make your facility stand out above the others.
2. Establish an annual advertising and promotion budget.
3. Determine the most effective way to sell your business (e.g., newspapers, radio, television, flyers, etc.).
4. Establish what approach will be used while staying within the predetermined budget.

Potential lenders will review this section closely to see what steps will be taken to attract customers. Preestablished membership goals, without promotional methods, will surely fall short of projections. A well-organized advertising plan leads to action—it gets people interested and makes them want to join. The purposes of advertising are listed in Figure 2.9.

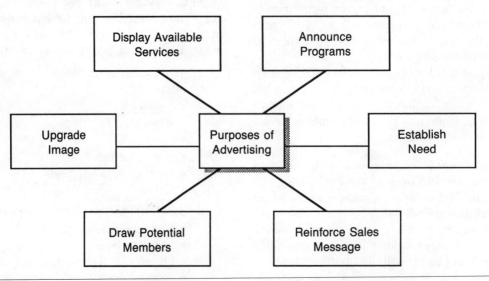

Figure 2.9. The purposes of advertising.

Management Plan. The management section of the business plan explains the organizational format of the business and the personnel involved. Unfortunately, many businesses often leave this section to the end because they become more interested in the marketing plan or financial projections. What must be remembered is that there will be no marketing plans or financial projections unless someone (i.e., management) makes them happen.

The management plan provides direction in carrying out tasks that were determined in previous sections of the business plan. These tasks establish the organizational structure and develop the management system. The organizational structure assigns responsibilities for each task to specific personnel.

Business Format. In forming a business, you must decide on the legal form of ownership. The choices that are available are the sole proprietorship, the partnership, and the corporation. Each of these is defined in this section. The form selected will affect liability, distribution of profits and losses, tax consequences, ability to raise capital, and method of control of the business. The pros and cons of each form must be researched carefully. The key is to select the one that best suits your needs as the owner of a new health/fitness business. You are well advised to get professional help in making these decisions.

A *corporation* is a legal entity that is recognized as being separate and distinct from its owners. As a separate entity, it can acquire, hold, and convey property; sue and be sued; and generally act in its own name. It derives its rights from state statutes and its article of incorporation and bylaws. Creditors generally may not look outside the corporation for the satisfaction of business debts.

An *S corporation* is a regular corporation except that it has elected special tax treatment under Subchapter S of the Internal Revenue Code. This special election results in the corporation being treated like a partnership. It has virtually all of the features of a corporation (e.g., limited liability). The S corporation acts like a partnership in that profits and losses typically flow directly to the individual shareholders, and it is their responsibility to report these gains or losses on their individual tax returns. Under the new tax law, many small health/fitness businesses are switching to the S corporation status.

A *partnership* is an association of two or more persons, who carry on as co-owners of a business for profit. Even though a partnership can be created by an oral understanding or implied by the conduct and acts of the purported partners, a written contract should always be used to create a partnership. The partnership is a unique business, frequently referred to as a *conduit*. A partnership is a conduit because, though persons have banded together for a profit-producing motive, it is not considered a legal entity separate from the partners. Thus a partnership may not sue or be sued in its firm name only, and partners are both individually and jointly liable for the debts of the partnership. There are two types of partnerships. The first, called a *general partnership*, contemplates that each partner participates in all profits and losses equally or according to some previously agreed upon ratio. Normally, a general partner has unlimited liability, which includes his or her personal assets outside the business association. In the second, a *limited partnership*, the liability of each partner depends on the extent of his or her capital contribution.

A *sole proprietorship* is a business completely and directly owned by a single person. As the sole owner of all the assets, the sole proprietor is entitled to all the profits and must bear the business' total liabilities and operational losses. Minimal legal formalities are required to bring this business into being. The major source of capital comes from operations and from the owner's borrowing capacity.

The schedule in Table 2.3 outlines some of the major nontax and tax characteristics of the different business forms. As you will see, each form has several specific advantages and disadvantages.

John McCarthy, executive director of the International Racquet Sports Association, stated that "85%-90% of the club industry was historically composed of single-club owners" (personal communication, January 2, 1987). However, in 1985, the picture changed; McCarthy noted that "75% of all athletic and racquet clubs are now corporations formed under limited partnerships." This change has resulted from large club acquisitions by such companies as Bally Manufacturing, Living Well, Inc., and Club Corporation of American.

Personnel. A successful health/fitness business is based on the following formula: success = facilities + promotions + programs + staff.

It is the belief among many fitness experts that the facility (i.e., atmosphere, equipment, indoor/outdoor appearance) and promotional activities initially draw individuals to join a health/fitness facility. However, once a person becomes a member, the facility loses drawing power, and the programs and staff must take over to help membership retention. Thus the composition of management and staff is important at this stage. Many owners and investors agree that a first-class management team is the most important component of the marketing strategy. Because fitness is considered an intangible product, the people responsible for selling the service are a key ingredient. The management plan should focus on the experience and competence of each staff member. The management organizational structure is shown in Figure 2.10.

ORGANIZATIONAL STRUCTURE OF DIFFERENT SETTINGS

The organizational structures of health/fitness programs differ among the corporate, community, and commercial settings due to the obvious differences in their purposes.

Corporate Setting

The health/fitness director usually reports to the personnel or medical department manager. In rare instances, the health/fitness director answers to the company CEO.

We recommend that you designate a project coordinator from within the corporation to be responsible for hiring the health/fitness director or contracting with outside resources to deliver the health/fitness program. The project coordinator usually is a member of the personnel or medical department. Figure 2.11 is an example of a typical management structure within a corporate setting.

Community Setting

Organizational structures in community health/fitness programs depend on the type of agency and the purpose of the service provided. For example, in a large YMCA that conducts both corporate and adult fitness programs, there may be two distinct departments with a director for each. These managers may work in equal line with a sports and recreation director. In a medium-sized YMCA, one person may manage a combined health/fitness program and another a sports/recreation program. In a small YMCA

Table 2.3 Business and Tax Considerations for Comparison of Corporations, S Corporations, Partnerships, and Sole Proprietorships

Factor	Corporation (regular corporation)	S corporation (small business corporation)	Partnership	Sole proprietorship
Life	Unlimited or perpetual, unless limited by state law or terms of its charter	Same as regular corporation. Election may be revoked or terminated without affecting continuity of life.	Generally set up for a specific, agreed term; usually will be terminated by death, withdrawal, insolvency, or legal disability of a general partner.	At death, business assets pass with proprietor's estate.
Entity	Completely separate from owners and recognized as such.	Same as regular corporation	Generally recognized as separate by the business community, but not for all purposes.	Generally recognized as separate by the business community, but not for all purposes.
Liability of owners	Limited. Stockholders are generally sheltered from any liabilities of the corporation.	Same as regular corporation.	Each general partner is fully liable as an individual for all debts. A limited partner's liability is usually limited to the amount of his or her capital contribution.	Owner has unlimited risk. Creditors can attach all personal assets for business debts.
Ease and effect of transfer of ownership interest	Generally, stock is easily and readily transferable, and transfer has no effect on the corporate entity.	Same as regular corporation. Consideration must be given to the effect of the transfer on the election to be sure it does not result in an unintended termination of S corporation status.	Transfer may require approval of all other partners and may cause termination of old partnership and creation of a new one.	Transfer terminates entity and creates new firm.

(Cont.)

Table 2.3 (Continued)

Factor	Corporation (regular corporation)	S corporation (small business corporation)	Partnership	Sole proprietorship
Availability of outside or capital financing	May sell stock or bonds to the public.	Limited in that there can be only one class of stock outstanding. The corporation can have "straight debt," which will not be treated as a second class of stock. Also, different voting rights are applicable.	Limited to borrowing from partners or outsiders, or to admitting new partners who contribute additional capital.	Limited to owner's personal assets and outside credit.
Management of business operation	Much flexibility. Control can be exercised by a small number of officers without having to consult owners, regardless of the total number of shareholders.	About the same as a regular corporation, except that more active participation by all owners can usually be expected since the total number of shareholders cannot exceed 35.	Usually, all general partners will be active participants in management. However, other partners may grant management control to one or more partners by agreement.	Owner has complete control.
Who is the taxpayer?	The corporation is taxed on its taxable income, whether or not it is distributed to the shareholders.[a]	The shareholders are taxed on the taxable income of the corporation, whether or not it is distributed to them.	The partners are taxed on the taxable income of the partnership, whether or not it is distributed to them.	The owner is taxed on the taxable income whether or not it is drawn by the owner.
Distribution of earnings	Taxable to shareholders as ordinary dividends to the extent of earnings and profits.[b]	No tax effect to shareholders, unless the distribution exceeds the shareholder's basis in the S corporation. Excess taxed as capital gain to shareholder until basis is reestablished.	No tax effect on partners, unless distribution exceeds partner's basis. Excess taxed as capital gain to partner.	No tax effect to proprietor.

Net operating loss	Deductible only by the corporation within prescribed carryback and carryover period.	Deductible by shareholders subject to adequate basis to cover losses.	Deductible by partners, subject to adequate basis to cover losses.	Deductible by owner, subject to adequate income to cover losses.
Salaries paid to owners	When owners are employees, salaries are taxable to them and deductible by the corporation. Salaries must be reasonable in amount in relation to services rendered.	Same as regular corporation. The question of unreasonably large salaries is not so important unless salaries are used as a device for shifting income among stockholders within a family group.	Generally, amounts paid are considered partial distributions of income. If the distribution is a guaranteed payment of salary, it will be deductible by the partnership and ordinary income to the partner.	Sole proprietorship is not an employee. Amount paid is considered a partial distribution of income.
Liquidation of the business	Amount received in excess of basis in stock is taxable as capital gain, unless the corporation is collapsible.	Same as regular corporation.	Normally no tax unless cash or equivalent exceeds basis in partnership interest. Excess is taxed as a capital gain, unless the partnership is collapsible.	No gain or loss until business or assets are sold to a third party.
Pension or profit-sharing plan	Owners are employees and can be included in a regular, qualified plan; after 1981, even if a qualified plan is maintained, employees may set up IRAs.[b]	Owners may participate only in a self-employed qualified plan, which must be more restrictive in its coverage and provisions; where no qualified plan is maintained, employees may set up IRAs.	Partners may participate only in self-employed qualified plan, restrictive in its coverage and provisions; where no qualified plan is maintained, employees may set up IRAs.	Same as partnership.

(Cont.)

Table 2.3 (Continued)

Factor	Corporation (regular corporation)	S corporation (small business corporation)	Partnership	Sole proprietorship
Capital gains and losses	Taxed to the corporation at a maximum rate of 28%. No capital loss deduction is allowable.	Generally, taxed to the shareholders as such, but may be taxed to the corporation in certain cases.	Taxed to the partners as such.	Same as partnership.
Tax on transfer of assets to business	Generally none if the transferors retain control of at least 80% of the corporation after the transfer (unless liabilities assumed by the corporation exceed transferor's basis).	Same as regular corporation.	None, unless liabilities assumed reduce transferor's basis in the partnership below zero.	None.
Allocation of net income or loss or different types of income and deductions among owners by agreement.	Not possible.	Not possible.	Can be done, so long as there is substantial economic substance to the agreement.	Not applicable.
Effect of death or sale of interest on basis of assets in business.	None.	None.	Election may be filed to adjust basis of partnership assets applicable to transferor partner's interest.	Upon death, basis adjusts to fair market value for heirs. Upon sale, basis adjustment not applicable.
Earnings accumulation	May be subject to penalty tax if accumulation is unreasonable	No limit because all income is taxed to the shareholders whether distributed or not.	Same as partnership.	

Passive investment income	May create a personal holding company taxed at penalty rates.	In limited cases, may disqualify the S corporation and cause termination of the election.	No effect.	No effect.
Selection of taxable year	No restriction.	Calendar year, unless justified business purpose and consent of the Commissioner to use fiscal year.	Must conform to that of the principal partners, unless consent of the Commissioner is obtained; Rev. Proc. 72-51 generally grants permission for 9/30 (or later) for calendar-year partners.	Same as that of the owner.
Sale of ownership interest	All capital gain unless corporation is collapsible, then ordinary income.	Same as regular corporation.	May be part capital gain and part ordinary income.	Same as partnership.
Charitable contributions	Deductible by the corporation limited to 10% of taxable income. Excess may be carried over.	Same as partnership.	Not deductible by the partnership on its return, but may be deducted by the partners on their individual returns subject to the limitations applicable to individuals.	Not deductible by the proprietorship, but may be deducted by the owner on the individual return subject to the limitations applicable to individuals.

(Cont.)

Table 2.3 (Continued)

Factor	Corporation (regular corporation)	S corporation (small business corporation)	Partnership	Sole proprietorship
Minimum tax on preferences	Tax preference items are subject to minimum tax at the corporate level.	Tax preferences pass through to the shareholders, except for certain capital gains subject to tax under Sec. 1378. No 15% cutback provision.	Tax preferences pass through to the partners.	Same as partnership.

Note. From *An Entrepreneur's Guide to Starting a Business* (pp. 5-7) by Arthur Andersen & Co., 1983, Chicago, IL. Copyright 1983. Reprinted by permission.

[a]The Tax Equity & Fiscal Responsibility Act (TEFRA) allows the IRS to allocate Personal Service Corporations (PSC) income back to the employee-owner. This also affects the corporation's pension plans. The use of PSCs is now diminished, and some individuals may decide their PSC is no longer advantageous. Liquidation normally would accelerate tax costs, but the new law provides special disincorporation relief for liquidations in 1983.

[b]The Tax Equity & Fiscal Responsibility Act (TEFRA) allows the IRS to allocate Personal Service Corporations (PSC) income back to the employee-owner. This also affects the corporation's pension plans. The use of PSCs is now diminished, and some individuals may decide their PSC is no longer advantageous. Liquidation normally would accelerate tax costs, but the new law provides special disincorporation relief for liquidations in 1983 and 1984.

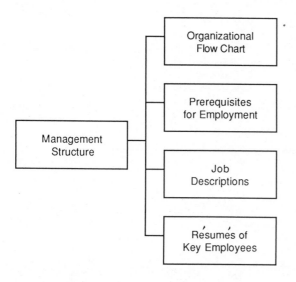

Figure 2.10. Component of a management organizational structure.

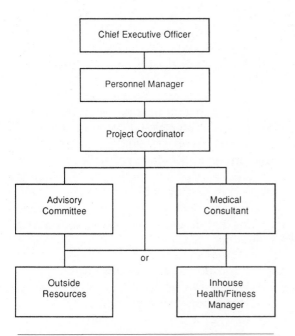

Figure 2.11. Sample health/fitness management structure within a corporate setting.

that focuses primarily on family recreation, one person can manage both the health/fitness and the sports/recreation programs. The organizational relationships of different-sized YMCAs are illustrated in Figure 2.12.

In a college or university that provides health/fitness programs for individuals in the surrounding community, the health/fitness program may be offered through the continuing education department. In most cases, however, the program is organized within the department of health, physical education, recreation, and dance (Figure 2.13).

Hospitals can take several approaches to delivering health/fitness programs both to inhouse hospital workers and to the outside community. In the past, health/fitness programs usually evolved from cardiac rehabilitation programs offered on an outpatient basis. The fitness components eventually were offered to hospital employees and to the community. In some hospitals, the health/fitness program now is under the administrative direction of the consumer/patient education department. In others, it is placed under the personnel department's employee assistance program (EAP) or the recreation division. In some instances, it is directed by the physical therapy department.

An interesting trend facilitated by the American Hospital Association is to have health promotion services, including health/fitness programming, placed under the consumer/patient education department, with services delivered both to employees and patients of the hospital and to consumers in the community (Figure 2.14).

Commercial Setting

Comprehensive health/fitness programs are provided by private health care organizations, health spas, and health studios. Usually, the

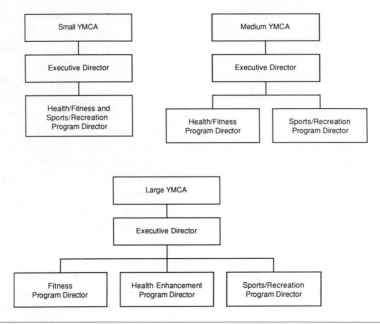

Figure 2.12. Sample YMCA organizational structure for health/fitness programs.

medical, education, and activity directors all are responsible for delivering health/fitness programs to the community; they report directly to the CEO (Figure 2.15).

In health spas and health studios, the marketing director, operations director, and activity director all share responsibility for the program (Figure 2.16). However, the burden of health/fitness delivery will probably be placed on the activity director, who is responsible for program development, that is, planning the types of activities to be offered. This individual usually has a background in health, physical education, or recreation.

The operations director is primarily responsible for the maintenance and safety of the facilities and equipment. The activity and operations directors should be familiar with each other's responsibilities so they can cover for one another. The sales director or promotion specialist is in charge of selling memberships to the club by promoting its staff,

programs, services, and facilities. The large, multipurpose commercial facilities are much more complex in terms of organizational structure (Figure 2.17).

The prerequisites for employment will vary with each health/fitness facility. Because there are no official standards for employment, each owner should determine early on the concept and staff responsibilities in their facility. This delineation will provide a better understanding of the type of employee needed for each position. Employee qualifications that should be considered include the following:

- Educational requirements
- Experience requirements
- Professional accreditation
- Emergency procedure skills
- Activity-related skills
- Communication skills
- Role-modeling image

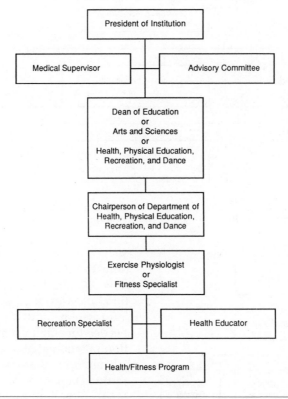

Figure 2.13. Sample organizational structure for health/fitness programs in the university setting.

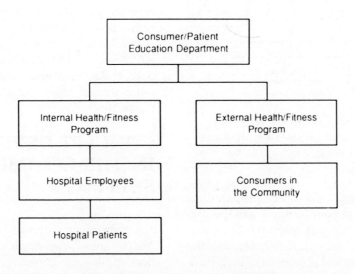

Figure 2.14. Sample hospital organizational structure for health/fitness programs.

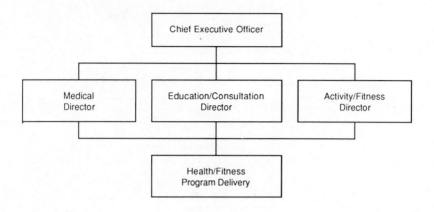

Figure 2.15. Sample private health care facility organizational structure for health/fitness programs.

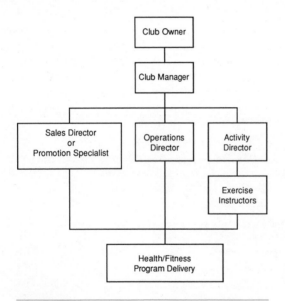

Figure 2.16. Sample health spa or club organizational structure for small health/fitness programs.

A job description should be prepared for every position in your facility. Take the prepared list of total staff responsibilities and analyze all positions in detail. Outline the specific job titles and objectives of each position, the duties and responsibilities, initial flow of authority, employee review information, and working hours. In addition to this information, add the special qualifications needed for employment, such as the information mentioned above. Examples of various job descriptions are provided in the appendix to this chapter.

To underline the qualifications of the management team in the business plan, include résumés of key personnel that list past experiences in the health/fitness field, professional accomplishments, educational background, publications, and professional affiliations. These résumés will show the potential investor that your plan to hire the right people from the start is being implemented.

CONCEPT DEVELOPMENT IN THE COMMUNITY SETTING

The community setting has various types of health/fitness programs (chapter 1). This section applies the generic model for concept

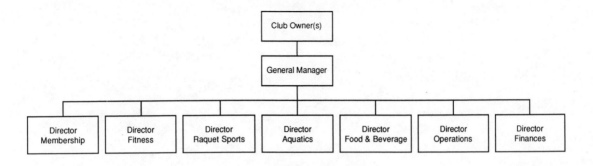

Figure 2.17. Sample health spa club organizational structure for large, multipurpose programs.

development to the hospital wellness program. A hospital-based wellness program in a community setting combines aspects of both corporate and commercial settings. The employee wellness component of the program is the corporate, or nonprofit, aspect, and the community outreach component is the commercial, or for-profit, aspect. Thus concept development must take these two characteristics into consideration and account for them both in the overall plan for the program. The typical hospital health/fitness program, marketing wellness to the community, sells a commercially oriented program but with a broader based content offering. Thus, in this setting, the best approach is to delineate the for-profit and nonprofit components of the program and then combine these elements in the various stages of concept development.

SUMMARY

This chapter presented the stages of concept development necessary for various health/ fitness settings: corporate, commercial, and community. In addition, it outlined the major functions of organizing and writing a fitness-related business plan. Whether you are involved in developing a health/fitness facility in a corporate, commercial, community, or clinical setting, the components mentioned can be adapted to provide the necessary information to present to potential investors. Every business plan will vary in length and content depending upon the stage of development, the complexity of the project, and the market it will serve. Financial discussions are so significant to the commercial business plan that the next chapter will be devoted to this subject.

Realistic planning is the key factor to the success of any health/fitness program. The corporate proposal serves to sell upper management and launch the program. The business plan serves as a management tool to provide short- and long-term goals, obtain financing, establish organizational and staff planning, and formulate the promotional and advertising plan.

CHAPTER 3

Financing Facilities

Financing is a major consideration when planning and developing a health/fitness facility. The complex network of the financial world provides a sobering glimpse of reality for those wishing to get involved in the health/fitness industry. Obtaining answers to such questions as how much capital is necessary, where the capital will come from, and where to obtain financial assistance can be confusing and is often the reason why many projects never get started.

Every business needs money to operate. The ability to obtain money when required is as necessary to the operation as finding a good location, providing quality equipment, obtaining reliable sources of supplies and materials, and having adequate personnel. Unfortunately, insufficient capital is a major cause of many early business failures (Burstiner, 1977, p. 71). Poor financial planning is the main reason why many health/fitness facilities go out of business (Berg, 1985, p. 28). For this reason, careful thinking and sound financial planning are essential if potential investors are to consider the venture.

The purpose of this chapter is to provide a systematic approach to financing health/fitness facilities. The specific topics discussed include (a) identifying capital needs, (b) preparing the financial statement, (c) identifying capital acquisition sources, and (d) obtaining financial assistance.

FINANCIAL COMPARISON OF VARIOUS FITNESS SETTINGS

The steps involved with financing a commercial fitness facility vary from setting to setting. The recent fitness boom has developed the commercial fitness business into an industry of nearly 7,000 health clubs nationwide (Poveromo, 1984). The main emphasis of a commercial health/fitness facility is to provide a consumer service, while at the same time showing a profit. The usual financing of commercial facilities is accomplished through investors looking for financial gain. Investors must be sold on the profit-making potential of the project. With the interest in today's fitness market, many development companies are finding that fitness facilities can be profitable in a number of ways. For example, companies are building fitness facilities in their developments as an incentive to help sell lease space. This type of an investment creates a large profit-margin capability for the developer.

As an alternative to building new commercial fitness facilities, large club acquisitions by such groups as Living Well, Inc., Bally Manufacturing, and Club Corporation of America have become a common practice. In 1985, the largest chain of health clubs was the 288-unit Health and Tennis Corporation (HTC), a wholly owned subsidiary of Bally Manufacturing. HTC's 1.4 million members average 4,861 per club, and the chain operates under 12 names, including Vic Tanney and Jack LaLanne (Kilburg & Strischek, 1985). The loan structure for such a club acquisition is a complex process. The combination of cash settlements, stock options, and various manager incentives based upon performance are often parts of the contractual arrangements.

Another practice of individuals wishing to enter the commercial fitness market is to lease either a new or an established facility. Leasing rather than buying allows many owners to stretch their capital by channeling more dollars into operating funds. Additional headaches such as paying building insurance premiums; meeting property tax liabilities; and repairing, heating, and air-conditioning the premises are usually the responsibility of the landlord. Also, the tax advantages and possible lease-purchase agreements are pluses of a lease arrangement. However, the disadvantages must also be considered. A landlord has the right to increase rent upon the expiration date of a lease. Lessees may even find that location has been lost to a higher bidder, even though they built up the location. Also, a lease agreement on a building sometimes includes a clause that indicates that a percentage of the business revenues is paid to the landlord. This amount often becomes a sore spot between the owners and the lessee. Finally, if equipment is leased it does not become an asset of the business, and thus no equity buildup is obtained.

Lease costs depend upon whether the individual contracts for just building space or negotiates for a totally operational facility. Today, most clubs operating in leased facilities pay from $5 to $15 per square foot for building space, or $15 to $25 per square foot

for a totally operational facility. It is important to remember that lease charges vary depending upon population density, building space availability, environmental conditions, and facility needs. As an example, lease space is generally more expensive in the downtown section of a city and becomes cheaper towards the outskirts of a city.

Financing Corporate Fitness Facilities

The financing of a corporate fitness facility is generally circulated through the corporate structure, and the allocation of funds is determined by a chairman of the board and/or board of directors. This arrangement is often established as an employee benefit that provides reduced health care costs and increased productivity for the company. Because there are no guidelines established for a corporate fitness program, each company's program will vary in appearance and approach depending on its resources and philosophy.

Corporations have found that the return on investment for a health/fitness program may not be immediate. The financial risk is not usually centered around what an employee fitness program will cost, but whether it will save money and whether such savings will outweigh the costs of the program. Generally, corporate officials have evaluated fitness programs in three major areas: program effects on work, program effects on health, and program effects on habits and behaviors. Although some of these areas are hard to quantify, management has been receptive to continuing health/fitness programs if any positive change results. Corporate investments into fitness have included funding for recreational organizations, in-house fitness programs, purchasing memberships in outside fitness facilities, and wide varieties of health promotion programs.

Financing Community Fitness Facilities

Community facilities, which include YMCAs, schools, and city recreation departments, are unique because they are usually based on a nonprofit tax-exempt financial structure. Monies derived from membership dues are placed back into charitable donations or individual scholarships so no profit can be shown. Funding for community facilities comes from community sources such as private foundations, community corporations, and capital campaigns. Additional funds can also be secured from federal, state, and local tax dollars.

CAPITAL NEEDS

The biggest obstacle to overcome in starting any new business, including a new health/ fitness project, is obtaining the necessary capital. Just as you can purchase a car for anything from $5,000 to $50,000, the same is true for start-up costs in the health/fitness business. You can get into the fitness business with anywhere from $100,000 to $10 million and operate profitably in either mode. Careful planning of all capital requirements should be formulated well in advance of approaching any potential lender.

Initial Capital

Prior to establishing a health/fitness facility, you should investigate all aspects of obtaining capital funding. The first question that must be asked is, How much money will be required? Traditionally there have been three types of essential capital: (a) initial capital, (b) operating capital, and (c) reserve capital.

Each of these capital resources plays a significant role in constructing, operating, and managing any new business.

Initial capital covers the start-up costs of building a health/fitness facility. Such items as construction costs, engineering and architectural fees, licensing and permits, franchising fees, and insurance are just some of the initial capital that must be determined. Also included are funds set aside for an open house or for promotional purposes. Although many of these expenses are easy to estimate, others will be more difficult to determine, and sometimes only an educated projection can be used. To guard against underfunding during this phase, it's a good idea to add a contingency (additional capital) to act as a buffer for any uncertain conditions that could arise. The following is a list of initial capital needs for the XYZ Health Club.

List of Initial Capital for the XYZ Health Club

Feasibility study costs	$_____
Architectural engineering fees	$_____
Construction contingency	$_____
Equipment/furnishings costs	$_____
Legal and professional fees	$_____
Licenses and permits	$_____
Printing costs	$_____
Landscaping	$_____
Construction costs	$_____
Total	$_____

There are typically six major components to a health/fitness construction project budget: construction costs, architectural/engineering fees, equipment costs, professional fees, financing costs, and miscellaneous fees and expenses. Although each of these items will vary greatly in content and magnitude for any given project, it is important to have some understanding of what each area consists of.

Construction Costs

These relate directly to the quantity and quality of the space or square footage developed. Early cost estimates, based on a square-foot-per-dollar basis, are further required as the scope of the project is developed in more detail. In the IRSA 1987 industry data survey, the average acreage for all free-standing fitness facilities ranged from 2.0 to 13.0 acres. Depending upon the contractual approach selected, an early guarantee of the construction cost can be obtained.

Cost estimates vary greatly depending on the quality of the facility, programs, equipment, and other considerations. Most often the construction costs include the actual building, mechanical systems (computer, energy system, ventilation design, public address [PA] system, and fire alarm arrangement), fixed equipment (front desk, storage shelves, and built-in furniture), and site development (paving, roads, landscaping, etc.) associated with the project.

Construction costs will also differ from region to region. For example, a club being built today in the Chicago area will cost from $50 to $100 per square foot, whereas in Meridian, Mississippi, a health/fitness facility can cost from $35 to $50 per square foot. These costs do not include land, construction, financing, start-up costs, mortgage points, and the like.

Architectural Fees

These are the costs associated with the following phases of a construction project:

- Schematic design
- Design development
- Construction documents
- Bidding or negotiation
- Construction phase
- Engineering development

A detailed explanation of these phases appears in chapter 6.

The architectural fees vary according to the complexity of the job. On the average, architectural fees range from 3% to 8% of the total construction costs, or an hourly rate of $50 to $100. This fee will be paid as the various phases of the project are completed.

Once the design phase of the project is completed, the architect becomes an on-site observer to evaluate the work completed and determine the amount owed to the contractor. The architect is also available to reject work that does not conform to contract documents.

Equipment Fees

The cost of equipment varies even more widely than construction costs. Estimates for equipment are based on quantity, quality, and space planning. Each division of a health/fitness facility must be considered when budgeting for equipment. For example, weight rooms, cardiovascular areas, locker rooms, clerical offices, computers, and so forth should be listed along with the prices of specific pieces of equipment needed for those areas.

In addition, there are alternative ways of acquiring equipment. The most popular method is purchasing new equipment. However, many facilities are investigating the possibilities of leasing new equipment or purchasing used equipment. Such considerations as tax benefits and financial negotiations make leasing and purchasing used equipment a consideration. Figure 3.1 represents the percent breakdown of how equipment is acquired in the health/fitness industry.

For an average fitness center, the equipment costs account for 10%-30% of the construction costs. For example, a study (*Corporate Fitness and Recreation*, 1983) on the purchase of weight room equipment found that budgets for corporate fitness operations ranged from $5,000 to $40,000. The data presented in Figure 3.2 represent the percent breakdown of weight room budgets for corporate fitness centers.

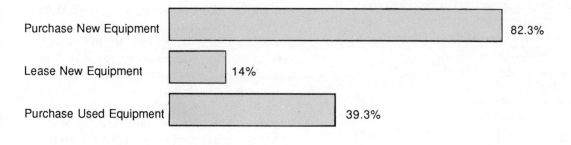

Purchase New Equipment   82.3%

Lease New Equipment   14%

Purchase Used Equipment   39.3%

Figure 3.1. Equipment acquisition for the health/fitness industry.

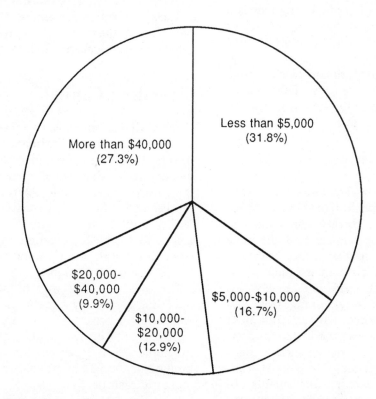

Figure 3.2. Weight equipment costs for corporate fitness programs.

Financing Fees

Such fees are associated with obtaining funds to pay for the project's construction. Generally, these fees are connected with paying interest on loans obtained from banks or other lending institutions. The total amount of the financing fees depends on market conditions at the date of financing and the equity contribution of the owner.

Because project financing can be accomplished through a number of ways, financing fees will be adjusted according to the various fees and reimbursable costs involved in obtaining these funds. For example, if a fitness center were built with tax-exempt bonds, the financing costs could include attorney fees, bond counsel, underwriter fees, auditors, and financial advisors.

The key to controlling financing fees is a well-planned and carefully budgeted facility development program. With a clear picture of what is to be bid by the contractor, you can determine a more realistic construction cost. For most construction projects a financing fee of 1%-3% is added to the total construction loan.

Professional Fees

These include additional funds associated with professional services for consultants, space planners, attorneys, construction managers, and the like. These services typically have reimbursable expenses that include traveling, printing costs, and on-site personnel supervision. Including fees and reimbursable expenses, professional services range from 10% to 15% of both construction and equipment costs. This figure varies according to the complexity of the job and whether such changes are included in other projected costs. It is important to remember that the benefits obtained by a good professional team often offset the additional fees incurred. Access to

specialized expertise provides a continual flow of advice and guards against the possibility of error.

Miscellaneous Fees

The other minor expenses associated with any capital budget are miscellaneous fees. To evaluate these costs accurately, the person responsible for the financial management must review each area and determine a budget figure for each item. Some examples of miscellaneous fees include printing costs, license and permits, and landscaping. Many of the miscellaneous fees are hidden in the operating expenses or sometimes just forgotten. Past experience has shown that neglecting these costs has caused projects to exceed their projected budgets and has led to early financial problems. Remember to consider every facet of the construction process when determining miscellaneous fees.

Operating Capital

Once the initial capital has been established, you should determine the financial needs for the first 12 months of operation. This process will determine the annual operating capital that must be generated. Operating capital represents the funds necessary to manage a facility until a profit begins to show. The ability to establish operating capital must come from listing and projecting costs for at least 1 year of operation.

The most effective way of determining operating costs is by a preliminary budget. Although the process of developing a working budget will be discussed in greater detail in chapter 13, it is relevant to mention the preliminary budget in the context of projecting early cash needs.

In its simplest form, a preliminary budget provides a plan for estimating future revenues and expenses. By projecting the initial cash flow needs early, you can turn financial expectations into actual goals for benefiting the facility. Through this form of early planning, you establish a better position for preventing crises.

To obtain the working capital required, a projection of the fixed and operating expenses must first be completed. Fixed expenses are those overhead expenses that do not vary with the volume of business activity. In other words, these are expenses that are incurred daily and are the result of preestablished decisions. By their nature, fixed expenses are generally recurred during every future accounting period. Some examples of fixed expenses are insurance, rent or debt service, interest on borrowed money, and depreciable expenses.

Operating expenses fluctuate with the changes in business volume. Basically, operating costs are the business expenses generated through promoting membership sales, and they fluctuate directly with the quantity of sales. Some examples of operating expenses include advertising, legal and accounting fees, maintenance/equipment repairs, and payroll taxes. Experience has shown that in the commercial fitness business, 60%-70% of the expenses consist of operating expenses, and the remaining 30%-40% comprises fixed expenses.

Once the expense items have been compiled, a similar list of projected revenues must be established. Approximately 60%-90% of the revenues in the commercial fitness industry come from membership dues and initiation fees. Additional revenues, which include storage locker fees, guest fees, activity fees, lessons, exercise classes, program fees, court time, pro shop, and food and beverage, represent the remaining 10%-40% of revenues.

When gathering the figures for a preliminary budget, you must begin with accurate information planning. If you have never developed a

budget before, contact an accountant or consulting firm for assistance. It is also recommended that you approach other professionals in the health/fitness field to discuss their ideas about financial planning. Their past experiences are useful when you are attempting to gather pertinent financial information. In addition, research the market to determine if any related surveys of industry data are available to aid in comparing and contrasting early projections of revenues and expenses.

The preliminary budget is of special interest to loan officers and prospective investors. The estimated cash flow needed to operate the facility is weighed and scrutinized closely. For this reason, each projection must be realistic and conform to industry standards. As an example, the International Racquet Sports Association (IRSA) provides an annual survey for health/fitness facilities. It's a good idea to obtain information of this type to support your financial projections.

The XYZ Health Club

The XYZ Health Club will illustrate the principles of a start-up budget for a commercial health/fitness facility. The preliminary information needed to establish the budget is as follows.

The club is constructed on a 7-acre tract of land in a large metropolitan suburban area. The facility is approximately 50,000 square feet. An owner/manager and an assistant manager are responsible for the operations of the facility, including a support staff of 16 full-time employees and 25 part-time employees. The facility is operational from 5:00 a.m. to 10:00 p.m. 7 days per week. The club charges an annual membership fee of $840 ($70 per month), with an initiation fee of $150. Additional revenues are collected from court fees, guest fees, and activity fees

Table 3.1 Sample Financial Worksheet for the XYZ Health Club

	Jan.	Feb.	March	April	May	June
Revenues						
Initiation fees	$ 15,000	13,500	12,000	10,650	8,250	8,250
Membership dues	$ 84,000	75,600	71,400	67,200	59,640	46,200
Court fees	$ 8,000	8,000	7,000	7,000	7,000	6,000
Guest fees	$ 1,000	1,000	1,000	1,000	1,000	1,000
Activity fees	$ 6,166	6,166	5,166	5,166	4,166	4,166
Other	$ 2,666	2,666	2,666	2,666	2,666	2,666
Total revenues	$116,832	106,932	99,982	95,032	85,122	68,282
Operating Expenses						
Advertising/promotion	$ 10,000	9,000	4,000	4,000	5,000	5,000
Maintenance/repairs	$ 1,000	1,000	2,000	2,000	3,000	3,000
Supplies	$ 2,500	1,250	2,000	1,250	1,250	1,000
Printing/postage	$ 500	500	500	500	500	500
Program expenses	$ 15,000	11,671	11,666	11,666	11,666	11,666
Utilities/telephones	$ 8,500	8,000	6,750	6,250	5,500	4,750
Payroll/fringe benefits	$ 5,875	5,875	5,875	5,875	5,875	5,875
Professional fees	$ 7,833	7,833	7,833	7,833	7,833	7,833
Management fees	$ 6,658	6,658	6,658	6,658	6,658	6,658
Total operating expenses	$ 57,866	51,787	47,282	46,032	47,282	46,282
Other expenses (fixed)						
Insurance	$ 2,087	2,083	2,083	2,083	2,083	2,083
Real estate tax	$ 1,674	1,666	1,666	1,666	1,666	1,666
Interest/debt service	$ 12,500	12,500	12,500	12,500	12,500	12,500
Depreciation	$ 5,000	5,000	5,000	5,000	5,000	5,000
Total expenses	$ 21,261	21,249	21,249	21,249	21,249	21,249
Total operating and fixed expenses	$ 79,127	73,036	68,531	67,281	68,531	67,531
Net income before taxes	$ 37,705	33,896	31,451	27,751	16,591	751

	July	Aug.	Sept.	Oct.	Nov.	Dec.	Total
Revenues							
Initiation fees	$ 7,950	7,500	9,300	7,500	7,650	7,950	$120,000
Membership dues	$44,520	42,000	52,080	42,000	42,840	44,520	$672,000
Court fees	$ 6,000	6,000	5,000	5,000	5,000	5,000	$ 75,000
Guest fees	$ 1,000	1,000	1,000	1,000	1,000	1,000	$ 12,000
Activity fees	$ 4,166	4,166	3,174	3,166	2,166	2,166	$ 50,000
Other	$ 2,666	2,666	2,674	2,666	2,666	2,666	$ 32,000
Total revenues	$66,302	63,332	73,228	61,332	61,322	63,302	$961,000
Operating Expenses							
Advertising/promotion	$ 5,500	5,500	3,500	3,500	2,500	2,500	$ 60,000
Maintenance/repairs	$ 4,000	4,000	5,000	6,000	7,000	7,000	$ 45,000
Supplies	$ 960	958	958	985	958	958	$ 15,000
Printing/postage	$ 500	500	500	500	500	500	$ 6,000
Program expenses	$15,000	11,667	11,666	11,666	15,000	11,666	$150,000
Utilities/telephones	$ 5,500	6,250	4,000	4,000	7,500	8,000	$ 75,000
Payroll/fringe benefits	$ 6,625	6,625	6,625	6,625	6,625	6,625	$ 75,000
Professional fees	$ 8,833	8,833	8,833	8,833	8,833	8,837	$100,000
Management fees	$ 7,508	7,508	7,508	7,508	7,508	7,512	$ 85,000
Total operating expenses	$54,426	51,841	48,590	49,590	56,424	53,598	$611,000
Other expenses (fixed)							
Insurance	$ 2,083	2,083	2,083	2,083	2,083	2,083	$ 25,000
Real estate tax	$ 1,666	1,666	1,666	1,666	1,666	1,666	$ 20,000
Interest/debt service	$12,500	12,500	12,500	12,500	12,500	12,500	$150,000
Depreciation	$ 5,000	5,000	5,000	5,000	5,000	5,000	$ 60,000
Total expenses	$21,249	21,249	21,249	21,249	21,249	21,249	$255,000
Total operating and fixed expenses	$75,675	73,090	69,839	70,839	76,673	74,847	$866,000
Net income before taxes	$ 9,373	9,758	3,389	9,507	15,351	11,545	$ 95,000

(i.e., daily exercise classes and activity programs). Other revenues include interest income, storage locker fees, and incidental charges. The first-year membership projection is to sell 800 memberships. Assuming that this membership goal is met, we can predict the first-year revenue budget (Table 3.1).

Notice that 82% of the total revenues are generated from initiation fees and membership dues. The remaining 18% of revenues come from support services. The total revenue goal for the first year of operation is $961,000. For this goal to be reached, the club would need to sell approximately 66 new memberships each month.

Also shown in Table 3.1 is the XYZ Health Club's list of operational and fixed expenses. The operational expenses include advertising/promotion, maintenance/repairs, utilities, and payroll. The total operational expense budget is $611,000, which is 70% of the total expenses. The remaining 30% consists of fixed expenses that include insurance, real estate taxes, debt service, and depreciation. The total fixed-expense budget equals $255,000. A total budget of $866,000 accounts for the first-year expenses.

If the proposed revenue and expense projections are achieved, the club records a net income before income taxes of $95,000. Always remember to apply realistic expectations when preparing an initial budget. If there is a question when determining a revenue or expense item, always lean toward conservatism in your projections.

Financial Statements

In addition to obtaining cash needs, you need to develop a set of various financial statements that provide realistic objectives for the new facility to follow. If money is to be borrowed on a short- or long-term basis, the lender needs to assess the projected financial position and determine its strengths and weaknesses. Specifically, a projected financial statement provides feedback to the owner and lender on what is to be expected financially over the next 1-3 years.

If you are the owner of the facility, you prepare the financial statement projections, because you are initiating the project. However, it is also recommended that you consider using an independent public accountant or a consulting firm that specializes in the health/fitness business. Financial statements developed by an unbiased, professional organization provide more credibility to potential lenders. There are at least two financial statements that are recommended: a balance sheet and a profit-and-loss statement.

Balance Sheet

A balance sheet is used to show the status of the business at a given point in time. It basically shows what is owned and what is owed for that day. A balance sheet is required for purposes of providing financial control, management decisions, and annual business goals. This report presents an updated list of assets, liabilities, and net worth. The owner dictates when the balance sheet should be completed; generally, one is prepared monthly, quarterly, or at the end of the fiscal year. Through interpreting the balance sheet, management can gain insight into planning and establishing short- and long-term financial goals.

Table 3.2 is a projected balance sheet for the XYZ Health Club. Note that the statement reveals the value and nature of the fitness center's assets, the size and character of its liabilities, and the amount of capital or equity that is available. The equity pertains only to the dollar value of the owner's capital, not to the cash fund or any other specific asset.

It is practically impossible to determine an owner's total investment among the assets shown on the balance sheet because it is most often split up among the building, land, equipment, and cash values.

Table 3.2 XYZ Health Club Balance Sheet

CURRENT ASSETS	
Money market	$ 75,000.00
Cash in bank	$ 10,000.00
Petty cash	$ 500.00
TOTAL CURRENT ASSETS	$ 85,500.00
FIXED ASSETS	
Exercise equipment	$150,000.00
Furniture	$ 30,000.00
Automobile	$ 10,000.00
Computer system	$ 10,000.00
TOTAL FIXED ASSETS	$200,000.00
TOTAL ASSETS	$285,500.00
CURRENT LIABILITIES	
Accounts payable	$ 10,000.00
Prepaid dues	$210,000.00
TOTAL CURRENT LIABILITIES	$220,000.00
CAPITAL	
Net worth	$ 15,000.00
Retained earnings	$ 5,000.00
TOTAL CAPITAL	$ 20,000.00
Current earnings	$ 45,000.00
TOTAL RETAINED EARNINGS	$ 45,500.00
TOTAL CAPITAL	$ 65,000.00
TOTAL LIABILITIES AND CAPITAL	$285,500.00

Profit-and-Loss Statement

A second financial statement is the profit-and-loss statement. In contrast to the balance sheet, a profit-and-loss statement reflects how the business is doing over a given period of time. Profit-and-loss statements are prepared at the beginning of each fiscal year and continue until the last day of the fiscal year.

Because a profit-and-loss statement provides excellent financial feedback, it should be prepared not only for the end of the year, but also monthly. This statement is often the only way a manager can keep up to date on what's happening financially and take steps to rectify any problems. A major element of the profit-and-loss statement is the bottom-line figure, which shows whether there was a monthly or yearly net profit or a loss. An example of a profit-and-loss statement is shown in Table 3.3.

A projected balance sheet and profit-and-loss statement for at least the first 3 years of operation should be included in the business plan. Ideally, these projections are extended to a 5-year plan. Past and current financial statements are included in this section if the fitness center has previously been in business. Such statements present both a history of operations and extended projections for the future of the facility.

Table 3.3 Profit and Loss Statement for XYZ Health Club, January 1, 1988–December 31, 1988

Income	
Membership dues	$ 775,000.00
Pro shop sales	$ 70,000.00
Food and beverage sales	$ 90,000.00
Activity fees	$ 50,000.00
Other income	$ 15,000.00
Total income	$1,000,000.00
Expenses (operating)	
Payroll and related costs	$ 270,000.00
Maintenance/repairs	$ 50,000.00
Utilities	$ 75,000.00
Other operating expenses	$ 145,000.00
Total operating expenses	$ 540,000.00
Expenses (fixed)	
Insurance	$ 25,000.00
Depreciation	$ 165,000.00
Debt service	$ 150.000.00
Real estate taxes	$ 20,000.00
Total fixed expenses	$ 360,000.00
Total expenses	$ 900,000.00
Net income/loss	$ 100,000.00

Reserve Capital

In addition to initial and operating capital, you will need reserve capital to cover unexpected situations and to maintain the business in case profits are not generated. Because most businesses fail within the first 12-18 months, it is important that your facility not become undercapitalized during this crucial period. It is not uncommon for owners to borrow enough cash to cover at least 1 year of operations, assuming no income is generated. Therefore, it's a good idea to plan ahead so enough capital will be available to give the business a chance to succeed. Figure 3.3 lists the capital requirements for the development of a health/fitness facility.

```
┌─────────────────────────────────┐
│  Initial Capital                │
│                                 │
│  1. Feasibility Study           │
│  2. Architectural Fees          │
│  3. Construction Costs          │
│  4. Equipment Costs             │
│                                 │
└─────────────────────────────────┘
   ┌──────────────────────────────────┐
   │  Operating Capital               │
   │                                  │
   │  1. Preliminary Budget           │
   │  2. Projected P&L Statement      │
   │  3. Projected Balance Sheet      │
   │                                  │
   └──────────────────────────────────┘
      ┌──────────────────────────────────┐
      │  Reserve Capital                 │
      │                                  │
      │  1. Most Businesses Start by Being│
      │  Undercapitalized                │
      │  2. Borrow Enough Cash for 1 Year │
      │  of No Income                    │
      │                                  │
      └──────────────────────────────────┘
```

Figure 3.3. Capital requirements for the development of a health/fitness facility.

CAPITAL ACQUISITION SOURCES

Once you have determined the cash needs, the next hurdle is to locate the required capital. In the health/fitness industry the traditional sources of potential capital include (a) personal funds, (b) banks, (c) government, and (d) venture capital. Each source has both positive and negative aspects to consider before borrowing any funds. Among the areas to investigate are interest rates, loan pay-back periods, availability of additional capital, sharing the business control, and lender

honesty. Information on each one of these areas must be obtained and then weighed accordingly before you decide which capital source to use.

The key to obtaining outside capital is convincing potential investors that you have the ability to run a successful business and that your projected venture has a good chance to succeed. In other words, you must become a salesperson for the project. Spend the necessary time on preparing for the financial presentation. Begin to obtain contacts and develop relationships with people in the financial field. An encounter with a prospective backer, investment group, or interested bank could occur in this environment. Most lenders are skeptics; you have to sell them on the importance and profitability of the business. An explanation of each of the four recommended sources of capital follows.

Personal Funds

Personal funds are the money and resources that an individual has on hand and can afford to put into a project. When seeking out banks or other lenders to invest in a fitness center, you will find that many are unwilling to lend money unless you are willing to risk personal funds. Among the areas that should be addressed are current cash position, sources of income (including salary), life insurance premiums, stocks and bonds, and other personal property. It's not necessary to disturb all savings. Loans can be established against savings accounts. Often the interest paid on a loan can be offset if a substantial balance is left in a savings account to continue to earn interest. Despite low cash availability, it's important to show prospective investors that the belief in the project is so strong that a portion of your personal funds is made available.

Bank Loans

Commercial banks are the major source of capital for new and continuing small business ventures. However, banks sometimes are reluctant to give loans to new businesses. The state of banking is changing constantly, and timing is a key issue when obtaining funds from a bank. Study the current banking environment and determine the best possible moment to approach your banker.

To increase the chance for obtaining a loan, prepare a business plan that includes all financial information, a description of the proposed fitness center, an explanation of the past and future trends for the fitness business, industry standards, and a feasibility study. The objective of any business plan should be to provide supportive data that will help sell your concept to the banker, while educating him or her about the health/fitness industry. The business plan is the single most important document that can be made available to the banker. A complete description of the process of preparing a business plan and the necessary steps involved in presenting it to the lender is given in chapter 2. The following are five areas that are important to a banker when considering a loan request:

1. Building location
   - high traffic location
   - commercially zoned
   - easily converted to other uses
2. Staff qualifications
   - past experience
   - education requirements
   - special skills
3. Personal collateral
   - show ability to pay back loan
   - provide personal guarantees
4. Individual equity
   - place personal funds into the facility
   - place profits back into the facility
5. Successful existing operation
   - yearly financial growth
   - periodic facility improvements
   - yearly membership increase

Another area that must be considered before approaching a banker is the normal debt/equity ratio. In the commercial health/fitness business the ratio is 60:40. This ratio means that normally you need to generate at least 40% of the start-up and first year capital needs from yourself and your partners before a financial institution will review the project. For example, if the total coast of a fitness center is $1 million, the investment owner or partners should not borrow any more than $600,000. Prior to going to the bank, the owner should have accumulated $400,000 in equity. This model prevents the owner from entering the industry and becoming over-leveraged from the start, especially considering that a fitness center takes approximately 2 to 3 years to generate a positive cash flow (McCarthy, 1986).

If a bank does not approve a loan request the reasons can be traced to one or more of the following problems:

- The basic business idea was considered unsound or too risky.
- There was insufficient collateral.
- There was no financial commitment on the owner's part—"all partners should be at risk."
- The projected use of funds was unclear.
- No business plan was prepared.
- The applicant demonstrated a lack of confidence and enthusiasm regarding the project.

When deciding upon a bank, never go with the first bank that you approach. Shop around and compare such things as interest rates, down payment amounts, collateral requirements, and other services that the bank provides. Many individuals like to try their personal banker first, or ask their attorney or accountant whom they might recommend. Allan Schwartz of the Tennis Corporation of America suggests that a title search of banks that have made loans to clubs or recreational organizations is another method for finding financing. A title search shows what bank actually owns a particular business. Also, never settle for a loan that is less than what the business plan calls for. Obtaining a loan is a two-way street; the bank provides the initial funding, but the owner must repay that loan with interest. An agreement equitable from both sides must be decided upon.

Government Loans

Congress has established several avenues to help provide financial assistance to many businesses. The Small Business Investment Corporation (SBIC) comprises special investment corporations chartered by the federal government to stimulate the formation and growth of small businesses. The SBICs must comply with regulations governing the size of companies that are invested in and the amount of equity that is obtained.

The Small Business Administration (SBA) was also established by Congress to aid small businesses in obtaining loans. The SBA generally provides financing through direct loans but prefers to work through a bank or insurance company. This arrangement benefits the lending institution, because the money is loaned from a bank or insurance company and the SBA guarantees up to 90% of the loan.

In 1985 the SBA granted 134 loans worth $16.1 million to health/fitness club owners and operators. That figure was an increase from 118 loans, valued at $13.8 million, in 1983. The total number of SBA-guaranteed loans increased from 17,198, worth $2.4 billion, in 1983 to 17,290, valued at $2.7 billion, in 1985. To secure an SBA-guaranteed loan, revenues over the past 3 years (or projected first 3 years for a new fitness center) cannot surpass a yearly average of $3.5 million. The applicant must also have been turned down by a bank to be eligible (Brox, 1986, p. 36).

Always investigate the loan limits and interest rates before securing an SBA loan. They vary depending upon the type of loan and whether it is secured by the SBA or through another lending institution. Currently, the maximum limit from the SBA for loan assistance is $500,000. It is important to check the loan limits periodically, because they can change with new tax laws or through federal intervention.

Venture Capital

Venture capitalists consist of five groups:

- Investment bankers
- Private partnerships and corporations
- Divisions of large corporations
- Small business investment companies (SBICs)
- Individual and family venture capitalists

These organizations or groups loan funds with one idea in mind—capital gains! Venture capitalists generally fund a business in any stage of development, whether it is a new project or an already established facility that needs additional capital for further expansion.

When searching for potential investors, seek the guidance of business associates, consultants, lawyers, accountants, or bankers. Be prepared to ask specific questions regarding the organization and always ask for references. Don't hesitate to approach several venture capitalists simultaneously.

Once the venture capitalists fund a project, they obtain partial ownership of the business until the loan is paid back. This relationship must be reviewed closely, because partial control of the business is held by the venture capitalist. Fortunately, many venture capitalists realize their expertise is not in the health/fitness field and leave the decision-making responsibilities to the owner.

Venture capitalists fund less than 2% of the business proposals that are reviewed. For this reason, the proposal you present should be as professional, concise, and appropriate as possible to receive funds.

OBTAINING FINANCIAL ASSISTANCE

Several organizations help with the financial planning for starting a health/fitness facility, including private consultants, the SBA, banks, and public accounting firms. For these groups to be of assistance, you must provide the right financial information. The variety of health/fitness centers continues to increase, but consistent financial parameters are slow in being established. As a result, the burden of obtaining the necessary financial information rests with the owner/manager.

The financial information requested by most lenders includes

- an explanation of how revenues will be generated;
- a financial feasibility study, including a projected pro forma;
- financial statements, either projected or from past years;
- estimated debt service;
- the projected break-even point; and
- the present value of the total project.

By providing this information, you will show lending institutions that you are serious about the project and that you have addressed all financial areas.

The value in obtaining financial assistance comes in preparing the documentation, providing projected operating statements, and determining an accurate pro forma. Most companies have had previous experience in adopting financing profiles to various business settings. It will be the responsibility of the owner/manager to educate the organization in the nature of the project being proposed. In the past, health/fitness projects have been notorious for not providing the necessary documentation to satisfy the lenders. As a result, many new facilities have been turned down on their requests for financial assistance.

Many of the organizations mentioned have developed computerized financial pro formas to assist in financial planning. The software packages available provide financial projections for Years 1 through 5 if requested. An effective financial pro forma requires a series of variables that provides the necessary ingredients to adjust standard software packages to a specific model:

- Total number of presale memberships
- Total number of new men and women per month in the first year
- Dues and initiation fees for men, women, family, and so forth
- Total number of staff and average monthly salaries
- Anticipated debt service or lease fee per month
- Anticipated utility costs per month
- Approximate size of building (square feet)

If you decide to pay a consulting firm to help you obtain financial assistance, you should enter into a written agreement of the work requested. Oftentimes costs can be reduced by agreeing to an oral report, backed by a written summary. The following are some points that should be covered in the agreement:

- The scope of the project clearly defined.
- Dates for specific phases of the financial documentation.
- The benefits that should be expected for the project (they should be measurable).
- A list of the financial materials that will be generated—lists, charts, tables, and so forth.
- A determination of the approximate fees.

By providing such an agreement, you ensure that both parties understand what is expected and nothing is left in question. Always remember that the caliber of work is of the highest concern. The professional appearance of all documentation is an important factor when lenders evaluate the financial presentation.

SUMMARY

This chapter outlined the major functions of financing a fitness facility. Whether you are involved with a corporate, commercial, or community setting, the components can be modified to provide the necessary information to present to potential investors.

The major steps in financing a facility are determining capital needs, conducting a budgetary analysis, preparing the financial statement, locating capital sources, and putting the financial package together. The discussion focused on the commercial health/fitness program, but many of the suggestions for obtaining capital apply to the corporate or community settings.

The key to capital acquisition is recognizing the need that both investors and financial institutions have for complete documentation. A combination of an experienced, professional person with a comprehensive business plan provides the necessary ingredients for proper capital acquisition. This process also provides short- and long-term financial goals for management to meet and compare to budgetary objectives.

PART II

Getting Built

The information in Part II should facilitate getting your health/fitness facility planned and built. Included in the discussion are criteria for selecting facility and program consultants, contractual and fee reimbursement procedures, and important considerations in working with an architect. We present key concepts for the design process and illustrate practical examples of good and bad design characteristics. We make note of important ideas to keep in mind during the construction process and provide a detailed checklist of each facility component. Although the technical aspects are only highlighted, you will gain a working knowledge of sufficient detail to assist you in working with the various professionals in the design and construction industry.

CHAPTER 4

Health/Fitness Facility Consultants

As is evident from previous chapters, the effective use of consultants is an important ingredient for the successful development of health/fitness facilities and programs. Numerous decisions will be made in the various stages of planning, developing, building, and constructing a facility, as well as during the formative stages of program development and management. During the development of a facility, the judicious use of consultants to supplement existing expertise in making decisions is invaluable. The purpose of this chapter is to assist you in maximizing the use of such consultants.

THE ROLE OF THE CONSULTANT

The role of the consultant in the health/ fitness field has changed greatly in recent years. Up to this time, when individuals wanted to develop and operate a health/ fitness facility they naturally looked to a local professional such as an athletic coach or YMCA director for expertise. There were no industry standards to use as benchmarks in making judgments about the merits of a business plan. Market research was very primitive in the health/fitness industry and posed a real challenge to the lender and the borrower alike.

Space planning was equally underdeveloped during these early stages. The facility planners available frequently resorted to modeling the plans for a new corporate or clinical facility after a local school plant or the YMCA. Personnel was frequently secured from local sources; for example, a successful high school coach in the community might be hired to start the health/fitness program. Such individuals were unfamiliar with the program objectives and clientele, causing the program to be doomed from the start because of inappropriate implementation techniques. This has all changed in recent years. Many talented and experienced health/fitness professionals are in the field, and consumers are far more informed about this growing industry. Also many competent consultants are available to facilitate the development and management of new facilities.

A real challenge confronts those trying to develop health/fitness programs, and consultants can be most helpful in this regard. Figure 4.1 illustrates the developmental process that occurs in health/fitness facility and program development. It is clear from the figure that each phase of the development could benefit from consultants as resources. A specific consultant may be needed to assist with business planning, whereas another may be brought in to perform space planning. Yet another consultant may be needed for personnel development and program start-up. The whole process is very complex and requires several specialists to put it together in a workable fashion. A team approach is best for using consultants effectively. Consultants who claim that they can be all things to all people should be viewed with great scrutiny. There is a trend

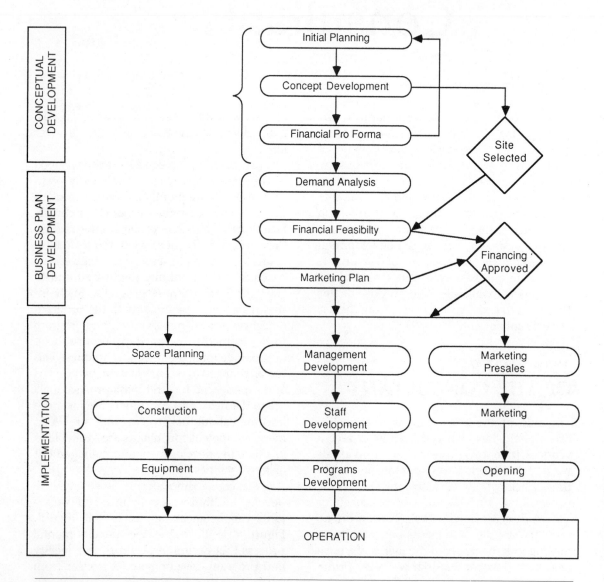

Figure 4.1. The developmental process of program development.

for consultants to form business associations and pool their talents and resources to better meet the changing needs of the health/fitness market.

Program Concept Consultant

A consultant is helpful in developing the program concept. In this regard, he or she is responsible for overseeing concept development, including developing a good planning committee, providing leadership for defining program objectives, and so forth. The following are questions for the consultant to address in developing the program concept:

- What is the main purpose of the project? Profit? Reduced employee health care costs? Morale? Community visibility?
- What image should be projected? Medical? Fitness? Wellness? Body building?
- Where should the resources be placed? Facility? Program? Staff? Marketing?
- Where will the programming occur? On-site? Off-site? Or will it be joint-ventured?

Marketing Research Consultants

The consultant is also a good resource in developing a market research program. The consultant has the options of conducting the market research on his or her own or referring the project to a market research company. In either case, numerous questions must be addressed at this juncture, including the following:

- What population is to be served? Geographic area? Income level? Age? Sex? Health status?
- What services do these people want? Fitness? Wellness? Sports medicine? Rehabilitation?

- What conveniences will the target population expect? Close proximity to work and/or home? Baby-sitting? Parking?
- What form of membership structure should be established? Cost? Corporate? Family?
- What kind of competition will the projected program have? Corporate? Commercial? Community? Clinical?

Business Plan Consultants

The consultant is instrumental in developing the business plan and the financial pro forma to present to potential investors. Some of the questions that a consultant can help to answer include the following:

- What are the capital needs for the project? Initial? Operating? Reserve?
- When will the project begin to break even financially? Projected income? Expenses?
- What kinds and amounts of expenses should be planned for? Personnel? Utilities? Insurance? Debt service?
- What kinds and amounts of revenues should be expected? Membership? Vending? Pro shop? Amenities? Entry fees? Equipment rental?
- Where will the members come from? Primary market? Secondary market? Competition?

Facility Planning Consultants

Consultants also specialize in facility planning and construction. Although this is discussed in greater detail in chapter 6 it is relevant to mention it here in the context of specific consultants' roles. Consultants are very important in the space planning phase of the facility development. Their familiarity with the health/fitness business is essential in the development of program statements, which define the parameters of the facility and include such concerns as numbers and types of facility users, peak periods of use, various space needs for programming, and the like. For example, knowledge of space requirements for lockers is critical. In this situation, you would need to know that there are different types and configurations of lockers on the market, each of which serves a useful purpose in a particular setting. The consultant will also know that different techniques are available to force-feed ventilation through lockers to prevent unpleasant odors, which is important in establishing the proper image for your facility. These examples stress the importance of being aware of the details of constructing a facility, either through your own expertise or through the expertise of a consultant. During the preconstruction phase of the project, critical decisions are made that influence the future success of the program, and you can benefit greatly from consultants in this regard. Some of the questions a facility planning consultant needs to address are as follows:

- What are the specific program requirements? Types of activities? Number of members serviced? Peak usages?
- What are the specific space requirements for the program activities? Lockers? Activity areas? Administration? Storage?
- What are the interrelationships of the various spaces? Administration? Activity? Lockers? Front desk?
- What are the best resources for architects? Trade journals? References from model facilities? Professional associations?

Space Planners

There are times when it is appropriate to hire a space planner in addition to hiring an architect. Space planners who specialize in health/fitness facilities can effectively collaborate with architects. This is more expensive than using only one consultant because some of their services overlap, but the final product may be worth the additional expense and may be the most cost-effective. At any rate, consultants who specialize in space planning are often needed during the design development, construction document, and bidding phases. The following are some of the questions to address during these phases:

- Is the design an efficient use of available space? Is circulation space minimized? Is programming space maximized? Is it ecologically efficient?
- Is the facility structurally and functionally sound? Is load-bearing floor capable of handling weight-lifting equipment? Are air exchanges adequate in humid areas?
- Is the facility capable of being expanded in the future, with lockers on exterior walls and activity areas on exterior walls?
- Do the construction documents meet all the specialized equipment and governmental code requirements (e.g., electrical, plumbing, air-conditioning, ventilation)?
- Does the design reflect the desired image including ambience, landscaping, and interior design?

Program and Management Consultants

Program and management consultants are available to operationalize the program once the facility is built by assisting in personnel recruitment and development, management start-up, marketing and promotional activities, equipment selection and installation, computerization of diagnostic and prescriptive activities, and records and management procedures. Consultants are available for managing health care costs in corporations, implementing specialized programs such as stress management, installing and supervising accounting systems, and so forth. Some of the more important questions to address during construction as well as after completion of the facility include the following:

- From where will the important personnel be secured? Professional associations? Placement services? Headhunters?
- How will we get ready for the management of the facility? External management contract? Internal management by program director?
- How will we promote and advertise the program? Consultants? Media? Special events?
- Who will implement the programming? Contract labor? Consultants? In-house staff?
- Who will keep track of all the records and cash flow? Consultants? Computers? Office staff?

As you can see, there are many different types of consultants, and each has a specialized form of service. Consider your consultants carefully, as there are a large number of vendors to choose from with varying amounts of expertise. Be sure to examine their qualifications and experience before securing their services. The following are some important things to look for when scrutinizing a consultant:

- Credentials. Does the consultant belong to an accrediting agency such as the American Institute of Architects?
- Licensure/certification. Does the consultant have licensure or certification, if appropriate, in his or her area of expertise?
- Reputation. What kind of reputation and references does the consultant have in the health/fitness field?
- Proximity. Is the consultant close enough that travel expenses will not become excessive?

- Colleagues. Does the consultant have other resources to draw from in the health/fitness field? Remember, no one person can meet all the needs of health/fitness consulting.

There are a number of resources to use in finding a good consultant. Professional associations frequently list consulting resources. The Association for Fitness in Business, for example, publishes an annual information directory that categorizes available consultants who pay for their listings. Several journals publish an annual buyer's guide, which frequently includes professional consultants. Included among these journals are *Club Business* and *Athletic Business. Fitness Management* provides a list of professional health/fitness consultants who meet a fairly stringent set of criteria for their being listed.

PLANNING TO USE A CONSULTANT EFFECTIVELY

It is important to plan on a long-term basis for the kind and amount of consultation that will be involved in the development and management of the program. Consultants as a rule are very expensive, with current costs ranging from $500 to $2,000 per day. You can easily get overextended by relying extensively on consultants. Yet, catastrophic mistakes can be made without them. The key is a balance. One way to achieve this balance is to plan ahead for the kind and amount of consulting services that will be needed for the project. The following developmental timeline shows long-range planning that might be used for consultants.

Developmental Timeline

CONCEPTUAL DESIGN	BUSINESS PLAN DEVELOPMENT	IMPLEMENTATION
Initial planning	Demand analysis	Program development-------->
Design model	Financial feasibility	Construction--------------------->
Financial pro forma	Marketing plan	Marketing, Phase I------------>

YEAR 1__/ __/ __/ __/ __/ __/ __/ __/ __/ __/ __/ __/ __/

Consulting activities: *Consulting activities:*   *Consulting activities:*

IMPLEMENTATION		OPERATION
Equipment procurement/layout---------> Opening		Facility/equipment maintenance
Staff development/training--------------> Programs begin		Programs/classes/special events
Marketing, Phase I-------------------------> Marketing, Phase II		--->

YEAR 1__/ __/ __/ __/ __/ __/ __/ __/ __/ __/ __/ __/ __/

Consulting activities: *Consulting activities:*   *Consulting activities:*

Once you have contacted the appropriate consultant(s) for your purposes, you have to make some decisions regarding contracts. Before running headlong into a contractual agreement, you should be aware of some of the preliminary items that you may have to deal with in the process of signing a contract.

CONTRACTUAL AGREEMENTS

There are probably as many different kinds of contracts in the health/fitness business as there are consultants in the field. Yet these contracts will undoubtedly share some common elements to deal with the terms of the more prevalent business arrangements. The following are some of these more common elements of a contract.

Party identification names the client and consultant.

Purpose of agreement states the terms and conditions under which the consultant will provide consulting services to the client.

Services provided specifies the type(s) of service(s) to be performed by the consultant.

Statement of confidentiality states that all services and information derived from such services will not be divulged. Failure to maintain confidentiality is subject to legal redress.

Compensation states the rate of compensation for services rendered by hour, day, week, month, or for the task(s) identified in the "Services Provided" section. It is customary for the contract to stipulate that travel and other business-related expenses be reimbursed by the client. Sometimes a clause for past due service charges is included.

Exclusivity states the degree of exclusivity or independence that can be assumed by the contract. Most consultants want to maintain independence in order to contract services with other clients.

Term of agreement states the duration of the agreement as well as the requirement for premature termination of the contract.

Attorneys' fees and costs states the prevailing party's entitlement to reasonable attorneys' fees, costs, and disbursements in addition to any other relief to which the party may be entitled.

Retainer fee is a one-time fee accorded the consultant to secure his or her services.

Miscellaneous provisions states any additional provisions necessary to consummate the agreement.

It is always prudent to secure the contract prior to initiating the consultant's services, because once the services commence a contract becomes more difficult to obtain. Although many services can proceed to completion without a hitch, an isolated nightmare with some party will outweigh by far the trouble of routinely securing contracts. Seek legal counsel before you make any contractual agreements; a lawyer should be actively involved in this stage. A sample consultant contract is included here to illustrate the basic elements of a contractual agreement between a client and a consultant.

HEALTHSCAPE, INC.
302A Thornridge
Argyle, Texas 76226
(817) 464-3700
CONSULTING CONTRACT

This agreement is made between Robert W. Patton, PhD, Coordinator of consulting specialists in a professional association known as ''Healthscape, Inc.,'' hereinafter referred to as ''Consultant,'' and _____, hereinafter referred to as ''Customer.''

Purpose of Agreement

The purpose of this agreement is to state the terms and conditions under which Consultant will provide consulting services to Customer from time to time.

Now, therefore, in consideration of the mutual promises herein contained, the parties hereto agree as follows:

Services Provided

1. Consultant agrees to provide professional services related to the design, implementation, and management of health/fitness and/or health promotion programs, facilities in either a profit or nonprofit setting for the Customer.

Such services shall include, but not be limited to, feasibility studies, planning new or evaluating existing facilities, program design and implementation, personnel recruitment and development, equipment purchasing and installation, management and operations development, and

(Cont.)

Consulting Contract (Continued)

marketing and business planning and implementation. Consultant will interact with Customer regarding specific service requirements.

Confidentiality

2. All information given by Customer to Consultant concerning statistical, financial, or personal data relating to the business of the Customer will be held in strictest confidence by the Consultant. Such obligations shall extend beyond the term of this contract, regardless of the nature of its termination. Should Consultant breach this obligation of confidentiality, Customer shall have the right to seek all legal redress necessary to protect its interests.

Compensation

3. Customer shall pay Consultant for all services rendered at the rate of $_____ per day or $_____ per hour, unless a retainer of $_____ per month is agreed upon. Customer shall also reimburse Consultant for all expenses incurred in the performance of his or her services. Such compensation and reimbursement shall be paid within 2 weeks of invoice receipt. A service charge of 1.5% per month (APR = 18%) may be applied to past due invoices.

Independent Contractor

4. Consultant is an independent contractor and not an employee, agent, or other representative of Customer. Consultant may contract services with other clients. Consultant has no authority to make any representations on the behalf of the Customer or perform any act on behalf of Customer except for the services outlined in this contract.

Term of Agreement

5. The term of this agreement shall begin upon execution and shall continue in force and effect thereafter. It is terminated by fifteen (15) days written notice by either party to the other at the addresses set forth above. In the event of termination by Customer, Consultant shall not incur additional expenses after receipt of notice of termination.

Attorneys' Fees and Costs

6. If any action at law or in equity is necessary to enforce or interpret the terms of this agreement, the prevailing party shall be entitled to a reasonable attorneys' fee, costs, and necessary disbursements in addition to any other relief to which such party may be entitled.

Miscellaneous Provisions

7(a). This agreement shall become binding upon signing by both parties. Consultant shall commence execution of services upon receipt of a retainer fee in the amount of $_____.

(b). This agreement shall be construed under and in accordance with the laws of the State of Texas, and all obligations of the parties created hereunder are performable in Denton County, Texas.

(c). This agreement shall be binding upon and inure to the benefit of the parties hereto and their respective heirs, executors, legal representatives, and assigns, where permitted by the agreement.

(d).   In case any one or more of the provisions contained in this agreement shall for any reason be held to be invalid, illegal, or unenforceable in any respect, such invalidity, illegality, or unenforceability shall not affect any other provision thereof and this agreement shall be construed as if such invalid, illegal, or unenforceable provision had never been contained herein.

(e).   This agreement constitutes the sole and only agreement of the parties hereto and supersedes any prior understanding or written or oral agreement between the parties regarding the within subject matter.

Executed this date _____

Consultant _____
          Robert W. Patton

Customer _____

A final point regarding contractual agreements between clients and consultants has to do with the accounting methods associated with long-term contracts. It serves both parties well to understand these matters because different methods have significantly different tax implications. Long-term contracts can have significant tax-deferral potential. Those eligible for long-term contracts should consider the following ways of reporting income. (Service contracts such as architectural, engineering, and the like are generally not eligible for these methods; however, see the section on "Advance Payment Elections" later in this chapter.)

Percentage-of-Completion Method

The most common method is percentage-of-completion, which is typically used for financial reporting purposes. The percentage-of-completion method recognizes income on the basis of the percentage of the job that is complete, based on cost or physical completion. Various criteria, including costs incurred, labor hours worked, and physical construc-tion completed, are used to measure job completeness. This method smooths out revenue earned over a number of periods and results in little, if any, deferral of income for tax purposes. It also promotes a stable cash flow if the consultant maintains a steady rate of work. The realization of periodic payments is a real incentive to the consultant.

Completed-Contract Method

The other general method is the completed-contract method, according to which contract income and direct and allocated contract costs are recognized only when construction is completed. As no income is recognized at all prior to completion, this method provides the maximum deferral of reporting income for tax purposes. In addition, it can be used for tax purposes even though the percentage-of-completion method is usually used for financial reporting purposes. Finally, advanced payments are ignored for the purpose of income recognition. Clearly, there is an incentive for the consultant to complete agreed-upon services as soon as possible to promote cash flow.

Accrual-Acceptance Method

A variation of the completed-contract method is the accrual-acceptance method, by which income is recognized on shipment, delivery, title transfer, or customer acceptance. Accrual-acceptance allows the use of regular inventory methods for accumulating costs of the contract. It is generally unavailable to most service-oriented consultants; however, it may be used for tax purposes even though another method of accounting is used for financial reporting purposes.

Advanced Payment Elections

Taxpayers who use long-term contract accounting methods, or taxpayers who receive payments in advance for goods or services to be provided in a subsequent year, have the ability to elect deferral options with respect to those payments. These elections provide the ability to defer the income until the services are provided, or when the revenue is recognized under the completed-contract method, even though the general rule requires inclusion of income in the year of receipt. This method is available to any company or consultant, not just those eligible for long-term contract methods. For example, service businesses of architects, engineers, and health/fitness consultants that use the accrual-acceptance method can defer advance payments for services to be performed in the following taxable year.

Although a description of accounting techniques may appear somewhat inappropriate in a discussion of consulting services, these procedures for accounting may influence the arrangements that are agreed upon between the client and the consultant. It behooves both the client and the consultant to be informed about such tax saving and cost-effective procedures. Moreover, there are incentive advantages of a different nature for each of the consultant payment systems.

WORKING WITH CONSULTANTS

Working with consultants can be both a challenging and a rewarding experience. The challenges are many. It is a challenge for clients to admit the need for a consultant, especially when they have been in the field and have more than a passing knowledge of the processes that they are suddenly paying consultants large sums of money to develop. Because of the above, it is a challenge to establish clear, direct, and specific lines of communication with well-understood expectations. A contract frequently helps clarify such problems. The client must retrieve all the essential information necessary to arm the consultant with enough data to give good counsel. For example, basic assumptions about program goals, member ceilings, expansion plans, and so forth should be addressed early in the consulting process. The client must also take the long-term view and invest in the numerous consultants that will be necessary to put together a project that will be viable in the distant future.

The consultant is faced with maintaining effective interaction between the client and his or her planning team. In addition, the consultant must interact and work with other consultants who perform related services on the project. Space planners and architects are, for example, synergistic consultants, yet they may have difficulty with turf struggles. Finally, it will be a challenge for the consultant to balance the conservation of the client's resources and the need to produce consulting revenue.

Ideally, the relationship between a client and consultant involves a lot of listening first by the consultant and second by the client—a rigorous dialogue should precipitate prior to conclusion of the consultation. The rewards of the joint venture between client and consultant are many, but they always revolve around the development of a model project. A final product that is pleasing to all concerned is the most important reward.

SUMMARY

In this chapter we have introduced you to the role of the consultant in facilitating concept development, business plan design, construction of a facility, and program implementation. The successful use of consultants will almost always require several different professionals. Some of the issues confronting the client and consultant were addressed and some methods of resolving these issues were presented.

CHAPTER 5

Facility Planning and Design Considerations

In this chapter we discuss important considerations in planning and designing health/fitness facilities. Most individuals comprising a good planning and design committee have some experience in facility development, construction, or management. For example, the investor may have been a college athlete and spent considerable time in gyms. The banker may be a long-standing member in a local health or country club. The architect/space planner may have designed other fitness-related facilities. You as a principal planner may have managed other health/fitness facilities. Each person involved in the development of a facility in the health/fitness industry usually brings different experiences and expertise to the project.

The design process requires that all of the principal players be involved, but in specific and appropriate ways. On the one hand, the size, nature, and programs of the facility must be appropriate to assure downstream profitability for the investor. On the other hand, the banker is concerned that the feasibility study for the facility should indicate sufficient immediate return to service the debt. The architect/space planner is concerned about many things, but ultimately wants to make a functional and aesthetic statement with his or her creative endeavor. You as a potential manager or operator are probably concerned about many things as well, but will naturally focus on the programming and personnel requirements of the space being planned. These particular concerns of key individuals will combine to complement your plans at times, but will force unwanted compromises at other times.

The ingredients for a successfully designed facility are a generous amount of expertise, a sprinkle of adventure, a pinch of fiscal reality, a flavoring of some pragmatic programming input, and a large dose of homework and elbow grease. This mixture of ingredients is only possible with the right blend of human resources operating with a common mission. This team of people can both enjoy and profit from the design process if properly conducted. Once this team is developed, it is wise to start with a common frame of reference. This is frequently accomplished by site visitations to recognized facilities of excellence similar in purpose to the one being planned. Your consultant and/or space planner can be a good resource for identifying such facilities. Good notes taken during such visitations can be invaluable in galvanizing the thoughts of the key individuals on the planning and design team. Moreover, many of the good features in the model facilities can be incorporated into the design of your complex. However, it is important to leave the design process in the hands of the designer once the basic parameters have been defined.

Thomas Wills, a prominent space planner, says that the design process is both an art and a science. There are many unmeasurable things that go into making the program participants excited about the facility besides nice equipment and hot showers. Most buildings don't leak. Most facilities have controlled temperatures and humidities. But, not all facilities give first-time occupants a sense of excitement and drama as they enter the spaces. A well-designed facility will not only satisfy the functional and technical requirements, but excite the human senses. This excitement has little to do with extravagant expenditure. It has much to do with the creative orchestration of all the functional requirements of a facility with a dramatic application of the right space, light, texture, color, and form. The right mixture creates the drama and excitement. This design process requires the unfettered talents of a professional. So, once all the information is provided, the wise client should let the designer perform the special magic that he or she alone can do. The planning committee should not interfere in this process. It can, however, be very effective in critically reviewing the designer's work and fine-tuning the space plan.

THE FACILITY DESIGN PROCESS

The facility design process can be divided into four phases: predesign, design, construction, and preoperation. (Penman, 1977). All of these phases are applicable to any type of

health/fitness facility: commercial, clinical, community, or corporate. The facility designer must select the components of each phase that are specific to the particular setting. None of these phases is distinct, as there is continual overlap throughout the process. However, there are certain activities that are easier to describe by assigning them to a specific phase. For example, you would not conduct a feasibility study in the final operation phase, nor would you conduct program evaluations in the design phase. They would occur in the predesign and preoperation phases, respectively. The facility design process is a continuum, in which certain activities follow others while important outside influences impinge upon the flow. The entire, four-phase process is shown in Figure 5.1 (Flynn, 1985; Penman, 1977; Penman, personal communication, 1985) and briefly described below. (Refer to chapters 2, 6, and 7 for more detail on the predesign, construction, and preoperation phases.)

It is reasonable to assume that a well-planned, well-constructed facility should take 6 months to 2 years to complete, depending on the size of the project. Thus each phase of the project contributes an approximate percentage of time to it:

Predesign: 25% or 6 months
Design development: 12% or 3 months
Construction: 50% or 12 months
Preoperation (start-up): 13% or 3-4 months

These phases overlap and so do their percentages of time (Figure 5.1). It is also possible to shorten any of these time spans at very substantial cost savings. For example, Healthscape, Inc., of Orlando has developed modularized facility elements such as showers, lockers, and other commonly needed facility components that can abbreviate significantly the time normally required to customize the construction of such elements. However,

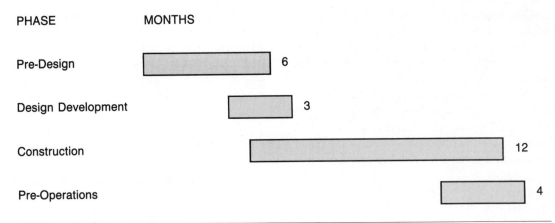

Figure 5.1. The facility design process.

decreasing the time allotment of any phase of the process just to save money should never be done at the expense of quality work. This only ends up being more expensive in the long run because something will have been missed or done incorrectly. It is best to proceed through the facility design process carefully, making certain that all aspects of the facility are covered. This chapter reviews the predesign phase and then focuses on the design and design development phases. Chapter 6 will cover the construction phase.

PREDESIGN PHASE

The predesign phase includes the program analysis, feasibility study, development of the master plan, selection of a site for the facility, and cost analysis.

Program Analysis

The predesign phase begins with a program analysis, which involves a comprehensive look at all the programs that the facility will offer, including physical activities, lectures, personal services, and specialty services. The

entire spectrum of the program offerings must be determined prior to designing the facility so that the structure can be built to accommodate the programs being planned instead of vice versa. (Athletic Business, 1985a; Bronzan, 1974; Demars, 1985; Flynn, 1985.)

It is too often the case that facilities are built and then programs are force-fed into the facility. This approach usually does not work for two reasons. First, because there was inadequate planning to accommodate various programs, the programs themselves will be presented ineffectively. Second, there is a better than even chance that the facility will have to undergo renovation to meet new program needs (e.g., free weight areas) and retrofit spaces in underutilized areas (e.g., racquetball courts). This is very costly, and in today's market, many facility managers and operators might choose not to offer the programs rather than undertake the cost of expansion or renovation.

It is for these reasons that a thorough program analysis must be performed first. Then, the facility is designed more functionally to fit the actual programs and the philosophy behind those programs. Furthermore, any future expansion needs are handled during initial construction, thereby keeping long-term costs down. The important thing to remember is that the health/fitness industry becomes very volatile at times, and customer needs can fluctuate rapidly. Therefore, it is recommended that the facility be designed to be as inherently flexible as possible. Accordingly, a feasibility study can be conducted to ascertain the likelihood of success of different types of programs for the intended market segment.

Feasibility Study

The feasibility study is the next step in the facility predesign process. The study is conducted to determine a location for the facility, the potential target markets, the programs these people are interested in, estimated usage, revenue figures and their sources, competitors, financial data, and pricing structures. A feasibility study answers one basic question: Is it feasible to build a fitness facility in a particular location so that maximum potentials can be achieved? (*Club Business*, 1984). These potentials relate to several things based on the objectives of the facility, but usually they include revenue, usage, and programs in commercial programs or member adherence in corporate programs.

Some of the analyses, if they are conducted thoroughly enough, form the basis of the master plan. This plan is vital for the success of any venture because it entails both business and marketing data. It also includes a description of the strengths and weaknesses of the company, along with a listing of the opportunities for and obstacles to success.

Master Plan

The master plan is a comprehensive business plan that extends the feasibility study into a more practical tool. The components and objectives of the plan are described in chapter 3 and elsewhere (Bronzan, 1974; Flynn, 1985; Gerson, 1985; Penman, 1977). As you can see from chapter 3, the master plan is a working document that is used throughout the design and operation of the facility. The planning and design team always knows that program and procedures are being followed toward stated objectives simply by comparing them with the master plan.

There is one aspect of the master plan that is unique to fitness facilities. Once everything has been written in detail, it is very instructive to develop a program plan outline (Flynn, 1985). The outline is basically a summary of the salient points of the master plan as they relate to the entire design process. It also serves as a quick reference for anyone who wishes to review the foundations upon which the master plan is based. A sample program plan outline follows:

Sample Program Plan

I. Basic assumptions
- The facility provides for a broad spectrum of lifestyle-enriching programs and activities serving the whole person.
- Equitable areas are provided for men and women.
- Facilities are used by a target population.
- Outdoor facilities, if any, are adjacent to the indoor facilities.

- There is a balance between active and passive program components.
- A qualified operator manages the facility.

II. Trends affecting planning process

- Current emphasis on health and fitness
- Other facilities in area
- Individual program providers and new products
- Expansion possibilities and capabilities
- Coed facilities
- Individualized instruction areas
- Space availability
- Target markets and usage

III. Current and proposed programs

- Instructional
  1. Exercise/aerobics
  2. Strength training
  3. Racquet sports
  4. Health promotion
- Service amenities
  1. Massage
  2. Facial/cosmetology
  3. Whirlpool
  4. Herbal wrap
  5. Loofa bath
  6. Swiss shower

IV. Program objectives

- Instructional
  1. Racquet sports
  2. Health promotion
  3. Strength training
  4. Exercise classes/aerobics
- Leagues
  1. Intramural
  2. Interclub
- Tournaments
  1. Intramural
  2. Public
- Community-based programs
  1. Health promotion
  2. Exercise

(Cont.)

Sample Program Plan (Continued)

V. Activity and service facilities

- Exercise/aerobics room
- Weight room
- Pool
- Racquetball/squash/tennis courts
- Locker rooms
- Showers
- Lavatories
- Drying area
- Laundry
- Clothing issuance area
- Storage
- Equipment rooms

VI. Preliminary data: Design specifications and space allocations

- Listing of areas
- Priority needs of areas
- Square footage per area
- Primary versus secondary spaces
- Auxiliary, storage, and maintenance spaces
- Initial design schematics

VII. Facility usage

- By room or area
- Multipurpose use
- Area size based on activity
- Types of activities

VIII. Space relationships

- Room to room; area to area
- Traffic patterns and accessibility
- Ease of supervision
- Handicap access

IX. Equipment and furniture list

X. Other considerations

Selecting an Architect/Space Planning Firm

Another factor to consider when the master plan is being developed is hiring an architect or space planner to serve as an outside resource on the planning and design team.

Many of the factors are discussed in depth in chapter 6 but are briefly presented here for emphasis. Many qualified architects and space planners build beautiful buildings, but how many have experience in the design and construction of health/fitness centers? This is a primary consideration when choosing an architect. Some firms provide a range of services from predesign (feasibility, master planning), design, construction, personnel development, and program development to facility management. The architect identified in such firms is usually well acquainted with the special needs of health/fitness facilities. Other factors in selecting an architect or space planning firm include

- membership in the American Institute of Architects (AIA),
- a license to practice in the location where the facility will be built,
- references from previous works,
- a business office that is close to the project site,
- the ability of the architect to work with the project team through all phases of the design process, and
- the ability of the architect to recommend and possibly hire qualified contractors and subcontractors.

These considerations will aid you in hiring an architect or space planner for a project. The designated architect should establish a positive rapport with all members of the planning and design team from the start, and the lines of communication should be open to everyone. The more knowledge each person has about other team members' responsibilities, especially the architect's, the smoother the operation will run.

A third important aspect of the master plan is the project completion schedule. This is a timeline that the architect and the planning committee use to estimate the starting and completion dates of every aspect of the project. The project completion schedule helps you adhere to the percentage-time allotments of the facility design process, develop budgetary strategies, plan for personnel requirements, and check to see whether the construction crew is completing each task on time. A sample project completion schedule is shown in Figure 5.2.

Site Selection

Site selection can occur at any time, but a proposed site should be analyzed in the feasibility study before a final site is determined. Where the facility is built must be based upon the three primary rules of real estate: location, location, and location. Choose the site wisely, and if the feasibility study for the proposed site says it will not work, find another one. Remember that people will only use the facility if they perceive it to be in a convenient location.

The ideal site for a health/fitness facility depends on a combination of things. What is the topography of the soil? Will it erode? Are there accessible feeder streets? Is there ample parking? What about sewage and drainage? How about wind factors? What are the weather patterns? Will the facility be visible from the street? What will traffic patterns be like entering and exiting the facility? These are only some of the questions that must be answered relative to the physical aspects of the site. There may be others, but the major concern is the actual cost of construction on a given site when all things are considered.

Cost Analysis

In general, the estimated total cost of the real estate should not exceed 20%-25% of the total project costs. There are exceptions to this rule, but most well-constructed, well-planned projects fall within these cost guidelines. When construction costs exceed initial projections, developers usually begin to try to save in other areas. When this happens, the entire facility suffers. Therefore, choose the site and plan the construction of the facility so that monies spent for completion do not exceed monies available.

It is extremely important to have a good estimate of facility costs before proceeding to the

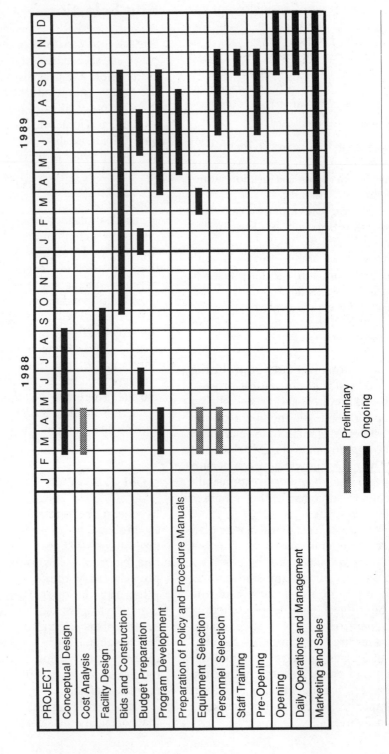

Figure 5.2. Sample project completion schedule.

design phase of a project. Facilities rarely cost less than originally planned. Thus it is best to perform a cost analysis prior to proceeding with the architectural renderings, which become very time-consuming and expensive. Many design firms have access to cost-analysis consultants who appraise the programming statements, rough schematics, and other information to provide a fairly accurate cost estimate for the project. This estimate is broken down into different program areas that are evaluated according to their cost-effectiveness. Deleting a pool, for example, at this stage is nearly cost-free, but such a deletion at a later stage of the design process is very expensive. The cost analysis permits you to temper your desires and adjust expectations to accommodate budgetary constraints. The wish list at this stage of development is pared down to a more realistic planning list. This, in the long run, enables everyone involved in the project to proceed with common goals, expectations, and budgets. It also avoids needless delays in redesigning the project because of facility deletions. Figure 5.3 is a cost-analysis summary that enumerates the elements defined as core programs and presents options that might be desirable but not essential items in the master plan. Such an approach to cost analysis enables decision makers to maximize program options with limited resources. After due deliberation and review of program and cost analyses, contracts are usually developed and signed during this predesign phase.

DESIGN PHASE

The design phase includes the primary activities of design development and the preparation of construction documents (Fitzgerald, 1982). An overriding activity is the continuous process of design review and revision that often occurs even as construction is going on. However, it is very important to minimize

structural changes in the facility during the construction process, as these create additional expenses. In general, every project manager should attempt to maintain cost controls through this phase and the entire life of the project.

Design Development

Design development is the actual process of designing the facility. Key people on the planning team, including the development project manager, architect, interior designer, facilities manager (if hired), and any consultants, meet to develop drawings from the schematics and the master plan. These drawings evolve into blueprints for both construction and interior design. Design development means different things to different people. In this discussion, we restrict its meaning to amplifying the technical drawings that an architect presents in the blueprints. Design development could also be construed to mean the subsequent technical drawings and documents necessary for engineers to execute the construction process. However, this information is presented in the next chapter. Additionally, the specification of equipment can be included in the design development process. The innovations of computer-assisted-design (CAD) systems have revolutionized the architectural field. Once specifications change, the data are input into a computer and the CAD system rapidly massages a schematic to desired specifications. The limits of such systems have yet to be realized, but it is clear that the CAD systems aid the creative process immensely.

There are certain design mistakes that can occur during the design development process. The most prevalent are listed in Table 5.1. To avoid these problems, make sure you have a clear idea of what to include in the facility before the preparation of construction documents begins.

IN	Sq. Ft.	Space/Area	Furniture Equipment	Construction	Total	Total
		CORE PROGRAM				
1	200	Public	4,522.00	9,480.00	14,002.00	
2	560	Administration	27,498.00	23,040.00	50,538.00	
3	1,110	Cardiac Rehabilitation	98,469.00	56,980.00	155,449.00	
4	1,215	Physical Therapy	168,827.00	79,000.00	247,827.00	
5	1,055	Shared Program Areas	62,917.00	62,230.00	125,147.00	
6	2,440	Exercise	172,976.00	148,950.00	321,926.00	
7	2,090	Showers/Lockers/Amenities	129,172.00	128,160.00	257,332.00	
8	1,330	Facility Requirements	85,020.00	63,105.00	148,125.00	
		Shipping Delivery & Installation @ 17.5%				131,145.18
		Taxes and Professional Fees Not Included				
		SUBTOTAL	749,401.00	570,945.00	1,320,346.00	1,451,491.18
9		**OPTIONS**				
	530	Daycare	11,830.00	25,000.00	36,830.00	
	5,200	Pool	11,717.00	400,000.00	411,717.00	
		Shipping Delivery & Installation @ 17.5%				4,120.73
		Taxes and Professional Fees Not Included				
		SUBTOTAL OPTIONS	23,547.00	425,000.00	448,547.00	452,667.73
	15,730	Total				
	5,730	OPTIONS				
	10,000	Total Building Square Footage				
		GRAND TOTAL (including options)	772,948.00	995,945.00		2,039,424.80

Figure 5.3. Cost analysis summary. *Note.* Courtesy of Healthscape, Inc., Orlando, Florida. Used by permission.

Table 5.1 Common Facility Design Mistakes to Avoid

Mistake	Comment
1. Inefficient traffic flow	1. Keep hallways and intersections to a minimum. Keep related areas together.
2. Inappropriate placement of service and activity areas	2. Never cross dry areas to go from one wet area to another. Keep service areas together near locker rooms. Keep activity areas together.
3. No aquatics areas	3. Be certain there are whirlpools. If possible, build a lap pool for swimming, an exercise pool, and plunge pools.
4. No facilities for disabled individuals	4. Install ramps, elevators where necessary, wide doorways, and handicap bathroom facilities and drinking fountains.
5. Inadequate administrative space	5. Provide offices for key personnel and testing.
6. Inadequate storage space	6. There is never enough storage space.
7. Failure to plan for future expansion of the facility	7. Build the facility so areas can be enlarged, floors can be added, and walls can be moved, with special attention being paid to the more permanent structures such as the locker rooms and the front desk area.

Space Planning

Space planning concerns the interrelationships of all the programming areas within the facility. The space planner considers the programs that will be offered; the number and types of spaces associated with those programs; and the function, size, and location of each space in relation to others. Space planning also mandates a determination of the goal of each space, more specifically, its purpose and use (O'Donnell & Ainsworth, 1984). For example, an office inside a shower room would not be evidence of good space planning; however, an office that overlooks both a hallway and a workout area is definitely effective planning. This office now serves several purposes, including administra-

tion, counseling, traffic control, and exercise supervision. Multifunction space planning is also cost-effective, especially because budgetary limitations exert a great influence on the entire facility design process. Additionally, multifunction space planning is very labor and energy efficient, because these areas can be supervised by a minimum number of people during slow periods. Thus it is easy to see why space planning is an integral part of the facility design. Space planning considerations should include the following:

- Design spaces to be user-friendly.
- Design spaces to accommodate peak usage hours.
- Define space uses by the design elements.

- Design spaces to be aesthetically attractive.
- Separate wet and dry areas.
- Soundproof classrooms and offices.
- Minimize hallways and intersections.
- Use open spaces wherever possible.
- Keep mechanical and maintenance equipment in separate areas.
- Allow administrative personnel to view entrance and exercise areas.
- Plan spaces for long-term use.
- Provide for future expansion.
- Provide facilities for disabled individuals.
- Keep traffic patterns direct and simple.

Development of Spaces

The development of areas within the facility is based on the traffic patterns through an area by both participants and staff (O'Donnell & Ainsworth, 1984), the location of the area, its purpose, the number of participants that will be using the area, the length of time each person will spend in an area, and the maximum number of participants an area will hold. These factors also influence the configuration and interrelationships of several spaces, and thus you must consider them when designing a facility.

The best way to emphasize space development is with an example. If all of the factors listed in the previous paragraph were taken into account, it would not be wise to design a facility in which a participant had to walk through a lounge, a plunge pool area, and a vanity area to get from the locker room to the showers. This is very poor space development and planning. A more appropriate configuration would place the showers adjacent to the locker room and separate the two areas by a drying area and a door. This configuration allows a more efficient traffic flow and encourages a desired behavior that links dress-

ing with showering (O'Donnell & Ainsworth, 1984).

Development of Floor Plans

Once the spaces in a facility are clearly defined, they are arranged in a particular configuration that conforms to the space that is available for the facility. This process is usually accomplished first by employing a *bubble diagram*, which is a technique designed to optimize the space available by reducing needless traffic patterns for users (see chapter 6 for details). Moreover, related programming and administrative activities are placed together in the plan. The effect of this technique is to streamline the placement of spaces within the facility.

The second approach in the design of the floor plans is to place the spaces in a block design that conforms to the exterior and interior constraints of the building. This is normally accomplished by the designer in concert with drafting support personnel. At some stage in this development, a CAD system frequently begins to assume some of the work of floor plan development. Ultimately, a floor plan is developed and this schematic is presented to the client for review and revision. This process continues in a cyclical fashion until the designer has produced a schematic that is satisfactory to the client.

Figure 5.4 represents two different types of floor plans. The first is for a commercial facility and the second is for a clinical or private facility (Patton et al., 1986). These plans adhere to many of the principles of facility design specified in this chapter. However, as with any facility design, flaws are evident. Table 5.2 lists four positive design elements and four negative elements of the floor plans. You may want to add more to each list. This is a good exercise in learning how to read and critique floor plans.

■ Commercial facility. ■

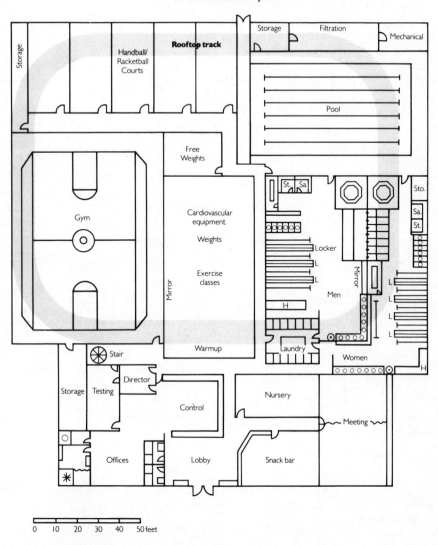

Figure 5.4a. Floor plans for a commercial and clinical facility. *Note.* From *Implementing Health/ Fitness Programs* (pp. 265 and 267) by R.W. Patton et al., 1986, Champaign, IL: Human Kinetics. Reprinted with permission.

■ Clinical facility. ■

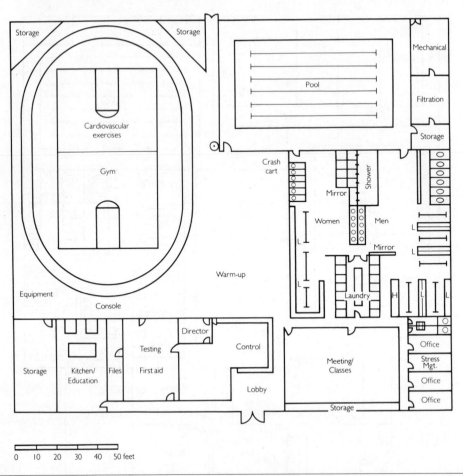

Figure 5.4b. Floor plans for a commercial and clinical facility. *Note.* From *Implementing Health/Fitness Programs* (pp. 265 and 267) by R.W. Patton et al., 1986, Champaign, IL: Human Kinetics. Reprinted with permission.

Table 5.2   Evaluating Floor Plans

Commercial facility

Positive design elements	*Negative design elements*
—Control desk near entrance	—Meeting room in high-noise area
—Offices in proximity to entryway	—Locker rooms of unequal sizes
—Sufficient storage space	—Crowding in exercise room due to equipment and participants
—Activity areas grouped together	—One entrance to men's locker room; in pool area, users must go from wet to dry area to enter

Clinical (private) facility

—Control center near entryway	—Locker rooms of unequal sizes
—Locker rooms have entry and exit doors	—Pool entry from workout area
—Traffic flow smooth through all areas	—Only one activity at a time can be performed in gym/cardiovascular exercise area
—Activity areas grouped together	—Placement of equipment, console, and crash carts should be together and in a more spacious area

Ambience

Ambience is an important consideration in the design development process. The intended user must be considered when designing the facility. If you want the consumers of your services to be upscale, affluent executives, you have to design a well-appointed and somewhat luxurious setting. The feeling that one gets when entering and using a facility must be well planned. This requires great attention to the design of both the exterior and the interior. The exterior is discussed elsewhere. Let's briefly discuss the interior in this last section.

The lighting plays an important role in the ambience of a facility. The type of lighting will influence the ambience. Fluorescent lighting creates much less warmth and charm than incandescent lighting. Consequently, offices and administrative areas benefit from the inexpensive and stark features of the fluorescent lights, but the locker areas, which are inherently personal spaces, should adopt in-candescent lighting whenever possible. Moreover, the intensity of the lights in a facility alters the moods of the user. Harsh and intense lights create difficulty in establishing a friendly mood among your members. A subdued lighting in the locker room, contrasted by a well-lit grooming area, sets the right mood to achieve both privacy while dressing and an upbeat mood when exiting the facility. The ambience of a facility should set the right mood for your market by providing a sense of privacy in some spaces, an opportunity for collegiality in other spaces, and a feeling of having a home away from home. This cannot be accomplished without the design efforts of a professional who is skilled in selecting the proper textures, materials, and colors for a given health/fitness facility.

SUMMARY

In this chapter we have discussed the basic aspects of the design process of a health/fitness facility. The process is normally broken down into a set of phases: predesign, design, construction, and preoperation. This chapter focused on the overall concerns of the predesign and design phases. The construction and preoperation phases in the process are discussed in later chapters. The predesign phase requires an analysis of the programs to be delivered and a feasibility study to validate the assumptions underlying those programs. It is important to be well aware of the target market, the kinds of services you need to provide, and the suitability of the proposed site of the facility before you launch a facility planning team into action. The architect requires a master plan that outlines these assumptions regarding target market and programs to proceed with preliminary design efforts. Equally important is the estimate of costs for the project; many inexpensive decisions regarding downsizing or upsizing a facility can be made at this juncture.

Once the contract is signed with the space planner, the design process begins in earnest. The space planner uses a bubble diagram to define the types of spaces and their relationships to each other. Space development is further refined to rough schematics through repeated drawings by hand or with the aid of computers until the final design is approved. Subsequent technical documents are then drawn, and the design development processes are implemented. The design process requires many individuals with differing talents. The success of such a process also requires a cohesive team, a common mission, and definitive leadership.

CHAPTER 6

Space Planning and Construction Considerations

As the health/fitness industry continues to expand and change, the chances of becoming involved in a construction project are likely. Depending upon the setting, a construction project ranges from a small renovation of an existing facility to the total construction of a new health/fitness center. The ability to design and construct a facility with concern to user-efficiency, budgetary parameters, maintenance, and program capabilities is essential when developing a health/fitness facility. As mentioned in chapter 5, the basic floor plan and ambience of a completed renovation or of a new health/fitness facility either entice people to exercise regularly or are the deciding factors in a person's choice not to exercise.

Often, the burden of success for a construction project falls upon the manager or director, who has good management and operational skills, but rarely has much experience or training in designing and building a fitness center. Unfortunately, most health/fitness professionals obtain their experience from being placed on a project that forces them to either succeed or fail. Although this situation happens frequently, it does not always provide the best results. Errors that are made at

this level are usually felt by the users for years to come.

This chapter complements the previous chapter on planning and design considerations by providing helpful insights into the actual construction of health/fitness facilities. The intent is not to provide an all-inclusive document of recommended construction principles, but to present a more conceptual approach to the overall construction process. The areas that are discussed in this chapter include

- selecting an architect,
- the schematic design phase,
- the design development phase,
- selecting a contractor, and
- facility considerations.

SELECTING AN ARCHITECT

Designing health/fitness centers has evolved into a specialized profession. Rarely have two fitness centers been built alike. Differences have always existed in activity facility requirements, requested amenities, spatial relationships, crowd flow, and security, but each fitness setting also has a special set of needs and problems that relates to demographics, financial parameters, and facility goals and objectives.

There are now specialized space planning firms that provide a wide array of architectural services. Some of these firms are owned by architects and some are owned by designers. We will refer to these professionals as architects in this chapter to avoid repetitious reference to the distinction between such professionals.

The selection of a competent architect can aid in solving many of the problems mentioned above, while also providing a design that not only is functional but follows a master plan established by management. The criteria for choosing an architect can vary from setting to setting. For example, a corporation that is interested in adding a new fitness facility might choose the architect who designed the original building. For a new commercial fitness center, the project manager might decide to use design competition to determine which architectural firm provides the best facility layout. These examples suggest different processes for choosing an architect, yet both are considered acceptable depending upon the particular setting.

Most people in the construction industry agree that the selection of the architect is probably the most crucial decision an owner will make in the entire process of building. Most often, the assurance of a successful project depends upon the special chemistry that develops between the client and the architect. Because choosing an architect is so important, the selection process should receive all the time and effort needed to assure a successful project.

There is no one established set of criteria for selecting an architect; however, the criteria outlined in chapter 4 for selecting consultants

and chapter 5 for selecting architects will prove helpful. A common recommendation is to become familiar with the alternatives and choose the one that best suits the needs of your setting (see Figure 6.1).

Before deciding upon an architect, you must first decide whether or not you want to hire a consultant. Chapter 4 provided a detailed explanation of the various types of consultants and indicated how to locate and choose a consultant based upon the needs of the health/fitness facility. The advantage of consultants is that they integrate their specialized expertise with the architect and add to the overall design of the new facility. The consultant's role is to draw upon the input of individuals who are involved in the project and combine his or her experience in establishing a plan for the overall design and operation of the new facility. The consultant acts in many capacities, but the most important function is to provide an independent professional opinion and plan based on an unbiased look at the total operation. Consultants should be able to facilitate all representatives in the design, construction, and various start-up phases (i.e., programming, management, and operations) of the project.

If you choose not to hire a consultant, then you are responsible for providing the information necessary for the architect to understand what you want. This process can be difficult if you have not had much experience in fitness facility design. The cost of hiring a consultant must be weighed against the possible funds that could be lost in additional architectural design charges and construction change-orders.

Direct Selection

The simplest procedure for choosing an architect is direct selection, based upon the recommendation of someone whom you trust and

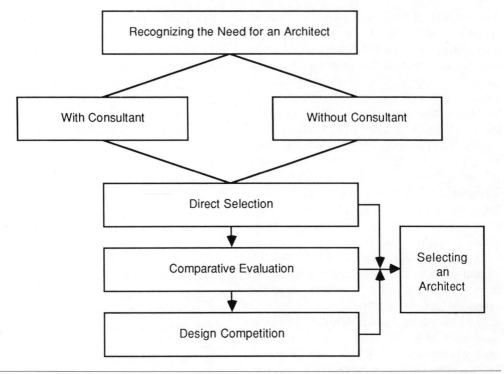

Figure 6.1. The process of choosing an architect.

who has had a good experience with a particular firm. Corporations that wish to construct a fitness facility often hire the same architect who designed the company's building. As in any personal service, outstanding past performance is the best criterion for selection. It is also recommended that a firm be chosen that has had experience in constructing health/fitness facilities and thus is aware of the problem areas associated with them. Ask questions that will help determine whether you can communicate with the individual who will be designing the facility.

Comparative Evaluation

Another method of architectural selection is a comparative evaluation of several firms.

This process begins with compiling a list of architectural firms, based upon the recommendations of friends and associates; other professionals in the field who have built similar projects; the local chapter of the AIA, which could submit a list of architects interested in constructing fitness facilities; or professional journals that list fitness-related architectural firms. Examples of the latter include *Club Industry*, *Athletic Business*, *Fitness Management*, *Optimal Health*, and *The Association of Fitness in Business*.

Once this list is compiled, contact the designated architectural firms and ask them if they are interested in building a health/fitness facility. If the firms are agreeable, ask for literature describing the companies' qualifications and experience. The firms usually respond to such requests by sending brochures that include photos and biographical data on key personnel. Often this process becomes frustrating and confusing, because most of the materials are done professionally and contain photos that will make all the companies appear to be excellent choices. To evaluate this material properly, look beyond the style of the material and make your analysis based on these questions: (a) have they built similar facilities, (b) what was the quality of past jobs, (c) are the references good, (d) what type of staff is available, and (e) what is the firm's professional status in the community? This process should help reduce the original list. The list should remain as balanced as possible by including firms that are large, small, and located within and outside the community. This allows for a greater basis of comparison when the interview process starts.

The interview is the opportunity for you to determine the suitability of each firm by asking questions. What experience does the architect have in designing health/fitness facilities? How busy is the firm? Does it have the capacity to do the work? Who will handle the work? It is important during this time to meet the particular individual who will be responsible for the project. Often in large architectural firms the person making the presentation is not necessarily the person in charge of the project. Remember, the ease of communication and the basic chemistry between the client and the architect are the essential keys to its success.

Design Competition

For major projects of great scope and complexity, the method of selecting an architect may be design competition. The architect is selected after you, or an established panel, evaluate the designs submitted by various architectural firms. For this method to be successful, it is imperative that you have a conceptual picture of the new building and submit a written plan of the desired facilities and general requirements and an analysis of designated space layout. These areas must be predetermined and explained so each architectural firm's design can be compared equally. This method of selection is the most expensive and time-consuming.

Methods of Payment

Once an architect has been selected, the next step is to develop a clear understanding of each party's responsibilities and obligations. This is formalized by signing an agreement or contract. However, before this can be accomplished there are a number of aspects that must be reviewed and agreed upon with the architect. These conditions include the scope of services that will be provided by the architect and the fee that will be charged for these services.

For many years the standard method for paying an architect was determined by a percentage of the project construction cost. The percentage varied depending upon the type, size, and complexity of the project. For example, a multirecreational, full-service activity center is more difficult to design and construct than a large gymnasium or auditorium, even though the square footage might be identical. Thus the design and construction costs are higher for the full-service activity center. Traditionally, the range used by architects for new facility design and supervision has been between 6% and 12% of the total construction cost, and higher if the project was a renovation.

However, both architects and owners have now found that a percentage method of payment sometimes appears to be a conflict of interest. Some owners suspect that the architect will increase project costs in order to increase the architectural fee. A preferable method is the lump sum compensation, according to which the architect is paid directly for the services he or she renders in developing the project. The architect and owner determine this amount by reviewing the services that are available and deciding upon the ones that are required for the project. The tasks assigned to the architect are then evaluated for time and cost. In addition to these direct costs are amounts for overhead and profit. The total of these costs provides the lump-sum fee to develop the project. If the owner and the architect agree, then this figure is the compensation for the architect. Table 6.1 compares and contrasts the two methods of payment.

The payment for the architect can be made in several ways, from a monthly direct personnel expense to a lump-sum payment. If the architect's services are hard to predict, then a multiple of the total architectural fee is the best form of payment. A monthly payment in proportion to the services performed, after an initial payment made upon the signing of the agreement or contract, is the most preferred method of compensating the architect.

The Contract

After you establish the scope of services, compensation, and method of payment, the next step is to enter into a contract or agreement for professional services. In addition to covering the method of payment, this document explains the responsibilities of both parties and provides a detailed description of the services to be rendered by the architect throughout the project, including the construction phase. The specific responsibilities of the architect are shown in Figure 6.2.

The AIA agreement forms (available upon request) were developed to standardize this legal process. These forms are used most often between client, architect, and contrac-

Table 6.1 A Comparison of Architectural Fee Methods

Percentage of construction cost

1) Total architectural fees range from 6% to 12% of the construction estimate, and higher for a renovation.
2) Fees are dependent upon type, size, and complexity of the project.
3) Owners are oftentimes suspicious of a conflict of interest between architectural fees and total project cost.
4) This method provides little negotiation between owner and architect. It is totally related to construction cost.

Lump-sum method

1) Architectural fee based upon a well-defined scope of work that describes the project.
2) Man-hours, direct and indirect costs, and profit are all applied to the single-price figure.
3) If the scope of the building changes, the architect must change fees based upon a range from $20 to $100 per hour.
4) The owner and architect must review all compensation forms and agree on the final architectural fee.

tor to explain the responsibilities of all parties. Finally, it is recommended that an attorney review all documents and suggest any changes before you sign any agreement.

In most architectural agreements the engineering fees are included in the total compensation of the architectural services. The architect will negotiate (i.e., subcontract) with the various engineers for their services and associated costs. This method is preferable because the owner does not have the technical expertise or experience to determine construction requirements from a blueprint. It is important, however, to be familiar with the

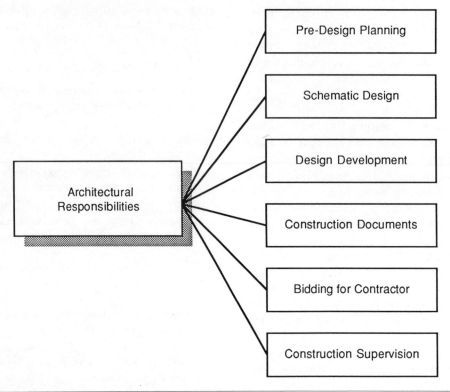

Figure 6.2. Professional responsibilities of an architect.

role that engineers play in the overall construction project. Table 6.2 lists the types of engineers and their responsibilities.

Additional services and fees include interior design costs, topography and site surveys, soil testing, printing costs, and professional renderings or scale model charges. Some of these fees are covered in the architectural or construction cost, whereas others are soft costs that must be added to a preliminary budget. It is your responsibility to address these services and determine how the costs are divided. It is extremely important to address these issues prior to signing the contract, as add-on costs can be financially devastating.

During the construction phase the architect assumes a variety of different roles. The primary role is to act as an agent to the owner. For example, the architect points out defective workmanship and communicates to the contractor what needs to be fixed. The architect also visits the site periodically to observe the amount and the quality of work completed. It must be understood, however, that the contractor or construction manager, not the architect, is responsible for managing the construction process. Although it is sometimes difficult to keep the roles separate, no action by you or the architect should ever interfere with the basic role of the contractor.

In addition to making occasional site visits, the architect has other duties. The architect establishes standards that the work must meet and determines whether the construction documents are being followed. Shop

Table 6.2   A List of Engineers and Their Responsibilities

Civil engineer:

1. Grading and land movement plans
2. Geometric layout of new improvements
3. Plans for new roads and street pavements
4. Utility plans
5. Plans for water collection system and sanitary sewers
6. Soil erosion control plans

Structural engineer:

1. Determine possible structural systems and materials
2. Provide cost of preferred systems and materials
3. Design final structure to meet architectural requirements

Mechanical/electrical engineer:

1. Specifications for heating and air-conditioning equipment
2. Provide drawings and specifications for power and lighting
3. Determine plumbing requirements
4. Responsible for the design of any communication system (security, PA, music, etc.)

drawings are also reviewed by the architect for requested building parts, materials, and equipment.

A final duty of the architect is to determine progress payments to the contractor. Each month the contractor submits a request for payment, listing the percentage of each area completed during the past month and the dollar value associated with that work. The architect then decides if the payment requested is actually representative of the work performed. It is important for the architect to make judgments without bias and to consider whether the work is consistent with the intent of the construction documents. Accordingly, it is helpful to all parties concerned to have a schedule of events by which to gauge project completion. Figure 6.3 is a typical schedule.

SCHEMATIC DESIGN PHASE

After you select an architect, the next phase is to begin designing the new activity center structure. During this phase it is the architect's responsibility to listen to your ideas and put them into written guidelines. Often, you will be asked to submit a statement of purpose, or a wish list of desired facilities and any special features that are to be designed into the drawings. This stage, discussed briefly in chapter 5, is the predesign planning phase and is one of the major responsibilities of the architect to complete.

During the predesign planning phase, a planning and design committee made up of the architect, consultant, owner, and various representatives meets to discuss the architectural possibilities and limitations of the building. This is also the time to consider the different activity programs that will be offered. Unfortunately, many facilities were not designed with activity programs in mind; the program planning frequently seems to be an afterthought. Adequate time should be spent discussing space requirements and owner needs. Once the architect has researched and interviewed the personnel involved, he or she should prepare a statement defining the various uses of the space. At that time you, the architect, and the consultant must decide upon the ultimate functional requirements of the proposed layout. The

Sample Construction Schedule

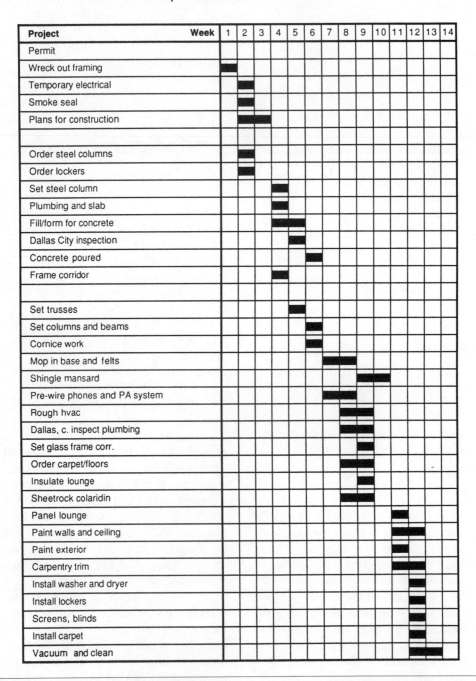

Project	Week	1	2	3	4	5	6	7	8	9	10	11	12	13	14
Permit															
Wreck out framing		■													
Temporary electrical			■												
Smoke seal		■													
Plans for construction		■■													
Order steel columns			■												
Order lockers		■													
Set steel column					■										
Plumbing and slab					■										
Fill/form for concrete					■■										
Dallas City inspection						■									
Concrete poured							■								
Frame corridor					■										
Set trusses						■									
Set columns and beams							■								
Cornice work							■								
Mop in base and felts									■						
Shingle mansard											■■				
Pre-wire phones and PA system								■							
Rough hvac									■■						
Dallas, c. inspect plumbing										■					
Set glass frame corr.										■					
Order carpet/floors									■■						
Insulate lounge									■■						
Sheetrock colaridin									■■						
Panel lounge												■			
Paint walls and ceiling												■■			
Paint exterior												■■			
Carpentry trim												■■			
Install washer and dryer												■			
Install lockers												■			
Screens, blinds												■			
Install carpet												■			
Vacuum and clean												■■			

Figure 6.3. A sample construction schedule.

master plan described in chapter 5 facilitates this predesign process immensely.

The next step is the schematic design phase in which the architect takes what is written in the master plan and subsequent program analysis and places it into a conceptual drawing of the new building. The architect begins with rough drawings of the interrelationships of requested facilities and space allocation. Sketch plans are then prepared showing the overall arrangement of areas and how they connect. A popular method used by architects to show how facilities interconnect is a functional bubble diagram (see Figure 6.4).

The schematic drawings include a site plan, which denotes the new building and how it coordinates with an existing or new site, and preliminary drawings of various floor plans showing the projected scope of the design layout. At this stage all drawings are in sketch form so that you or the architect can easily make revisions. It is important to take the time to understand every aspect of the initial design. It is your obligation to ask questions and consider every facet before approving the drawings.

Also at this stage, a preliminary estimate is made of construction costs. This figure is obtained by adding the estimated square-footage costs for each activity and service area. Because this amount fluctuates throughout the construction phase and across geographic regions of the country, a higher estimate is inserted so the project cost will not exceed the early budgetary figures. This prevents you from underestimating your financing projections. As mentioned in chapter 5, construction cost consultants are available to assist in this process. Using such consultants is much better than relying upon subjective judgments of individuals with limited knowledge of such matters.

It is not uncommon to begin a construction project with a preestablished budget that was determined by the owner or management. This process indicates to the architect that his or her design must fit within the confines of the budget figure. A good example of this approach is found in a hospital or corporate setting where other fiscal considerations must be weighed against a new construction project. Figure 6.5 represents the areas that the architect must consider during the schematic design phase.

Spatial Relationships

One of the first tasks that an architect must perform is to visualize the size of each activity area as it relates to the total design. The best way to approach this is to begin estimating gross square footage for each area. The gross square feet of a particular room is the total room size, including the nonassignable areas (walls, partition thickness, and mechanical shafts). Architects use gross square feet to properly determine the actual volume and costs associated with the proposed design. Table 6.3 is a list of the projected gross square footage of each area of a multipurpose health/ fitness facility.

Site and Parking Development

A proposed site plan should always show the relationship of the new structure to the overall site development. How does the new building fit into an existing or new plot? Is it symmetrical to other facilities? Is the view and access from the main thoroughfares good?

A close evaluation should be made of the access of traffic to the building areas. Special consideration should be given to potential

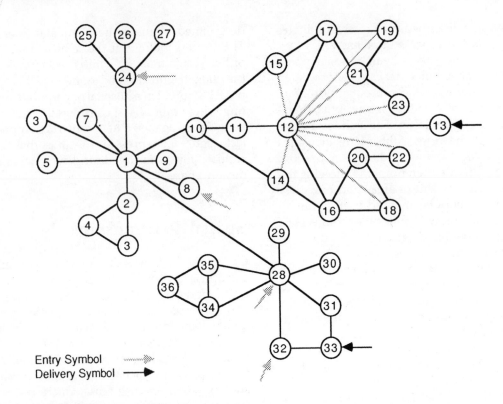

Functional Bubble Diagram

1. Gymnasium
2. Gym Control Counter
3. Staff Offices
4. Staff Restrooms
5. Workout Room
6. Racquetball Courts
7. Pro Shop
8. Gym (Member Entry)
9. Gym Janitorial Room
10. Dressing Control Room
11. Kit Bag Storage
12. Laundry & Attendant Room
13. Storage & Equipment Room
14. Women's Kit Lockers
15. Men's Kit Lockers
16. Women's Day Lockers
17. Men's Day Lockers
18. Women's Toilets/Lavatories
19. Men's Toilets/Lavatories
20. Women's Wet Area
21. Men's Wet Area
22. Steam, Sauna, Whirlpool Mech. Control
23. Steam, Sauna, Whirlpool Mech. Control
24. Gym Field Exit
25. Swimming Pool
26. Tennis Courts
27. Track Start
28. Main Lobby
29. Lobby Janitorial
30. Member Lounge
31. Dining Room & Restrooms
32. Kitchen
33. Administration Offices
34. Testing Rooms
35. Restrooms & Shower

Figure 6.4. Functional bubble diagram.

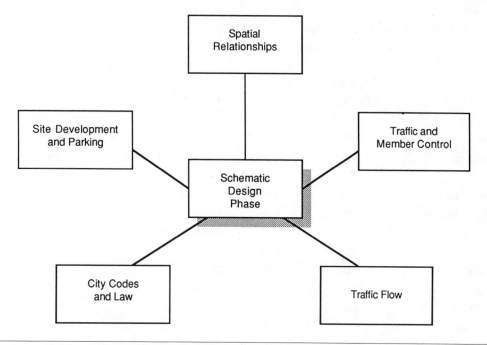

Figure 6.5. Architectural considerations during the schematic design phase.

liability areas, such as outdoor jogging tracks that cross roadways. Parking lots should be designed to accommodate traffic patterns during all hours, but especially during peak usage hours. Local city parking codes have been established to help clarify various parking requirements. As an example, the parking ratio for Dallas, Texas, is one parking spot for every 150 gross square feet of building space. It is not uncommon for many health/fitness consultants to suggest adding 10% to the required numbers of parking spaces as a buffer for special events. Table 6.4 is a checklist of factors to consider when evaluating a specific site.

Review Codes and Laws

Architects and engineers must have a good working knowledge of various building codes and city laws pertaining to construc-

tion. National and state building codes vary with each location and type of building. Zoning codes relate to the type and occupancy of the building, parking requirements, height maximums, use classifications, and lot coverage.

Prior to granting a building permit to start construction, city officials must have approved the architectural drawings for facility classification, fire and exit review, and all safety standards. Following the construction phase, the city must again approve the new facility before a certificate of occupancy can be obtained.

Traffic/Member Flow

The setting of a health/fitness facility will determine whether it has single or multiple entranceways from surrounding parking lots to local streets. For example, in a corporate

Table 6.3 Sample Space Requirements for a Multiuse Fitness Center

Ground floor:	Square footage	% of total footage	Second floor:	Square footage	% of total footage
Lobby	1,124	2.0	Gymnasium	6,980	13.0
Auditorium	2,170	4.2	Racquetball	1,848	3.5
Play area	939	2.1	Aerobics	2,673	5.1
Women's kit lockers	440	0.8	Storage	440	0.8
Women's lockers	3,408	6.6	Offices	1,045	2.2
Pool area	4,876	9.4	Weight lifting	3,393	6.6
Lounge	1,232	2.4	Fire stair	250	0.5
Electrical	160	0.3	Chase	250	0.5
Toilets	483	0.9	Toilets	160	0.3
Juice bar	260	0.5	Stairs	352	0.7
Cardiovascular	196	0.4	Elevator	50	0.1
Mechanical	468	0.9	Check in	176	0.3
Men's lockers	4,564	8.8	Waiting	196	0.4
Men's kit lockers	745	1.0	Subtotal	17,793	34.0
Laundry	840	2.0	Circulation	714	1.0
Storage	150	0.3			
Offices	527	1.0	Total	18,507	35.0
Administration	315	0.6	Mezzanine:		
Pro shop	252	0.5			
Check in	300	0.6	Running track	6,798	13.1
Elevator/basement	80	0.1	Warm-up and stairs	308	0.6
Stair/basement	223	0.4			
Stair/fire	223	0.4	Total	7,106	13.7
Stair/activity	352	0.7	Grand total:		
Elevator/activity	50	0.1			
			Ground floor	26,219	50.0
Subtotal	24,377	47.0	Second floor	18,507	36.3
Circulation	1,842	3.0	Mezzanine	7,106	13.7
Total	26,219	50.0	Gross square feet	51,832	100.0

Table 6.4   Checklist of Factors in Site Evaluation

Regional factors

1. Demographic factors
2. General character of region (rural, industrial, residential)
3. Distance to competitors in sports events
4. Traffic and transportation
5. Potential for recruitment

Local factors

1. Character of environs (urban, suburban,)
2. Community acceptance
3. Accommodations for visitors
4. Character and quality of adjacent structures
5. Civic services (fire, police protection, health care)
6. Access
7. Traffic and transportation
   * Access from major highways and local streets
   * Existing traffic volumes and patterns
   * Public transportation
8. Climate

Features of the site

1. Acreage
   * Must be adequate for buildings, parking, playing areas, etc.
   * Additional acreage for expansion
2. Shape
   * Generally rectangular usually best shape
   * Acute angles or odd shapes may be wasteful of space
3. Topography
   * Generally level terrain desirable
   * Consider extent of earth-moving in adapting to steep slopes
4. Soil and subsoil
5. Vegetation
6. Drainage
   * Essential that site be well drained
   * Possible recharging basin
   * Method of disposing of runoff
   * Environmental regulations
7. Climate
   * Precipitation
   * Prevailing winds

* Climatic extremes
8. Zoning regulations
   * Permitted use
   * Parking
   * Setbacks, buffers
   * Height limitations
   * Allowable coverage
   * Procedures
9. Access
   * From principal roads
   * From local streets
   * Traffic capacity of streets
   * Ability to accept additional volume
   * Pedestrian routes and crossings
   * Truck and bus access
   * Emergency access
10. Security considerations

Site utilities

1. Sewerage
   * Capacity of municipal system
   * Location of sewage lines
   * Possible on-site plant
2. Electric power
3. Water
   * For buildings
   * For site sprinklers
   * For fire protection
4. Storm drainage
5. Energy sources
6. Telephone
7. Solid wate disposal

Economic factors

1. Acquisition costs
2. Taxes
3. Financing
4. Development costs

Developmental constraints

1. Restrictive zoning
2. Easements
3. Covenants
4. Other legal constraints
5. Community resistance

or hospital setting a single entryway is preferable for reasons of security and traffic control. In private commercial settings where convenience and easy member access are more important, multiple entrances are common. Easy access should also be available for members entering the fitness center facilities. Although multiple entrances to and exits from the facility are preferable, greater difficulty with member control may be a deterrent to this type of design. Some owners opt instead for a large single entrance and exit doorway, which provides an easy check-in system for members and prevents nonmembers from using the facility.

A health/fitness facility should be designed so new members can easily orient themselves within the building. All activity areas should be readily accessible, with very little travel distance from one to another. Architects generally don't design compartmentalized fitness centers; instead, they prefer more open spaces so members can see where the activity areas are and prospective members can easily view the facility.

Maximum separation is suggested for building and food service trash removal. Defined routes should also be established for all suppliers and food deliveries so there will be no interference with the movement of the members.

Control

Member control and security are major concerns that face today's health/fitness owners. Thefts, nonmember usage, and a lack of overall security are enough to cause member adherence and new membership sales to suffer. During the schematic phase, all possible security problems should be addressed as they relate to the overall design. The following areas are essential for member control and security:

- A large check-in desk, so anyone entering or leaving the facility can be observed.
- A minimum number of corridors and long hallways, which reduce the view of members and staff.
- A minimum number of entrances and exits.
- As many activity areas as possible open to observation by staff or members.
- Parking lot review to identify potential security problems.

Prepare Detailed Cost Estimate

The design development phase can have a positive or negative effect on the overall cost of the project. During this phase, every element of the building should be reviewed with the architect. You must feel confident that the design provided is the best for the construction dollars.

Cost estimates are reviewed on a regular basis until the final bid documents are completed. As the project becomes more defined the discussions turn from projected costs to actual costs. Construction cost revisions are an expected part of the design development phase and should be updated as often as possible.

As explained earlier, the estimated costs during the schematic design phase are very general. Construction costs are based on a cost-per-square-foot basis. Currently, the cost per square foot for a health/fitness center in the Dallas, Texas, area ranges from $75 to $125. This range is greatly affected by the building structure, physical finishes, and fixed equipment. As an example, Table 6.5 represents estimated construction costs during the schematic design phase for a women's locker room renovation.

Table 6.5 Renovation Costs for Women's Locker Room

Work	Cost
Demolition	$ 769.00
Remove siding and flooring at sauna.	
Remove shower partitions	
Remove doors at whirlpool.	
Remove 195 square feet of ceramic tile.	
Remove one (1) door to exercycle room.	
Remove one (1) coat rod and shelf.	
Remove toilet partitions.	
Credit for mechanical door.	
Drywall	$ 1,771.00
Frame and sheetrock 23 linear feet of additional walls.	
Drywall fill two (2) door openings.	
Frame and wonder board 21 linear feet of shower walls.	
Relocate and repair ceiling at access.	
Furnish and install four (4) metal frame and wonder board benches.	
Credit for 20 linear feet of drywall frame and sheetrock.	
Ceilings	$ 225.00
Furnish and install 60 square feet of 2' × 4' ceiling with R-19.	
Doors	$ 930.00
Furnish and install 1 panel door and frame to exercycle room.	
Furnish and install 1 hardware set, lock, hinges, push pull, and closer.	
Credit for hollow metal doors and hardware at sauna.	
Credit for laminate.	
Carpentry	$ 1,375.00
Install a 5' × 8' ramp made out of 3/4 inch plywood at hall.	
Furnish and install four (4) louvered salon doors with hardware.	
Glass and mirrors	$ 3,013.00
Furnish and install four (4) shower doors and sidelite, opaque.	
Furnish and install one (1) 2'6'' × 6'8'' glass door frame at sauna.	
Furnish and install one (1) 2' × 6'8'' aluminum panel door and frame at mechanical room.	
Credit for one (1) 10' × 6' mirror.	

(Cont.)

Table 6.5 (Continued)

Work	Cost
Paint and wallcovering	$ 2,016.00
Paint 2 (2) doors and frames.	
Tape, bed, and repair at access at ceiling.	
Tape and bed 120 square feet of additional drywall.	
Tape and paint 432 square feet of wall at exercycle room.	
Furnish and install 700 square feet of vinyl wallcovering at massage room and toilet.	
Paint 4 linear feet of shelving.	
Electrical	$ 875.00
Furnish and install four (4) fluorescent lights.	
Furnish and install four (4) incandescent down lights.	
Plumbing	$10,888.00
Remove four (4) existing toilets.	
Furnish and install four (4) floor-mounted tank toilets.	
Furnish and install one (1) floor drain at sauna—lining.	
Relocate four (4) shower drains—lining.	
Relocate four (4) shower heads to wall.	
Furnish and install four (4) new shower heads and faucets.	
Relocate one (1) watercooler.	
Sawcut and break 49 square feet of plumbing.	
Masonry and concrete	$ 438.00
Credit for masonry.	
Add 40 square feet of concrete pour at plumbing.	

As the project enters the design development phase, costs are estimated based on the actual quantities of materials, equipment, and systems indicated in the plans and specifications. When the design development is completed, the majority of the building systems and components will be sufficiently detailed, so a contractual bid can be prepared and presented for construction bids.

DESIGN DEVELOPMENT PHASE

Once the schematics have been approved, architectural design becomes more technical and concise. Sketch drawings are prepared in more detail to illustrate all aspects of the proposed fitness center design. All work performed during this design development phase is an elaboration on ideas developed in the programming and schematic phase. The following are the areas that are completed during the design development phase:

- Floor plan design
- Building elevations
- Specification development
- Equipment and furniture arrangements
- Detailed building cost
- Construction documents

Floor Plan Design

The floor plans indicate all rooms drawn to scale and in their designed shape. As the architect draws each room or activity area, it is important for him or her to consider the following four factors (Whitehead, 1986):

1. Intended users and uses for each space
2. Physical requirements
3. Relationship with other spaces
4. Equipment

These considerations will insure room justification and prevent wasted space.

Once a floor plan has been completed, it is reviewed for traffic flow, crowd control, entrances and exits, city codes, space utilization, storage, and potential security problems. Often consultants will meet with their clients at this stage and perform a *walk-through*, which consists of evaluating every step that a given member would experience on a daily basis, including facility entrance, parking, check-in, locker room entrance, access to all activity areas, and facility exit. Countless design errors have been caught and remedied during this process, because it provides a design assessment of the facility through the eyes of a member. It is important to consider each type of member that will be using the club, including senior citizens, the handicapped, and children. The overlapping use of space by these different types of members influences the design as well. Many major design problems can also be alleviated if you and the consultant complete a close evaluation of the floor plans before granting written approval to the architect. Figure 6.6 is an example of a health/fitness facility floor plan.

Building Elevations

Exterior drawings of how each side of the new facility will look are the principal reason for providing elevations. Windows, roof lines, columns, and building shadows are all reflected in the elevation design. Environmental factors of sun, shading, insulation, cost, and aesthetic appearance are all elements to consider when evaluating building elevations. An example of building elevations is shown in Figure 6.7.

A building section is useful for viewing exterior and interior relationships of the facility. The section, or cut-through, of the facility provides visual relationships that can assist in determining such things as ceiling heights, equipment and furniture arrangements, and space allocation. Building sections also provide a multilevel reference so you can visualize relationships between floors. As an example, building sections are especially helpful to show how a raised indoor jogging track fits into the total scheme of a gymnasium. Figure 6.8 is an example of a building section.

Specification Development

Specification development is an outline that is prepared and presented by the architect of all building materials, room finishes, and a

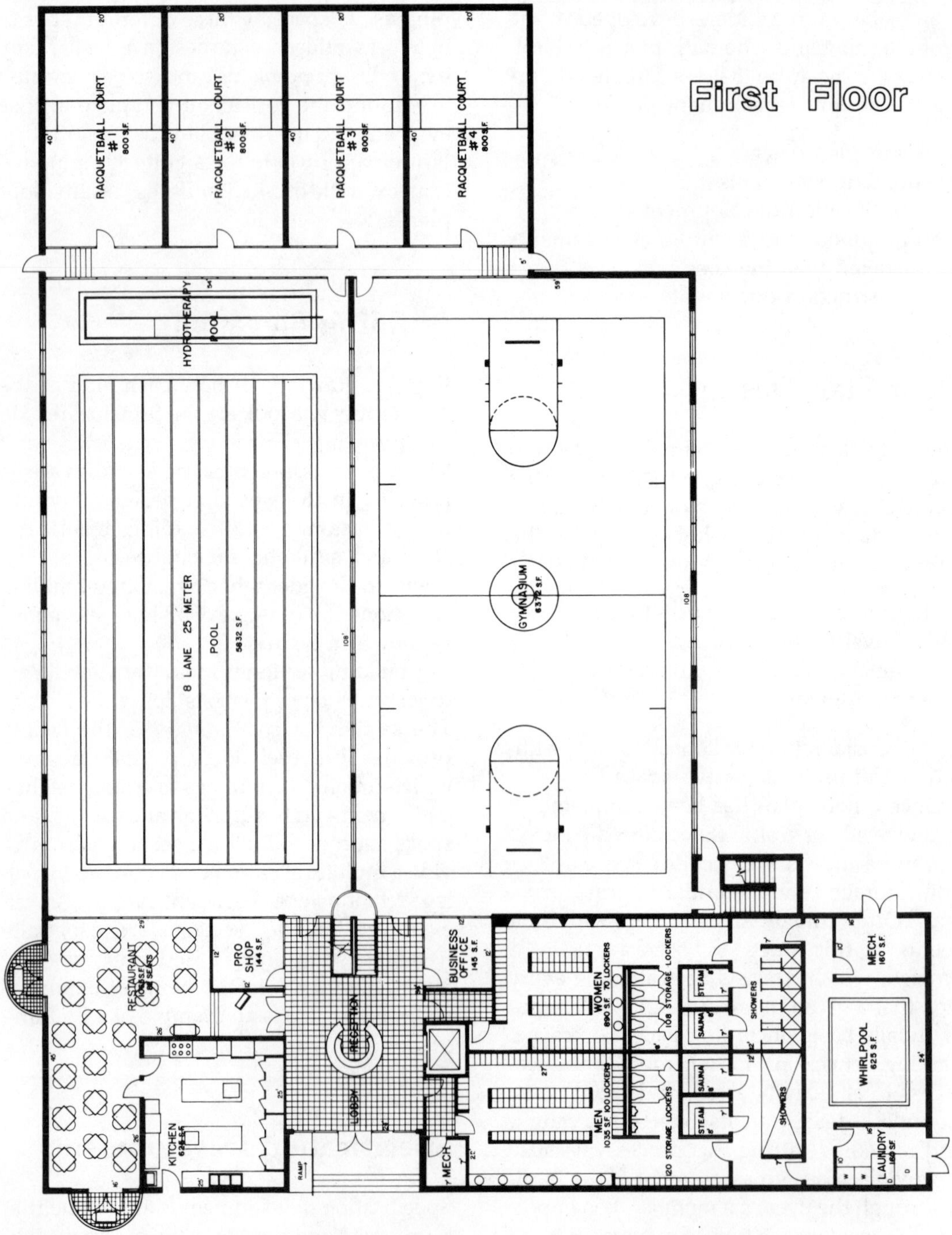

Figure 6.6a. Health/fitness facility floor plan.

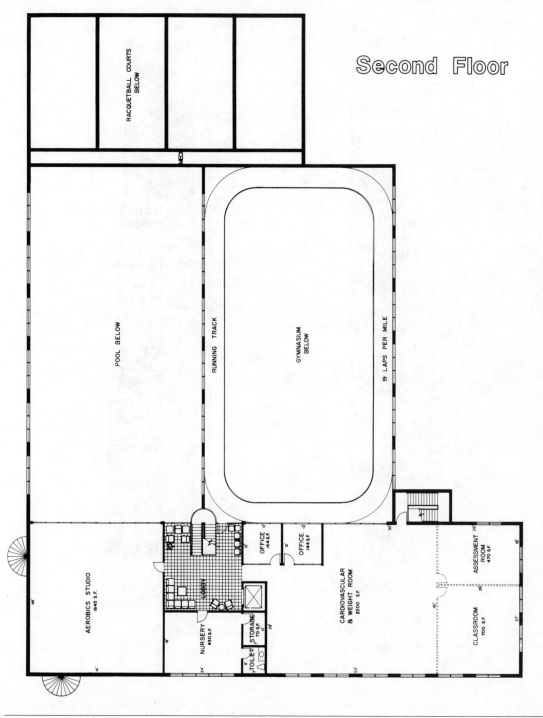

Figure 6.6b. Health/fitness facility floor plan.

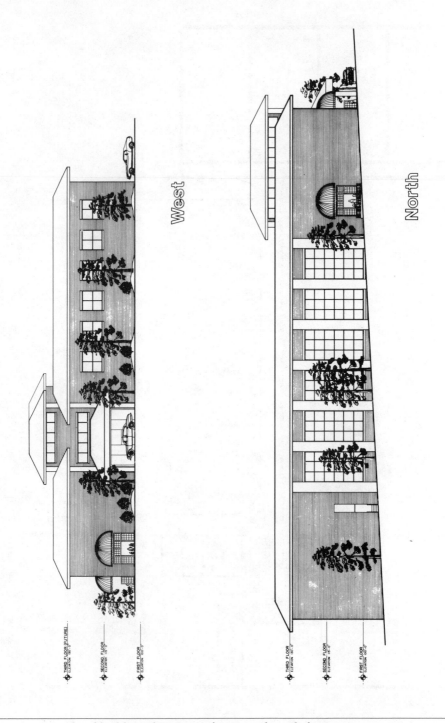

Figure 6.7a. An example of building elevations of west and north faces.

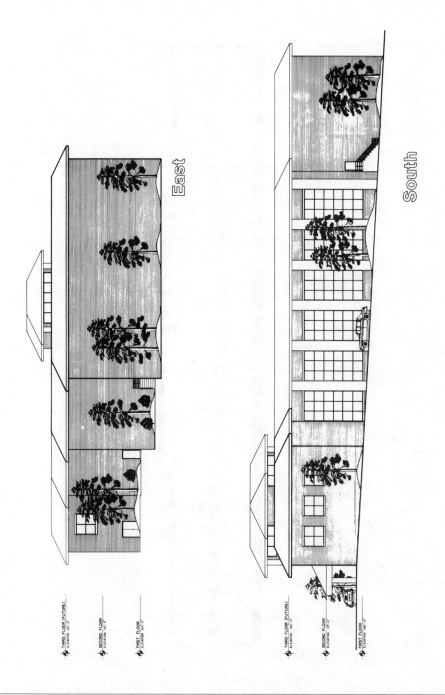

Figure 6.7b. An example of building elevations of east and south faces.

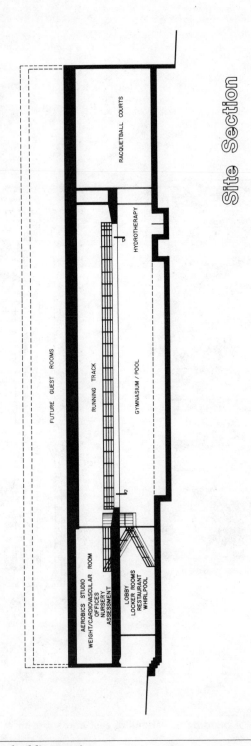

Figure 6.8. An example of a building section.

general description of the mechanical and electrical systems. Special consideration must be given to building frame (e.g., wood, steel, prefab), windows, exterior and interior finishes, selected materials that meet maintenance and durability requirements, and cost.

It is the responsibility of the architect to have a good working knowledge of materials used in health/fitness facilities. These recommendations, once you approve them, are placed in a written instruction manual that describes in detail the work to be performed by the contractor. The specification manual and construction drawings serve complementary functions. The drawings represent the size, shape, and location of the building components. The specifications exhibit the quality and performance standards of the materials and equipment items identified on the drawings. Figure 6.9 is a typical page from a specification manual.

Equipment and Furniture Arrangements

Health/fitness facilities require careful attention to equipment and furnishings that are either movable or fixed to implement the operational program. Early in the design phase the architect should interview you and the staff to determine specific room use and, especially, equipment requirements. This information helps the architect determine room size, utility services, lighting, and crowd flow. Once the equipment and furniture items are decided upon it is the responsibility of the architect to submit a list of equipment requirements for each room.

Detailed Building Costs

Estimating preliminary building costs is perhaps the most important step in deter-mining the feasibility of any construction project. Only when these costs are detailed can a developer complete the financial phase of the business plan and determine whether the construction of the building can be accomplished. Although everyone realizes the importance of obtaining accurate building costs, the process necessary to secure these figures consists of an orderly progression of steps from the building's conception to the completion of the design development phase.

During the early design phase of a construction project, rough estimates of square footage are determined by listing the projected floor space for all activity and service-related areas. The total building square footage is determined from this list, and that figure is then multiplied by the average construction cost of a similar building in the city where the project is to be built. To assist in obtaining comparative costs, you might visit other fitness centers that are representative of the type of facility to be built. This approach provides a chance to inquire about the overall building cost and the average square-foot price after the facility was completed. In addition, you can contact professional health/fitness organizations that have constructed similar facilities and ask about their general building costs. The object of this approach is to obtain as much preliminary information on building costs as you can so that you can at least come up with a ballpark figure for early cost projections.

As the design of the facility is refined you can request a more detailed cost estimate from your architect. Often the architect contracts with a cost estimator to assist in obtaining more exact construction costs. The cost estimators use construction reference manuals that list square-foot costs of different types of construction and what these structures would cost to build in different cities. These manuals include square-foot, systems, and unit costs of items in specific areas of the

Section 8C—FINISH HARDWARE

8C.01 SCOPE:

Work under this heading consists of furnishing all materials, tools, equipment, supplies, transportation, and facilities and performing all labor necessary for, required in construction with, or properly incidental to the furnishing and delivery of all items of finish hardware as provided herein and as noted and/or detailed on the drawings.

If any doors or other movable articles are not specifically mentioned, hardware like similar openings shall be furnished. All other hardware necessary for proper fastening and operation of all movable parts of building (other than mechanical equipment) shall be furnished hereunder.

Thresholds and weather-stripping are specified in this specification.

This contractor is to supply hardware templates to manufacturer of hollow metal steel frames.

8C.02 GENERAL:

After hardware is delivered, the general contractor shall take care of, order, receive, and be responsible for same until completion of the work.

All hardware is to be properly set by the general contractor, and the building is to be left completely equipped and with all hardware properly adjusted and in working order. Any additional hardware such as hooks and so forth to be set by contractor without additional charge.

Delivery of keys: The hardware contractor shall tag all keys with permanent name of number of room. Exterior door keys to be noted "EXT."

8C.03 INSTALLATION

A. An allowance of twelve thousand five hundred dollars ($12,500.00) shall be made the general contractor for the purchase of all finish hardware which is to be selected by the owner and architect. This amount is to be included in the contract sum.

The sum of the allowance shall be included in the contract sum and any lesser amount spent in the purchase of the finish hardware shall be credited to the owner; any greater amount spent shall be billed to the owner as an extra to the contract.

Figure 6.9. Typical page from a specification manual.

country. Although the figure obtained from this procedure is considered more accurate, it is still only an estimate of what the building will actually cost.

The final and most precise step in estimating building costs occurs after the contractor has been hired and the final set of construction documents has been completed. The contractor takes these plans to various subcontractors, structural engineers, plumbers, electricians, and so forth to derive costs. Once these figures have been obtained, the contractor and the architect will present you with their final bids. Because cost estimating is not an exact science, a construction contingency should be included to absorb any cost overrides or additional building charges. Even the most accurate cost estimate can be wrong by as much as 4%-6%. For this reason the recommended contingency for the construction of a new facility is 8%-10%; the contingency for a renovation is 12%-15%.

The steps mentioned above are traditional methods for obtaining building costs. However, consultants in the health/fitness industry have recently adopted new and innovative ways for estimating construction costs. For example, Thomas Wills and Associates of Deland, Florida, developed a facility data planning package that identifies all the elements that would go into a facility: entrances, control desk, reception area, fitness activities, storage, lockers and showers, and so forth. Once this information is defined, a computer program provides a per-area cost breakdown and a total cost of the project. This process allows the building developer to obtain estimated costs at any stage of the project. Variations of this facility planning package will likely become a common procedure among consultants in the future.

Construction Documents

The detailed drawings and specifications are called construction documents. The drawings provide the graphic design of the facility, and the specifications provide a verbal description of the project. A new fitness center could not be built without the simultaneous use of both documents. The construction documents ensure a coordinated effort among the general contractor, subcontractors, and engineers. The architect submits the facility design, project requirements, and various interpretations of city codes to the general contractor. Specifications are then developed from the construction drawings. Ideally, the specifications explain physical properties and performance criteria for each item incorporated into the new facility.

Table 6.6 provides an outline from a set of working construction documents. The initial title sheet explains the project, followed by supplemental sheets that are broken down into trades, such as A-1 for architectural drawings, S-1 for structural drawings, P-1 for plumbing, M-1 for mechanical, and E-1 for electrical. Also included is the site plan and a detailed drawing of how the new facility is located on the land development. In short, the construction documents are sectionalized into special areas to aid the contractor and various subcontractors in completing the project as designed by the architect.

SELECTING A CONTRACTOR

Once the construction drawings and specifications have been prepared, the next step is choosing the right contractor for the project. You or the consultant can hire the contractor, or you can hire a construction manager to oversee the construction phase of the project. The majority of health/fitness centers have been constructed by a general contractor who was chosen by the owner.

There are several methods of selecting a contractor, the most common of which is

Table 6.6 Organization of Construction Drawings

Code numbers	Explanations
Cover	Project title
	Index
Civil	Drawings in this category shall be arranged in the order indicated. The first plan shall be numbered C1-1 and additional plans shall be numbered consecutively C1-2, C1-3, C1-4, and so on.
C1-1	Location plans
C1-2	Site plan
C1-3	Demolition
C1-4	Grading
C1-5	Paving and drainage
C1-6	Sitework details
C1-7	Landscaping (if involved)
Architectural	
A1-1, A1-2, etc.	Plans
A2-1, A2-2, etc.	Elevations and general sections
A3-1, A3-2, etc.	Finish schedule
	Door schedule and details
	Equipment schedules (millwork, material, etc.)
A4-1, A4-2, etc.	Wall sections and exterior details
A5-1, A5-2, etc.	Interior details
A6-1, A6-2, etc.	Reflected ceiling plans
Structural	
S1-1, S1-2, etc.	Plans
S2-1, S2-2, etc.	Schedules
S3-1, S3-2, etc.	Details
S4-1, S4-2, etc.	Elevations and general sections
Mechanical	
M1-1, M1-2, etc.	Plans—Heating and air conditioning
M2-1, M2-2, etc.	Plans—Plumbing and special systems
M3-1, M3-2, etc.	Schedules
M4-1, M4-2, etc.	Details and schematics
Electrical	
E1-1, E1-2, etc.	Plans—Lighting
E2-1, E2-2, etc.	Plans—Power and special systems
E3-1, E3-2, etc.	Schedule
E4-1, E4-2, etc.	Details and diagrams

competitive bidding. It is the responsibility of the architect to prepare the drawings, specifications, invitations to bid the project, instructions on how to bid the project, and bid forms. The following information is then sent to contractors who are recommended by the architect or owner.

In competitive bidding, the contractors who will be involved are first asked to provide information on experience, financial condition, and ability to be bonded and to submit references. After this initial screening, all contractors submit their bids, including the price of the project, within a preestablished time period. Traditionally, the lowest bidder is selected for the project. However, it is not always advisable to go with the lowest bidder. Considerations should be given to references, previous work completed, personnel involved, and the overall construction market before such a decision is made. The key to competitive bidding is starting with reputable construction firms so that any firm you eventually select is considered acceptable.

Although competitive bidding is the most frequently used method of hiring a contractor, it has also been known to cause problems for the contractor, architect, and owner alike. Oftentimes, contractors who need the work underbid the project to get the job and then recapture dollars through change-orders. This results in a very frustrating construction period of claims and counterclaims between the architect and the contractor. The best way to prevent the adverse effects of open competitive bidding is to screen the contractors in advance and establish a list of acceptable bidders based on recommendations of other owners of health/fitness facilities.

You may choose instead to hire a construction manager for the project. A construction manager serves as a consultant to the owner

in a number of ways. If hired during the design phase, the construction manager provides his or her expertise to the owner and architect in such areas as proper building materials, electrical and mechanical systems, scheduling, and construction cost analysis. When the construction phase begins, the construction manager is responsible for the construction subcontractors, coordinating and supervising their work. Construction managers have become so popular that many architectural firms have chosen to provide this service. Generally, construction managers are hired on a cost-plus-fee basis, because their services vary from project to project. The fixed cost is usually between 5% and 8% of the total construction cost, whereas the additional fees include reimbursable expenses and services not covered in the general agreement.

A negotiated contract between the owner, architect, and preferred construction company is another method of selecting a contractor. This process allows you to select a contractor who has a reputation for building quality health/fitness facilities. As a result, the contractor becomes a valuable collaborator throughout the project. The firm chosen must obviously be well known and trusted by both yourself and the architect. If a firm of this nature is not available, then competitive bidding is the preferred method. The main disadvantage to a negotiated contract is that there is no incentive for the contractor to limit the cost of the work. Thus you should establish a guaranteed maximum on the project so the total project costs will not exceed a predetermined dollar value.

You and the designated contractor work together to establish the terms of the agreement, which are formalized by signing a contract. This agreement details the responsibilities and expectations of all parties involved in the project. The architect assists you, your attorney, and an insurance adviser in the preparation of the contract. The AIA has published standard forms that cover most types of contractual arrangements. Because the general conditions of the AIA contracts have been approved by the Associated General Contractors of America, it is best to use these forms wherever possible.

Methods of Payment

During the contractual phase, you will need to negotiate the financial arrangements with the contractor. Traditionally, the negotiated contract is either a lump sum or the cost of work plus a fee. The lump-sum fee is based entirely on a well-defined scope of work that describes the total construction. Material costs, labor, overhead, and profit are all parts of the lump-sum value prepared by the contractor. Construction costs average between 50% and 60% of the total project cost. This fee is dependent upon whether the project is a new building or a renovation of an existing facility.

The lump-sum fee is preferable to the owner, because it allows a predetermined amount to be used for budgeting purposes. Realizing that this figure should not deviate drastically during construction should enable you to feel more confident about the initial projections.

The cost-plus-fee arrangement reimburses the contractor for his or her direct and indirect costs of the construction and, in addition, pays a fee for his or her services. The fee is usually a stipulated sum or a percentage of the construction cost. The stipulated sum is a matter that is negotiated with the contractor but usually entails the contractor's direct and indirect personal expenses plus any additional fees that are charged against

the project (e.g., consulting or construction management).

Once the contract has been signed, you must rely on the architect to supervise the construction, and the contractor must meet the quality and quantity standards described in the construction drawings. Any changes or design deviations during the construction phase can be very costly. For this reason, a contingency fee of between 10% and 15% of the total construction cost is recommended. This fee should cover any charges above the original construction agreement.

FACILITY CONSIDERATIONS

This section includes specific suggestions and guidelines for the design phase that was introduced in chapter 5. Owners and architects can use this information during the design phase of a fitness center project. The examples below draw from facilities that are primarily designed for commercial, community, and corporate health/fitness centers.

Testing Room

A testing room should be included in the design of any health/fitness facility. Testing can include a basic fitness appraisal (body composition, functional capacity, strength, and flexibility) or a more sophisticated exercise stress test analysis. The rooms must be designed accordingly, and a testing protocol will facilitate the determination of the specific space needs. We normally find that non-clinically-oriented services such as general fitness testing are offered.

A fitness testing room should be at least 100 square feet but preferably 150 square feet of air-conditioned, well-lit space. Sufficient space is needed for a bicycle ergometer, a flexibility tester, a desk, two chairs, and perhaps a file cabinet. There should be enough room between the pieces of equipment and furniture to move about freely.

The stress testing room should be at least 150-200 square feet of air-conditioned, well-lit space. Space is needed here for a treadmill, control console, examination table, crash cart, metabolic cart, storage cabinet, and ease of traffic flow. Both testing rooms should be private and acoustically controlled.

The location of this space should generally be convenient to the locker areas for the members being tested. If the space is not serving as the office space for the technician, it should also be located near the staff office area.

Gymnasium

Prior to designing a gymnasium, you and the architect must first answer a number of preliminary questions so that you can develop a well-planned and functional scheme for your facility.

- What planned activities will be provided in the gymnasium area?
- What is the estimated number of participants that will be using the gymnasium area?
- Will the gymnasium serve purposes other than fitness-related activities (lectures, dances, etc.)?
- What relationship will the gymnasium have to other activity areas? Will the gymnasium serve as an area that others are built around or will it be placed at the end of the building?

Because the size of a gymnasium ranges from 2,000 to 20,000 square feet, an area that uses this amount of space must be properly discussed and planned out. A good gymnasium design provides easy access to all participants, flexibility of activities, and good member control for security. Those involved in designing the gymnasium must address the following design issues:

- structure (ceilings and walls),
- floors,
- lighting,
- storage, and,
- indoor and elevated jogging tracks.

Structure

The ceilings of a gymnasium should be built high enough to accommodate games like basketball and volleyball. Generally, the ceiling height should be approximately two stories, or at least 24 feet. This height will have to be modified if an elevated jogging track is planned for the area above the gymnasium floor. The ceiling should be a light color so that a ball or object can be easily spotted by a participant. Also, support structures should be kept to a minimum and be the same color as the ceiling.

Traditionally, gymnasium walls have been built with a durable material, such as concrete block or concrete. However, contemporary designers are attempting to improve upon the aesthetic appearance of gymnasium walls by using shatterproof glass or durable wood materials. The material that you select should be durable, but not abrasive, and should be easy to keep clean (Flynn, 1985).

Floors

A variety of floor surfaces is available for gymnasiums, but the major decision is whether to choose a wood surface (maple, beech, etc.)

or a synthetic material (polyurethane or rubber). There are advantages and disadvantages to each system, but it is beyond the scope of this chapter to go into such detail on the various floors. In general, you should identify the purposes and needs of the floor before you make a decision. Also, consider the floor lines that will be necessary to accommodate the desired activities.

Lighting

Most gymnasiums have direct or indirect lighting, or a combination of both. The system you choose must produce at least 50-100 footcandles and provide an even light distribution throughout the room. Although there are many systems to choose from, considerations should be given to purpose, cost, bulb availability, and ease of replacement.

The more popular lighting systems include mercury vapor, metal halide incandescent, and fluorescent. Because replacing bulbs in a gymnasium is time-consuming, you would do well to pay more for a bulb with a longer life than to purchase a cheaper bulb and replace it more often.

Storage

Gymnasiums use various types of equipment (e.g., standards, exercise mats, and sound systems and apparatus) that require proper storage space. The storage areas should be accessible from the gymnasium through large double doors. The size of the storage area will vary depending upon the setting and the activities. Generally, an area of 100-300 square feet is adequate for most storage space requirements.

Indoor and Elevated Jogging Tracks

Indoor jogging tracks have made great technical advances in recent years. In addition to traditional carpet or concrete for indoor tracks, today there are many rubber-based and synthetic surfaces from which to choose. Prior to selecting an indoor track surface, you need to consider initial cost, life of the surface, quality of materials, reputation of the manufacturer, ease of maintenance, and reliability of the installer.

Surface materials range anywhere from $3 to $6 or more per square foot for rubber-based and polyurethane synthetics, and $7 to $12 for wood surfaces. In addition to a high-grade surface, synthetic materials require a prepared base. For indoor tracks this base is predominantly concrete and is generally designed into the structural phase of the construction project.

If a banked track is planned, the raised areas are created by either building a graduated support structure under the track material or having the architect design the angle of embankment into the concrete support structure. Because most track materials are troweled or laid on over the base, concrete has proven to be an excellent base surface.

For an elevated track over a gymnasium, the lanes should be 3 feet wide and constructed 12-15 feet above the gymnasium floor. The track should be large enough so that at least 12 laps per mile are necessary to avoid injuries associated with excessive turning. Timing devices and graphic displays are helpful additions. Support structures should be designed from the concrete base to the ceiling or wall, with reinforced handrails for added security.

Exercise Studio

As the popularity of group exercise classes continues to increase, a properly designed exercise studio has become a high priority for many health/fitness facilities. The ideal exercise studio takes into account room size, floor surface, lighting, ventilation, climate control, sound system, and furnishings.

The size of an exercise studio is dictated by the number of projected participants and space availability. Although room dimensions vary from setting to setting, it is generally accepted that 36 square feet is the minimum space that should be allowed per participant. Rectangular and square-shaped rooms are the most popular designs. Keep in mind the current interest in group exercise classes and design the room to be large enough to accommodate needs.

Floor surfacing has become a prominent issue in aerobic exercise studios. This has primarily been the result of the high incidence of instructor and participant injuries. There are now a number of highly recommended floors with a variety of good surfaces. Industry professionals and sports medicine specialists identify five items as essential criteria for selecting a safe flooring system (Exerflex, 1986):

1. Compliance (shock absorption): How does the floor yield or bend? Does it have good shock-absorption capabilities?
2. Foot stability: Will the floor provide a stable base for foot impact?
3. Surface function or traction: Will the floor allow dissipation of side-to-side stresses during horizontal glide or slide movements?
4. Resiliency (energy return): Does the floor have the capability to rebound or spring back into shape after impact?
5. Impact independence: Does the flooring system isolate the absorption of impact energy, keeping the deflection of the floor to a small area?

Currently, the most widely used surfaces are wood and carpet. These floors are constructed with either a high-density foam or a spring-loaded wood overlay between the concrete base and the surface. A good aerobics floor system costs between $5 and $12 per square foot. Always consider other activities that might be held in the studio, because these programs will affect the floor system that is purchased as well.

Temperature control is another important consideration in an exercise studio. Unfortunately, this item is often overlooked until after the studio is in use. Body heat of exercising members increases the cooling load up to three times that of a normal room. A separate heating and cooling system with an independent control for both temperature and humidity should be placed in the studio. The average temperature setting is between 68 and 72 degrees Fahrenheit and humidity setting between 50% and 60%.

All aerobic studios should be well lighted and well ventilated. Incandescent lights are preferred over fluorescent lights, and natural lighting (skylights and windows) is preferred when possible. Artificial lighting should feature dimmer switches to increase the variety of uses for the room. The inside air should be well ventilated with the proper exchange of outside air. The circulation of air is accomplished with a good blower system or ceiling fans. Always consider the noise factor when such systems are installed.

The proper stereo system is a very integral part of the aerobics room. Seek the assistance of an acoustical engineer when designing and selecting a stereo system. Speaker placement, instructor microphone systems (including instructor-mounted remote units), and component placement should all be discussed with the instructors who will be conducting the classes.

Careful planning and feedback from all individuals involved is the key to a successful studio. The following can serve as a checklist to facilitate the architectural development:

• Ideally, the room should be at least 1,200 square feet, with 36-40 square feet per person used as a minimum guideline.

- The floor should be either spring-loaded hardwood or low-pile, bonded-layered carpet on top of 100-ounce padding. Both have been shown to be acceptable. Furthermore, there are synthetic and specially made aerobics floors that can be used as alternatives.
- The ceiling should be made of acoustical material. It should be at least 8 feet high if no fans are to be hung and 10-12 feet high if fans will be used.
- There should be at least two to four ceiling fans in a 1,200-square foot room to help circulate air.
- At least one wall should be covered with a 6-foot-high mirror, but two or three wall mirrors would help students view their alignment and technique.
- An oak ballet bar, 42 inches high, 1.5-2 inches in diameter, and 6-7 inches from the wall, should be mounted on at least one, but preferably two, of the walls.
- There should be a separate sound system for this room including an amplifier with a tuner, turntable, dual cassette deck, and four speakers. The speakers should be hung from the ceiling or placed on shelves high up in the corners of the room.
- It is not necessary to build a stage for the instructor.
- Light controls should be on rheostat.
- There should be two doorways to enter and exit the room.

Strength Training Areas

Another area that has increased in popularity is the strength training room. You should expect a mixture of dedicated bodybuilders, recreational weight trainers, and novices who are just getting interested in weight training. Also, there are as many women involved in strength training programs as men. The per-son responsible for designing a strength training area must consider all these variables and create a room that will fit the needs of all groups.

Designing a strength training area is essentially the same as designing a gymnasium or aerobics studio. The first step is to define the use of the space. Answers to the following questions will help determine room size, equipment preference, structural requirements, and interior design:

- What programs (e.g., circuit training, free weights, etc.) will be offered in the strength training area?
- What is the size of membership in the facility and what is the approximate demand on the strength training area?
- What equipment preferences are there, and will there be a mixture of free weights and machines?
- Is there a high demand for separate men's and women's strength training areas, or is a coed strength room acceptable?
- Is the anticipated space for the strength training room in a structurally sound area of the facility?

The areas of primary importance during the design phase of the strength training include

- room size and facility placement,
- floor,
- equipment and equipment layout, and
- interior design

Room Size and Facility Placement

With the increasing interest in strength training, it is recommended that the room contain a minimum of 1,600 square feet of floor space. It is not uncommon to see weight training areas of 3,000 to 10,000 square feet in many community and commercial health/fitness facilities. Unfortunately, many new weight training rooms are outdated when they open, because the architect and/or the owner did not perceive the popularity of the activity during the design stage. A square or rectangular room with little or no structural obstacles is best.

Consideration should also be given to designing one large coed weight room or providing separate men's and women's weight areas. Privacy has become an important issue with many new commercial fitness facilities. As an example, separate weight rooms from the coed areas are now being designed in both men's and women's locker rooms. A close evaluation should be made of the membership characteristics and availability of space before making such a decision.

The live-load of a new strength training area is another concern that could affect the room placement. City building codes are established to prevent excessive weight loads from being placed on building structures that are not originally designed for this purpose. Commercial structures typically have a 60-pound-per-square-foot load-bearing capacity, but exercise areas normally demand at least 100 pounds per square foot. The areas of major concern are weight rooms that are designed over a gymnasium or on a floor of a building other than the ground floor. Perimeter placement of weight machines alleviates some of the load-bearing problems in these instances; however, the improper placement of a weight room could produce a weight overload and cause significant structural problems. Structural problems should not occur if the room is located on a ground floor or structural concrete slab.

Floor

The type of flooring depends on the type of equipment selected. If the weight area is equipped primarily with machines (Nautilus, Universal, Hydra Fitness, etc.), an easily cleaned, durable carpet is best. However, if the room is predominantly equipped with free weights, a resilient rubber surface is recommended. This material comes in sheets or tiles that can be glued on top of the existing concrete slab.

Equipment and Equipment Layout

The decision regarding which weight equipment to purchase will depend upon space requirements, member preference, and cost (see chapter 9 for an in-depth discussion of weight training equipment). Manufacturers of weight equipment provide necessary information on their equipment and consulting assistance with equipment layout.

A primary rule to remember when arranging weight training equipment is not to overcrowd the space. Provide fewer stations if there appears to be a crowding situation. A recommended lower limit of 46 square feet should be given for each piece of single-station strength equipment. This figure includes the dimensions of the equipment and the distance between stations and averages out the large and small equipment items in an area.

It is also best to keep all machines, free weights, and stretching mats in separate areas. Some health/fitness facilities have incorporated separation walls approximately 4 feet high to divide these sections. This design provides traffic control without the visual shrinkage a full wall creates. Others have designed separate rooms for both free weights and machines.

It's a good idea to make a scaled-down version of the room and equipment layout based upon the kinds of equipment involved. Manufacturers provide the dimensions for each piece of equipment and even provide scale models that can be placed on graph paper. This process allows you, the architect, and the contractor to view the room and equipment layout before the beginning of construction.

Interior Design

The appearance of the strength training room is very important. The right ambience entices members to exercise while enjoying their surroundings. At least one wall should be mirrored. Special consideration should be given to lighting, carpeting, graphics, and skylights. Carpeting that extends on a side wall to wainscoting height serves as an excellent acoustical buffer as well as a protective surface in a free weight area. The color schemes of walls, equipment upholstery, and flooring must all be coordinated to appeal to the user. Assistance in this area is provided by experienced interior designers and consultants.

Racquetball Courts

The dimensions of a racquetball court are 40 feet long and 20 feet wide, with a front wall and ceiling height of 20 feet and a back wall that is at least 12-15 feet high. The overall playing surface for a racquetball court requires 800 square feet. Although the dimensions of a racquetball court are standardized, the court components vary from facility to facility. Six major areas must be considered in the initial design and construction of a racquetball court:

- Walls
- Ceilings
- Floors
- Lighting
- Doors
- Ventilation system

Walls

The most common wall systems to choose from are panels, reinforced fiberglass concrete, plaster, poured-in-place cement slab, and shatterproof glass. Before deciding on a wall system, discuss the following items with the architect and consultant: material cost, land considerations (moisture and stability), overall appearance, maintenance, and ball action (i.e., sound and speed). Comparing these characteristics in each of the preferred wall systems will facilitate your decision.

Although plaster has been around for many years, the maintenance costs have proven to be too expensive. A poured-in-place concrete slab has not been used very often; the cost is prohibitive, and obtaining a straight wall from a slab that is poured on the ground and then erected is difficult to accomplish. Reinforced fiberglass concrete is the newest material on the market and has great promise for the future, but its applications have been inconsistent. Plexiglass walls provide a panoramic view of the activity but are too expensive for many facilities. All things considered, the system with the best reputation is a panel system designed from compressed wood. The advantages of this system far outweigh the disadvantages. The resiliency of the panel systems on the market varies widely, and care should be exercised in getting the highest level possible.

Ceilings

Racquetball court ceilings are often constructed from the same material as the walls. An alternative is a combination of the wall material for the front half of the ceiling and acoustical tile for the back half. The acoustical tile deadens the sound of the ball. Another ceiling alternative is sheet rock that is covered by paint or a glazed material.

Floors

Traditionally, racquetball courts have been covered with a wood floor surface. Maple wood floors look nice, provide a consistent ball bounce, and absorb the shock to the feet. The only disadvantage is that if moisture enters the wood it will buckle the system and cause a swelling of the floor. This becomes an important consideration when subterranean structures are built in areas with porous soil. The only other system available is a synthetic floor. The new polyurethane materials have been used with favorable results. Polyurethane floors are poured and troweled over the concrete floor slab.

Lighting

The lighting choices available for racquetball courts include mercury vapor, fluorescent, and metal halide. The favored system in many facilities is mercury vapor because the consistency, intensity, and life of the bulb is so superior. A racquetball court should provide 50 to 75 footcandles of light. Light fixtures should be easy to install, easy to maintain, energy efficient, and recessed with a protective covering. Always check the maintenance guidelines of various fixtures, because they vary considerably.

Doors

A full-height, solid-core court door that has the same ball action characteristics as the front and side walls is ideal. The door should be flush with the back wall and have no protruding edges. All hinges and door handles should also be flush with the door. A small viewing window 4 inches by 6 inches of shatterproof glass, mounted into the door at approximately the height of an average male adult, is also advisable.

Ventilation System

The ventilation and climate controls of a racquetball court should not be overlooked.

Complete court air exchanges should be made at least four to six times per hour, with humidity kept between 60% and 70%. All ducts for heating and air-conditioning should be recessed and installed at the edge of the front wall and ceiling or located at the rear of the court.

Tennis Courts

The construction of a tennis court is not a simple matter. Construction requirements and materials depend upon the environment in which the courts are to be built. Some minor distinctions are also made between indoor and outdoor tennis courts. A combination of these makes constructing a tennis court difficult.

What is the best method of building tennis courts without experiencing the pitfalls? The first suggestion is to obtain a good tennis court consultant who has had experience with various court surfaces, lighting, court placement, and drainage. Another recommendation is for you to learn about the basic components that encompass good tennis court construction. These components include site considerations, surfaces, drainage, backstops, and lighting. An understanding of these areas assures the quality of tennis courts and avoids costly repairs.

The dimensions of a single and double tennis court are 36 feet by 78 feet. Including the clearance on each side of the court (10 feet) and the clearance between the baseline and the fence (21 feet), a total area of 60 feet by 120 feet encompasses one tennis court. The total surface area for one court is 7,200 square feet. If indoors, the ceiling height should be at least 30-35 feet from the middle of the court.

Site Considerations

Taking the time to plan the placement of outdoor tennis courts minimizes construction costs, avoids potential drainage problems, and reduces the effect of winds. Outdoor tennis courts should be elevated from the surrounding area. If a high area is not available, then you should have one made. Wind studies should be performed to determine the average tendencies and velocity of the wind on the proposed site. Natural or man-made wind protection, including trees, bushes, shrubbery, and windscreens, should be used to protect the courts.

Tennis courts are only as good as the soil base on which they are constructed. It is essential to determine if water, expansive soil, organic material, or loose fill that could cause earth settlement is underneath the surface. Soil compaction tests should be performed by an engineer to determine the stability of the proposed site.

A soil base must have an adequate slope to assist in water drainage. Tennis courts should drain in either one direction or four directions from the center of the court down. Drainage sloping should be 1 inch in 20-30 feet for porous courts and 1 inch in 10 feet for nonporous courts.

For indoor tennis courts the playing surface is flat, because water drainage is not a problem. Generally, the courts are placed over a structural concrete slab reinforced with metal rods to prevent movement. A similar soil base compaction test is also recommended for indoor courts, because moving earth, splitting, and eroding can also happen underneath the slab of an indoor court. An asphalt surface is usually installed on top of the concrete base to provide good cushion, easy adherence to synthetic materials, and prevent water penetration.

Surfaces

The purpose of a tennis court surface is to provide good and consistent action of the ball,

to maintain safe footing, to have an appearance that is satisfying, and to minimize maintenance problems. Although there are over 100 different tennis court surfaces available, not all provide a desirable combination of these important factors. Before purchasing any surface, visit a number of installations and determine how each surface plays and how it stands up under heavy use.

The primary objective of a good design for a tennis court surface is to create a predictable ball bounce. This can be accomplished through either a porous or a nonporous system. A porous surface allows water to penetrate the surface and is predominantly used for outdoor tennis courts. A nonporous system prevents the water from penetrating the surface and generally drains off or evaporates. This surface is used for both indoor and outdoor courts. Table 6.7 compares porous and nonporous tennis court surfaces.

The factors involved with selecting a tennis court surface are

- surface costs (i.e., construction and re-surfacing),
- player recommendations,
- maintenance,
- durability,
- effect of weather (drying time),
- ease of resurfacing, and
- ball action (hard surface, soft surface).

The surface colors of a tennis court encompass a broad spectrum. Every color or color combination imaginable has been used to surface a tennis court. There are no standard recommendations that specify against the use of certain colors. However, it is suggested that a color not be too light, as it causes a glare against the surface. Always consider the contrast of the color of the surface to the ball, so the eye can constantly stay in contact with the ball. Also, determine if the color can be readily accessible for maintenance touch-ups.

Lighting

The recommended lighting for tennis courts is mercury vapor or metal halide. The light intensity should range from 30 to 50 foot-candles. Each light should be covered with a safety grill. The current trend is to extend the lights and poles over the fence into the court clearance area, so more direct light is positioned over the court. This system prevents light pollution from occurring around a multicourt arrangement.

Backstops/Windscreens

Tennis court backstops are constructed of anodized aluminum, with a chain-link fence that is usually 10- to 12 feet high. The backstops should be buried deep enough to provide support for the windscreens during heavy windstorms. Backstop poles should be placed in concrete filled holes that have a depth of 25%-40% of the length of the pole above ground.

A dark-colored windscreen is best for providing a good background against which players can follow a ball that is in play. Vented screens and open mesh curtains are also suggested, so the wind escapes through the screens and doesn't cause heavy tension against the frame of the backstop.

Pools

Swimming has often been called the perfect exercise because cardiovascular, musculo-skeletal, and flexibility benefits are all derived from the one activity. Additional rehabilitative benefits have also resulted from swimming, because water provides a non-weight-bearing environment and aids in the therapy of orthopedic injuries. Combine these advantages with the recreational aspects of a swimming pool, and you can easily see why the number of swimming pools in health/fitness facilities has doubled since 1970.

As a result of the interest in water activities, pools of all sizes and shapes have been built in corporate, commercial, and community settings. Many owners and developers of commercial and community facilities are constantly faced with the decision of whether to build a pool or an aquatic complex. The best way to determine the type of pool structure to design is first to decide on the goals and objectives of the pool area and then discuss the various aquatic programs that will be offered. Prioritize the goals and programs and design the pool with these priorities in mind.

It is beyond the scope of this text to mention all the various designs of swimming pools. For the purpose of this section, a lap rectangular pool, 4- to 6 feet deep and 25- to 50 yards long will be used for discussing pool design considerations.

The quality of the pool's design depends on your choice of an architect and contractor. The procedures mentioned in the first section of this chapter are the steps to follow for this process. Oftentimes the architect and contractor chosen to build a new health/fitness complex are also given the responsibility of designing and building the pool. This process is not always recommended, because pool design demands specific expertise in pool construction materials and an understanding of hydraulic systems. If an architect has never designed a pool, seek the assistance of a consultant or obtain an architect with pool design experience.

The designated firm must be familiar with all state and local codes and have experience in commercial, not residential, pool construction. A review of all the recommended guidelines presented by professional organizations and pool manufacturers must also be performed. Finally, all safety considerations

Table 6.7 A Comparison of Various Tennis Court Surfaces

Court type	Repairs may be costly	Glare	Average time before resurfacing	Other uses	Surface hardness	Ball skid length	Ball spin effective
Porous							
Fast dry	no	no	10 years	yes	soft	short if damp court	yes
Clay	no	generally	5 years	yes	soft		yes
Dirt	no	yes	3 years	yes	soft	long (dry court)	yes
Grit	no	yes	3 years	yes	soft		yes
Grass	no	no	indefinite	yes	soft	moderately long	yes
Special (porpous concrete	yes	no	3 years (if colored)	yes	hard	medium	yes
Nonporous noncushioned							
Concrete	yes	no (if colored)	3 years (if colored)	yes	hard	long if glossy court finish	no if glossy finish
Asphalt Plant Mix (colored)	no	no	5 years	yes	hard	medium if gritty court finish	yes if gritty finish
Asphalt Job Mix (colored)	no	no	5 years	yes	hard		
Asphalt Penetrated Macadam	no	no	5 years	yes	hard	short	yes
Wooden	no	no	indefinite	yes	hard	long	no
Nonporous cushioned							
Asphalt Bound System (colored)	no	no	5 years	no	soft	long if glossy finish, short if gritty finish	no if glossy, yes if gritty finish
Synthetic	no	no	varies	yes	soft	medium to short	yes
Synthetic carpet	no	no	varies	yes	soft	short	yes
Removable	no	no	varies	yes	soft	varies, shortest to longest	yes

Maintenance of all nonporous surface types is very minor. Porous types, with the exception of porous concrete (very minor) require daily and annual care.

Colors	Drying time after rain	Is ball bounce uniform	Stains ball	Abrasive surface (hard on balls, shoes, and rackets)	Humidity problem indoors	Slide surface	Uses affect ball bounce
green	fast	yes (if maintained)	some do	no	yes	yes	yes
red (varies)	slow	yes (if maintained)	yes	no	yes	yes	yes (if tapes)
varies	slow	yes (if maintained)	yes	no	yes	yes	yes (if tapes)
varies	slow	yes (if maintained)	yes	no	yes	yes	yes (if tapes)
green	slow	irregular	yes	no	won't grow	yes	no
wide variety	fast	yes	no	yes	no	no	no
wide variety	fast	depends on installation	no	varies	no	no	no
wide variety	fast	yes	no if colored	no if colored	no	no	no
wide variety	fast	yes	no if colored	no if colored	no	no	no
wide variety	fast	yes	no if colored	no	no	no	no
wide variety	fast	yes	no	no	no	no	no
wide variety	fast	yes	no	no	no	yes	no
green	fast	yes	no	no	no	slight	no
green	fast	yes	no	no	no	no	no
variety	fast	yes	no	no	no	slight	no

Note. From *Planning Facilities for Athletics* (p. 87) by Athletic Institute and American Alliance for Health, Physical Education and Dance, Washington, DC. Used by permission.

should be incorporated into the design of the pool.

The areas of consideration in designing a pool include

- pool placement,
- pool shell structure,
- gutter/overflow system,
- pump/filter system,
- lighting, and
- air movement.

Pool Placement

One of the essential aspects of the placement of an indoor or outdoor pool is that the locker rooms and pool area be next to each other. This arrangement allows easy access to dressing facilities and provides shower capabilities before entering the pool. This design satisfies health department standards as well.

Outdoor pools should be placed with concern to environmental elements. Consideration should be given to the section of a city or town in which the pool will be constructed. Developers should avoid areas that have high traffic usage, heavy industry, and open fields. Heavy winds can carry dirt and debris into a pool, thus building or environmental barriers should be considered to block the wind. A close evaluation of the movement of the sun should also be performed to determine shadows throughout the day. Generally, a north-south location is best.

Adequate parking space must also be available for both indoor and outdoor pools. Many owners of health/fitness facilities have unconsciously restricted the usage of their pools by providing inadequate parking. City codes should be followed in determining the numbers of parking spaces. The recommendation for parking spaces per square feet for a pool arena is approximately one space for every 100 square feet.

Finally, make sure there is enough area for deck and storage space. If a pool is to be built outdoors, consideration should be given to a sun-deck area that is large enough to accommodate lounge furniture and still provide easy participant access. Minimum deck width should be 10 feet. A storage room should be designed into the pool scheme so pool apparatus (brushes, vacuums, leaf nets, etc.) can be placed together close to the pool.

Pool Shell Structure

The construction of the walls and floor of a pool shell is an important aspect of any pool construction. Most pools have been constructed with concrete in a monolithic style, where no seams are found between the walls and the floor surfaces. Concrete that is either poured or applied through a Gunite process (forced pressure) is the standard construction method used for most commercial pools. However, today both steel and aluminum pools are becoming quite popular. Because soil conditions are often unstable and movement can occur, iron reinforcement rods are also recommended to provide additional stability and longevity to the pool structure.

The exterior finish of a pool consists of plaster, ceramic tile, or an epoxy coating. These finishes are applied over the concrete shell and must be roughened or scratched to provide traction for individuals using the pool. A slip-resistant, glazed or unglazed tile is the best surface for finishes and trim for both indoor and outdoor pools. A high-grade colored tile is also recommended. Pools built with a steel basin must be painted with a waterproof paint. Aluminum must be either painted or covered with tile.

Gutter/Overflow Systems

The purpose of a gutter or overflow system is to allow the water that is displaced by swimmers to be stored and reinstated into the pool via the filter pumps. There are three common overflow systems that are used by pool contractors.

- Perimeter overflow systems: Water height is monitored at deck level.
- Roll-out overflow systems: Gutter is open and water washes into the system.
- Recessed overflow systems: Gutter is recessed into the pool walls and water is washed into the system.

Various techniques of storing overflow water have been developed for each system mentioned above. Examples include using large storage tanks, surge trenches around the perimeter of the pool, and large gutters that can store the displaced water. The architect and engineer designing the pool will determine which system is preferable in light of cost, storage space, and pool use (recreational or competitive).

Pump/Filter Systems

A pool's hydraulic system consists of a pump and filter unit. This system circulates pool water through a series of pipes and through a filter where the water is treated and then reinstated into the pool. State health departments dictate how often the pool water must be completely recycled. Turnover rates can range from 4 to 6 hours depending upon the use of the pool. There are three filter systems that are used in the design of a pool.

- Cartridge filter systems: Stringy cylinders trap materials in the water as they pass through.
- Sand filter systems: Water passes from the top and seeps through the sand as it is circulated out; impurities are caught on top of the sand and stored until cleaned.
- Diatomaceous earth filter systems: Particles in the water are removed as the water passes through a thin layer of diatomaceous earth.

Lighting

For liability reasons, any pool being used at night must have adequate lighting in and around the pool area. It is recommended that 50 to 60 footcandles be used for lighting around outdoor pool decks, whereas 100 footcandles are needed for indoor pools.

Proper attention should be given to the type of light used and the placement of the lighting. High-intensity mercury vapor lamps are the preferred lights among pool owners. Pool lighting must be placed so the direct beam of light does not interfere with the vision of swimmers. All circuits should be no-fault grounded to prevent any electrical problems that could result from weather conditions or man-made hazards.

Final considerations in swimming pool design include the following:

- Provide the proper drainage pitch for drains and the gutter system.
- Evaluate and design the proper safety features into the pool.
- If the pool is heated, provide a system that can maintain a pool at 80 degrees Fahrenheit. Common ways to heat a pool include gas, electricity, and oil.
- Provide the proper number of inlets and outlets to circulate water effectively in the pool.
- Construct pool decks with a material that prevents slipping and is not uncomfortable to the feet during the hot days of summer.
- Design lap pools with eight-foot-wide lanes and a center stripe marked by a dark tile.

Air Movement

The humidity of an indoor aquatics area can cause problems throughout the facility. Careful planning to maintain relative humidity of a pool area in the 55% to 60% range can now be accomplished with separate exhaust systems and differential air movement systems in the wet and dry areas. A negative pressure in the wet area with respect to the dry area can present undesirable humidity moving from the wet areas into the dry areas.

Locker Rooms

The locker rooms of many health/fitness facilities have changed dramatically over the last 10 years. The participants involved in today's activity centers desire space, comfort, function, and an aesthetically pleasant locker room. It has been estimated that participants of a fitness facility spend 20% to 30% of their total workout time cooling down, showering, dressing, and relaxing. The image of a locker room plays a major role in selling prospective individuals and conveying the members' overall attitude toward a facility setting.

Unfortunately, the locker room has traditionally been an afterthought in the design planning stage. Locker rooms have always suffered when budgetary cutbacks are required, and they seem to get the last consideration when a club is being built. What people don't realize is that a locker room is an important social area that can dictate an atmosphere that can sell people on the facility or turn them off. As competition for the membership revenue and member approval increases, attractive locker rooms become a necessity.

The amount of attention paid to designing a locker room depends on the type of facility and the number and type of individuals it will service. The number of members determines both the number of lockers and showers required and the amount of space necessary to build them. The architect should always consider space needs during peak usage times. Such planning is often overlooked, and thus many facilities are built with an inadequate number of lockers and showers. Locker rooms and parking spaces almost always represent the rate-limiting factor in facility use. If people can park and get suited up, they will find a way to exercise.

The following are specific areas to consider during the design phase of a locker room:

- Layout and design
- Wet and dry areas
- Locker areas
- Lockers

Layout and Design

A well-designed locker room entails extensive planning during the design phase so most mistakes and problems can be avoided. The factors involved in designing a locker room include space, convenience, function, security, ease of maintenance, and aesthetics.

The design of the locker room depends on the answers to the following questions: How many participants (men and women) will the locker room serve? What size of lockers will be used? What specific amenities will be provided (sauna, whirlpool, massage, steam room, toiletries, etc.)? Where will the locker room be placed in relation to activity areas? What will the budget be for the locker room?

By answering these questions you establish a facility philosophy that provides an idea of the basic accommodations required. Various settings differ in their approaches to locker room layout. Some provide a very plush, high-class appeal to their clientele, whereas others prefer to project a spartan-style locker room. Neither approach is wrong, as long as it reflects the philosophy of the particular setting.

Perhaps the most important factor of a well-designed locker room is space or the appearance of space. Space is essential in both the actual locker area and the section between the wet area and the locker area. A drying-off area, placed between the wet area and the locker room, is suggested to act as a buffer zone. The space should be arranged to allow a minimum of congestion and bottlenecks during peak usage hours or projected special events. Figure 6.10 is the recommended floor plan of a locker room.

A successful locker room design also offers convenience to the participants. The locker area is centered around as many of the activity areas as possible. This provides easy access and minimizes the time spent in activities other than exercise. Additional convenience factors include the placement of amenities, storage, and laundry facilities. These also have an effect on the participant's perception of the locker room design.

Wet and Dry Areas

A major aspect of a good locker room design is how the ventilation system controls mois-

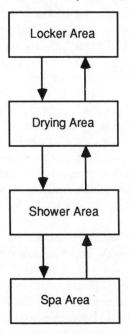

Figure 6.10. Recommended floor plan for a locker room.

ture. The object of a well-designed ventilation system is to maintain dry, rather than humid, inside air. An improper ventilation system affects mechanical systems, the structural system, electrical fixtures, and floor and wall finishes.

Locker rooms contain both hot and humid wet areas and dry dressing areas in proximity to one another, and thus a separation must be provided. The first separation comes from independent mechanical systems that provide at least 60% outside air in the dry area and exhaust fans that provide complete air exchanges in the wet area. It is often difficult to determine how many air exchanges are adequate. The volume of ventilation depends on the size of the facility and the atmosphere; state codes are available to provide such information. Sometimes the recommended volumes are too low and thus should be reviewed closely by a mechanical engineer and increased if necessary.

A system designed to create a negative air pressure in the shower area helps control moisture and facility odor. A way of creating this pressure change is to install doors between the wet and dry areas and assure that the mechanical systems for air movement create the appropriate pressure differential. Increased ventilation is also obtained by adding ceiling or circulation fans.

Floors and wall surfaces in the wet areas should always be designed with safety, maintenance, and aesthetics in mind. Abrasive, nonslip tile is the best surface for floors. Because a buildup of soap and dirt can develop, a beige- or brown-colored grout is recommended to keep the tile in good condition. All floors should be pitched away from the dry areas and directed towards a drain. Tile is also recommended for the wall areas.

Alternative surfaces include epoxy sealants over waterproof sheet rock or concrete block. These surfaces have proven to be satisfactory in dressing room, sink, and commode areas.

All corners of these areas should be rounded so moisture cannot penetrate the seams. Make sure that ceilings are moisture-resistant. Epoxy-painted surfaces or moisture-resistant acoustical tiles are best in this area. Lights should have waterproof fixtures and be centered over the showers and walkways (Hayes, 1986).

Privacy in a health/fitness facility is a recommended feature in the shower and drying areas. If the budget will allow for it, separate shower stalls should be designed into both the men's and the women's locker rooms. If this is not possible, a communal shower is recommended for men and a private shower and drying area for women.

Shower partitions are constructed with ceramic tile or stainless steel. Less expensive, modular fiberglass shower stalls have also been used with good success. Figure 6.11 shows modular fiberglass showers that can be connected and assembled during construction of the facility.

Vanity and sink areas should be large enough to handle peak crowds, be well lit, and have wall-mounted power sockets and hair dryers (Jolly, 1983). A separate makeup area for women that is large enough to provide space for hair curlers, cosmetic bags, and hair dryers is also recommended.

Dry Areas

All materials in the locker area should combine easy maintenance with hygiene considerations. Materials should be durable and able to withstand moisture and dirt. Aesthetics must also be considered, because this area often sells the facility to interested participants.

The floor of the locker room is a major concern for interior decorators and designers. Because mildew and mold are constant prob-

lems, materials should be able to withstand long periods of moist conditions and show little or no sign of delamination. A 100% nylon carpet is the flooring material of choice for many health/fitness settings. Carpeting provides a pleasing appearance that is maintained with daily vacuuming and periodic shampooing, providing it is mildew resistant and Scotch-guarded.

Wall coverings in the locker area most often consist of epoxy-coated paint, vinyl, or wallpaper. The material chosen must be resilient and not show dirt. Consideration should also be given to corner and wall-to-wall molding to prevent cuts and black marks that will occur with heavy use.

Ceilings are finished with moisture-proof, hand-finished paint. Acoustical materials are also used in conjunction with the paint to reduce the noise levels in the locker room. It is also recommended that the ceiling be approximately 9 feet high.

Lighting is another special consideration as it often establishes the atmosphere of the locker room. Natural lighting is preferred by most designers, and this is accomplished by making the best use of windows and skylights. Ambient and indirect lighting is also suggested because it provides a soft, reflective source of light. The goal of the lighting scheme is to provide adequate lighting while creating a pleasant atmosphere. Different intensities of lighting can effectively provide a sense of privacy in dimly lit dressing rooms and a sense of buoyancy in well-lit grooming areas.

Adequate seating must also be provided in the locker areas. Fixed benches or stools are the most common methods of seating in most locker room facilities. Although there are positives and negatives associated with each, stools take up less room than benches and provide a more appealing look to participants.

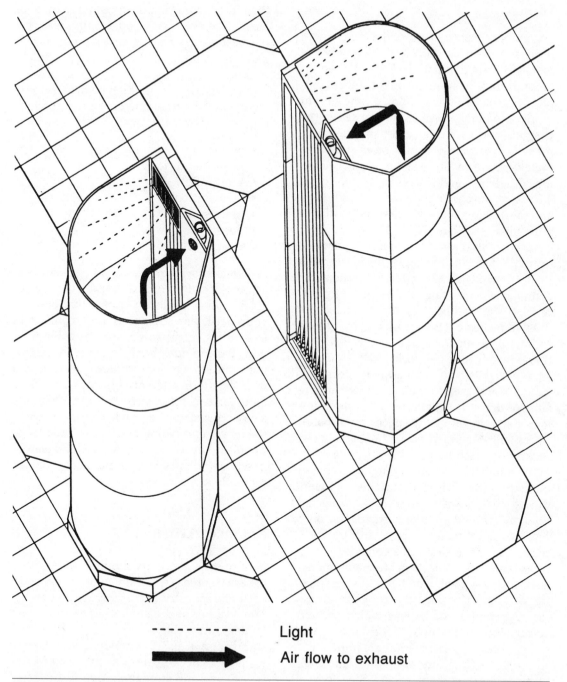

- - - - - - - - - - Light

➡ Air flow to exhaust

Figure 6.11. Modular fiberglass showers. *Note.* Courtesy of Healthscape, Inc., Orlando, Florida. Used by permission.

Lockers

Lockers are considered one of the more crucial purchases the health/fitness facility will have to make. An individual's locker is the center-point of his or her outlook on the entire complex. For this reason, additional time should be given to purchasing lockers that satisfy the clientele and create an enjoyable environment. Locker systems should be evaluated on their appearance, noise factor, ease of cleaning, durability, and resistance to moisture.

Prior to purchasing a locker system, you and the designer must decide whether to provide full-size lockers (12″ × 18″ × 72″) that can be used as day lockers for storing clothes, or reduced lockers that allow for more space in the locker area. An effective system for commercial, corporate, and community settings is the use of permanent kit lockers (twelve inches by fifteen inches by twelve inches) in a separate area and full-size or three-quarter size day lockers. Participants keep valuables and extra athletic attire in a kit locker and use the day lockers for hanging suits or dresses. An alternative is the mini-locker system with hang spaces for apparel. Space efficiency and cost are the two biggest concerns in selecting a locker system.

The number of lockers to purchase is based on either the projected number of users during peak hours or 10% of the projected total of men and women participants. Both figures are estimates at best, and an additional allowance should be considered.

Six basic types of lockers are made: metal/steel, stainless steel, wood, wood/steel, plastic, or glass. The majority of health/fitness facilities choose wood, metal, or a fabricated combination of the two. Wood lockers provide the best appearance but are impractical in a high-traffic facility where the daily wear and tear damages them quickly. Steel lockers have stood the test of time and hold up well under moist and humid environmental conditions. Two disadvantages to steel lockers are their institutional appearance and their noise factor. The plastic or wood laminate is probably best suited for the fitness industry. It looks appealing and does not dent, scratch, or rust.

Once you decide on the type of locker you want, consider these factors before purchasing:

- Service
- Layout and design
- Warranties
- Size and color
- Maintenance
- Security
- Cost.

Each locker system has advantages and disadvantages. By considering all these variables, you can select a system that best fits your particular setting. A new concept in lockers by Healthscape, Inc., is a modular unit that provides bench, ventilation, lighting, and storage lockers in a prefabricated unit (Figure 6.12). This system is not only modularized. It can be configured to provide a moving wall to alter the lockers available to the men's and women's areas in a matter of minutes. This is a particularly helpful feature in settings where special events are conducted regularly.

Service Areas

Facility considerations should also be given to service areas, which include the check-in desk and laundry and storage locker areas. The location of the service areas should be strategically designed for easy access and staff supervision. A common design flaw is to have a check-in desk at the front of the facility and the storage lockers in the rear. The service areas should be close to each other and project a predetermined traffic pattern for participants to follow.

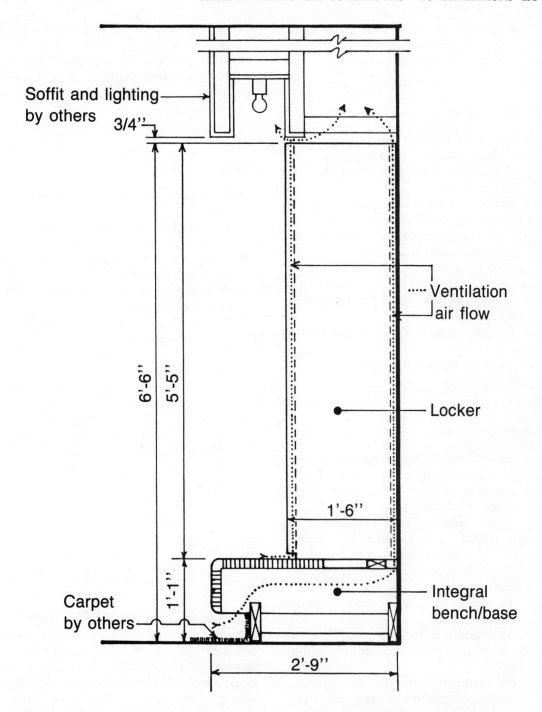

Soffit and lighting by others

3/4"

6'-6"

5'-5"

Ventilation air flow

Locker

1'-6"

1'-1"

Carpet by others

Integral bench/base

2'-9"

Figure 6.12. A modular unit that provides a bench, ventilation, lighting, and storage lockers in a prefabricated unit. *Note.* Courtesy of Healthscape, Inc., Orlando, Florida. Used by permission.

The following are lists of specific guidelines to consider when designing the check-in desk and laundry and storage locker areas.

Check-In Desk

- Design an area that provides high visibility for security and easy access.
- Control the PA and sound systems from this area.
- Locate the burglar and fire alarm panels behind the check-in desk.
- Design facility monitoring equipment to be viewed from this area.
- Make phones available for court reservations.
- Include storage areas for equipment check-out.
- Design a system for locker key check-out.
- Locate computer feedback systems in this area.

Laundry

- Determine space requirements based on the type of equipment that is used, volume of work done, and number of personnel available.
- Locate laundry close to check-in desk so personnel can be divided for both duties.
- Use nonskid concrete floors.
- Slope floors toward drains. Make sure that doorways are wide enough to allow for laundry carts and equipment placement.
- Acoustically treat walls so that sound does not permeate to other areas of the facility.
- Build worktables into the laundry area.
- Allow for sufficient hot and cold water supplies.
- Design all plumbing for easy maintenance.

- Provide adequate ventilation and exhaust fans for displacing odors and heat.
- Have an engineer design electrical needs. The commercial washers and dryers and wall sockets should all have varied electrical currents.

Storage Lockers

- Locate lockers close to the check-in desk area.
- Determine locker size by the size of articles placed into each locker.
- Use a lock system in this area for maximum security.
- Provide good ventilation in the room and open lockers if necessary.
- Design adequate lighting for easy locker identification.
- Select lockers with sloped tops so dust doesn't accumulate.
- Construct large doorways so participants can have easy access to their lockers.
- Construct walls and ceilings of drywall and coat them with a heavy, water-resistant paint.
- Place lockers on a frame to provide easy access to bottom lockers.

SPECIAL CONSIDERATIONS

This section addresses special design and construction recommendations that an owner and architect should consider prior to the building phase. Many of these topics are either forgotten or not discussed seriously during the planning stages. By paying necessary attention to these areas, you will ensure that a more functional and efficient facility will be constructed.

Acoustics

The correct balance of an audio environment is often overlooked in the design of a health/fitness facility. Heavy reverberation, sound absorption and reflection, and the noise generated from various activities are just some of the factors that an acoustical engineer must attempt to control during the design stage. For example, extending a carpet from the floor-wall junction up to the wainscot level buffers sound tremendously and requires low maintenance. Many owners of fitness facilities have found that, by not taking the necessary time to investigate potential acoustical problems, their buildings were limited in their overall capabilities. Also, these owners have discovered that trying to correct acoustical problems after a facility is constructed is far more expensive than designing acoustical solutions into the original building.

It is the owner's responsibility to apprise the architect or acoustical engineer of the various uses of each area. The architect must in turn communicate to the owner what acoustical materials will be used and in what areas acoustical treatments will be applied. Often, a written statement of the acoustical importance is included in the agreement between owner and architect.

The selection of proper building materials and good structural design are the two main ingredients for audio control. Unwarranted noise can be transmitted through walls, ceilings, and floors that are constructed of inadequate materials. Attention should be given to the following:

- Insulating and lining ventilating ducts and pipes.
- Providing proper floor materials (synthetic, carpet, or wood) and a good subfloor (concrete, asphalt, or wood).
- Providing wall insulation between building studs.

- Placing sound-absorption materials over suspended ceiling partitions and using accepted sounding tiles for all suspended ceilings.
- Using oil paint to absorb sound levels.
- Using strategically placed acoustical tiles in areas that require additional sound absorption (e.g., gymnasiums, exercise studios, and swimming pools).
- Paying close attention to the location and installation of all mechanical systems and providing double walls, soundproof doors, and good mountings for all equipment.

Lighting

The proper lighting of a health/fitness facility is dependent not only on the quantity of light, but also the quality of the light. Providing adequate illumination is difficult because each area has specific lighting requirements. A large gymnasium has significantly different lighting needs than a locker room, yet the lighting specified must accommodate the specific purpose for that area.

Three basic lighting systems are used in most buildings: incandescent, fluorescent, and high-intensity discharge (HID). The HID lights include mercury vapor, metal halide, and high-pressure and low-pressure sodium. Incandescent and fluorescent sources are primarily used inside the facility. Their applications include illuminating offices, locker areas, meeting rooms, dining areas, and pro shops. The HID lamps are used in large activity areas such as the swimming pool and racquetball courts, as well as for outdoor lighting of tennis courts and walkways.

In addition to the quantity and quality of light provided, these factors should be considered: maintenance requirements, bulb availability, repair and replacement capabilities, cleaning requirements, and cost. Each light system has advantages and disadvantages. The architect in association with an illuminating engineer can assist in determining the best sources of light for each area of the facility. As the owner of the facility, you should consider the following questions:

- What is the base cost of operating the total lighting system, including energy charges, lamp replacement, and labor costs?
- Is the visual effect created by the lighting pleasing to the participants?
- Does the lighting provide sufficient illumination so that safety is not compromised?
- Is the lighting necessary to maintain member and property security?

Climate Control

A major concern for all owners of health/fitness facilities is the control of all heating, air-conditioning, and ventilation systems. The goal for every mechanical engineer should be to provide an even distribution of heating and cooling throughout the complex. To accomplish this, consideration must be given to the projected number of participants and the usage for each area of the building.

Areas of high activity sometimes dictate additional mechanical equipment and independent control systems. Examples of these areas include exercise studios, racquetball courts, and weight rooms. Special equipment can also be designed to increase the circulation and intake of outside air to ventilate these areas properly.

When selecting equipment for climate control needs, consider the following guidelines:

- Economy of operation
- Flexibility of control
- Operating noise
- Capacity to meet air control needs

- Maximum occupancy of the area to be controlled
- Special needs for geographical locations

Security

As the number of health/fitness facilities continues to increase, so will the number of security-related problems. Proper care must be given to design a facility that reduces unauthorized use, vandalism, theft, and misuse of equipment. A successful facility not only incorporates good operational procedures, but also determines potential security limitations and corrects these problems during the design phase.

Security objectives should be established while a facility is still in the planning stages. The objectives should take into consideration the specific areas that must be protected. For example, an owner should always want to protect the participant and equipment. The architect can then keep these issues in mind while developing the building layout.

Identifying the specific problem areas of a health/fitness facility is another task that must be determined by the owner and the architect. This can be achieved by drawing upon past experiences, discussing security problems with other facility owners, and obtaining professional law enforcement assistance. Once the problem areas have been identified, measures should be taken to design around them.

The following is a list of security suggestions that should be considered during the planning stages of a health/fitness facility.

- Design one entrance and exit doorway. If multiple entrances and exits are required, control them with lock systems that fit fire code requirements.
- Consider including strategically placed cameras throughout the facility, both in-

doors and outdoors, to frighten away thieves.

- Provide a check-in desk that is situated so that participants and guests must pass by to enter the facility. This area is also where all equipment check-out is located.
- In the specifications of the facility, provide lockers that have a safe lock system. The majority of lock systems used in fitness centers include key lock-token lock and combination lock systems.
- Install a sophisticated burglar alarm system that is activated when the facility is closed. Usually, this system is located in the check-in area for easy staff access when entering or leaving the premises.
- Specify a heavy-duty lock system for entrance and exit doors. Also, make sure that all doors are made of high-quality steel materials.

Landscape

The landscaping of a health/fitness facility is another important aspect that is determined during the design phase. A master plan of the outdoor landscaping should be adopted with the assistance of the architect or landscape architect. The developed plan should reflect the placement of all plants, bushes, or trees and the design of all entrance and exit walks, drives, and parking areas. Special consideration should be given to the climate, heavy usage times, drainage, and maintenance aspects of the facility while preparing this plan.

A code requirement in many cities is that a landscape plan be submitted to a city planning board for approval before any new construction takes place. Also, the submittal of a revised landscape plan must accompany the request for building renovation changes that would alter the existing site plan. This code requirement forces the owner and the archi-

tect to contemplate the outside appearance of the facility and decide what is compatible with the facility image, aesthetically pleasing, and easily maintained.

Sufficient time should be taken by both the owner and the architect to consider the proper landscaping that will fit the location, philosophy, and land conditions of the facility to be built. There exists a wide variation of plants, bushes, flowers, and trees to decide upon. Seek professional assistance when making these decisions and aim for providing a look that will attract people to the new facility. Many nursery owners provide cost-free services when their products are purchased.

Fitness Trail

An outdoor fitness trail is a nice addition to a health/fitness facility, provided there is enough land available. Trails can be of any length, but it is preferable to make them at least 1-mile long. This allows a user to get both a cardiovascular and a conditioning workout. One recent approach that is popular is a perimeter placement on the facility property arranged in a greenbelt concept. This is an attraction to local traffic and is a good marketing tool. The major problem with this concept is pedestrian traffic across automobile ingress and egress.

Fitness trails consist of a series of exercise stations spaced along a running path. The path is usually made of bark chips or cinder, but it can also be concrete or synthetic. The stations vary in number based on the length of the trail. Longer trails can have 16 to 21 stations, whereas shorter ones may be designed with only 4 to 8 stations. In fact, workout clusters have been designed to accommodate shorter trails. The workout cluster is a group of similar exercise stations placed in one area so the user can do all those exercises at one time before proceeding to the next cluster.

Many companies produce fitness trails, and many vendors are available to select a suitable system. Durability and maintenance considerations, as well as the exercise station configuration, should be given serious consideration.

Amenity Areas

The amenity area has recently experienced resurgence of popularity in many health/fitness facilities. Combining a sauna, steam room, or whirlpool with a daily workout provides the physical conditioning, relaxation, and social exchange that are all positive qualities of a successful fitness setting. Owners should realize that these areas provide the reward following the exercise bout, and members actually look forward to their use.

Despite the enhancement of participation and the relaxation aspects, the spa area can turn into an owner's nightmare if not properly designed and constructed. The following information provides insights into the best methods of constructing these areas.

Saunas

Saunas can be either built from preassembled units or constructed by a carpenter. The walls, ceilings, and floors are made of soft wood. Generally, redwood is preferred, but cedar, spruce, kiln-dried pine, and clear pine have been used as well. Thicker walls provide better heat retention; a 1 1/2-inch thickness is considered sufficient. All benches should be screwed from underneath rather than nailed or stapled from the top, because nails and staples transmit heat and work loose due to expansion and contraction of the wood.

Ventilation is also important. Openings, either under or near the heater and between the upper and lower benches, have been used with good success. A complete air exchange should be made six to seven times an hour.

To help monitor sauna use, install a glass window on the door so that a fitness director can easily supervise the area. Make sure to include sufficient lighting; most sauna packages provide just one light, but two lights are recommended for adequate visual supervision.

Heater units are designed to fit in the sauna room. Regulated temperature controls should be placed in a lockbox for liability purposes. The recommended temperature setting is approximately 175 degrees Fahrenheit. An accurately functioning thermostat, properly positioned, is a high priority for all fitness settings. The heating element should be Underwriters Laboratories-approved and designed appropriately for the room size.

Whirlpools

Designing a whirlpool involves many of the same considerations as designing a swimming pool, only on a smaller scale. A whirlpool represents a greater investment than a sauna and has more things that can go wrong. In general, whirlpools are very labor intensive.

Whirlpools come in a wide variety of shapes, sizes, and materials. Most whirlpool shells and linings are acrylic, fiberglass, or high-impact plaster. An insulation layer is recommended around the inside shell before the lining is installed. A textured tile surface on the bottom assures walking without slipping. Additional safety features are a handrail and steps that are easily seen. A ceramic tile band around the perimeter is ideal for appearance and ease of maintenance.

The mechanical system of a whirlpool consists of a filter, motor, pump, and heater. Additional elements include an air blower, or supercharger, to increase water pressure. The heater should easily maintain a temperature of 104 degrees Fahrenheit. The mechanical room should be designed close to the whirlpool, but out of sight, and easily accessible for maintenance. Some fitness facilities have even designed a crawl space underneath the edge of the whirlpool to allow repair work around the pipes and jets.

An assortment of whirlpool jets provides varied airflow rates and nozzle adjustments. Whirlpools that are constructed by an experienced pool contractor have jets designed to hit strategic areas of the body, including knees, lower back, and shoulder regions.

The area in which the whirlpool is placed should be lined with tile on the floors, ceilings, and walls. In some cases, mirrors are attached to the walls to make the room appear larger. Proper ventilation should also be included, because the humid atmosphere is a constant problem in this area. A change of air at least eight to ten times an hour is recommended. A mechanical engineer should be advised of any excessive heat and humidity in the whirlpool room and be instructed not to underdesign the heating, ventilation, and air-conditioning system.

Steam Rooms

Steam rooms provide the greatest facility concern for owners and managers of health/ fitness facilities. Wherever there is water, there are problems! A steam room consists of a closed, tightly sealed, tile area that is fed hot steam from a generator located in an adjoining room. The generator is thermostatically controlled and maintains an environment of approximately 120 degrees Fahrenheit and 98% humidity (Lauffer, 1986).

The most important part of a properly designed steam room is the interior and exterior applications on the walls, ceilings, floors, and benches. The building materials used and the process of applying these materials are the keys to a maintenance-free steam room. It is best to hire an experienced contractor who has previously constructed wet areas to construct your steam room.

The floor of a steam room should be covered with a liquid rubber material that is applied over the concrete slab. A layer of fiberglass fabric is laid over the rubber material, followed by another coat of liquid rubber. The floor should be sloped toward a drain. This system protects against water leaks and expands with floor movement.

The walls and ceilings should be covered with a cement building board and taped with a fiberglass tape. This wall surface should be placed on Wolmanized lumber or galvanized metal studs. Remember to slope the ceiling so moisture runs off rather than drips on those using the room. This system is very durable and resists rot and mildew.

A floor pan should be placed between the exterior and the interior walls. This system catches any moisture running down the walls. The recommended material has changed from the standard lead pan to a synthetic monolithic membrane.

The tile you select must be attractive and durable. A textured nonslip tile should be used on floors, whereas a glazed ceramic tile can be used for the ceilings, walls, and benches. The tile is set with a latex mortar for additional protection from water seepage. Finally, a strong epoxy group is applied over the tile (Rubenstein & Reed, 1985).

The door frame should be constructed of an anodized aluminum. The remaining part of the door should be glass for observation purposes. The door enclosure should be strong enough to keep a tight fit, even with heavy usage. If a steam room is constructed with these methods in mind, water problems should be minimized.

Massage Room

The massage room should be a minimum of 8 feet by 10 feet, with carpeted or tiled floors; an acoustical ceiling; cabinets for storage of lotions, linens, and towels; a sink; a mirror;

a rheostat-controlled lighting system; and a standard massage table. A massage is considered a dry service, as opposed to a wet one. Therefore, the massage room should be located either within the locker room or directly adjacent to it. Clients should not have to go from a locker room through a shower room or whirlpool (wet areas) to get to the massage room. This is consistent with the earlier design requirement of keeping all wet and dry areas separate.

Facial Room

The design specifications of a facial room are identical to those of a massage room. The only difference is in the equipment. A facial room requires either a facial chair or a lounge, and some facilities opt for expensive facial equipment. The latter is not always necessary, although it lends a nice touch to the area. Facial rooms do require storage space so that cosmetics are readily available to the operator and a sink so both the operator and the client can wash up after the facial.

Herbal Wrap Room

An herbal wrap is a relaxation service where the guest lies on a bed and is wrapped in steamed, scented sheets for 10 to 15 minutes. The room is dark and quiet, thereby promoting greater relaxation. The design specifications of the room are based on the number of beds (i.e., massage tables) to be placed in it. For example, an 8-foot by 10-foot room allows enough space for one bed and the steam pot to heat the sheets. An 8-foot by 15-foot room allows you to put three beds in comfortably and to squeeze in a fourth if necessary. Whatever size room you decide on, the floor should be nonskid tile, the ceiling must be acoustical and moisture resistant, the walls can be tiled or covered with moisture resis-

tant wallpaper, and the lighting system should be on a dimmer control. Herbal wraps are considered a wet area service, and the room should be placed in an area of the facility with other wet services.

Loofa Bath Room

A loofa bath is a wet area service that involves scrubbing and massaging a guest with soapy, warm water and loofa sponges or mitts. The room should be no less than 8 feet by 10 feet; the floor and walls must be covered with nonskid tile; and there should be a hose bib, a floor drain, and a grease trap in the room. The lighting can be either incandescent or fluorescent. There should also be a door to ensure privacy.

The most important design specification for this room is the loofa bed. It can simply be a massage table covered with vinyl that has a moisture-proof backing. Otherwise it must be constructed of cement and covered with either tile or marble, and possibly a pad for comfort. The constructed bed can be built to standard massage table measurements or you can use these figures as a guide: 28 to 30 inches wide and 30 to 32 inches high. This allows the operator to work on the guest without bending over too much. It is recommended that the loofa bath be given after a massage to further cleanse the oils from the body.

Swiss Shower

The Swiss shower is also called a needle shower because of the flow of the water from the shower heads. It is a standard-sized shower with 17 spray heads placed in it. The top head is a regular overhead spray. The other 16 heads are fine, needle sprays; 4 heads are placed high in each corner of the shower. The distance between the heads can vary from 12 to 15 inches. The controls can be placed either outside the shower, which would require someone to operate them for the user, or inside, which would enable the user to control the water flow. The premise is to adjust the water continuously from warm to cool to hot to cold to provide an invigorating feeling along with a water-massage effect.

Cosmetic/Beauty Salon

There is another new trend in the design of health/fitness facilities. This trend is more evident in the multipurpose health club than in the clinical, corporate, or community facility. The inclusion of cosmetic or beauty salons has become another way for clubs to attract both salon customers and new members. It seems to make good sense. Everything a person could need for their health and fitness is available at a club, so why not something to enhance their beauty? This is true for both men and women.

The typical salon services include hair care, manicures, pedicures, skin care, and specialty services geared more to women such as color and wardrobe consulting. It is a mistake to believe that salon services are designed only for women. There is a proliferation of men's beauty products on sale in every department and specialty store. Men are as concerned about their health and their outward appearance as women. Therefore, the salon should be designed to accommodate both men and women. It should also be promoted as an additional benefit of belonging to a particular club.

The importance of a salon as a member attraction feature cannot be underestimated. A recent survey by IRSA revealed that over 10% of current member clubs had plans to add a cosmetic or beauty salon to their existing facility. Some may begin by adding tanning booths or rooms, but eventually a full-service salon may become as integral a component of a multipurpose facility as the aerobics room or weight training area.

The design of a salon area varies according to how much space is available. Usually, a salon provides adequate service in 200 to 500 square feet. Some clubs have the room to build salons up to 1,000 square feet or larger, but that is not necessary. The minimum requirements for a salon include appropriate electrical power, water supply, styling station, shampoo sink, storage space, and a dryer. Although 200 square feet may seem very small, two operators at their own styling stations can work in that space very comfortably. The salon operators must also adhere to some local health department codes and department of professional regulation requirements. These vary among states, so it is wise to investigate all the requirements before putting a salon in a facility.

The larger salons can include separate areas for manicures and pedicures, makeup consultations, a reception desk and waiting area, and facial rooms and tanning booths. Again, the amount of equipment and the types of services that are offered in a cosmetic/beauty salon are often dictated by the space that is available. This is especially true if the salon is an addition to an already existing facility. Ideally, when a new facility is being planned and designed, the salon should be included in the original plans. Then, the salon space can be allocated and customized to the desired services.

SUMMARY

This chapter described the various methods of selecting an architect. The methods include (a) direct selection, (b) firm comparison, and (c) design competition. When interviewing architectural firms, you can facilitate the selection process by considering (a) whether they have built similar facilities, (b) what the quality of their past jobs has been, (c) whether there were favorable references, (d) what type of staff is available, and (e) the professional status of the firm. Perhaps the most important issue of hiring an architect is the ease of communication and mutual understanding between the owner and architect.

Architectural responsibilities were discussed as they related to initiating a health/fitness facility concept and generating this concept into actual construction drawings of the new building. The responsibilities consisted of (a) predesign planning, (b) schematic design, (c) final design, and (d) construction documents. This phase of designing a health/fitness facility is the most demanding, because all the decision making must relate to cost, space availability, and program desires.

The next consideration is the factors involved in hiring a contractor. Many of the methods used for hiring an architect are also useful when selecting a contractor. The most commonly used method is competitive bidding. Special consideration should be given to screening all contractors in advance and establishing a list of acceptable bidders. A

construction manager may also be considered for the project.

The chapter concluded with information on specific facility considerations that should be addressed with the architect and general contractor during the design and construction phase of a health/fitness facility. Each activity or service area mentioned was divided into checklist items followed by recommended guidelines. Emphasis was placed on the importance of determining the goals and objectives for every activity or service-related area.

The process of designing and constructing a health/fitness complex is complicated. It entails moving through various stages and involves many people from concept development to reality. As a result, problems should be expected to occur. However, the key to a successful result is the relationship of mutual understanding, communication, and trust built between the architect and the planning team members.

A checklist of specific considerations to cover in each facility area is provided as an appendix to the chapter. Careful attention to such details prior to and during the construction process will avoid costly oversights.

APPENDIX A

Checklist For the Facility Design Process

_____ Involve and organize all the individuals who will have a role in planning the facility. This might include consultants, financiers, and people who will be operating and using the facility.

_____ Conduct a comprehensive program analysis to determine present and future needs, then realize that the need for future facilities may fluctuate based on the expansion of existing activities or the creation of new ones, and determine how you will proceed.

_____ Conduct a feasibility study.

_____ Write a comprehensive business plan, including information concerning space needs, programming trends, existing facilities, modern facility innovation, and available equipment.

_____ Write a detailed description of the services to be provided, their associated needs, and their manner of functioning. This can be an extended portion of the program plan.

_____ Select and hire a well-qualified planning team.

_____ Write the detailed qualitative and quantitative space requirements necessary to accommodate the proposed services.

_____ Develop the financial pro formas for the facility in conjunction with the business and marketing plans.

_____ Develop a well-defined and realistic project completion schedule.

_____ Review carefully the architectural drawings and specifications at each stage.

_____ Select and hire reputable contractors for the construction of the facility.

_____ Complete the facility under the control of a well-qualified project supervisor.

_____ Hire well-qualified and competent staff.

_____ Formally accept the facility, install the fixed and movable equipment, and orient the staff.

_____ Occupy the facility and initiate the service.

APPENDIX B

Facility Design Checklists

General Features

It is assumed that the facility design process has been carried out as described and these checklists will serve to verify that appropriate procedures have been followed. These lists will also help to prevent costly design mistakes.

_____ A comprehensive master plan has been prepared on the nature and scope of the program, and the special requirements for space, equipment, fixtures, and facilities have been dictated by the activities to be conducted (form follows function).

_____ The facility has been planned to meet the total requirements of the program, both present and future, as well as the special needs of those who are to be served. Any possible future additions or expansions are included in the present plans to permit economy of construction and costs.

_____ The plans and specifications meet the codes of all governmental agencies (city, county, state) whose approval is required by law.

_____ The plans of the facility conform to accepted standards and practices.

_____ The facility site is as close to the center of the membership market as possible.

_____ The following factors have been considered for the proposed facility and site:
- feeder streets (new or existing)
- parking areas
- electrical supplies
- water supplies
- sewage lines
- gas lines
- storm drainage
- soil topography

_____ The selection of equipment and supplies has been based on a cost-per-use ratio, as well as ongoing maintenance costs.

_____ Sufficient attention has been given to fire codes, fire and security systems, and emergency escape routes.

_____ Window heights are appropriate for privacy, safety, maintenance, and the use of natural light.

_____ Floor and wall surfaces have been selected according to the following criteria: year-round usage, multiple uses, dust and moisture resistant, stainless, inflammable, nonabrasive, durability, resiliency, safety, maintenance, and cost-per-use.

Indoor Facilities
General

_____ All passageways are free of obstructions so two-way traffic can occur. Every effort has been made to eliminate hazards.

_____ Buildings, specialty areas, and facilities are clearly identified.

_____ Locker rooms are arranged for ease of supervision and utilization.

_____ Administrative offices, exercise rooms, and service facilities are properly interrelated. The same is true for medical, first-aid, and emergency rooms.

_____ Special needs of the physically handicapped are met, including a ramp into the building at a major entrance.

_____ Storage rooms are of adequate size and are accessible to appropriate areas. All dead space is used, such as areas under stairwells.

_____ Low-cost maintenance features have been considered.

_____ All areas, courts, facilities, equipment, climate control, security, and the like conform rigidly to detailed standards and specifications.

_____ Drinking fountains are conveniently placed in the locker rooms and workout areas or immediately adjacent to them.

_____ Provision is made for repair, maintenance, replacement, and storage of equipment.

_____ A well-defined program for laundering towels and uniforms is included in the plan.

_____ Antipanic hardware is used on doors as required by fire regulations.

_____ Properly placed hose bibs and drains are sufficient in size and quantity to permit flushing the entire wet area with a water hose.

_____ A water-resistant, covered base or carpet is used under the locker base and floor mat and where floor and wall join.

_____ Space relationships and equipment are planned in accordance with the type and number of users.

_____ Warning signals—both visible and audible—are included in the plans.

_____ Ramps have a slope equal to or greater than a 1-foot rise in 12 feet.

_____ Minimum landings for ramps are 5 feet by 5 feet, they extend at least 1 foot beyond the swinging arc of a door, and have at least a 6-foot clearance at the bottom.

_____ Dressing space between lockers is appropriate. Also, the design of dressing, drying, and shower areas keeps wet foot traffic to a minimum and establishes clean, dry aisles for dressing.

_____ Toilet facilities are adequate in number and are located within both wet and dry areas.

Climate Control

_____ There is climate control throughout the building (i.e., heating, ventilation, and air-conditioning, or HVAC).

_____ Special ventilation is provided for locker, dressing, shower, drying, and toilet rooms.

_____ HVAC systems are on both a zone control and an individual room control system.

_____ Temperature and humidity are specific to a particular area.

Electrical

_____ Lighting intensity meets approved standards.

_____ An adequate number of electrical outlets are appropriately placed throughout the facility. They should be 3 feet above the floor, unless otherwise specified.

_____ Service area lights are controlled by dimmer units.

_____ Locker room lights are mounted above the space between lockers and shine into the aisles.

_____ Lights are shielded when special protection is needed, such as in court areas and showers.

_____ Natural light, when used, is controlled properly to reduce glare.

Walls

_____ Electrical wall plates are located within the wall where needed and are firmly attached.

_____ Materials that clean easily and are impervious to moisture are used where moisture is prevalent.

_____ An adequate number of drinking fountains are provided and are properly recessed in the wall.

_____ One wall (at least) of the aerobics room has full-length mirrors.

_____ All corners in locker rooms and showers are rounded.

_____ Wall coverings are aesthetically pleasing and match the overall decor of the facility.

Ceilings

_____ The ceiling height is adequate for the activities to be performed in a given area.

_____ Ceiling support beams are designed and engineered to withstand stress.

_____ Acoustical materials impervious to moisture are used in moisture-prevalent areas.

_____ All ceilings except those in storage areas are acoustically treated with sound-absorbent materials.

_____ Skylights in exercise rooms are impractical and therefore are seldom used because of problems in waterproofing roofs and controlling sun rays.

_____ Ceilings and crawl spaces are easily accessible for maintenance and repair purposes.

Floors

_____ Floor plates placed where needed are flush-mounted.

_____ Lines and markings are painted on floors before sealing is completed on racquetball and squash courts.

_____ A water-resistant, rounded base where the wall and floor meet is used in locker and shower rooms.

_____ Nonskid, slip-resistant flooring is used in all wet areas (e.g., laundry, pool, shower, and drying rooms).

_____ Floor drains are adequate in number and are properly located. The floor is sloped for proper drainage.

Service Area Checklists

Locker Room

_____ The main locker room is strategically located for the practical use of all facilities, such as drying room, showers, and toilets.

_____ The locker room is of sufficient size to accommodate peak loads.

_____ There is adequate ventilation in the locker room.

_____ The floor surface is safe and easy to clean and maintain.

_____ The electrical switches and sockets are waterproofed and are installed so as to eliminate dangers from shock.

_____ The lockers are of quality design and construction, are mounted off the floor, and have been placed for traffic control and dressing comfort.

_____ A public address system is included.

_____ Adequate grooming areas have been provided.

_____ Lighting fixtures are vapor-proof and centered between aisles. When fixtures are placed over lockers, the beam should be aimed at the aisle.

_____ Windows, if used, are high enough so valuable wall space is not lost. Also, if skylights are used, they are centered between aisles.

Shower Room

_____ The shower rooms are centrally located in relation to the dressing rooms and to other areas.

_____ The shower room and drying room have sufficient capacity to handle peak loads.

_____ The hot water supply is sufficient to meet peak load requirements.

_____ The shower heads are mounted at the ideal height and angle for various users. A single control is used to regulate water temperature for each shower.

_____ The plumbing is designed for economical maintenance.

_____ Soap receptacles are provided even if a soap dispenser system is planned.

_____ The doorways in the shower room are wide enough for two-way traffic.

_____ The walls and ceilings are moisture-resistant, can be maintained easily, and have rounded corners for efficient cleaning.

_____ The floors are covered with a nonskid material and pitched away from the dressing area and toward adequate drains.

_____ An efficient ventilation system has been installed.

Storage and Issuance Rooms

_____ The storage areas conform to fire laws.

_____ The storage and issue areas are centrally located and are of sufficient number to handle peak periods effectively.

_____ The doors to storage areas are wide and do not have a riser.

_____ The storage areas have appropriate security.

_____ Storage areas have adequate ventilation.

Laundry

_____ The laundry is located directly off a corridor, close to other plumbing services, and near the locker and issuance rooms.

_____ There is adequate space to house the machines, provide for storage of the clothes and supplies, provide for the performance of routine tasks, and allow for maintenance and repair of the machines.

_____ The floor is made of nonskid material, is sloped, and has adequate drains.

_____ The room has been soundproofed, the walls and ceilings are moisture-resistant, and there is adequate ventilation.

_____ There is easy access for laundry to be transported from the building.

Activity Areas Checklist

_____ The floor area and dimensions are determined by the activities to be conducted.

_____ Adequate space or buffer zones are provided between activity areas.

_____ Wall surfaces were selected to allow their use for activities, cleaning, and maintenance.

_____ The floor surface material has been selected to allow for a maximum variety of uses.

_____ Adequate storage rooms are conveniently located near activity areas.

_____ Acoustical standards are met for all rooms.

_____ Lighting quality meets all standards.

_____ There are provisions included for an emergency safety lighting system.

_____ There is a properly installed, high-quality public address system.

_____ There are provisions for an intercom system that may be connected with the public address system.

_____ There are adequate climate control systems.

_____ Floor plates have been installed.

_____ There are provisions included for repair, maintenance, and installation of ceiling fixtures.

_____ There are provisions included for proper and necessary signs, both illuminated and nonilluminated, pertaining to areas, exits, and participants.

_____ There is a suitable lock-key system for doors, storage rooms, light controls, sound system controls, intercom controls, climate controls, and public address systems.

Provisions for the Handicapped and Disabled

_____ Necessary provisions should be present for parking, loading, and unloading areas, and ramps should be provided wherever necessary. (Elevators should also be considered.)

_____ All doorways and passageways are of sufficient width to accommodate wheelchairs. The feasibility of electrically operated doors has been considered.

_____ All thresholds are flush.

_____ All doorways or entryways to toilets, telephone areas, food and refreshment areas, locker rooms, and special rooms are sufficient to accommodate wheelchairs.

_____ Restroom facilities are provided for the handicapped.

Amenity Areas Checklist
Massage Room

_____ The room is sufficiently large so the operator can work comfortably on each side of the table.

_____ There is a sink in the room.

_____ The floor is nonslip tile, vinyl, or carpet.

_____ The table is adjustable.

_____ There are storage shelves/cabinets for linens, towels, and supplies.

_____ There is a mirror in the room (optional).

_____ Lights are controlled by a rheostat.

_____ Soft music is played (optional).

_____ The room is private.

_____ The room is soundproof (optional).

Sauna

_____ The room is either redwood or cedar.

_____ The temperature is set at approximately 108 degrees Farenheit.

_____ The door creates an adequate seal.

_____ The lighting is sufficient so the room does not appear dark.

_____ There is a wooden door handle on the inside.

_____ There is an emergency button in the room.

Steam Room

_____ The steam generator is set at a temperature of no more than 120–140 degress Farenheit.

_____ The floor and benches are nonslip tile.

_____ The ceiling is pitched for drainage down the walls.

_____ The floor is sloped for appropriate drainage.

_____ There is a cold water shower with a rope pull-chain in the room.

_____ The lighting is sufficient to see clearly through the steam.

_____ The door creates an adequate seal.

_____ There is an emergency button in the room.

Whirlpool/Plunge Pools

_____ The tub is Gunite construction covered with nonslip, decorative tile, or made from acrylic or other synthetic materials.

_____ The therapy jets are set at appropriate heights.

_____ The tubs can be drained for cleaning and then refilled.

_____ There is a handrail next to the stairs entering the tub.

_____ The floor around the tub is nonslip tile and sloped for proper drainage.

_____ There are benches for the clients to sit on.

_____ The water temperature for the whirlpool and hot plunge pool is 102–105 degrees Farenheit and room temperature for the cold plunge.

_____ There is proper drainage on the floor surrounding the pools.

Herbal Wrap

_____ The steamer is electric with an outer jacket liner and an emergency shutoff valve.

_____ There is a direct water line to the steamer, along with a direct drainage hose.

_____ The floor is nonslip tile and sloped for proper drainage.

_____ The tables/beds are spaced so the attendant can move freely between them.

_____ Lights are controlled by a rheostat.

_____ There is storage space for towels and linens.

_____ Ice for cold compresses is readily available.

_____ Soft music is played (optional).

_____ The room is either fully private or semiprivate.

Swiss Shower

_____ The water temperature is controlled by a unit next to the shower stall.

_____ There are 17 shower heads in the stall.

_____ The shower heads are 12-15 inches apart and located in the four corners.

_____ The overhead shower is a spray nozzle.

_____ The floor outside the shower is nonslip tile.

Loofa Bath

_____ The loofa bath room must be a minimum of 8 feet by 10 feet.

_____ It must contain a hose bib, water drain, and grease trap.

_____ The loofa bed should be either a regular massage table or a concrete bed covered with tile and a rubber vinyl top sheet. The table should be 28-30 inches high and 24-30 inches wide.

_____ Lighting in the room is provided by a standard ceiling fixture with a 60–100 watt bulb.

_____ The room should have a door or a draw curtain for privacy.

_____ The walls should be tiled so that the water and moisture in the room will drip to the floor.

_____ The floor should be a nonskid tile.

APPENDIX C

The facility design measurements in the following table are considered to be the industry standards. Our own personal experiences as consultants in the design of fitness facilities have shown these figures to be accurate. *Note.* Compiled from *New Concepts in Planning and Funding Athletic, Physical Education and Recreation Facilities* by R.J. Brogan, 1974, Danville, CA: APER. Copyright 1974 by APER. Adapted by permission. *Planning Facilities for Athletics, Physical Education and Recreation* by R.B. Flynn, 1985, Reston, VA: AAHPERD. Copyright 1985 by AAHPERD. Adapted by permission. ''Facility Design'' by M.P. O'Donnell and T. Wills, 1984, in M.P. O'Donnell and T. Ainsworth (Eds.), *Health in the Workplace*, New York: John Wiley & Sons. Copyright 1984 by John Wiley & Sons. Adapted by permission.

Facility Design Measurements

Square footage per member for the building (excluding tennis courts):

> 10–15 square feet — average
> 6– 8 square feet — high density (8–10 square feet preferred)
> 8–10 square feet — medium density (10–12 square feet preferred)
> 10–12 square feet — low density (12–14 square feet preferred)

Square footage per participant:

> 36–40 square feet — for aerobics
> 40–50 square feet — for floor work or weight training

Space allocations as percentage of total space:

> 40% for exercise and activity areas
> 35% for locker room and shower facilities
> 25% for administrative and service areas

Locker room space per member during peak usage

> 10–20 square feet; 8–10 feet between locker rows

Number of lockers: Peak usage number plus 10%, or one locker per 10 users.

Peak usage: 10% of total member population

Furniture and fixtures

> Tabletop — 30 inches high
> Sink — 36 inches high
> Vanity counter — 32 inches high
> Seating clearance — 60 inches minimum for smooth flow
> Desk — 34 inches for chair and 26–34 inches to pass by

PART III

Gearing Up

Part III of the book is intended to help you gear up for operating your facility and programs. The first step in gearing up is to hire a good staff. We present staff development procedures for determining job descriptions, recruiting and selecting staff, and developing a professional management team. The next step in gearing up is to develop a strategic plan of action, including planning, implementing, and evaluating programs. Next in the gearing-up phase come equipment selection and maintenance. We discuss purchasing procedures, criteria for selecting equipment, and the many important maintenance considerations. The key ideas presented will help you launch your newly developed facility into action as a viable, vital, long-term business.

CHAPTER 7

Staff Selection and Development

The design and construction of a facility, along with its programs, are important contributors to the success of the operation. However, one of the most significant factors leading to success or failure is the staff members who will operate the facility. The people who run the facility, who are responsible for its daily operation, who initiate and maintain client contact, and who implement the programs will determine the success of the operation. These people must be leaders in every sense of the word, as it is often poor leadership that causes programs to fail. It is not the programs themselves, nor is it the facility; you can have great programs and the world's most lavish facility, but if you do not have the staff to tie it all together, the entire operation will falter.

A successful operation is based on the selection of a qualified staff. Qualifications include education, experience, and certification, but the intangible skills of motivating and managing others and the ability to bring programs to life must also be considered. Although technical knowledge is vital in the health/fitness industry, it is just as important for the health/fitness professional to possess a variety of people skills, including leadership, communication, interpersonal relations, and role modeling. These people skills enable health/fitness professionals to motivate others to change and improve their lifestyles and to maintain their new programs over time.

In this chapter, we describe both the technical and the sociopsychological skills necessary for a health/fitness professional. We consider education, certification, experience, and age, along with position descriptions, selection procedures, and training processes. We also briefly discuss the skills of leadership, communication, interpersonal relations, and role modeling. Finally, we provide resource information on where to find health/fitness professionals to staff your facility.

STAFFING CONSIDERATIONS

The first step in the selection of staff members is to determine the actual position titles, their associated job descriptions, and how many people will be needed to fill each position. It is imperative to know what is required of a person to fulfill the responsibilities of a job before that person can be hired. It is also important to know how many people will be required on payroll to provide adequate coverage in all areas throughout the daily operating period of the facility. This knowledge also helps determine your budget figures, as discussed in chapter 3. Examples of several health/fitness job descriptions are provided below.

Job Descriptions

POSITION: *Executive Director-Clinical or Corporate Setting*

QUALIFICATIONS:
1. Doctoral degree (PhD or EdD) or MS in physical education, exercise physiology, or related field with evidence of publication.
2. Minimum of 2–5 years experience as director (manager, supervisor) of a spa, health club, or fitness facility.
3. Knowledge and experience in development and implementation of health promotion programs.
4. Knowledge of budget preparation, revenue projection, financial review, and personnel management.
5. American College of Sports Medicine certification as program director or health/fitness director.

RESPONSIBILITIES:
1. Report directly to vice president.
2. Develop and supervise all operations and programs, and hire and train personnel.
3. Provide staff for all health promotion, wellness, and fitness programs.
4. Develop yearly budget.
5. Conduct monthly and annual financial reviews.
6. Develop public relations, advertising, and marketing strategies.
7. Conduct ongoing training workshops for the staff.
8. Conduct departmental staff meetings.
9. Conduct employee evaluation interviews.
10. Develop departmental performance standards.

POSITION: *Fitness Supervisor*

QUALIFICATIONS:
1. Master's degree in physical education, exercise physiology, or related field.

2. Minimum 1 year supervisory experience of a fitness staff in community, commercial, corporate, or clinical health/fitness facility.

3. Knowledge of administrative procedures and personnel management.

4. Background in health promotion, specifically stress management, nutritional awareness, and lifetime fitness.

5. American College of Sports Medicine certification: Health/Fitness Instructor or Exercise Specialist.

RESPONSIBILITIES:
1. Report to executive director.
2. Supervise operations of fitness center.
3. Supervise all department heads.
4. Develop fitness evaluation tests and protocols.
5. Develop exercise prescriptions and programs.
6. Develop counseling procedures.
7. Hire and train fitness staff.
8. Conduct departmental meetings.
9. Conduct employee evaluation interviews.
10. Conduct ongoing training workshops for staff.

POSITION: *Exercise Physiologist/Fitness Instructor*

QUALIFICATIONS:
1. Bachelor's degree in physical education, exercise physiology, or related field. Master's degree preferred.
2. Minimum 1 year experience as an instructor in a community, corporate, commercial, or clinical health/fitness facility.
3. American College of Sports Medicine certification: Health/Fitness Instructor.

RESPONSIBILITIES:
1. Report directly to fitness supervisor.
2. Conduct client interviews.
3. Perform fitness tests.
4. Develop exercise prescriptions and programs.
5. Teach exercise classes.

POSITION: *Registered Dietitian*

QUALIFICATIONS:
1. Bachelor's degree in nutrition, public health, or related field. Master's degree preferred. Registered Dietician certification a must.
2. Minimum 2 years experience in nutritional counseling, dietary management, and meal planning.
3. Previous experience in health/fitness facility desirable.
4. Knowledge of food preparation and kitchen function helpful.
5. Registered with American Dietetic Association.

(Cont.)

Job Descriptions (Continued)

RESPONSIBILITIES:
1. Report to executive director.
2. Design calorie-controlled menu plans and recipes.
3. Provide individual and group counseling for clients.
4. Develop seminars in basic nutrition, the role of vitamins and minerals, and weight control.
5. Prepare nutrition information kit for clients.
6. Update and revise personal plans on either a quarterly, semiannual, or annual basis.
7. Develop an at-home food management program for each client who requests one.
8. Implement individualized weight control techniques for a proper weight loss program.

POSITION: *Sales Director*

QUALIFICATIONS:
1. Minimum 1-3 years sales experience, preferably in a health club.
2. Previous health club operations experience helpful.
3. Good communication skills.
4. Ability to work variable hours.

RESPONSIBILITIES:
1. Supervise membership sales staff.
2. Conduct personal sales of memberships.
3. Prepare weekly, monthly, and annual sales projections and reports.
4. Assist operations manager with running the facility.

POSITION: *Operations Manager*

QUALIFICATIONS:
1. Minimum 2-3 years health club experience.
2. One year supervisory experience.
3. Knowledge of facility operations, including front desk, programming, scheduling, and membership sales.
4. Bachelor's degree in physical education or business helpful.
5. International Racquet Sport Association management training.

RESPONSIBILITIES:
1. Supervise all facility operations staff.
2. Schedule work hours, programs, and special events.
3. Provide member services.
4. Prepare monthly financial reports.

POSITION: *Secretary*

QUALIFICATIONS:
1. Minimum 2 years experience, preferably with a fitness facility.
2. Ability to type 60 words per minute.

3. Bookkeeping knowledge helpful.

4. Supervisory experience desirable, but not necessary.

RESPONSIBILITIES:

1. Report to executive director.

2. Type all correspondence.

3. File all materials.

4. Answer telephone.

5. Schedule appointments.

6. Take dictation.

7. Maintain accurate bookkeeping records.

8. Train and supervise reception desk personnel.

9. Conduct weekly staff meetings.

10. Maintain positive guest relations with clientele.

Once you determine the job requirements, you can begin to look for the appropriate personnel. Health/fitness professionals tend to have expertise in either health promotion or fitness leadership areas. Health promotion specialists demonstrate competencies in needs assessment, program planning, implementation, and evaluation in areas such as risk factor identification, stress management, nutrition and weight control, substance abuse, exercise programming, and smoking cessation. Fitness leadership specialists show proficiency in exercise testing and prescription, fitness training, and exercise class leadership. It is also not uncommon for specialists in either area to possess skills that overlap. Additionally, there are both education and certification programs that lead to skill development in these areas, and it is recommended that health/fitness professionals have a degree in the field, be certified, or both. It would also be ideal to have a staff person with business training who could serve as the facility manager or director.

STAFF QUALIFICATIONS

The health/fitness professional should have a minimum of a bachelor's degree; and when necessary, a master's or a doctoral degree may be preferred or even required. The educational background of a potential staff member is very important because the health/fitness field is now expanding very rapidly. It is vital that any applicant being considered for a position have training in as many of the following course areas as possible (Breuleux, 1982; Gerson, 1986).

- Accounting
- Adult fitness
- Athletic facilities and management
- Athletic training
- CPR/first aid
- Behavior modification
- Exercise leadership
- Exercise physiology
- Financial management
- Health behaviors/psychology
- Health tests and measurements
- Health promotion and wellness
- Human anatomy and physiology
- Human motivation
- Basic nutrition
- Stress management
- Human movement theory
- Fitness internship
- Kinesiology
- Marketing management

- Organization and administration of physical education
- Personnel management/organizational behavior
- Public relations
- Sport psychology
- Exercise testing and prescription

Certified Fitness Instructors

Many organizations, such as the Aerobics and Fitness Association of America (AFAA), American College of Sports Medicine (ACSM), International Dance Exercise Association (IDEA), and YMCA, offer primary and secondary certifications in the health/fitness field. In fact, over 50 other organizations claim to offer some type of certification, and this is a major reason why certification has become such a hotly debated topic.

Certification implies that an individual possesses a basic body of knowledge and skills in a particular health/fitness area. The issue is whether or not the certification process has become diluted due to the number of providers, the cost of obtaining certification, the ease with which some certifications can be obtained, and the question of which certification is best to have. We would like to focus on the four organizations mentioned above, as their certification programs are widely accepted and respected throughout the profession.

AFAA Certification

This is a primary, grass roots program for aerobic exercise instructors. The program involves an intensive weekend of training in such areas as anatomy, exercise physiology, body composition, cardiovascular aspects of exercise, injury prevention, safe and effective teaching techniques, and basic nutrition.

There are also practical workshops where participants demonstrate their teaching styles and their exercise routines. Participants must pass a standardized written examination and a practical test involving the proper demonstration of exercises. Finally, everyone must hold a current CPR card to complete the certification process.

IDEA Certification

This process is formulated on similar grounds as AFAA, but there is a major distinction. AFAA provides training whereas IDEA does not. IDEA sees itself as an educational organization trying to unify the aerobics industry. IDEA provides a written, standardized test that covers the areas mentioned in the preceding paragraph. However, no practical test is given with the certification. It wants other organizations and facilities to train the instructors and then use its test to demonstrate a knowledge base. Despite the differences between the certification processes of these two organizations, both are acceptable by aerobics instructors, other fitness professionals, employers of instructors, and end users (participants). However, it should be remembered that the aerobics industry is still young, still looking for respect as a separate profession, and trying to stand alone as a distinct aspect of the overall health/fitness profession. The key to developing a recognized and accepted aerobics certification will be largely based on which organization can actually unify a divided industry.

YMCA Certification

A third organization offering certification is the YMCA. It offers competency tests for fitness instructors, back care specialists, and YMCArdiac Therapy. These programs are time-tested and well respected. However, they are only offered to employees of the YMCA. As such, outside individuals in the health/fitness profession cannot participate in this certification process.

ACSM Certification

Of all the certification programs provided, we strongly recommend that you consider those applicants with an ACSM certification. This certification has become the gold standard, the one by which all other certification programs are evaluated.

ACSM divides its certifications into two tracts; preventive and rehabilitative and simply preventive (ACSM, 1986). The preventive and rehabilitative tract includes the exercise test technologist, exercise specialist, and program director. The preventive tract includes the fitness leader, health/fitness instructor, and health/fitness director. A brief description of the preventive and rehabilitative tract follows.

Exercise Test Technologist. Administers exercise tests safely and demonstrates knowledge in functional anatomy, exercise physiology, pathophysiology, electrocardiography, and psychology in order to perform tasks such as preparing the exercise test station for the administration of exercise tests, preliminary screening of participants before the test, test administration and data recording, administration of emergency procedures when necessary, and summarizing test data and reporting the results to appropriate professionals.

Exercise Specialist. Possesses all the skills of the exercise test technologist and health/fitness instructor plus the ability to lead exercise for persons with medical limitations as well as asymptomatic populations. The specialist must also be able to design an exercise prescription based on the results of an exercise test, evaluate participants' responses to exercise and conditioning, educate patients, and interact effectively with appropriate professionals.

Program Director. Possesses the knowledge and skills of *all* other certifications plus demonstrates the knowledge and skills associated with administering preventive and rehabilitative exercise programs, educating the program staff and community, and designing and conducting research. The program director must also possess management skills along with the capabilities to organize and administer all types of programs in any situation.

Descriptions of the preventive tract would include the following:

Fitness Leader. Demonstrates a basic knowledge of exercise physiology, exercise programming, emergency procedures, health appraisal and evaluation techniques, exercise leadership, psychology, aging, risk factor identification, anatomy, and kinesiology. Additionally, this person specializes in an area such as dance exercise.

Health/Fitness Instructor. Possesses all the knowledge and skills of the fitness leader and serves as a supervisor, exercise leader, health counselor to participants, and exercise programmer. The minimum educational prerequisite is a bachelor's degree in an allied health field or the equivalent.

Health/Fitness Director. Possesses all the knowledge, skills, and capabilities of the previous two certifications plus the ability to administer and supervise preventive programs, and the leadership ability to train and supervise personnel. The minimum education prerequisite is a graduate degree in an allied health field and an internship or period of practical experience of at least 1 year.

The applicant who possesses a college or graduate degree in the field along with one of these certifications has had the training and experience necessary to become a qualified health/fitness professional. Now that you know what you are looking for in terms of job descriptions, education, and certification, you can begin the staff selection process.

STAFF SELECTION PROCESS

The actual staff selection process has been described by Vander Zwaag (1984) as a four-step approach. First, the position must be advertised. This is usually done in professional trade journals or in career placement newsletters, such as AFB's *Career Educational Placement Institute* (CEPI), ACSM's *Career Services Bulletin*, or AAHPERD's *Job Exchange*. These three are the primary sources job applicants review to learn of position openings in the health/fitness field. It is a wise move for any employer to consider advertising in one or more of these publications. Because a facility is also interested in hiring operations and sales personnel, the club manager should consider advertising in several trade journals. Some of these include *IRSA's Club Business*, *Club Industry*, and *Fitness Management*. There are obviously many other places in which advertisements can be placed, but these magazines appear to be the most widely read by the general fitness and health club industry.

The position advertisement usually describes the job by title and responsibilities, mentions academic and experiential requirements, may provide a salary range, and certainly identifies to whom applicants should send their letters of inquiry and résumés. An example of a job advertisement is as follows:

XYZ Corporation has an opening in its fitness department for an exercise physiologist. Responsibilities include exercise testing and programming, health promo-

tion instruction, and exercise leadership. Master's degree in exercise physiology required, ACSM certification preferred. Minimum 1 year experience in corporate fitness setting. Salary range $20,000-25,000. Send résumé and three letters of recommendation to Fitness Director, XYZ Corporation, Anytown, U.S.A.

Once the position has been advertised, résumés and letters of application will start arriving. The second step in staff selection is to process all these résumés and letters. This can be done by the individual to whom the candidate will report or a search/selection committee. The processing involves comparing the résumés with the job description, by using either a linear rating system (e.g., 1-10 for certain characteristics) or some type of matrix system that cross-checks qualifications against job requirements. Any number of methods can be used as long as they achieve the desired goal: reducing the résumé list to the three or five best candidates.

The third step in staff selection is to verify references and previous employment. Again, this responsibility can be handled by the department head, the selection committee, or, if the company is large enough, the personnel department. This step is vitally important and should not be glossed over. Accurate checking of references and unreferenced work on the candidate's résumé can provide insights about the candidate that are not readily apparent from the résumé. These insights can turn out to be negative, which would be a disappointment because the candidate was selected in the top group as a potential employee. However, most reference checks result in positive recommendations for the candidate. This leads to the fourth step in the process: the interview.

The formal interview is scheduled at a time that is mutually convenient for the candidate and the employer. Usually, the candidate arranges personal schedules to meet the employer's time frame, but both parties should remain flexible. Once the interview is scheduled, company policy determines if the candidate is to be reimbursed for travel expenses to the site. This assumes, of course, that the candidate must travel from out of town. There is also the question of lodging and meals. Some other expense items that must also be considered are reimbursements for second and third interviews, if required, and relocation expenses. It is wise for a company to have clear guidelines concerning these policies prior to interviewing for a position. Unclear policies can create unnecessary obstacles between a potential employee and the employer. Therefore, make all your interviewees aware of the company's policy on expense reimbursement.

The candidate should always be interviewed by the person to whom he or she will report and by the personnel department, if one exists. However, we recommend that several people from other departments with which the interviewee would have contact, along with at least one person from senior management, also interview the candidate. Interviewers may wish to use some of the questions that follow in "Structured Interview Questions." Each interviewer can provide a different perspective on the candidate. All of these suggestions can then be taken into account when the hiring decision has to be made. One way to coordinate different interview perspectives is to have each interviewer complete a rating sheet, such as the "Employee Interview Checklist" on page 182, on every candidate. Then, the ratings can be correlated before the hiring decision is made.

STRUCTURED INTERVIEW QUESTIONS

1. How did you originally get your job with the your present company?
2. How long have you been employed by them?
3. Briefly describe your present job responsibilities.
4. What are some of the most enjoyable aspects of your job?
5. What are some of the things you enjoy the least?
6. In what way has your job changed since you began?
7. Why do you want to leave your present position?
8. How would your colleagues and your supervisor describe you?
9. Was there anything you did not like about your employer?
10. How long have you known you were going to leave your present position?
11. What would be some personal advantages to you if you joined our company?
12. What would be some advantages we would receive by hiring you?
13. How does the position you are applying for fit in with your personal and professional goals?
14. What can you do for us that someone else could not do?
15. What are the three best reasons for us to hire you?

Note. Questions have been adapted from a variety of sources, including the work of the Robert Half Agency and of Human Kinetics Publishers, Inc.

Employee Interview Checklist

Applicant name: _____ Date: _____

Position applied for: _____

Salary range: _____ Salary requested: _____

Category	Rating (1–5)
Education (degree: _____)	_____
Certification (type: _____)	_____
Experience (years: _____)	_____
Appearance	_____
Alertness	_____
Knowledge	_____
Enthusiasm	_____
Communication skills	_____
References	_____

Comments: _____

_____

_____

_____

Rating:	1	2	3	4	5
	poor	fair	good	very good	excellent

Candidate is qualified to fill the position. Yes ( ) No ( )

The decision to hire a candidate is made by the department head, the personnel office, the selection committee, or any combination of these. It is strongly suggested that the department head (fitness director) have the greatest input into the hiring decision as he or she will be working with the candidate on a daily basis. The primary candidate is then contacted with the position offer. If the candidate accepts, then the other candidates must be contacted, told that the position has been filled, thanked for their interest, and informed that their information will be kept on file for future consideration. The people who were not selected may be contacted by letter, telephone, or both. However, the possibility always exists that the primary candidate will refuse the offer. If this occurs, you may offer the position to the second or third choice candidate, and so on down the line if everyone refuses the offer. If you are unhappy with the second and third choices, it is wise to open the position again and repeat the entire staff selection process.

This staff selection procedure is effective for any position in a health/fitness facility. However, upper level personnel, such as supervisors, managers, program directors, or department heads, are more often found through external formal procedures. These include recruitment agencies (headhunters), executive placement services, national professional associations, or other health/fitness consultants. It may be extremely helpful, especially if your primary candidate(s) have refused your offer, to contact schools and community agencies about your job opening. They can often recommend candidates for various position levels. In any case, try not to omit a resource for job prospects, as we have found that you may be pleasantly surprised.

It is sometimes necessary to speed up the selection process due to time demands for filling a position. Regardless of the time frame, employers should look for the following characteristics in their health/fitness personnel (Institute for Aerobics Research, 1981):

1. Good role model. The applicant displays a positive image of good health and fitness—a nonsmoker, with below average body fat, moderate eating habits, and a high level of physical activity.
2. Physically fit. The applicant scores better than average on all fitness tests.
3. Positive attitude. The applicant is creative, enthusiastic, adaptable, and highly

motivated in the delivery of programs, plus has the ability to motivate others.
4. Dependable and trustworthy. The applicant shows a history of job loyalty and commitment and is able to maintain client confidentiality.
5. Desires professional growth. The applicant is active in professional organizations, shows interest in publishing and performing research, and has well-defined career goals.
6. Exercise leadership. The applicant can supervise and teach a variety of exercise programs, including aerobics, weight training, water classes, and flexibility.

There are other qualities to look for beyond these six. Patton et al. (1986) have suggested that the health/fitness professional should be both inspired and inspiring, be concerned about matters vital to human health, have a good sense of humor, possess good communication skills, and show a desire to develop the management skills necessary to administer a program. Finally, work experience should be a determining factor in the selection process, as this can reduce staff training time.

Several additional factors influence the hiring process. Employers may require a prospective candidate to perform an audition, demonstrating skills directly related to the job, such as leading an exercise class, simulating procedures for graded exercise tests, or conducting a mock client interview. The audition allows the employer to view the candidate under hypothetical work conditions.

Some companies require an individual to pass a preemployment physical. The physical is only a basic screening device, but it can identify various degrees of health status. Hospitals and large corporations, more so than traditional fitness centers and community centers, often require this preemployment physical. Some agencies require mental test batteries and drug screening as well.

The final hiring of health/fitness personnel must be done in accordance with affirmative action and equal opportunity laws. No candidate may be discriminated against because of race, creed, color, nationality, age, or gender. Some companies even have a minority hiring quota. Be aware of the personnel and labor laws that are applicable to your facility when hiring health/fitness personnel. You must also be aware of your company's own personnel policies and procedures.

Finally, you must be prepared for a variety of common questions that usually arise, either during the actual interview or after the job offer has been extended to the candidate. These include starting salary, performance review (time and procedure), salary increments, vacation time accrual, sick days, personal days, secondary employment, job security, and contractual arrangements. The last point, the use of contracts or letters of agreement, is a difficult one to assess. Contracts have their positive aspects, in that everything from job responsibilities to terms of employment is spelled out so that no one can make a mistake in interpreting performance, roles, and responsibilities. However, contracts also have a negative side in that when they end, they end. Contracts are not always renewed. They also can create negative or harsh feelings between the employer and the new employee, especially if the new person demands a contract when the company policy is against contracts.

Once the health/fitness staff members have been hired, it is time to begin their training program. Staff development is crucial to the success of any operation. The staff must be trained in all company procedures as well as in running the fitness department. If the newly hired staff members are operations or sales people, then their training must focus on running the facility and selling memberships. The initial staff training as well as the on-going personnel development will determine the level of success of your program.

STAFF DEVELOPMENT

Staff development can be divided into three major areas: training, supervision, and growth. Most organizations emphasize one of these areas, but it is vital to the success of an organization that the three be integrated into a total development package (Nash, 1985). After all, it is highly ineffectual and inefficient to spend time training new employees and then allow them to perform their new jobs totally without supervision. All people need some form of guidance and feedback (see section on "Supervision") to inform them of their performance and to give them the opportunity to grow. Without these, most people will falter in their jobs within a short period of time, causing the individual staff member, the clients, and the entire facility to suffer. Therefore, it is imperative to the health and success of the individual and the organization that staff development always include training, supervision, and the potential for growth (Blanchard & Tager, 1985).

Training

Training procedures are needed in every health/fitness facility for each new staff member, regardless of his or her background and experience. New people must be introduced to the organizational philosophy, departmental objectives and goals, current operating procedures and requirements, existing staff, club members, and the new staff members' *exact* job responsibilities. Additionally, the training process must include a review of the staff member's job description and the standards of performance that are used for evaluation purposes. Finally, the new staff member must actually practice the job skills and receive ongoing feedback, orientation up-dates, and continuing education. The following orientation checklist and listing of job standards of performance are effective forms to use in this process.

Checklist for Inducting a New Employee

Name _____   Department _____

Job title _____   Hire date _____

Supervisor: Indicate information discussed with new employee.

Employee records	**Date**	**By whom (initial)**
Application and personal history		
Tax withholding W-4		
Insurance card		
Employment information		
Duties		
Working hours		
Rate of pay		
Probationary period		
Employee benefits		
Group insurance		
Holiday pay		
Pension		
Vacation policy		
Leave of absence		
Credit union		

(Cont.)

Checklist for Inducting a New Employee (Continued)

Miscellaneous information

Parking		
Bulletin boards		
Safety program		
Where to put personal effects		
Fellow employees (introduction)		
Exact working hours		
Lunch and rest periods		
Smoking rules		
About leaving the job		
When and where to report accidents		
Reporting lateness or absence		
Reporting address change		
Use of telephone		
Organizational chart		
Policy regarding pay raises		
Housekeeping		
Care and use of equipment and supplies		

SUPERVISOR: Return this page to personnel immediately after completing.

Hospital XYZ
Job Responsibilities/Standards of Performance

Job Classification _____ *Exercise Physiologist* _____ Dept. _____ *Wellness*

Supervisor Title _____ *Wellness Coordinator* _____ Effective Date _____ *4/1/86*

Job Summary *The Exercise Physiologist will function under the direction of the Wellness Coordinator with regards to all phases of wellness and health promotion. Exercise Physiologist will participate in client education and testing and under the direction of the Coordinator will instruct and guide the client in prescribed exercise activities. Will also participate in activities of all wellness programs.*

Exercise Physiologists' Responsibilities/Standards (Continued)

Weight Assigned	Job responsibility	Standards of performance	Total points
20	1. Performs fitness assessments, interprets results from metabolic cart tests, conducts lifestyle counseling sessions, and writes exercise prescriptions for clients.	1a. Conducts fitness assessments and graded exercise stress tests on clients.	1 2 3
		b. Writes exercise prescription according to American College of Sports Medicine Guidelines.	1 2 3
		c. Designs individualized programs for each client based on test results.	1 2 3
		d. Conducts preexercise and ongoing client interviews.	1 2 3
		e. Modifies client programs according to their preferences and/or physician recommendations.	1 2 3
			15
15	2. Participates in activities of health promotion programs.	2a. Conducts health promotion classes on assigned topics.	1 2 3
		b. Assists staff members in their corporate presentations and programs.	1 2 3
		c. Assists in the implementation of other programs.	1 2 3
		d. Performs screenings and assessments for program participants.	1 2 3
			12
10	3. Provides and reinforces patient/family/client teaching and counsels them in all aspects of wellness according to established standards.	3a. Conducts initial wellness assessments on all clients.	1 2 3
		b. Reviews lifestyle assessment questionnaires and health risk appraisals with clients.	1 2 3
		c. Develops behavioral change programs for clients to improve their health.	1 2 3
		d. Motivates clients, through teaching and role modeling, to maintain healthy lifestyle practices.	1 2 3
			12

Note. The remainder of weighted factors not shown could be developed in a similar format.

Orientation procedures usually include familiarization with the company, the facility itself, its hours and procedures of operation, equipment, programs, and other personnel. Orientation also includes learning company policies, available fringe benefits, accepted behaviors and dress codes, the job responsibilities of others, chain of command, and accepted reporting procedures. Some companies provide more information during their orientation process whereas others provide less. The main purpose is for the new employee to learn how the company and the facility operate and exactly what is expected in his or her new job position. Usually, the orientation process is considered part of the probationary period, which lasts anywhere from 30 to 180 days. You should expect new staff members to make mistakes during the training period and to learn from those mistakes.

Communication lines must be open during training so that new employees can always learn from those who are more experienced. Communication channels can be either formal or informal, such as scheduled staff meetings or ongoing open discussions whenever necessary. Whatever the method of communication, the lines must be available to the new staff member at all times. Nothing turns a person off more than to need help, seek it, and not be able to receive it because no one is listening, knows the answer, or is willing to spend time with the new employee. Remember, the people make the programs succeed and bring life to the facility. Treat those people with respect, communicate with them, give them as much responsibility as they can handle at the current time, and watch them perform an extraordinary job (Peters & Austin, 1985; Peters & Waterman, 1982).

In summary, make the training program comprehensive but break it down into small pieces (*Athletic Business*, 1987). Give the new employees a chance to experience some early successes on the job. Teach them about things they know first, such as exercise testing for the fitness staff or front desk operations for the facility staff. Your new staff members will feel comfortable with this as a first venture, and then the other aspects of the training program will not seem so difficult to learn. Also, keep communication lines open, talk to the people, and, more importantly, listen to what they have to say. It makes the job of supervising much easier.

Supervision

Supervision is the next important area of staff development. Basically, supervision involves guiding and helping people to achieve a goal. It does not mean doing a job for them, nor does it involve leaving employees to flounder on their own. A good supervisor or manager is a support figure whom employees know they can come to for help. Additionally, the supervisor who provides guidance to employees, rather than constantly telling them how to do their jobs, earns their respect and maintains it to a much greater extent than the person who is always giving orders.

A supervisor performs a variety of other roles besides training and guidance. These include, but are not limited to, recruiting, hiring, and terminating staff; setting objectives and goals to develop their potentials; scheduling job assignments; delegating tasks; coordinating responsibilities; motivating staff members; and evaluating job performance. Appendices A and B of this chapter provide a series of checklists and forms that can be adapted for use in evaluating and terminating employees.

Being a supervisor is not an easy task, but it certainly can be a very rewarding one. There is no one best technique for managing people. Recommendations abound, including 1-minute management (Blanchard & Johnson, 1982), management by walking around (Peters & Austin, 1985; Peters & Waterman, 1982), humanistic management (Herzberg, 1966; Maslow, 1965; McGregor, 1967), and standard management practices such as management by objectives (Drucker, 1980). All these recommendations have their merits, but none of them will always work for every supervisor in every situation. It is probably best to have an understanding of management theory and techniques, and then select those that you believe fit your personality and behavior patterns. Better yet, if you do not want to learn all of these theories and techniques, you may want to manage simply by what feels good. Treat people in ways that make you feel good and that would make you feel good if you were in their positions. This helps staff members to achieve their individual goals as well as those of the organization.

There are two supervisory techniques that we strongly recommend because we know they work and because research supports their successful usage: motivation (Nash, 1985; Tarkenton, 1986; Zigler, 1986) and goal setting (Locke & Latham, 1984). Because volumes have been written on motivation and goal setting, and because an in-depth discussion of each is beyond the scope of this chapter, we will provide the following suggestions for management through goal setting. Briefly, the supervisor should be certain the staff understands what needs to be accomplished (individually, as a group, and as an organization), when the tasks need to be completed, how each staff member's skills and abilities match up with portions of the whole task, what type of guidance they will receive during the performance of the task, how and when they will receive feedback, and what the reward and incentive systems are for any and all tasks. These factors must be communicated clearly to all staff members, both old and new, for goals and objectives to be accomplished. When the supervisor meets these parameters, he or she can be assured

that the staff will maintain a high level of motivation, exhibit quality job performance, and express a strong desire for growth.

Growth

Everyone who accepts a job position is interested in its growth opportunities, both personal and professional. These include room for advancement, salary increments, memberships in professional organizations, attendance at professional meetings, continuing education, and committee service. There are also other ways that people view job growth, such as interacting with other professionals and clients, having the opportunity to speak to public and professional groups, and receiving on-duty time for in-service education.

Growth comes about through learning and change. Both of these activities are facilitated by constant communication between the department supervisor, or manager, and the employee. At specified times during the course of the year, a formal performance evaluation is given to the employee. The supervisor reviews a staff member's performance, applies both a subjective and an objective rating to it, discusses the evaluation with the employee, and then decides to take one of four actions with regard to the employee's behavior:

- Make no change.
- Change the job requirements.
- Change the variables affecting the job.
- Change the employee's position (promote, demote, transfer, or discharge) (Patton et al., 1986).

Evaluation

More than anything else, a performance evaluation should be a tool for growth. Nothing should occur during the evaluation session that will be a surprise to either the employee or the supervisor. If it does, then the supervisor has not done his or her job of maintaining constant communication with the staff. Furthermore, the performance evaluation should never be at a time when the supervisor looks to get even with an employee. It is always best for both parties to enter the session with open minds and to maintain objectivity as long as possible. The areas that should be covered in a performance evaluation include the following:

- Job knowledge, training, and experience
- Willingness to accept responsibility
- Planning and organizing work
- Quality and quantity of work
- Cost consciousness and control
- Relationships with others
- Leadership qualities
- Initiative and resourcefulness
- Originality and creativity
- Soundness of judgment
- Dependability
- Personal appearance, speech, and habits
- Attendance and punctuality
- Support for organization goals and policies
- Career objectives

A sample performance evaluation is provided in Appendix A of this chapter. The evaluation session must end with the employee's coming away with new goals, objectives, and suggestions for improved job performance and professional growth.

Professional growth is very important to people in the health/fitness industry. Supervisors, managers, and department heads should encourage all of their employees to join professional organizations; attend state, regional, and national meetings; and make presentations at these meetings. These associations and meetings are also excellent opportunities for networking and trading resources.

Some organizations even have job placement centers at their conventions. Two that were mentioned previously are the ACSM and the AFB. Whatever the reasons for joining an organization or attending a meeting, the results depend upon the effort and input involved. The same is true about the job. A person can always find growth opportunities and continue to develop if a positive attitude is maintained, goals are properly set and achieved, feedback is provided, and communication channels are kept open.

SUMMARY

This chapter described the staff selection and development processes. Selection involves considering the job requirements and the candidates, interviewing, and then making the final hiring decision. Development involves training, supervision, and growth, which includes performance evaluations. Within these developmental categories lie the skills most often required of managers: leadership, communication, interpersonal relations, and role modeling. Leadership in today's health/fitness industry means coaching, influencing, and persuading people to follow you in the performance of their jobs so that they and the facility receive the maximum benefit. Communication is essential so that everyone knows what is expected of him or her and how he or she should perform to achieve personal goals. Whenever there is a breakdown in the actual operation of a facility, and this does not refer to an equipment breakdown, it is usually due to improper or incorrect communication. More often than not, employees hear what they want or expect to hear. The same holds true for managers. It is imperative that staff members be certain that the message they are sending is being received exactly as it was intended. This is the only way to guarantee that proper communication is occurring.

Interpersonal relations is a key ingredient when interacting with fellow employees and clients. Health/fitness professionals must always realize they are in a service industry, and they must be able to speak well and listen better. Additionally, staff members must always try to see the other person's side of an issue. They should create win-win situations for everyone in every area of the facility so that all benefit. This is especially true when dealing with members or clients, but it is also of the utmost importance when interacting with other staff members. The goal of the facility manager is to make every staff member a part of a team that is working toward a unified objective. The goal of every staff member is to serve as an integral part of that team, making contributions and foregoing his or her personal gain for the benefit of the team. Finally, all health/fitness professionals should be excellent role models for their colleagues and clients. People working in this industry must literally live the lifestyle to the fullest and believe in it wholeheartedly. That is the only way they can ever hope to effect positive changes in their clients. Health/fitness personnel must always be prepared to provide advice or counseling whenever it is requested by a member or client, but their own personal actions must always speak louder than their words. It is the only way they can continue to grow as individuals in their chosen profession.

We have provided you with techniques to help you make the best decision possible on whom to hire as well as how to help that person become the best employee possible. The bottom line, with employees and clients, is to treat people with respect, give them responsibility and room for growth, acknowledge their accomplishments, and provide them with opportunities to excel. This creates a happy, competent, and satisfied staff and a very successful organization.

APPENDIX A

Employee Evaluation Forms[1]

The Performance Evaluation

I. What is a performance evaluation?

    A. A discussion with a subordinate to review how he or she is doing.

    B. A time for constructive criticism—not a fault-finding session.

    C. An opportunity to set mutually agreeable goals and standards for the coming year.

    D. A chance to gain understanding with your subordinates on what you expect of them in their work performance.

II. Advantages

    A well-defined systematic evaluation program, properly administered, can do the following:

    A. Improve job performance.

    B. Serve as an aid in promotions and/or transfers.

    C. Establish the need for training in specific areas and/or functions.

    D. Improve morale; give a sense of direction to individuals.

    E. Improve relationships between management and subordinates.

    F. Identify candidates for development, promotions, and other considerations.

    G. Increase competence when people

        1. know what is expected of them.

        2. know what they expect of themselves.

        3. know their own limitations.

        4. know where to get help.

        5. feel a part of the decision-making process.

        6. view outside worth.

III. How do you give an evaluation or performance review?

    A. Schedule a meeting with the person to be evaluated so that an office or some other suitable location for privacy can be acquired.

    B. Put subordinate at ease if necessary.

    C. Explain purpose of evaluation:

        1. A review of last year's performance or performance since he or she joined the department.

            a. Where he or she has done a good job.

            b. Where he or she needs improvement.

---

[1]These forms, and others like them, are standardized and available from any office supply store.

2. A discussion of problems the subordinate may be having and an attempt to develop solutions.

3. A chance to set goals for the coming year.

IV. Evaluate the employee, applying the following principles:

A. Take your time and do a thorough job.

B. Evaluate the employee from the point of view of his or her value to the company rather than how much you like or dislike the employee.

C. Evaluate the employee on actual performance and not on what you think he or she can do.

D. Avoid overrating the subordinate you trained yourself and underrating those you did not train.

E. Rate the individual in the category best describing his or her performance. Rating too low does the employee injustice. Rating too high does an injustice to other employees who also receive that rating but are more qualified than he or she is.

F. Discuss the differences between the self-rating the employee gives and the rating you give. Where the variance is significant, a sincere effort must be made to determine the reason. Remember, however, that the review is not a negotiating session. You must evaluate the employee honestly from your view of him or her in your role as supervisor.

V. Why you are holding the evaluation. Discuss the following:

A. What is expected of the employee in the job.

B. Strong points, areas where improvement is needed, and so forth.

C. How job performance can be improved.

D. What advancement the employee is looking for.

VI. Proceed with review of performance.

A. Maintain a positive approach.

B. Temper poor performance comments or constructive criticism with accomplishments.

C. Be sure of what you are going to say—a good practice is to have your comments summarized on a separate sheet of paper.

D. The success of the review depends on how well you have prepared for the interview. It normally takes more time to prepare than it does to conduct the interview.

E. If needed, give the employee a chance to talk about a definite problem area that has been encountered. Try to develop an agreeable solution.

F. This is a counseling and performance review session, not a time for reprimand. Give the employee a chance to talk.

G. Discourage gossip. Do *not* make comparisons with other employees.

H. Do not put the person reviewed on the defensive. Be positive and constructive.

I. End on an optimistic and friendly note.

J. Summarize. Use the "Comments" section of the performance evaluation, emphasizing accomplishments and areas in need of improvement.

Remember

It should be noted that the real value and significance of the performance evaluation lies in the counseling interview or face-to-face discussion that follows. *Every* employee wants to know "How am I doing?" The performance evaluation is a device to give the supervisor and the subordinate the opportunity to sit down together to talk over the subordinate's progress and find areas for improvement.

In conducting these all-important interviews, you would do well to remember the following:

A. Where subordinates are reviewed on the result of their work, and where an attempt is made to orient the discussion to the job, the relationship between the supervisor and the subordinate is healthy.

B. Where appraisal focuses on personality traits, appraisal interviews are carried out half-heartedly in an atmosphere of mutual embarrassment, and with little wholesome effort, the relationship between the supervisor and subordinate is unhealthy.

Always keep in mind that performance appraisal never fails, but the people who use it sometimes do.

EMPLOYEE EVALUATION

DATE

NAME	TITLE

DEPARTMENT	SECTION

INSTRUCTIONS:
Listed below are rating factors to evaluate the assigned employee. Extreme care should be taken to check the box for the appropriate descriptive phrase to eliminate "Average" tendency or "Halo" effect. Each block represents a point count. Upon completion show total point count and overall performance.
The evaluation should serve as a tool to assist in developing improvement in performance through a mutual Supervisor-Employee program. In the event that the Reviewing Authority changes a rating factor he will initial his entry instead of using a check mark.
Please return this form to Employee Relations within ten working days from the above indicated date.

1. ADAPTABILITY

Unable to perform adequately in other than routine situations (1)	Performance declines under stress or in other than routine situations. (2)	Performs well under stress or in unusual situations. (3)	Performance excellent under extreme stress. Meets the challenge of difficult situations. (4)	Outstanding performance (5)
☐	☐	☐	☐	☐

2. APPEARANCE

Very untidy. Poor taste in personal grooming. (1)	Sometimes careless and untidy. (2)	Generally neat and well groomed. (3)	Good taste in dress and general appearance. (4)	Exceptional grooming and neatness. (5)
☐	☐	☐	☐	☐

3. ATTENDANCE

Often absent, frequently reports late or leaves early. (1)	Careless or lax in attendance or reporting on time. (2)	Generally present and meets work period requirements. (3)	Regular and prompt in attendance. (4)	Very regular and prompt. Volunteers for overtime as needed. (5)
☐	☐	☐	☐	☐

4. COMMUNICATION

Unable to express thoughts clearly. (1)	Expresses thoughts clearly on routine matters. (2)	Usually organizes and expresses thoughts clearly and concisely. (3)	Consistently able to express ideas clearly. (4)	Outstanding ability to communicate ideas to others. (5)
☐	☐	☐	☐	☐

5. COURTESY

Discourteous, impolite, rude. (1)	Occasionally tactless. (2)	Pleasant and amiable. (3)	Always helpful and polite. (4)	Extremely courteous and pleasant. (5)
☐	☐	☐	☐	☐

6. DRIVE

Works without purpose or goals. No sense of urgency. (1)	Goals established too low. Little effort toward accomplishment. (2)	Average objectives and usually makes effort to reach these. (3)	Strong motivation for achievement. (4)	Establishes high goals and continually strives for accomplishment. (5)
☐	☐	☐	☐	☐

7. EFFECTIVENESS IN WORKING WITH OTHERS

Does not get along with people. Hinders effectiveness. (1)	Sometimes creates friction. Has difficulty getting along with people. (2)	Has average skill at maintaining good human relations. (3)	Pleasant, promotes harmony. Excellent team worker. (4)	Outstanding ability to promote harmony. (5)
☐	☐	☐	☐	☐

8. KNOWLEDGE OF DUTIES

Requires continuous assistance and direction. (1)	Knows only routine duties. Sometimes requires prompting. (2)	Usually performs all necessary tasks. Possesses some knowledge of other related positions. (3)	Has mastered all duties with good knowledge of related positions. (4)	Has mastered all duties with extensive knowledge of related positions. (5)
☐	☐	☐	☐	☐

EMPLOYEE COUNSELING RECORD

This form should be completed *IN FULL* for all employees in violation of company policy or standards. (See Counseling Policy)	DATE:

EMPLOYEE NAME:	POSITION:	HIRE DATE:

DEPARTMENT:	SUPERVISOR:	EXTENSION:	JOB DATE:

REASON FOR COUNSELING:	COUNSELING STEP: ☐ 1 ☐ 2 ☐ 3 Probation	THE NEXT INCIDENT MAY RESULT IN TERMINATION.

• • • COUNSELING INTERVIEW • • •

Include all pertinent factors leading to employee being placed on counseling and corrective action to be taken. (For attendance, include day and occurrences.)

• • • EMPLOYEE COMMENTS • • •

This form has been completed to advise you that you are in violation of company policy or standards.
- Counseling procedures provide guidelines dealing with employee performance, attendance, conduct of similar problems.
- The use of formal counseling procedures is discretionary and there may be occasions when immediate termination of employment will be considered.
- These procedures should not be construed as a guarantee for continued employment, which remains at will, and may be terminated at any time by either party.

EMPLOYEE ACKNOWLEDGMENT:	FOLLOW-UP DATE:	MGR/SUPV SIGNATURE:	EMPL RELATIONS REVIEW:

• • • FOLLOW-UP INTERVIEWS • • •
Explain employee performance since the last counseling session. (For attendance counseling include days/occurrences)

APPROPRIATE COUNSELING STEP: (AT THIS TIME) ☐ 1 ☐ 2	EMPLOYEE ACKNOWLEDGMENT:	NEXT FOLLOW-UP DATE:
☐ Probation (THE NEXT INCIDENT MAY RESULT IN TERMINATION)	SUPERVISOR/MANAGER'S SIGNATURE:	DATE:

APPROPRIATE COUNSELING STEP: (AT THIS TIME) ☐ 1 ☐ 2	EMPLOYEE ACKNOWLEDGMENT:	NEXT FOLLOW-UP DATE:
☐ Probation (THE NEXT INCIDENT MAY RESULT IN TERMINATION)	SUPERVISOR/MANAGER'S SIGNATURE:	DATE:

APPROPRIATE COUNSELING STEP: (AT THIS TIME) ☐ 1 ☐ 2	EMPLOYEE ACKNOWLEDGMENT:	NEXT FOLLOW-UP DATE:
☐ Probation (THE NEXT INCIDENT MAY RESULT IN TERMINATION)	SUPERVISOR/MANAGER'S SIGNATURE:	DATE:

APPENDIX B

Employee Termination Forms

NOTICE OF TERMINATION OF EMPLOYMENT

INSTRUCTIONS:

TO THE EMPLOYEE: *Complete upper portion of form in your own handwriting and return promptly to to your supervisor.*

TO THE SUPERVISOR: A. *Where employee has completed his portion of form:*
(1) *Complete supervisor's statement and send immediately and directly to Personnel Adminstration Department.*
(2) *Call exit interviewer to arrange appointment for exit interview.*
B. *Where employee is not available to complete his part of the form:*
(1) *Complete first two lines of employee's statement and own portion.*
(2) *Advise exit interviewer by phone and send form immediately and directly to Personnel Administration Department.*

EMPLOYEE'S STATEMENT

NAME OF EMPLOYEE (Please print)	EMPLOYEE'S NO.	EFFECTIVE DATE OF TERMINATION (Last day of work)
☐ MR. ☐ MRS. ☐ MISS		

DEPARTMENT

EMPLOYEE'S PRESENT ADDRESS	(City)	(State)	(Zip code)

EMPLOYEE'S FORWARDING ADDRESS AFTER TERMINATION DATE IF DIFFERENT FROM PRESENT ADDRESS (Include Zip Code)

C/O	EFFECTIVE DATE OF ADDRESS CHANGE

EMPLOYEE'S STATEMENT SUPPORTING NOTICE OF TERMINATION

I AM VOLUNTARILY RESIGNING FROM MY POSITION WITH   ON THE ABOVE EFFECTIVE DATE
FOR THE FOLLOWING REASONS:

CHECK (✓) ONE

☐ I INTEND TO ACCEPT OTHER EMPLOYMENT AFTER (Date)   ☐ I DO NOT INTEND TO ACCEPT OTHER EMPLOYMENT

EMPLOYEE'S SIGNATURE	DATE

SUPERVISOR'S STATEMENT

DATE EMPLOYEE GAVE NOTICE	EMPLOYEE'S LAST DAY OF WORK	VACATION PAY DUE
		DAYS

THIS PORTION MUST BE COMPLETED. INCLUDE AVAILABLE INFORMATION AND YOUR OPINION FOR EMPLOYEE'S TERMINATION; ALSO INDICATE YOUR RESPONSE TO ADVERSE COMMENTS, IF ANY, AND DETAILS OF EMPLOYEE'S NEW JOB WHERE APPROPRIATE.

EMPLOYEE SUBMITTED HIS/HER RESIGNATION:	RE-EMPLOYMENT RECOMMENDED	
☐ AS ABOVE ☐ BY TELEPHONE ☐ BY LETTER (Letter attached)	☐ YES ☐ NO (As per reasons above)	
SIGNATURE OF SUPERVISOR	DEPARTMENT	DATE

SEND IMMEDIATELY COMPLETED FORM DIRECTLY TO PERSONNEL ADMINISTRATION DEPARTMENT.

DATE RECEIVED	DATE OF EXIT INTERVIEW	SIGNATURE OF EXIT INTERVIEW

EXIT INTERVIEW

EMPLOYEE NAME:	POSITION TITLE:	GRADE:

SEPARATION DATE:	LENGTH OF SERVICE:	DIVISION/DEPARTMENT:	IMMEDIATE SUPERVISOR:

STATEMENT	cares about your opinions. That's why we ask you to complete the questions on this form. Your answers will be used to develop recommendations for improvement to the Corporation. Please answer each question candidly.

Please give in detail your most important reason for leaving.

If a good friend of yours was looking for a job, would you recommend _____ to him/her? ☐ Yes ☐ No

Why?

Were you given a good idea of what your job would be like when you were hired at _____ ☐ Yes ☐ No

PLEASE CHECK (✔) THE BOX WHICH BEST EXPRESSES HOW YOU FEEL ABOUT:

		DESCRIPTION	DISSATISFIED		Neutral	SATISFIED	
			Very	Slightly		Very	Slightly
THE JOB	1	OPPORTUNITY TO USE YOUR ABILITIES AND SKILLS					
	2	RECOGNITION FOR THE WORK YOU DID					
	3	THE AMOUNT OF RESPONSIBILITY YOU WERE GIVEN					
	4	HOURS OF WORK PER WEEK					
	5	SCHEDULE OF HOURS					
	6	YOUR WORK LOAD					
	7	YOUR SENSE OF ACCOMPLISHMENT					
	8	OPPORTUNITY TO DO CHALLENGING AND INTERESTING WORK					
	9	YOUR PAY					
	10	YOUR PAY COMPARED WITH THE PAY FOR SIMILAR JOBS IN OTHER COMPANIES					
	11	TRAINING YOU RECEIVED WHEN YOU STARTED YOUR JOB					
	12	TRAINING YOU RECEIVED WHILE IN YOUR JOB					
YOUR SUPERVISOR AND CO-WORKERS	1	YOUR SUPERVISOR'S MANAGERIAL COMPETENCE					
	2	YOUR SUPERVISOR'S TECHNICAL COMPETENCE					
	3	YOUR SUPERVISOR'S AWARENESS AND UNDERSTANDING OF YOUR PROBLEMS					
	4	YOUR SUPERVISOR'S INTEREST IN YOUR CAREER DEVELOPMENT					
	5	YOUR SUPERVISOR'S RECEPTIVENESS TO NEW AND ORIGINAL IDEAS					
	6	YOUR SUPERVISOR'S REVIEW OF YOUR PERFORMANCE					
	7	COOPERATION OF CO-WORKERS					
	8	TECHNICAL COMPETENCE OF CO-WORKERS					

(Cont.)

Exit Interview (Continued)

		DESCRIPTION	DISSATISFIED Very	Slightly	Neutral	SATISFIED Very	Slightly
COMMUNICATION POLICIES & PRACTICES	1	FREEDOM TO EXPRESS IDEAS AND SUGGESTIONS					
	2	THE OPPORTUNITY TO TALK WITH YOUR SUPERVISOR					
	3	INFORMATION YOU RECEIVED ON COMPANY POLICIES AND PROGRAMS					
	4	INFO YOU REC'D ON DEPARTMENTAL POLICIES & ORGANIZATIONAL STRUCTURE					
	5	PROMOTION/TRANSFER POLICIES/PRACTICES (CAREER OPPORTUNITY PROGRAM)					
	6	OVERTIME POLICIES AND PRACTICES					
	7	SALARY REVIEW POLICIES AND PRACTICES					
	8	PERFORMANCE REVIEW POLICIES AND PRACTICES					
	9	WORK MEASUREMENT STANDARDS					
WORKING CONDITIONS AND BENEFITS	1	PHYSICAL WORKING CONDITIONS					
	2	JOB SECURITY					
	3	OPPORTUNITIES FOR CAREER DEVELOPMENT					
	4	OPPORTUNITIES TO PARTICIPATE IN DECISIONS					
	5	AS A PLACE TO WORK					
	6	AS A PLACE TO LIVE					
	7	OVERALL COMPANY BENEFIT PROGRAM					
	8	VACATION PLAN					
	9	YOUR OVERALL JOB					
	10	THE COMPANY AS A PLACE TO WORK					

Do you have any comments not mentioned that you would like to make? If so, please indicate below:

NOTE   verifies   job title and dates of employment only. Nothing of a personal nature, including answers to these questions, will be communicated to your future employer.

EMPLOYEE SIGNATURE:

DATE:

---------------------------------- (DO NOT WRITE BELOW THIS LINE) ----------------------------------

INTERVIEWER'S CHECKLIST

- Benefit Conversion Review   ☐ Medical   ☐ Long Term Disability   ☐ ISP
  ☐ Life Plans   ☐ Dental   ☐ Savings Bonds
- Credit Union Loans/Savings   Current   ☐ Yes   ☐ No
- Company Property Returned   ☐ Badge   ☐ Keys   ☐ Manuals
  ☐ Corporate Card   ☐ Medical I.D.   ☐ Other

REFERRED TO BENEFITS SPECIALIST:

ON (DATE):

- Explanation of final check, vacation pay, severance pay ☐
- Type of Termination   ☐ Voluntary   ☐ Involuntary

INTERVIEWER:

DATE:

CHAPTER 8

Strategic Program Planning and Development

Besides developing and managing a health/fitness facility, management's major function is planning and developing the programs that comply with the organization's mission. Health promotion programs must make business sense in all of the corporate, community, clinical, and commercial settings if they are going to survive as parts of the health care system (*Optimal Health*, 1987). The programs must be strategically planned to contribute to the bottom line of the overall organization. Even in nonprofit community and corporate health/fitness programs, the manager should be able to show how the programs might impact the bottom line of the organization.

In a community setting, the bottom line for a health/fitness program may just involve service reports. If this is the case, the health/fitness manager should strategically plan the programs to meet that service bottom line. If the ultimate goal in the community setting is serving as many people as possible, then the programs should be planned accordingly.

The bottom line in the corporate setting may be cost containment, that is, prevention of health care expenditures that affect insurance premiums or self-insurance costs. The health/fitness programs in the corporate setting should then be strategically planned to help cut the health care costs of the employees.

The bottom line in the commercial and clinical settings is profit. Obviously, the manager should plan the programs to make money. The question that often arises in this management plan is, How soon will the programs make a profit? Some clinical managers use health/fitness programs as "loss leaders." They have the goal of running as many people as possible through the program because they want the visibility. They are willing to take a loss in the health/fitness promotional programs with the hope of gaining substantial revenue on other more profitable medical care services.

Strategic planning helps the manager evaluate the market's demand for health promotion and position product lines to meet that demand. It doesn't matter whether the manager is in a corporate, community, clinical, or commercial setting; the market's demand comes from all people—employees, citizens, patients, and members. The manager must take the input information and design products (programs) to meet the demands of the end users.

The health care and health promotion industry is in a constant state of flux. The manager should be good at strategic planning to see things as they will be in the future—not necessarily as they are now. The lack of strategic planning causes organizations to make shortsighted decisions. In the commercial and clinical settings, these shortsighted decisions may make short-term money but actually hurt the program in the long run by resulting in possible financial problems. A good example of this is advertising several types of membership deals and discounts with claims and promises of spectacular improvements in the participants' levels of health and fitness. Many health clubs promote such ideas only to discover eventually that the members become disenchanted with poor service and no program substance. Thus the members drop out and the club goes bankrupt—all over a shortsighted goal of making quick money. Programs can be strategically planned to make money in the future even though they may have to be initiated at a loss. In the community and corporate settings, shortsighted decisions may attract people to programs with a hurry-up, quick-fix approach. Quite often, the programs aren't handled properly, and that hurts the overall business in the long run.

Health/fitness programs are often low-margin businesses because most managers in the commercial, clinical, community, and corporate settings come up with the same approaches to the marketplace (*Optimal Health*,

1987). Thus the market becomes price/method competitive. Managers should consider new and innovative ways to provide health/fitness programs that attract participants. This requires strategic planning that goes a long way in getting the jump on the competition. Develop a plan that fits into your organization's mission, and don't plan the program in isolation—it must fit into the mainstream of the entire organization.

A strategic management plan is a four-step, iterative process that involves

1. assessing needs and interests,
2. planning the programs,
3. implementing the programs, and
4. evaluating the programs to ensure that the organization's health/fitness mission is well organized and purposeful.

The iterative process means that the manager constantly cycles through these four stages. As programs are implemented and evaluated in the third and fourth stages, information is gathered on how future programs can be offered. Information obtained on one program is used to design another follow-up program. The manager then cycles through the four stages on the follow-up program and so on. The four-stage management process is illustrated in Figure 8.1.

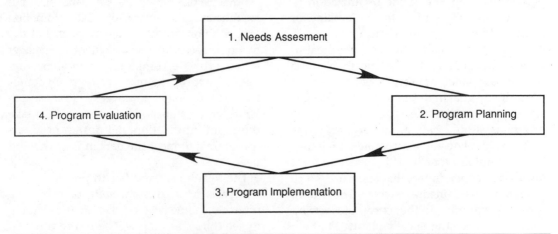

Figure 8.1. A four stage management process.

A good strategic plan is like a road map with checkpoints along the way to evaluate how the plan is working (*Optimal Health*, 1987). A good strategic plan has built-in flexibility to change if needed. The following are some questions to ask and issues to explore in planning and developing health/fitness programs:

- What is the market demand?
- What are the needs and interests of the participants?
- How will the market change?
- How is the competition positioning itself?
- What are the organization's capabilities?
- How will the programs be evaluated?

We will now examine these questions and issues using the four-stage management process.

NEEDS ASSESSMENT

The first stage in planning and developing health/fitness programs is to decide what types of programs to offer to fulfill the needs and interests of the clients. After all, the clients support the program and there would be no program without them. Regardless of whether the clients are from a corporate, community, clinical, or commercial setting, a needs assessment should be conducted to discover what types of programs will interest them. The types of needs assessments that could be conducted in the various settings are illustrated in Table 8.1.

Commercial Setting

In a start-up commercial setting, a market analysis should be conducted to determine which specific health/fitness services the clients will purchase. An outline of the essential items used in a market analysis is provided in the box on pages 204-205. Such a market analysis can cost between $5,000 and hundreds of thousands of dollars, depending on the scope of the project and how well the objectives are defined before the consultant is called. The more information that is provided to the consultant, the less the cost will be.

Table 8.1 Types of Program Needs Assessments Used in the Commercial, Community, Clinical, and Corporate Settings

Commercial setting	Community/clinical setting	Corporate setting
1. Conduct a market survey	1. Conduct a market survey	1. Management's perception of needs
2. Owner(s) perception of needs	2. Input from AHA, ACS, ALA, Red Cross, and so forth	2. Employee interests and health habits
3. Investor(s) perception of needs	3. Physician(s) perception of needs	3. Input from advisory committee
4. Board of directors perception of needs	4. Feedback from existing programs (Parks and Recreation)	4. Results from health screening, medical evaluation, fitness tests
5. Survey current members	5. Survey current participants	

Outline of Essential Items for a Market Analysis

1. Demographic analysis
   - Service area
   - Population data—age, sex, income, family dwellings
   - Employment—major employers, growth, major occupations
   - Travel time—to work, to health/fitness center

2. Competitor analysis
   - Types of competitors—multipurpose clubs, health clubs, athletic clubs, sports clubs, fitness centers, hospital wellness programs, clinics, community programs, and the like
   - Size of competitors—number of participants
   - Location
   - Membership characteristics
   - Competitive success factors
   - Staffing and facility requirements

3. Primary market analysis—consumer survey
   - Current participation

     Type, frequency, duration of exercise
     Time of day
     Place of exercise
     Reasons for exercise (health, fitness, fun, etc.)
     How many club memberships currently own
     How much will pay for membership fee and dues
   - Appealing features of a health/fitness program

     Screening
     Testing
     Counseling
     Health promotion (weight control, nutrition, smoking cessation, stress management, etc.)
     Leadership
     Full-service facility—equipment
     Structured group programs
     Individual programs
     Location
     Cost
     Other
   - Demographics of individuals surveyed

     Age, sex
     Education, occupation, income
     Marital status, children
     Zip code

4. Secondary market analysis—referral sources
   - Physicians
   - Hospitals
   - Physical therapy/rehabilitation
   - Other

5. Demand projections
   - Consumer membership
   - Referrals—source and mechanism
   - Turnover

6. Financial considerations
   - Product design
     Programs and services (fees, dues, testing, rehabilitation, classes, food and beverage, guest fees, pro shop, other)
     Operating expenses (salaries, benefits, taxes, rent, utilities, equipment, advertising, general, and administrative)
     Nonoperating revenues and expenses (interest income and expense, depreciation, amortization)
   - Marketing strategy
     To consumers
     To referrals
     Pricing and discount schemes
   - Preliminary financial analysis—pro forma

7. Recommendations—plan of action

In addition to market analyses, favorite program ideas are generated by the organization's owner(s), investor(s), and board of directors in the needs assessment of commercial programs. For existing commercial programs, current members should be surveyed to establish the needs for future programs.

Community and Clinical Settings

In community and clinical settings, the needs and interests of the potential clients are also discovered through market surveys and analyses. The same essential items shown in the market analysis could be used here. In addition, needs of the community are identified by the local health agencies such as the Public Health Department, American Heart Association, American Lung Association, American Cancer Society, and Red Cross, as well as the physicians practicing in that community. Community programs offered through parks and recreation departments and special events such as health fairs also provide channels of feedback information in identifying community needs and interests in health and fitness. Another source of needs/interests information is participants in an existing health/fitness program.

THE HEART TEST™
A RISK FACTOR ANALYSIS

Please answer
ALL questions.

1. To insure accuracy in transcribing, please PRINT clearly!

Name _____ Last _____ First _____ Initial

Title _____

Company _____

Address _____

City _____ State _____ Zip _____

Telephone: (___) ___ — ___
Area Code _____ Number

Age ☐☐ Years

Sex ☐ Male ☐ Female

Social Security Number (Optional) ☐☐☐

Date ___ / ___ / ___
Month / Day / Year

2. Read the questions below. Determine your own "point score" for each question, and write your score clearly in the box provided.

1. Age/Sex

Male—Age	51 and over	10
	35 - 50	6
	34 and under	1
Female—Age	51 and over	5
	35 - 50	2
	34 and under	0

2. Family History

If you have parents, brothers, or sisters who have had a heart attack, or heart bypass surgery.
At age 59 or BEFORE 5
At age 60 or AFTER 3
None of the above or don't know 0

3. Personal History

If you have had a heart attack 20
If you have not had a heart attack but have had angina, heart bypass surgery, angioplasty, stroke or blood vessel surgery 10
None of the above 0

4. Smoking

CURRENT cigarette smoker:
and you smoke 25 or MORE cigarettes a day 10
and you smoke 24 or LESS cigarettes a day 5
PREVIOUS cigarette smoker within last TWO years:
and you smoked 25 or MORE cigarettes a day 5
and you smoked 24 or LESS cigarettes a day 3
Never smoked or quit smoking more than TWO YEARS ago 0

5. High Blood Pressure

If you have had your blood pressure taken in the LAST YEAR
and it was Elevated or High 6
and it was Borderline 3
and it was Normal 0
None of the above or don't know ...... N

6. Diet

Which of the following BEST describes your eating pattern:
One serving of red meat and/or fried foods daily, more than 7 eggs a week, and consumption of butter, whole milk and cheese daily 6
Red meat 4 to 6 times weekly, 4 to 7 eggs weekly, some margarine, low fat dairy products, cheese and/or fried foods 3
Poultry, fish, little or no red meat, 3 or less eggs weekly, some margarine, skim milk, and skim milk products 0

7. Diabetes

Have you ever been told that you have diabetes?
YES at age 40 or BEFORE .. (Male 3-Female 6)
YES at age 41 or AFTER .. (Male 2-Female 4)
NO 0

8. Weight

The Body Mass Index is used to determine if you are overweight. This index uses two factors, height and weight.
Please enter your height and weight and the result will be calculated.
In general, if you are over your ideal weight:
25 pounds or OVER you will receive 3 points
BETWEEN 10 to 24 pounds you will receive 1 point
9 pounds or UNDER you will receive 0 points

Height ☐ ft. ☐ in.

Weight ☐ lbs.

9. Exercise

Do you engage in any aerobic exercise such as brisk walking, jogging, bicycling, racquetball, or swimming for more than 15 minutes:
Less than ONCE a week 3
ONE to TWO times a week 1
THREE or more times a week 0

10. Stress

How well do the following traits describe you:
"COMPETITIVE", "BOSSY", "EASILY ANGERED", "PRESSED FOR TIME"
VERY WELL 6
FAIRLY WELL 3
NOT AT ALL 0

11a. How many YEARS since your last complete medical evaluation. ☐

11b. Check this box if you are currently under the care of a physician. ☐

Health Interests:

Check which of the following health areas are of interest to you or your spouse.

Interested In:	Yes	
	Self	Spouse
12. Blood Pressure and/or Cholesterol Check	☐	☐
13. Comprehensive Medical Check-up	☐	☐
14. Personal Fitness Assessment/Custom Exercise Program	☐	☐
15. Reducing Risk Of Heart Attack/Stroke	☐	☐
16. Better Nutrition	☐	☐
17. Exercise/Aerobic Sessions	☐	☐
18. Weight Loss	☐	☐
19. Stress Management	☐	☐
20. Stop Smoking	☐	☐
21. Fitness Facilities/Equipment	☐	☐
22. Family Doctor or Specialist	☐	☐
23. Health Referral Service	☐	☐
24. Self-Help Guides To Better Health	☐	☐

That's all there is to it!

Now mail your completed questionnaire back to us for analysis and preparation of your heart test report.

Figure 8.2. A sample health screening instrument. *Note.* From *The Heart Test: A Risk Factor Analysis* by National Health Enhancement Systems, Inc., 1987, Phoenix, AZ: Author. Copyright 1987 by National Health Enhancement Systems, Inc. Reprinted by permission.

Corporate Setting

In the corporate setting, needs are identified by a combination of management's perception of those needs, results from employee surveys, and input from a company advisory committee. Results from health screening, medical evaluations, and fitness tests should also be used to identify needs and shape programs in the corporate setting. An example of a health screening and interest instrument is illustrated in Figure 8.2. The Heart Test (National Health Enhancement Systems, 1987) is a 10-item cardiovascular disease risk identifier that also includes a health promotion interest survey. The risk scores of the employees are used to classify which areas of health promotion need the most attention (e.g., exercise, stress management, blood pressure control, nutrition, weight control, or smoking cessation). The areas of need are then compared with the areas of interests to see if there is a match. Often, the areas of interest override the areas of need because the interest selections reflect what programs the participants might actually attend. This type of a screening and interest survey is also appropriate for use in the commercial, clinical, and community settings in identifying participants for the various programs.

PROGRAM PLANNING

Program planning involves using the information from the needs and interests assessments to define the specific program goals and objectives. Establishing these goals and objectives from the needs and interests of the participants shapes the kinds of programs that will be offered. All health/fitness staff members should be involved in program planning, especially because they have the responsibility of carrying out those programs. Their input

as to what works and what doesn't is valuable. Several staff meetings should be held with the manager to review survey results and other information from the needs assessment process. Questions to answer in the planning process include the following:

- Who is interested in the program?
- What long-term and short-term goals are to be achieved?
- What are the internal and external resources?
- What are the staffing needs?
- What are the program options?
- Who will develop the programs?
- How will the programs be marketed and promoted?
- How will the programs be delivered?
- Who will supervise the programs?
- How and when will participants be enrolled?
- What medical screening procedures will be used?
- How will feedback be given to the participants?
- What follow-up procedures will be used?
- What motivational techniques will be used?
- What special events will be conducted?
- What are the anticipated obstacles to program implementation?
- What is the estimated budget?
- What is the timing of program implementation?
- What are the adherence motives?
- How will the programs be evaluated?

Marketing and Promoting Health/Fitness Programs

Developing the strategic plan for marketing and promoting the programs is a very important step. The best of programs will not succeed if nobody knows that they exist. In the past, health/fitness specialists have been trained to know program content and how it is delivered. They have not been trained in marketing and promoting the programs. An increasing number of health/fitness professionals are becoming proficient at marketing and promoting, and these concepts are now being taught in several preparatory education programs.

The same careful planning methods used in program implementation should be used for marketing the programs. Generally, the marketing plan should have

- objectives,
- strategies of how programs are to be promoted,
- staff assignments in the promotional efforts,
- target dates and a timetable of tasks, and
- resources to be used in the promotion of programs.

Basically, the task of marketing is to show clients what you have. Therefore, you should design your promotional efforts to reveal the main features of your services and products. The theme of your organization should be evident in the marketing materials. The quality of your staff, programs, facilities, and equipment should be illustrated in your promotional information. Marketing is projecting the image of how you want your program/ organization to be perceived by the end users. The following are some promotional techniques used in marketing:

- Brochures
- Print advertisements
- Direct mail
- Public service announcements
- News releases
- Posters
- Gift certificates
- Audiocassettes
- Videotapes

- Referrals
- Radio and TV commercials
- Speaking engagements

When promoting a new program, the health/ fitness manager should consider doing an in-house pilot project to provide the staff with an opportunity to become familiar with how the new program works before it is promoted and delivered to consumers.

Medical Screening Procedures

In any health/fitness program, careful attention should also be paid to the procedures for medically screening clients and handling those clients as a result of that screening. Safety of the participants is of utmost importance! Because health/fitness programs usually involve exercise, there should be a medical management model for handling the participants.

Guidelines for exercise testing and prescription have been published by the ACSM (1986). A joint task force of the American College of Cardiology and the American Heart Association also has published guidelines for exercise testing (Schlant, 1986). We have combined recommendations from these two sources and present a medical management model for handling clients in Figure 8.3.

In this medical management model, participants are identified through the marketing and promotional efforts and then screened by a health questionnaire and risk factor analysis. The "Health Screen Form" (page 210) used by the YMCA of the USA (1987) is a good example of a health screening questionnaire. It addresses the major factors involved in potential cardiovascular problems. Any person with potential health problems should see a physician and obtain medical clearance before undertaking any fitness testing or exercise activity.

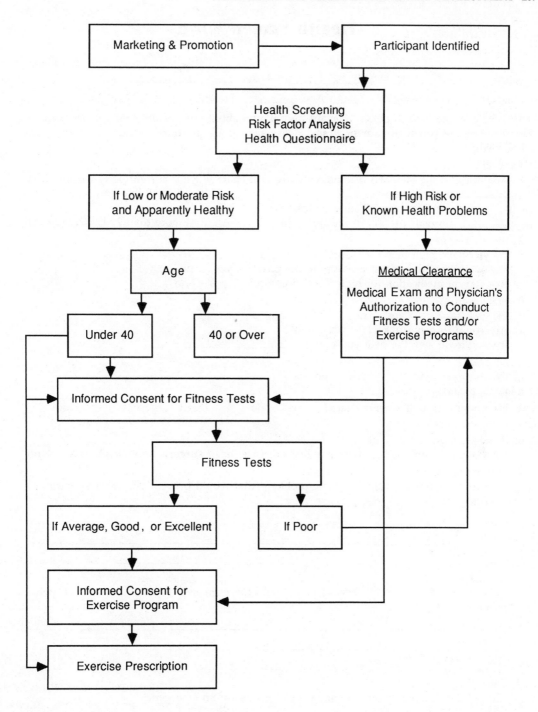

Figure 8.3. A medical management model for handling clients.

Health Screen Form

Name _____ Date _____

Male _____ Female _____ Age _____ Height _____ Weight _____

This form is intended to obtain relevant information about your health that will assist the staff in helping you with your program. Please answer all questions to the best of your knowledge.

1. Weight
   According to the attached recommended weight chart, is your current body weight
   _____ underweight?   _____ 5 to 19 lb overweight?
              (more than 5 lb under ideal)
   _____ normal? (± 5 lb of ideal)   _____ more than 20 lb overweight?

2. Blood Pressure
   Do you have high blood pressure?   yes   no
   Have you had high blood pressure in the past?   yes   no
   Are you on medication for high blood pressure?   yes   no

3. Smoking
   Do you smoke?   yes   no
   Are you a former smoker?   yes   no
   If yes, please give the date you quit. _____

4. Diabetes
   Do you have diabetes?   yes   no

5. Heart Problems
   Have you ever had a heart attack?   yes   no   Heart surgery?   yes   no
   Angina?   yes   no

6. Family History
   Have any of your blood relatives had heart disease, heart surgery, or angina?   yes   no

7. Orthopedic Problems
   Do you have any serious orthopedic problems that would prevent you from exercising?
       yes   no   If yes, please explain.

   _____

   _____

   _____

8. Other Problems
   Do you have any reason to believe you should not exercise?   yes   no   If yes,
   please explain.

   _____

   _____

   _____

9. Emergency
   Please list a relative whom we may contact in case of an emergency:

   Name _____ Telephone _____

   Relation _____

Note.   Adapted from *Health Enhancement for America's Work Force: Program Guide* with permission of the YMCA of the USA, 101 N. Wacker Drive, Chicago, IL 60606.

Medical Clearance Form

Dear Doctor:

_____ has applied for enrollment in the fitness testing
name of applicant
and/or exercise programs at the YMCA. The fitness testing program involves a submaximal test for cardiorespiratory fitness, body composition analysis, flexibility test, and muscular strength and endurance tests. The exercise programs are designed to start easy and become progressively more difficult over a period of time. All fitness tests and exercise programs will be administered by qualified personnel trained in conducting exercise tests and exercise programs.

By completing the form below, however, you are not assuming any responsibility for our administration of the fitness testing and/or exercise programs. If you know of any medical or other reasons why participation in the fitness testing and/or exercise programs by the applicant would be unwise, please indicate so on this form.

If you have any questions about the YMCA fitness testing and/or exercise programs, please call.

Report of Physician

____ I know of no reason why the applicant may not participate.

____ I believe the applicant can participate, but I urge caution because

_____

_____

____ The applicant should not engage in the following activities:

_____

_____

____ I recommend that the applicant NOT participate.

Physician signature _____ Date _____

Address _____ Telephone _____

City and State _____ Zip _____

Note. Adapted from *Health Enhancement for America's Work Force: Program Guide* with permission of the YMCA of the USA, 101 N. Wacker Drive, Chicago, IL 60606.

Informed Consent for Fitness Testing

Name _____
(please print)

The purpose of the fitness testing program is to evaluate cardiorespiratory fitness, body composition, flexibility, and muscular strength and endurance. The cardiorespiratory fitness test involves a submaximal test that may include a bench step test, a cycle ergometer test, or a one-mile walk test. Body composition is analyzed by taking several skinfold measures to calculate percentage of body fat. Flexibility is determined by the sit-and-reach test. Muscular strength may be determined by an upper-body bench press test and a lower-body leg extension test. Muscular endurance may be evaluated by the one-minute, bent-knee sit-up test or the endurance bench press test.

I understand that I am responsible for monitoring my own condition throughout the tests, and should any unusual symptoms occur, I will cease my participation and inform the instructor of the symptoms.

In signing this consent form, I affirm that I have read this form in its entirety and that I understand the description of the tests and their components. I also affirm that my questions regarding the fitness testing program have been answered to my satisfaction.

In the event that a medical clearance must be obtained prior to my participation in the fitness testing program, I agree to consult my physician and obtain written permission from my physician prior to the commencement of any fitness tests.

Also, in consideration for being allowed to participate in the fitness testing program, I agree to assume the risk of such testing, and further agree to hold harmless the YMCA and its staff members conducting such testing from any and all claims, suits, losses, or related causes of action for damages, including, but not limited to, such claims that may result from my injury or death, accidental or otherwise, during, or arising in any way from, the testing program.

_____   _____
(Signature of participant)   (Date)

_____   _____
(Person administering tests)   (Date)

Note. Adapted from *Health Enhancement for America's Work Force: Program Guide* with permission of the YMCA of the USA, 101 N. Wacker Drive, Chicago, IL 60606.

Informed Consent for Exercise Participation

I desire to engage voluntarily in the YMCA exercise program in order to attempt to improve my physical fitness. I understand that the activities are designed to place a gradually increasing work load on the cardiorespiratory system and to thereby attempt to improve its function. The reaction of the cardiorespiratory system to such activities can't be predicted with complete accuracy. There is a risk of certain changes that might occur during or following the exercise. These changes might include abnormalities of blood pressure or heart rate.

I understand that the purpose of the exercise program is to develop and maintain cardiorespiratory fitness, body composition, flexibility, and muscular strength and endurance. A specific exercise plan will be given to me, based on my needs and interests and my doctor's recommendations. All exercise programs include warm-up, exercise at target heart rate, and cool-down. The programs may involve walking, jogging, swimming, or cycling (outdoor and stationary); participation in exercise fitness, rhythmic aerobic exercise, or choreographed fitness classes; or calisthenics or strength training. All programs are designed to place a gradually increasing work load on the body in order to improve overall fitness. The rate of progression is regulated by exercise target heart rate and perceived effort of exercise.

I understand that I am responsible for monitoring my own condition throughout the exercise program and should any unusual symptoms occur, I will cease my participation and inform the instructor of the symptoms.

In signing this consent form, I affirm that I have read this form in its entirety and that I understand the nature of the exercise program. I also affirm that my questions regarding the exercise program have been answered to my satisfaction.

In the event that a medical clearance must be obtained prior to my participation in the exercise program, I agree to consult my physician and obtain written permission from my physician prior to the commencement of any exercise program.

Also, in consideration for being allowed to participate in the YMCA exercise program, I agree to assume the risk of such exercise, and further agree to hold harmless the YMCA and its staff members conducting the exercise program from any and all claims, suits, losses, or related causes of action for damages, including, but not limited to, such claims that may result from my injury or death, accidental or otherwise, during, or arising in any way from, the exercise program.

_____   _____
             (Signature of participant)   (Date)

Please print:

Name _____ Date of birth _____

Address _____
                    Street   City   State   Zip

Telephone _____

Name of personal physician _____

Physician's address _____

Physician's phone _____

Limitations and medications _____

_____

Note. Adapted from *Health Enhancement for America's Work Force: Program Guide* with permission of the YMCA of the USA, 101 N. Wacker Drive, Chicago, IL 60606.

The Heart Test on page 206 is a computerized risk factor analysis that can be used as a stand-alone questionnaire or in combination with clinical measurements of height, weight, blood pressure, cholesterol, and blood glucose. The clinical measurements override the individual's response on the questionnaire in terms of scoring risk. The total risk score can be used to classify an individual as low, moderate, or high risk for cardiovascular disease. All high-risk individuals should obtain medical clearance before fitness testing or exercise is allowed. The risk factor analysis can also be used to single out any one particular risk factor, such as personal history of heart disease or high blood pressure, along with the overall risk score for all 10 factors.

Both the health questionnaire and the risk factor analysis should be computer coded for ease of storing participant records, reporting test results, and tracking individual progress over time. More information on the use of computers for documentation is available in chapter 12.

In the medical management model, results of the health screening are examined to see if the participant is apparently healthy, with low or average risk for disease, or if the participant is at high risk. As mentioned previously, high-risk individuals need medical clearance before undertaking fitness testing or exercise. Every health/fitness organization should either have a medical director or medical consultant who provides medical clearance for the participants or directs participants to their own personal physicians for medical clearance. The form on page 211 is one that the YMCA of the USA (1987) uses for medical clearance. This is one example of how medical clearance can be provided in a program. The exact medical clearance policy used in your program should be established by your medical director and attorneys.

After a participant has been medically cleared by a physician, he or she should sign informed consent forms before any fitness testing or exercise programs are conducted. Pages 212 and 213 show examples of informed consent for fitness testing and exercise provided by the YMCA of the USA. Again, your medical director and attorneys should word these informed consent forms specifically to your unique situation.

The informed consent form is not a legal document that protects a program in a court of law. It is part of a safe procedure used to show that the participant has been informed of the risks of fitness testing and exercise programs. Some programs use a waiver of liability, but this document will not stand up in court either. If the participant/family can prove that program staff members were negligent in an injury/death event, informed consent or waiver of liability will not legally protect the defendant. These documents do help, however, illustrate that participants have been informed of program procedures and risks of participation.

More information on the legal liability issues associated with health/fitness programs is available from Herbert and Herbert (1984). Generally, to reduce legal problems in a program, you should

- be aware of your legal liabilities,
- select certified exercise instructors to lead exercise classes and supervise exercise on equipment,
- use good judgment in planning and implementing programs and provide written guidelines for medical emergency procedures,
- inform participants about the risks and dangers of exercise and require written informed consent,
- follow safe procedures in screening participants for fitness tests and exercise programs,
- instruct staff not to practice medicine but instead to limit their advice to their own areas of expertise,

- provide a safe environment by following building codes and a regular maintenance schedule for equipment, and
- purchase adequate liability insurance for the staff.

Next, we will examine how to manage a participant who is at low or average disease risk and is apparently healthy. Referring back to Figure 8.3, we see that the *age* of the low-risk participant is examined under these circumstances. The medical management guidelines state that if a participant is over age 40, then medical clearance including a diagnostic electrocardiographic (ECG) stress test is recommended before that individual is allowed to proceed to fitness testing or exercise programs.

If the participant is under age 40, the American College of Cardiology/American Heart Association guidelines state that there may not be a need for fitness testing and the individual could proceed directly to an exercise program. However, we believe that fitness testing can provide some valuable information about the participant's exercise tolerance, heart rate, and blood pressure responses. This information helps the health/fitness counselor write a more accurate and personal exercise prescription for that participant. Therefore, an entry to fitness testing for individuals under age 40 has been illustrated in Figure 8.3.

When planning the fitness testing part of the health/fitness program, you should make sure that the four health-related areas of physical fitness are included:

1. Cardiovascular-respiratory test(s): treadmill, bicycle ergometer, step bench, or walk/run tests
2. Body composition analysis: fat/lean ratio
3. Flexibility test(s): range of movement
4. Muscular strength and endurance tests: upper body, lower body, sit-ups, push-ups, and so forth

Detailed descriptions of these types of tests are available from the YMCA of the USA (1987) and the ACSM (1988).

The health/fitness program content should be planned to include the major health promotion areas of exercise, weight control, nutrition, back care, stress management, and elimination of substance abuse (e.g., tobacco, alcohol). Content objectives for these programs usually include the following:

I. Exercise

    A. Education component
    B. Exercise history
    C. Health screening
    D. Fitness testing
    E. Goal setting
    F. Implementation of training principles

        1. Overload of work
        2. Specificity of exercise
        3. Frequency of exercise
        4. Intensity of exercise
        5. Duration of exercise
        6. Type of exercise
        7. Warm-up
        8. Cool-down

    G. Motivational techniques
    H. Follow-up

II. Weight control

    A. Etiology of obesity
    B. Readiness questionnaire for weight control program
    C. Knowledge assessment for diet and exercise program
    D. Estimating percent body fat
    E. Recommended weight
    F. Nutrition principles
    G. Dangerous diets
    H. Behavior modification suggestions
    I. Guidelines for weight loss programs

III. Nutrition
   A. Basic nutrition principles
   B. The basic four food groups
   C. Fiber, vitamins, and minerals
   D. Dietary evaluation
   E. Nutritional recommendations and guidelines

IV. Back care
   A. Triage of participants to primary and secondary prevention of back pain programs
   B. Back pain knowledge and behavioral inventories
   C. Tests to assess the strength and flexibility of key posture muscles
   D. Relaxation tests and techniques
   E. Treatment of back strain

V. Stress management
   A. Stress and distress
   B. Individual versus group programs
   C. "Stress-pertise" test
   D. Coping with stress
   E. Tension rating
   F. Personality assessment
   G. Positive stressors
   H. Scales of satisfaction, frustration, and social readjustment
   I. Sample course outline for a stress management program

VI. Smoking cessaton
   A. Smoking questionnaire: identification of smoking types
   B. Motivation, dependence, and predicted ability to stop smoking
   C. Life change inventory
   D. Community resources for smoking cessation programs
   E. Types of treatments
   F. How to motivate a smoker to quit
   G. Smoker's self-testing kit

In the planning phase of the management process, determine how you are going to evaluate the programs you choose to implement. The evaluation procedures that could be used are explained later in this chapter.

PROGRAM IMPLEMENTATION

The implementation of health/fitness programs in the corporate, community, clinical, and commercial settings involves

- reviewing the planned objectives set for the program,
- scheduling the program tasks to meet those objectives,
- marketing and promoting the programs, and
- carrying out the assigned tasks.

In this section, we are going to examine staff leadership, marketing and promoting, internal and external resources, and follow-up plans.

Leadership

Obviously, the program tasks do not happen by themselves—professional health/fitness staff members are needed to carry out those tasks properly. In fact, if all aspects of a health/fitness center in any setting were to be ranked in order of importance, *leadership* by the professional staff would be the key to a successful program.

The consumer, whether in a corporate, community, clinical, or commercial setting, responds positively to professional leaders who show a caring attitude and expertise in guiding and motivating the consumer. In fact, the health/fitness professional should be very skilled at motivating participants. Consumers need the guidance and assistance of the health/

fitness professional staff. The participant doesn't always know what to do or how to get started. Herein lies the key challenge for the health/fitness professional: to *motivate* that participant to action.

Well-qualified professional leaders generally know what programs are best for the various settings. The staff should work hard, however, at implementing the program plans carefully to ensure their success. Under these circumstances, the consumer often accepts less developed facilities and equipment provided that the staff is well organized in the implementation of programs. Too often, organizations developing health/fitness centers consider first which gadgets, bells, and whistles should be built or purchased to promote the program, which may be ill-defined until people start using the center. Then, after the facility and fancy equipment priorities are achieved, the staff is hired to oversee the programs.

The priorities in the above scenario are backward. Selection of professional staff should be considered first. The staff should then conduct the needs assessments and carefully plan the proper programs to achieve the objectives and mission set for the health/fitness center. With this knowledge in hand, the professional staff can help design facilities and equipment to carry out those programs. Take note that health promotion is very competitive—you have to have the right kind of people with the right kind of expertise to keep pace with the demands of the marketplace.

Marketing and Promotion

In the implementation of programs, the timing of the marketing and promotional efforts is very critical. Programs should be marketed and promoted well enough in advance so participants can plan their schedules accordingly. However, the time period between the intensive marketing/promotional efforts and the start of the program should be neither too long nor too short. Scheduling the exact amount of time between the two is an art. It really depends on the nature and the setting of the program; however, some common-sense principles prevail. For example, in some commercial settings, a new racquetball league can be advertised and promoted 3-4 weeks in advance of the program's start. However, a special event involving a racquetball tournament may have to be announced and promoted months ahead of the scheduled date.

Internal and External Resources

The implementation of a health/fitness program in the corporate setting raises the question of whether to develop in-house expertise or purchase outside provider services. In most cases, though, both internal and external resources are combined to implement a cost-effective program.

For example, a program coordinator within a company may be selected to coordinate all the available resources to implement the program. Some internal experts may be hired to supervise exercise programs (e.g., exercise instructors), whereas other health promotion specialists like psychologists may be contracted to deliver stress management programs. Developing internal expertise to conduct all aspects of a health/fitness program is expensive for small to medium-sized companies. For the most part, this is feasible only in very large corporations.

Consider the fact that medical and health/fitness professionals are required to conduct health screening, medical evaluations, fitness tests, and exercise programs and add the fact that various health promotion specialists such as psychologists, dietitians, nurses, and physical therapists are required to conduct weight control, nutrition, back care, stress management, and smoking cessation programs, and it is easy to see the extensive costs involved in developing all those as internal resources. It is more cost-effective to use many of these resources as fee-for-service programs. They already exist as providers in the community, and thus there may not be a need to reinvent the wheel in these program areas. To be very cost-efficient, many of the providers in the community, clinical, and commercial settings are joining forces to reduce overhead and offer reasonably priced services.

As an example, many hospitals are joint-venturing with health clubs. The evaluation, prescription, and behavior modification aspects of the health/fitness program are provided by the hospital. The fitness facilities for carrying out the exercise programs are provided by the health club. Some hospital wellness centers are built to be very comprehensive providers of health/fitness programs by including the exercise facilities as well as all of the other aspects of the program. These centers are very costly due to the comprehensiveness of the program offerings.

Selecting an outside resource and purchasing the provider service to implement a health/fitness program, or parts thereof, require careful planning. The American Heart Association (1984) separates outside resources into low-, medium-, and high-cost categories (see Table 12.1). According to these guidelines, it is apparent that exercise programs can be implemented at virtually no cost by using facilities that already exist in the community. For example, walking, jogging, and cycling paths in parks and around lakes are now available at no charge in many communities. Par course systems are also included with many of the jogging trails for strength, flexibility, and endurance development. Some public schools open their facilities, such as outdoor tracks, to the public at no charge.

Many colleges and universities now offer health/fitness programs through their continuing education departments or their departments of health, physical education, and recreation. Because the schools provide the programs as part of their commitment to community service, the fees are usually reasonable and would fit into the low- or medium-cost categories.

Contract exercise instructors, hospital wellness centers. and YMCA health/fitness centers are also examples of outside resources that fit into the medium-cost category. Contract exercise instructors are now available to implement fitness programs for organizations. The instructor's credentials should be checked carefully to make sure the person is professionally qualified to provide a safe program.

Hospital wellness centers usually have professionally qualified personnel to conduct comprehensive health/fitness programs. Many offer their preventive medicine services in the medium-cost range in an effort to promote good public relations in the community and therefore encourage use of the hospital when treatment of illness is required.

YMCAs are perhaps the largest single providers of exercise programs in the United States. Small and medium-sized companies are the primary users of YMCA programs. The YMCA of the USA (1987) promotes a health enhancement program for America's work force to all of its member affiliates.

Private fitness centers, health clubs, and dance/exercise studios also serve as outside resources for the implementation of health/fitness programs for other organizations. Their primary emphasis is usually on the use of high-tech equipment for exercise and the use of saunas, steam baths, and massage for relaxation. Dance/exercise studios include exercise classes to supplement the machinery.

The American Heart Association (1984) provides an excellent summary of how to evaluate outside resources before purchasing their services. When seeking help from an outside provider to implement a health/fitness program, you should use the guidelines in Table 8.2 to evaluate the provider and ask the following questions of the provider:

Staff

Are the staff members professionally trained in physical education, exercise science, health promotion, or medicine? Are staff members certified by a national organization such as the ACSM or any medical certifying body? Do staff members have consulting expertise and experience? Do staff members have experience at administering exercise programs?

Programs

What program components are offered? Will the program components meet the goals and objectives set for the buyer of the services?

Facilities

What facilities are offered by the outside provider? Will the facilities meet program requirements?

References

What present and previous clients has the outside resource serviced? Will a list be provided for reference check?

Ownership

Who owns the organization providing the service? How long has the current ownership been in place? What is the turnover rate in ownership and staff at the outside resource?

In addition to answering all of the above questions to satisfaction, the buyer of a service should consult legal counsel before signing any agreements. The providers of health/fitness programs in the community, clinical, and commercial settings would be wise to meet the qualifications listed in Table 8.2 and to be able to answer all of the above questions positively.

Follow-Up

Follow-up is a very important part of program implementation that is often overlooked, especially in commercial settings. Health/fitness programs should be designed to provide some type of feedback and scheduled follow-up sessions for motivating the participants. Follow-up sessions may include repeating a fitness profile, reviewing progress in an exercise program, or counseling in a behavior modification program.

In the process of follow-up fitness testing, the evidence of change in fitness level can serve as important reinforcement to the participant. Reviewing progress in an exercise program can be an excellent opportunity to recognize individual achievements. Incentives, rewards, and special events serve as excellent motivators in the follow-up system. Shirts, equipment bags, warm up suits, plaques, trophies, tournaments, leagues, fitness months, fitness days, and recognition banquets can be used to motivate participants to higher levels of activity.

The follow-up component of program implementation is the bridge to evaluation of the program. In fact, some managers believe that follow-up is part of the evaluation process. Either way, it is a very important part of the overall program and should be carefully planned.

Table 8.2 Guidelines for Evaluating Outside Providers of Health/Fitness Programs

Staff qualifications	Program components	Facilities

• Physical education/ exercise science degree
• ACSM or other medical certification
• Health promotion/ medical specialty
• Recreation specialty
• Program administration expertise
	• Evaluation
	  -health screening
	  -medical clearance
	  -fitness testing
	• Exercise prescription
	  -cardiorespiratory
	  -flexibility
	  -strength
	  -individual programs
	  -group programs
	• Back care
	• Weight control
	• Nutrition
	• Stress management
	• Smoking cessation
	• Follow-up
	• Documentation
		• Locker/shower rooms
		• Exercise areas
		• Gymnasium
		• Weight training room
		• Outdoor/indoor tracks
		• Courts
		• Swimming pool
		• Classroom(s)
		• Child care center
		• Medical clinic

PROGRAM EVALUATION

The fourth step in the iterative process of managing a program involves evaluation. Program evaluation is classified as (a) process evaluation and (b) outcome evaluation. Both types can be used in any of the corporate, community, clinical, or commercial settings. Basically, these two types of evaluation involve analyzing the implementation tasks that were assigned to the staff to see (a) if the tasks were accomplished (process evaluation) and (b) if the objectives of the program were met (outcome evaluation). A summary of the process and outcome evaluation techniques is presented in Figure 8.4.

The health/fitness staff members should meet and go over the evaluation of a program periodically throughout the program and immediately after it is completed. Careful records should be kept during each program to evaluate it accurately. Microcomputers and data base software are now available to facilitate the documentation and evaluation of programs. More information about the documentation of programs is available in chapter 12. It is strongly recommended that all participant records and registration, screening, and testing forms be computer coded for ease of entry and data analysis.

Staff members should be assigned specific tasks in the evaluation process. Those assignments might include keeping various records and then evaluating the data.

The outcome evaluation is usually dependent on the process. If a program is conducted well, the outcome will reveal that fact. Sometimes, however, the outcome (e.g., how many individuals participated in each

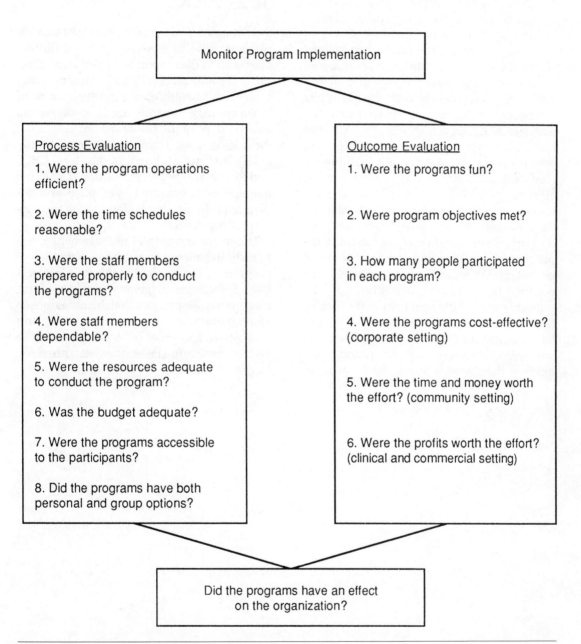

Figure 8.4. Summary of the process and outcome evaluation techniques.

program) doesn't seem to be impressive, although the process of offering and conducting the program was deemed quite successful. In this case, the process evaluation is viewed separately from the outcome evaluation. Occasionally, a popular program may be well attended (good outcome evaluation) in spite of a poorly conducted program (process). The manager does gain valuable information from the process evaluation and can then plan to conduct the program differently next time to solve the problem discovered by process evaluation.

In other cases, both the process and the outcome evaluations are viewed together to see if a particular program was successful. If the program was well conducted and there was an acceptable number of participants, the program is considered successful.

Examination of the results from the evaluations then determine which procedures are to be used next for assessing needs, planning, and implementing a new or different program in the iterative management process.

SUMMARY

This chapter outlined the processes used in planning and implementing health/fitness programs in the corporate, community, clinical, and commercial setting. The ultimate success of the health/fitness center in any of these settings depends on the professional qualifications of the personnel involved. That includes a range from the owner(s), manager(s), investor(s), board of directors, CEO, and fitness and health promotion staff to the maintenance personnel. Who plans and implements the programs determines the success of the center.

The major function of management is administrative planning and implementation of programs to meet the organization's objectives. Effective management involves a four-stage iterative process that includes needs assessment, planning, implementation, and evaluation. Examples of techniques used in each of these four stages have been provided in this chapter.

Health/Fitness Equipment

The selection, purchase, maintenance, and operation of exercise equipment are all parts of a very important process in the health/fitness profession. These represent a significant investment of both time and money, and if poor decisions are made during the process, they can come back to haunt you later. There is a wide range of products in varied price ranges on the market from which to choose. In this chapter, we provide the potential buyer of exercise equipment with some criteria for selecting equipment, as well as some ideas about purchasing, maintaining, and operating it. In addition, we offer some insight into the possible future of fitness equipment.

SELECTING HEALTH/ FITNESS EQUIPMENT

The selection of health/fitness equipment is a baffling process for the average buyer because of the multitude of vendors and types of products on the market. Canvassing classified advertisements in trade journals and visiting exhibits at trade shows will certainly confuse all but a few professionals who spend most of their time dealing with such matters. Indeed, there are certain criteria that must be employed by the potential buyer if good decisions are to be made. The following information is presented without regard to priority because each buyer has different priorities, depending on his or her situation.

Function

A piece of exercise equipment is normally designed for a particular function or purpose. For example, a bicycle ergometer is designed to function as an exercise station for cardiovascular endurance development; a free weight bar and the attached plates are designed primarily to develop muscular strength and endurance. Most equipment, however, can be used to accomplish secondary functions. For instance, the free weight equipment can be used with low resistance to accommodate a high number of exercise repetitions in order to achieve cardiovascular endurance. Thus deciding which functions a piece of equipment will serve is probably one of the first decisions you must make. When determining what kind of programming spaces a facility must have, you had to make arbitrary decisions about the need for strength development equipment, cardiovascular development equipment, and diagnostic/testing equipment, as well as for support equipment such as laundry, computers, and office equipment. The focus of this chapter will be on exercise-related equipment.

The selection of equipment should match the marketing image you want to project. The hard-core power lifting studio would probably be dominated by free weight equipment, whereas the executive fitness center would probably have selectorized, weight-stacked equipment predominating. Thus the basic questions to ask in the early stages of decision making are what kind of image do you want to project, who will be using the equipment, what is the basic purpose of the equipment, and will there be an emphasis on strength or endurance equipment? These questions can only be answered if a clear mission is defined and solid market research has been conducted.

Cost

The cost should also be a consideration in selecting exercise equipment. A single piece of exercise equipment ranges from a few dollars to several thousand dollars. Both pieces of equipment can be essentially designed for the same basic purpose. A dumbbell, for example, can be used to assess forearm strength and endurance at a cost of only a few dollars, whereas the same type of assessment can be accomplished by the Tygr equipment, a high-tech computer-oriented product line, for several thousand dollars. The difference, of course, is the degree of sophistication involved in the measurement. The Tygr equipment senses and alters forces, repetitions, elapsed time, and so on and can then be programmed to provide concentric and eccentric workouts in variable modes such as a pyramid or a maximal effort routine. Most of the sophisticated equipment interfaces with a computer system for logging and tracking purposes. A similar situation could be devel-

oped for bicycle ergometers and treadmills in the cardiovascular area.

Caution should be exercised when selecting equipment. It is probable that there is a point of diminishing returns when upgrading older equipment lines for newer products. The cost of equipment can easily place a program in financial difficulty, because expensive equipment can place such a burden on the budget that other important areas of the program, such as personnel, might have to suffer. Yet, equipment is a highly visible marketing tool, especially in the early stages of program development. Personnel, on the other hand, become critical in member adherence and renewals. A balance of expenditures is essential. A general guide to scale equipment costs against other expenses is that equipment should not represent more than 3%-5% of the total start-up costs for a facility.

Payment for exercise equipment is usually required prior to, or at the time of, delivery. Although delivery dates frequently extend to 8 weeks or longer, the large expenditures of money over short periods of time are sometimes burdensome. Alternatives to outright purchase of new equipment should be considered by anyone under the pressure of heavy expenditures.

One alternative to purchasing new exercise equipment is to buy used equipment. A series of phone calls to the manufacturer of the equipment you have chosen as desirable may provide you with contacts for trade-in equipment. Many vendors are a good source for used equipment because they frequently have trade-in agreements with their customers.

Another alternative to purchasing new equipment is to recondition your used equipment. Various companies now can rather quickly restore your old equipment to a nearly new condition and save you about 30% of the cost of new equipment.

A combination of used and new equipment is an option during the start-up period. If the new equipment is made more visible to the members, the general impression will be that all new equipment has been purchased for the facility. Although this arrangement is less than ideal, it can frequently be a necessary compromise when investors are seeking an early break-even period and a quick return on their investment. Likewise, a lease or a lease/purchase arrangement is another possibility. Again, these arrangements can be favorable to impatient investors.

Several companies are now emerging as vendors of used and rental exercise equipment. Locations for these companies can be obtained through trade journals or even local classified advertisements. A general rule for trade-in of equipment is 35-65 cents on the dollar. There are even leasing companies now that re-lease repossessed equipment. One such company (First Equipment Leasing Corp., Needham, Massachusetts), has arrangements with creditworthy clients for lease/purchase contracts to buy highly discounted equipment at approximately 10% of its original price. Several other businesses offer such services to the persistent and creative consumer of exercise equipment.

Space

The amount of space needed or available often determines the type and/or amount of equipment selected in a health/fitness facility. A rule of thumb for designing exercise spaces is that one station of exercise equipment occupies approximately 46 square feet of floor space. This accounts for circulation of participants and averages the space for larger items such as treadmills and smaller items such as bicycle ergometers, as well as large free weight racks and single-station selectorized equipment. Should the facility be planned for nothing but multistation selectorized equipment, such as a 12-station Universal Gym,

then the above assumptions are invalid. In this case, you should consult the vendor. In general, 46 square feet per exercise station is a guide in space planning for exercise equipment. It should be noted that most manufacturers of exercise equipment offer space planning services that are invaluable in the space planning process, especially if you are planning to use only one brand of equipment.

To optimize the space utilization, plan for as many exercise patterns in one space as possible. For example, arrange a circuit on Nautilus equipment around a group of ergometers to accommodate a supercircuit if a member wants to train in both areas simultaneously.

Durability

Durability is an important consideration when selecting exercise equipment. There is no ironclad way to calculate the useful life expectancy of a piece of exercise equipment in your setting. Equipment of a particular type enjoys more use in some settings than it does in others. Also, the consumer/user is a fickle person. He or she may drift from one type of exercise equipment to another in search of one that yields large gains with no pain. Some trendy equipment will experience intense periods of heavy use for short times, which are followed by periods of little or no use. However, we offer some generalizations to use as a guide for determining probable durability of a given type of equipment.

The warranty on the equipment serves as a rough indicator of the life expectancy of a particular item. For example, manufacturers of selectorized strength equipment frequently warranty the structural frame for life, the moving parts for a year, and the upholstery for 90 days. Each material obviously has a different projected life span. You should take care to read the small print in a warranty that promises a lifetime guarantee. Very little in this world is guaranteed for life, especially in the realm of exercise equipment. The manufacturers are very careful to extend a warranty to customers that requires very low repair activity at their expense. Therefore, you can assume that expected deterioration rates of equipment under normal conditions will exceed the warranty period advertised by the manufacturer.

Another indicator of durability is your competitors' experiences with the equipment. A canvassing of the other similar-sized programs in your area that serve a similar clientele can give you a good idea about the durability of a given type of equipment. This type of evaluation, coupled with trade journal commentary, will assist you in making the right decision about exercise product durability.

Safety

The safety of intended users should be your first consideration when making decisions about exercise equipment. Formal law and legal precedent dictate that agencies and administrators of health/fitness programs have a responsibility to provide a reasonably hazard-free environment for exercise experiences. "Safe Place" statutes in some states, which entitle the users to safe environments, place an extra burden of care on activity providers. In any event, it is important that the equipment you purchase is as safe as possible for the intended users. The following suggestions should help you avoid some of the trouble spots for exercise equipment on the market.

Weight Machines

- Cable systems should have plastic-coated cables, which are less likely to fray.
- Movable attachments should not have soft metal pulleys.
- Movable parts should be able to be easily lubricated.
- Frames should have the capacity to be anchored to floor or wall.
- Frames should have several welding marks at junctions.
- Equipment should be coated with corrosion resistant paint.
- Safety stops in selectorized machines should be aligned.
- Cotter pins should not be difficult to place in stack.
- Nonslip surfaces should surround lifting area.
- Lifting area should be free of clutter.
- Floor surface should be of high-density shock-absorbing material.
- Plates, bars, and collars should be stored after each use.
- Appropriate fasteners of free weights should be available.
- Sleeves for bars should not be bent or frayed at the ends.
- Preset barbells and dumbbells should be welded in place.
- Benches should be sturdy enough to support anticipated loads.
- Bench bolts and nuts should be welded in place.
- Bench surfaces should be padded to avoid splinters and the like.

Cardiovascular Equipment

- Electrical plugs should be grounded.
- Ground-fault interruptors should be on power source.
- Treadmills should have an emergency stop button on handrail.
- Spotter's platform should be available on treadmills that elevate.
- Cycles and rowers with turbines should have protective guards.

- Countdown timers should automatically stop equipment.
- Treadmills should have guardrails on three sides.
- Instructions for safe use should be permanently mounted on unit.
- Preventive maintenance should be easily accomplished (e.g., lubrication).

Versatility

Look for versatility when purchasing health/fitness equipment. Each piece must be able to perform more than one function. For example, the equipment should be capable of diagnosing ability, rehabilitating injury, or training the injury-free members in a club. In addition, the exercise equipment should be reliable so that the same information is obtained on the same subject in repeated tests. It should also be accurate in that it should truly measure what is intended in the test (e.g., treadmills may best measure running ability). Finally, the equipment should provide objectivity; the same results should be achieved when two different people test a member.

The equipment should be somewhat portable. Frequently, a piece of equipment must be moved from one location to another in the club, and this is facilitated if the unit is on casters or rollers. Although you may see this as an unnecessary extra, it may become a significant factor when equipment emergencies arise.

A major consideration for any equipment purchase is the ability to modify the equipment for different populations. Can children, women, and large men use the same piece of equipment effectively? If not, then you might want to seek alternative product lines. Some vendors offer products that can accommodate a wide range of body sizes and types. Unfortunately, many manufacturers have developed their equipment for the standard man and/or woman, and such equipment cannot comfortably accommodate different populations with unusual sizes and shapes without the use of pads, pillows, and other devices to adjust the user to the equipment design. The versatility of product design should weigh heavily in your decision making.

User Appeal

The intended user must find the equipment appealing if it is to be successful in the club setting. Several factors are involved in making a piece of equipment appealing. For instance, name recognition is one important appeal factor. Nautilus equipment, for example, has instant credibility and appeal among many users. A buyer seeking selectorized equipment would probably have high acceptance with any Nautilus equipment brought into a facility. Indeed, some buyers purchase a few Nautilus units and supplement the remainder of the equipment with other product lines for whatever reason in an effort to appease the customers' demand for Nautilus.

Free weights have recently enjoyed a groundswell of support. Although no particular product line has emerged as a consumer leader, sturdy and massive-looking equipment is desired by many devotees of the power lifting circles. This appeal is generally consistent with the concern for function in preference to appearance. Most free weight users are more concerned with results than with convenience and appearance of the equipment. The harried club member, in contrast, may be concerned with getting a quick but effective workout by using the selectorized equipment that doesn't require a spotter and that can be accomplished in a minimal amount of time and fuss. Time-urgent users will be concerned about efficiency as much as power lifters are concerned about the effectiveness of the equipment available. All of these considerations must be dealt with when selecting exercise equipment.

Maintenance Contracts

Some manufacturers offer service contracts at the time of purchase. This is an important consideration for those buyers who don't have access to maintenance and repair personnel. Typically, the maintenance contract dovetails with the warranty, and the fees are associated with the amount of equipment to be serviced. An average facility with a full complement of resistive and cardiovascular equipment should plan on spending about $100-300 per month for external maintenance contracts. Although this removes many of the headaches for the club, it places an extra burden on the budget. If the buyer has access to good maintenance personnel, the maintenance contract will not be a significant consideration in the decision-making process. It is strongly recommended that you investigate the availability of parts and service prior to the purchase of any equipment. A regional service center located nearby should place that vendor at an advantage over competing product lines of equal price and quality but at greater distances from the club.

PURCHASING HEALTH/ FITNESS EQUIPMENT

Purchasing equipment is a complex process that is influenced greatly by the setting in which you are located. The procedures that must be employed to secure the type and amount of equipment that you need will vary depending on whether the facility is corporate, community, clinical, or commercial. Insti-

tutions, for example, may have a purchasing department that is governed by state or federal laws as to the manner in which equipment is purchased. Hospitals may have corporate purchasing guidelines if they are members of a large group of hospitals. A community hospital, in contrast, may have more latitude in the purchasing process. Commercial fitness centers may be similar to hospitals, in that chain fitness centers often have centralized purchasing to enjoy the economics of scale in large-volume buying. Smaller, sole-proprietorship programs may have greater latitude in decision-making and procedural processes regarding equipment purchases. Thus it is very difficult to generalize about purchasing procedures. This difficulty is compounded when one considers the geographic setting (concentration of indoor vs. outdoor equipment), the intended user market (upscale, single-station units vs. downscale, multistation units), the desired image (lavish vs. spartan), and a variety of other factors that clearly influence the decision-making processes when purchasing equipment. Notwithstanding these limitations, let's examine some of the broad concerns that most programs will need to address when purchasing equipment.

Taking Inventory

Unless you are opening a new facility and are purchasing new equipment, it is important that you begin the purchasing process by taking an inventory of all the equipment in your facility. Equally important is determining the condition of each inventory item. A complete list of equipment and its condition will tell you not only what is needed at the moment, but also what will be needed later. It is important to plan ahead when purchasing equipment for many reasons, including member needs, tax planning, program planning, and budget planning. Table 9.1 illustrates a sample format for taking inventory of equipment that is adaptable to most settings.

The "poor" category in the equipment inventory should be an automatic item for replacement consideration when planning for next year's budget. The average category should be a red flag for ordering replacement parts to repair pads, cables, motors, and other repair-prone equipment. This inventory keeps track of equipment condition, assures quality control of equipment condition, and permits a good system for equipment budget planning.

Reviewing the Equipment Market

Taking stock of the available equipment on the market is no small task. It seems as if half of

Table 9.1 Sample Format for Equipment Inventory

Equipment items	Good	Average	Poor
Treadmill, No. 1	X		
Treadmill, No. 2	X		
Treadmill, No. 3			X
Cycle ergometer, No. 1		X	
Cycle ergometer, No. 2		X	
Cycle ergometer, No. 3			X
Rower	X		
Minitrampoline		X	
Stairclimber			X
Ski trainer, downhill		X	
Ski trainer, cross-country	X		
Recumbent trainer		X	
Quadripedal climber			X

the products at trade shows are computerized to operate a myriad of bells and whistles. One approach to avoiding purchasing errors in such a high-tech field is to hire an equipment consultant. A 1-hour consultation fee is money well spent to avoid costly mistakes such as buying inappropriate, obsolete, or high-maintenance equipment. A second approach is to contact vendors who represent a large variety of product lines and who are in a position to offer comparative opinions about available equipment. It is wise, however, to get a second vendor's opinion in this regard to account for the potential bias created by different profit margin agreements between manufacturers and vendors. A third approach is to study the equipment on the market personally by spending a lot of time at trade shows and by reading the journals in which the equipment is advertised. Many facility managers/owners take interest and pride in having expertise regarding exercise equipment. A better approach for the internal surveillance of equipment on the market might be to assign your staff members various areas of responsibility and get input and/or feedback from them before you make final decisions on equipment purchases.

Writing Specifications

Once you have determined what kind of equipment you want in your facility, it is very important that you write down clear specifications to assure that you get exactly what you want. Equally important, you want to get the equipment for the least amount of capital expenditure. If you use a bidding system to purchase equipment items, then clear and precise specifications are essential. The inability to develop good specifications is often the greatest source of purchasing mistakes. These mistakes can be avoided by following the suggestions described below.

The first step in writing good specifications is to get as much information about the desired equipment as possible. This can be your best defense against demanding club members, owners, and purchasing agents. Armed with the details of the equipment features and construction, you can write lock-out specifications for the equipment type and model you want to purchase. On a bid sheet, it is not sufficient to state merely that you want "Brand X, Model B, or equivalent." Substitutions are commonplace among purchasing agents trying to save precious dollars. You may also be deceived by a lower bid and buy what turns out to be an undesirable piece of equipment. Be specific! State the previous information, but be careful to add the size, color, materials, design, and performance characteristics that are necessary. This lessens your chance of disappointment, but does not always guarantee satisfaction. To guarantee satisfaction, you must provide all of the necessary information and indicate that no substitutions or alternate models are acceptable. Unfortunately, this is not permissible in many purchasing environments unless the equipment is an accessory to a previously purchased item that needs an attachment. In addition, it is helpful to contact the manufacturers of the equipment you want, because they can help prepare the specifications.

There is a trend toward listing not only the brand, model, and detailed characteristics of a piece of equipment, but also two or three acceptable brand names and models that meet the specifications. For example, Nautilus single-station exercise leg extension equipment may have been listed in the description, but David and Eagle may be included as acceptable brands that have models to serve as substitutes or alternatives that meet the specifications. This gives the bidder the flexibility to offer competitive bids on acceptable equipment items.

The detailed specification of equipment can also have the effect of intimidating potential bidders. If you write absolutely locked-out specifications, without providing alternative brands and models, there will be little variability and competitiveness in the bid returns. Indeed, such tight specifications deny you the opportunity to learn of legitimate alternatives to the product identified as acceptable. One approach that you can take when a good price on an alternative item comes in well under the price of the originally identified item, but meets the specifications, is to ask for a nonreturnable sample that can be field-tested by the staff and club members prior to the final decision for equipment purchase. Many manufacturers will accommodate serious requests for field-testing of a new product or product line. In fact, strategically placed products in prestigious facilities are frequently viewed by vendors and manufacturers as cheap advertisement.

Getting Bids

Getting bids is not a simple process. It is important to issue the bids far enough in advance to attract responsible bidders. Cut-rate vendors, eager to submit alternative, and frequently unacceptable, equipment bids, can often respond on a moment's notice. The responsible bidder requires enough time to evaluate adequately the specifications, service, and warranty requirements of the bid. To deal with this issue, a bidder list should be developed.

The bidder list is very important to the purchasing process. It effectively defines the competition you want involved in providing the needed equipment and sometimes the follow-up service of warranty performances. The list of criteria for suitable bidders should include past history on delivery and service, dependability, size of inventory, financial stability, and promptness in financial matters. The bidder list is further reduced if you insist that the bidder assist in installation and provide on-site repair, backup parts in stock, and a 2-year warranty period. All of these requirements add to the cost of the equipment and should therefore not be imposed in the specifications unless they are really necessary to the operation of your program. It is handy to put the bidder lists on a computer where a data base management system can update your list with minimum fuss. You may wish to notify the bidders on your list that you are accepting bids by using a form similar to the "Notice to Bidders" form that follows.

There is, in some situations, a distinction between informal and formal bidding processes. The informal bidding process frequently involves a matter of phone calls to bidder list vendors, and this process can get down to repeated calls to negotiate the final price. Such arbitration is very effective in many situations, if permitted. The sole proprietorship uses this process to the maximum, as large volume purchasing is not possible. The formal approach necessitates that a bid sheet be developed and distributed to a number of the vendors on the bidder list. Many large programs and institutional settings require that competitive bidding is assured by having a minimum of three bidders. Even in a formal bidding process, it is customary to invoke an informal communication at the end to

Notice to Bidders Form

(For use in advertising)

The board of education of _____ School District

(legal name)

No. _____ of the Town(s) of _____ popularly known as

_____, (in accordance with Section 103 of Article 5-A of the General

Municipal Law) hereby invites the submission of sealed bids on _____

for use in the schools of the district. Bids will be received until _____ on the _____ day

(hour)   (date)

of _____, 19_____, at _____,

(month)   (place of bid opening)

at which time and place all bids will be publicly opened. Specifications and bid form may be

obtained at the same office. The board of education reserves the right to reject all bids. Any

bid submitted will be binding for _____ days subsequent to the date of bid opening.

Board of Education

_____ School District No. _____

of the Town(s) of _____

County(ies) of _____

_____

(Address)

By _____

(Purchasing Agent)

_____

(Date)

Note: The hour should indicate whether it is Eastern Standard or Eastern Daylight Saving Time.

maximize the competition between very close bids. This assures that you receive the very lowest bid, and this brings us to the letting of the bid.

The lowest bidder will usually get the contract to supply the equipment. After all, the competitive process was established to get the lowest price for tightly specified equipment. Often, the lowest bidders will have cut their profit margin in order to get your bid and thus they will be less likely to overwhelm you with follow-up service calls if there is little profit in the offing. This is one reason why service is frequently built into the bidding process. Another factor that influences the selection of the lowest bid is the proximity and past history of the bidders. A local bidder with whom you have had a good relationship over the years might justifiably be selected over an outsider with whom you have never done business. However, exceptions to accepting anything but low bids are rare, and your local vendor should be apprised of his or her being underbid. If you ever get in the habit of buying from one vendor, you can forget competitive bidding. Temper your decisions about letting bids to the low bidder only with good judgment. One last comment regarding the letting of bids is that if everything is equal, you should stay with a standardized equipment line. The more equipment you have from a single manufacturer and/or vendor, the better.

Purchasing the Equipment

The actual purchase of the equipment is relatively straightforward, depending upon your fitness settings. For institutions that must adhere to legal procedures and policies the process becomes more complicated than the simple phone call from the sole proprietor of a local fitness center. In any event, the purchasing process should begin well in advance of the need for the equipment. It should follow a reasonably consistent order of procedures. The procedures listed here are tailored to a medium-sized institutional setting, but they are generally applicable to all settings:

Initiation—A request is made to the manager to fulfill, augment, supplement, or improve the program.

Request review—The manager and/or central office approves or rejects the request after careful consideration of needs and budget.

Budget review—The manager reviews the request and, if approved, assigns a code number to the equipment item in the budget category identified.

Specifications prepared—Detailed specifications are prepared and made available to vendors.

Bid evaluation—Bids are evaluated to assure quality requirements and examination of the lower bids to make recommendations for purchase.

Purchase order development—Purchase orders are developed and sent to the vendor.

Payment—Check is cut and mailed upon delivery and performance of contract.

Payment schedule—General rule is 50% down and 50% on receipt of equipment. Sometimes COD can be arranged. Plan on freight/installation to be added on to cost. Withhold 10% of payment for 30 days to encourage prompt, effective installation.

MAINTAINING HEALTH/FITNESS EQUIPMENT

Once the equipment has been purchased, the endless process of maintenance begins. The stress of 500 to 1,000 users per day on the equipment in a facility is considerable. The life span of equipment parts and materials can be very short if proper maintenance procedures are not employed on a periodic basis.

Internal Maintenance

The day-to-day maintenance of equipment is considered internal maintenance. External maintenance is established through contractual agreements with vendors and professional service companies that maintain exercise equipment in a given service area. The internal maintenance of equipment is extremely important because it limits the amount of external service needed and preempts and/or delays costly breakdowns. Moreover, many of the internal maintenance procedures are also considered cleaning procedures. Cleanliness is imperative in the health/fitness business and cannot be overemphasized. Therefore, internal maintenance must be a highly organized and ongoing process. The following are some guidelines to follow when internally maintaining equipment:

Equipment Frames

Tighten all nuts and bolts.
Use chrome polish on chrome—glass cleaner shows fingerprints.
Use car polish on painted surfaces.
Use fine steel wool to remove rust, then use nonabrasive polish.

Upholstery

Clean daily with upholstery cleaner.
Wipe clean frequently with warm water and mild soap.
Remove pad for repair at the first sign of hairline crack.

Have back-up pads available for high-use equipment.
Wax upholstery on monthly basis with hard floor wax.
Rotate cushions if possible.
Remove chewing gum by careful scraping and wiping with kerosene.
Remove ballpoint ink with rubbing alcohol.
Remove shoe polish or paint with kerosene or turpentine and rinse.

Pulley Systems

Inspect all parts and connections regularly.
Replace damaged pulleys and frayed cables immediately.
Adjust cables and chains regularly for proper tension.
Watch for and correct slack developing in pulley systems.
Wipe chains and cables regularly with oiled cloth.
Don't spray system with oil as it will drip onto floor and soil clothes.

Treadmills

Adjust rear drums to ensure proper belt tracking.
Put dance wax between belt and platform bed periodically.
Lubricate all moving parts regularly, except sealed bearings.
Mount control panel away from railing system if possible, as vibrations are major cause of control panel repairs.
Clean treadmill belt regularly with mild soap and water.
Inspect electrical cords and plugs regularly; replace as needed.
Locate equipment near electrical outlets to avoid injury to members and damage to equipment.

Bicycle Ergometers

Keep gears lightly lubricated.

Replace worn belts and chains as needed.

Clean upholstery and frames daily with mild soap and water.

Wax upholstery periodically with a hard wax.

Polish painted surfaces periodically with car wax.

External Maintenance

The first aspect of external maintenance should be considered before the purchase: Don't buy anything you can't get repaired. If the equipment is mechanical, you should anticipate problems in advance and plan on breakdowns. Pay attention to warranty conditions and durations and the location of the nearest service center. Warranty conditions are calculated by taking the average amount of maintenance-free service for a given product; therefore, service demands should be expected to increase at about the time the warranty period expires. Location of service centers in the immediate area is considered a favorable factor when buying a product or product line.

Another external maintenance consideration is the service contract. In large metropolitan areas, start-up companies are emerging to meet the equipment service needs of the health/fitness profession. Any and all equipment services can be contracted, including many of the internal maintenance procedures identified earlier. The fees vary, depending upon the degree and amount of services required. Typically, a service contract ranges from $100 to $300 per month for a medium-sized club with an average amount of new equipment.

SUMMARY

In this chapter we have provided some guidelines for selecting, purchasing, and maintaining exercise equipment. Each of these considerations is extremely important. The rate of change in the industry is such that an outside consultant may be helpful in the selection process. There are many considerations you must be aware of when purchasing equipment, and bidding procedures almost always prove to be cost-effective. Once the equipment is purchased and installed in your facility, the ongoing process of maintenance begins. Internal maintenance procedures must take place on a day-to-day basis, and external maintenance considerations are equally important. The availability of vendor-endorsed repair service, service contracts for major overhaul, and periodic maintenance are some important things to remember when maintaining exercise equipment. Without good equipment that is well suited to the membership and properly maintained and serviced, a club cannot function effectively.

Staying Well

Part IV is meant to help you launch your program into a mode of operation that will assure long-term success. We present proven techniques of promotional marketing practices along with advertising, public relations techniques, and other marketing principles to help you position your program for success in the marketplace. We outline the day-to-day program operations you need to carry out to successfully maintain and operate a facility that is perceived as pleasing and functional by a service-conscious clientele. We present documentation procedures for maintaining an efficient and effective system for managing paperwork, automated monitoring systems for program management, and methods of evaluating the cost-benefit ratio of corporate programs. For those interested in commercial programs we detail the financial considerations of the business of fitness, including budgeting, financial statements, insurance, and taxes.

Part IV also addresses trends and issues in developing and managing health/fitness facilities and programs. We present project facility trends and discuss the forces acting on the health/fitness profession that can be expected to exact future change. By being prepared, you can make proactive responses to such trends and issues and stay on the leading edge of the industry, rather than having to react in response to changes forced by your competition.

10 Marketing Health/Fitness Facilities, Services, and Programs

Marketing a health/fitness facility requires a well-written plan that very often is the determining factor in the success of the facility, regardless of whether it is a clinical, commercial, community, or corporate setting. The marketing program is an outgrowth of the market analysis section of the business plan, in which existing markets, competitors, and potential new customers are identified. The marketing plan serves as a blueprint of how the target populations will be reached. This also includes the promotional component of the marketing program, which encompasses advertising, public relations, and sales techniques. The purpose of these latter elements is to create an awareness of the services and programs offered at the facility.

All of these components are described in detail in this chapter. Following this, a checklist is presented to help identify the characteristics of a good marketing program. Lastly, a brief summary of the comprehensive marketing program is described. It is then up to you to put the theory into practice and make it work.

THE MARKETING PROGRAM

A good marketing program is based on an understanding of the concept of marketing. Marketing is the exchange of activities (products, services) conducted by individuals and organizations for the purpose of satisfying consumers' needs and achieving marketers' goals and objectives (Assael, 1985; Murphy & Enis, 1985; Reibstein, 1985). The definition simply means that two parties exchange an item voluntarily, and both believe they will benefit from the exchange. Additionally, the exchange must occur through some channel of distribution (marketplace) as a result of a communication (advertising, promotion) process. For example, in a health/fitness club context, where the goal is to sell memberships, the final step in the marketing program is the exchange of the right to use the facility for the price of a membership. This does not include any advertising or promotional efforts that were used to convince the new member to enter the facility and buy the membership, because these actions occurred early on in the marketing process. The same principles and relationships hold true when any vendor, a hospital for example, is trying to convince a customer (corporate client) to purchase health promotion and fitness programs. The marketing process achieves one of its goals when the purchase is made.

The consumer (client, member, employee) views marketing as a vehicle to satisfy personal needs, wants, or desires. The service provider (clinic, club, consultant, or corporation) sees marketing as the means to help the consumer achieve those objectives. The key in this relationship is the ability of the service provider to identify, through analysis and planning techniques, those consumer needs that must be satisfied and then to develop the products or services that will satisfy those needs. Or, if the product (health promotion program or exercise class) is already available, the provider must select an existing market that is in need of the product. In either case, the marketing program begins with an identification of the types of markets the service provider would like to concentrate on in order to sell the services (e.g., exercise classes, stress management, and weight control) of a health/fitness facility.

Preliminary Marketing Questions

The marketing program focuses the operation of the health/fitness facility on its desired goals and objectives. The program defines the services, products, customers, competition, strategies, and tactics that are necessary for success. The best way to create these definitions is first to answer some preliminary questions. If the business plan has already answered these questions, so much the better. However, if this is not the case, the marketing program can be facilitated by the responses to these initial inquiries (Blake & Bly, 1983).

What Is the Nature of My Business?

This question must be clearly answered to determine a path of action. A health/fitness facility is selling a service first, and a product or program second. Identify the type of service, such as memberships or racquetball, or program, such as stress management or weight control, that is being sold and then concentrate on becoming successful in that area.

Where Is the Market Area?

Decide where (geographically), how (physically), and to whom (demographically) the services of the facility will be offered. Will the market concentration be local, county, state, regional, or national? Will these markets be penetrated by an individual, or will a marketing/sales team be developed? For example, a club owner decides to build a facility that will cater to upscale residential and business clients, and that facility will be built in an area that is easily accessible for these types of clients.

Who Are the Customers?

Define and describe the consumer market. Will it be individuals, families, youths, the elderly, executives, line workers, or businesses such as corporations or hospitals? Be specific in identifying client characteristics, as these will determine the marketing approach, price structures, and how services will be provided. Services and programs vary in both content and price if they are provided in a blue-collar environment as opposed to a white-collar setting.

Who Are the Competitors?

Know who the competitors are and what services and programs they provide. Then, evaluate their strengths and weaknesses and specify the advantages of belonging to your facility. Make a comparison chart that is objective and easily readable. The chart not only gives a clearer picture of a competitor's services compared to your own, but also becomes an excellent presentation tool to potential clients. A completed comparison chart is shown in Figure 10.1.

How Will Services Be Distributed?

This answer is very important because you and your customers must know how the services will be delivered. Will all programs be individualized and professionally led or supervised? Can participants supervise their own programs? Will there be testing, counseling, or a referral system? Can people come to the facility and exercise on their own with no screening program or personal exercise prescription? Describe these answers in detail so a clear understanding of what can be expected will exist.

When Should Services Be Distributed? (When Should the Facility Be Opened?)

Enter the marketplace only when all the products and services are ready. Do not enter haphazardly, as poor or untimely provisions of service will hurt the company or the facility. This is becoming more and more evident as numerous health clubs and fitness consulting companies open and close within the same year. This trend also parallels the national statistics for other small businesses. Too many of them open before they are fully prepared to service their clients; then they cannot handle the business properly and they have to close. The quickest road to failure is being unprepared for most, if not all, of the possible eventualities of running a health/fitness business.

What Image Should Be Created for the Facility?

Remember that health and fitness is a service business. Thus, how staff members look, dress, speak, and interact with people will determine what those people think of the facility and its programs and services and

Company	Initiation Fee	Monthly Dues	Medical Supervision	Degreed Instructors	ACSM Certified Instructors	Comprehensive Fitness Evaluations	Personal Exercise Rx	Supervised Workouts	Computerized Training Equipment (Type)
Health Club A	$100	$35	no	1	0	no	no	yes	Lifecycle, Stairmaster
Health Club B	$250	$50	no	5	3	yes	yes	yes	Windracer, Liferower, Stairmaster
Wellness Center	$150	$30	yes	5	5	yes	yes	yes	Stairmaster, Liferower, Treadmills, Biocycle, Lifecycle
Aerobics/Dance-Exercise Studio	$50	$25	no	2	AFAA IDEA	no	no	yes	None

Figure 10.1. Competitors comparison chart

whether they will do business by becoming club members or program participants. Always be friendly, courteous, prompt, and neat and provide follow-up service after the sale. In addition, decide on the appearance of the facility. Will it be luxurious and well maintained, or will it be like an old high school gymnasium? Create the proper image in order to sell the facility properly.

What Are the Financial Requirements?

A marketing program requires financial planning, including start-up costs, operational expenses, advertising and promotion costs, staffing, predicted revenue generation, and cash flow. The success of the facility is often dependent on the financial projections of the marketing plan. It is for this reason that serious consideration must be given to the financial planning aspect of the marketing program. Additionally, funds must be allocated from the total revenue and expense budget to the marketing function. It is wise to use between 10% and 15% of revenue for marketing in a start-up operation and 5% and 10% in mature, ongoing operations. The exact percentages for a preopening situation are much more difficult to specify because there is no available basis for this operation to determine how much money is needed to be spent to attract a specific market share (number of members/program participants).

Once these questions have been satisfactorily answered, at least to the best of the planner's capabilities, it is time to develop the formal marketing plan. It is true that the developmental process can be arduous, but it is the only way to begin and maintain a fitness service business over a long period of time. The following components are recommended for inclusion in the plan, even though a variety of formats may be used when writing the actual plan (Gerson, 1988). Just be sure to include the answers to the preceding questions. A good marketing plan is actually an extension of a good business plan, and marketing strategies, tactics, and techniques will flow from that plan.

Market Analysis

The formal marketing program begins with a market analysis, which determines the critical path the health/fitness facility manager will follow to identify and secure clients, sell and distribute products and services, advertise and promote the facility, and forecast sales goals for the coming year. It is imperative that this analysis be done carefully and thoroughly, because the information provided will often determine success or failure of the business.

The components of a market analysis include the following:

Market Scope

The scope refers to the areas of service, and they may be local, regional, national, or international. Most fitness facilities use a local scope, whereas service providers may expand into a regional marketplace.

Market Distribution

Regardless of the scope, procedures for the distribution of health/fitness services to clients must be specified. Compare your methods of distribution with those currently being used in the industry. Will personal contact be a method of choice, or will direct mail, telephone sales, flyers, audiotapes and videotapes, or individual referrals make up the distribution method for membership and program sales?

Market Segmentation

Market segmentation is the process of dividing the total potential market into more manageable portions. The various methods that can be used to segment a market are discussed in the next section in greater detail. When the market segment has been defined, four questions must be answered before proceeding with any further development:

1. Are there enough prospective clients in the specified market segment to make the penetration worthwhile? In other words, are there enough people in the area who will become members in a club or are there enough employees interested in participating in a company wellness program?
2. Do the potential clients in this market segment recognize their needs and the ability of our facility to satisfy those needs? Do they know that they need to exercise more and lose weight and that we can help them realize and achieve their goals?
3. Do they have the ability to pay for services? Are the prices for the memberships or program participation reasonable for the area in which the services are being provided?
4. Are the people accessible? Can we reach them with our communication efforts (i.e., advertising and promotions)?

Market Demand—Changes and Trends

Many significant changes have occurred in the demand for health/fitness services in the past few years. Some of these were changes in the relative size of the market (dramatically increased), changes in the geographical distribution of the market (as people become more mobile, they still choose to take their health/fitness programs with them), the emergence of new market segments (e.g., children and the young-old), the disappearance of old segments, and the request for new and more advanced services. Furthermore, other trends will lead to future changes (e.g., computerization, water exercises, and programs for the physically challenged), and these must also be identified.

Major Customers

Who are the major customers for these health/fitness services and what are their key characteristics? Identify them clearly. Make a prospective list of potential clients that includes individuals, corporations, industries, and government agencies. It is also a good practice to rank potential clients by the percentage of sales each represents. For example, if individual clients represent 60% of all sales revenue and corporations provide 15% of the revenue, then the primary sales effort should be geared toward individuals rather than companies.

Sales Tactics

Describe the sales methods that will be used to offer the services to consumers. Will they include personal selling of memberships and programs, direct mail, telephone sales, or sales representatives? Will customers receive any special discounts or sales terms for early or full payments, as well as payment by cash or credit? Many clubs offer these kinds of arrangements as part of their membership sales programs. Describe what the normal sales terms will be and then identify any possible variations. These items must be specified in order to develop consistency in pricing and policies.

Price Structures and Policies

Price structures and policies must be established very carefully. The price must be right to help penetrate the market (acquire members), maintain market position (keep current members and attract new ones), and still produce a profit. Pricing memberships, programs, and services correctly can be the single most important reason people choose to do business with a club or a company.

The development of a price structure is usually based on the four Cs:

Consumers—Target market, audience
Costs—Resources, suppliers
Competition—Other facilities' competitive and market positions
Controls—Public and company policies, rules, and regulations

Once prices are formulated along these lines, it is recommended that pricing policies be set strategically. This is accomplished by doing the following:

- Competing on a nonprice basis, while maintaining a profit margin. This means providing more service to the client for every dollar that is spent.
- Pricing competitively if you cannot compete on a nonprice basis. Underpricing is not always the most effective way to get new members or clients. They may view the low price as indicative of a low-quality program. It is very wise, in certain situations, to price higher than the competition, even if they are well established. This provides the new market entrant with a positive value-due-to-high-price image and may attract more customers.
- Charging separately for extras. Provide the basics of a program in the quoted price, but do not give away the store to get new customers.
- Including provisions in the sales contract for price escalations. Just be certain that the new client/member is aware that the

possibility of price increases does exist. No one likes surprises, especially when they cost money.
- Using consumers to establish the price schedule. The market research study should disclose how much consumers would be willing to pay for certain specified health/fitness programs and services. If they will only pay $300 a year to join a facility, charging $600 will definitely not attract the majority of the potential members.

Finally, the payment terms must accurately reflect the price structure and policies. Do not price memberships, programs, or services in a facility so high or so low that the company goes out of business due to poor pricing at either end of the spectrum. One of the best ways to set payment terms is to identify the pricing and payment trends in the health/fitness industry over the last 3-5 years. How does your situation compare with the rise and fall in these industry trends? Also, does your price structure reflect inflationary adjustments? These questions must be answered honestly to create a competitive position.

Distribution Channels

Describe how the health/fitness services will be distributed to clients. For example, will there be a facility for people to join, or will programs be given in-house at company sites? Will facilities be rented on a per-use basis to provide programs and services? What other methods will be used to distribute health/fitness services?

Promotion and Advertising

How will the facility be promoted? Will someone give free speeches and presentations or make public appearances, or will the facility sponsor events? What advertising channels will be used—print, radio, or television? What will be the initial method of client contact—direct mail, trade publications, personal contact, or telephone solicitations? How will the projected and actual costs of the promotion and advertising campaign be determined? Who will pay these costs? Will the old formula using advertising costs as a percentage of sales or revenue be used, or will advertising be viewed as a method to generate sales? If the latter method is used, a predetermined advertising budget is needed that results in a certain amount of revenue.

Major Competitors

Identify major competitors to obtain key information about how to position the facility in the marketplace. What other health/fitness clubs or programs are in the area and are competing for the same dollar? What other personal needs of the clients may be competing for their health/fitness dollar? Determine the strengths, weaknesses, sales techniques, revenues (if possible), growth rate, and the portion of the market share for every competitor. Then, compare these results with the goals set for your facility. Finally, how do your competitors' market shares relate to the total health/fitness industry, and where do you fit in?

Market Share

What is your present or desired market share in the health/fitness industry? What percentage of the industry do you want to own? The following are common definitions of market share:

- A percentage of all service users (e.g., members or employees) for a defined geographic area.
- A percentage of service users from a defined segment of the health/fitness market.

- A percentage of a competitor's defined market segment or geographical area for a selected service or program activity.
- A percentage of all service users on a national basis.

Any one of these definitions can be used to predict market share and market sales. Market sales are the estimated sales, either in units of service or in dollar amounts, to a specific geographical area within a given time frame (Murphy & Enis, 1985). The estimates are based on the number of clients, their acceptance and renewal rates of the health/fitness services, the size of the total market, trends in the health/fitness market, and the competition, be it another club or a service provider.

The estimates are best described as sales forecasts that are presented in graph form. The graphs represent anything from membership revenues, program revenues, and number of memberships sold to number of programs sold, depending on the variable of interest. Figure 10.2 shows how to set up a sales forecast graph, Figure 10.3 shows monthly trends of sales, and Figure 10.4 shows sales forecasts on a yearly basis. These graphs are guides that must be modified according to the specific needs of the clinic, club, community, or corporate setting in the health/fitness industry.

The completion of these forecasts finalizes the market analysis section of the marketing plan. This must now be followed by the strategic analysis of the plan, which describes the strategies, tactics, and techniques for attaining business objectives and goals. It specifies the exact action plans that should be followed to gain a significant market share of the health/fitness industry and to be successful.

Strategic Analysis

Strategic analysis involves the development of goals and objectives and the techniques

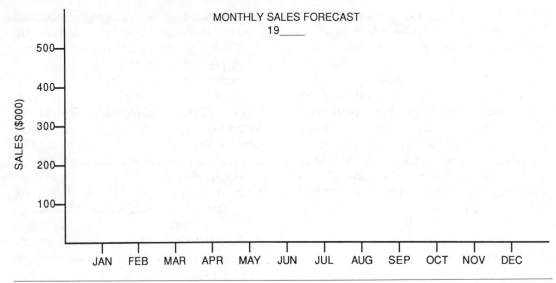

Figure 10.2. Sales forecast worksheet.

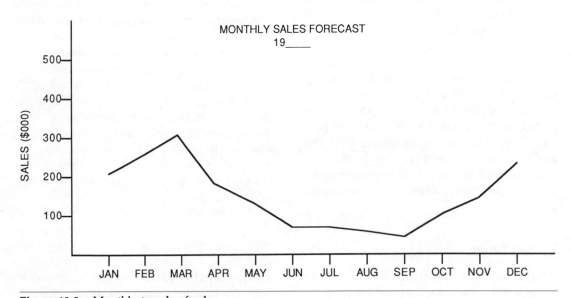

Figure 10.3. Monthly trends of sales.

required to achieve them, the identification of obstacles and pitfalls to avoid, and the determination of strengths upon which to draw. The strategic analysis provides guidelines for success in the health/fitness industry (or any other business). Careful attention must be paid to the action plan so that the desired outcomes are obtained.

√ Goals

Properly describe both long- and short-term goals. These should be specific, set within a certain time frame, and achievable through the strategies identified in the business plan. Therefore, goals must be objectively determined rather than being subjective or un-

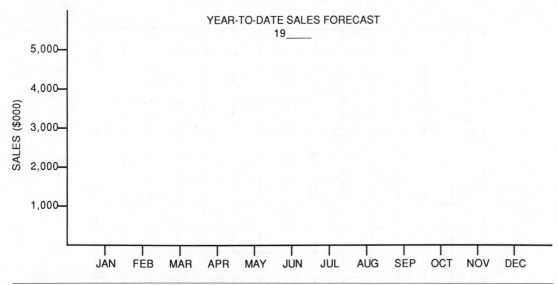

Figure 10.4. Sales forecast on a yearly basis.

realistic dreams and wishes. An example of a properly stated goal would be for a corporate fitness center to have 50% of its employees participating in its programs within 1 year of its opening.

Key Performance Indicators

These are the indicators, both financial and nonfinancial, that will be used to track the facility's performance toward its stated goals. Some of these indicators include sales revenue (either memberships sold or programs sold), profitability, advertising and promotion costs, number of employees required to provide the services, and the staff-to-client ratio. The smaller this ratio, the better, but most programs cannot be cost-effective by being labor intensive.

Project Completion Schedule

This chart represents the milestones that must be achieved, their deadlines for achievement, and who, if anyone, is responsible for completion of each project (Gerson, 1988). This schedule demonstrates the company's ability to plan systematically for goal attainment, minimize the risks involved by clearly defining each project, and reach its objectives in an organized fashion. The chart on p. 246 provides a blank "Project Completion Schedule," which is completed by filling in the project column and marking off the completion dates for each activity. This form is very similar to the one presented in chapter 5 on facility design, but serves a slightly different purpose.

Operating Assumptions

These are the expected external conditions under which the health/fitness facility or programs will operate. The conditions that are most important to the health/fitness industry must be identified, along with the trends that will occur during the time frame covered by the business and marketing plan. As a guide, operating assumptions can be categorized as economical (overall growth, inflation price trends, service costs), industrial (growth

Project Completion Schedule

Project	Jan.	Feb.	Mar.	Apr.	May	Jun.	Jul.	Aug.	Sep.	Oct.	Nov.	Dec.	Jan.	Feb.	Mar.	Apr.	May	Jun.	Jul.	Aug.	Sep.	Oct.	Nov.	Dec.

rates, new products and services, changes in distribution patterns, changes in consumer behavior, changes in the behavior of competitors), and influential (regulatory agencies, product suppliers). Other assumptions that are relevant to the health/fitness industry, such as price schedules, new ideas, or new training procedures, should also be specified.

√ Strategic Opportunities

These are situations that must be exploited and used to the facility's benefit. The strengths and weaknesses have already been identified, as were the market opportunities and risks. Now, the direction the company must move in and the outcomes it hopes to achieve must be specified. The marketing thrust is supported by the business strategies, so all the opportunities must be reviewed to develop appropriate tactics.

√ Strategic Obstacles

Certain problems exist that cannot be resolved within the lifetime of the plan. These must be identified so that they can be resolved later, either by the company or with outside help. Whatever is done, do not forget about these obstacles because they will not go away. Eventually, action must be taken to overcome all obstacles. A good example of an obstacle everyone encounters is a steadily dwindling budget. It takes a good manager to make a facility or programs work as the available funds decrease.

The strategic analysis must be geared to the chosen market segment—those customers who are most likely to join a facility, participate in a program, or purchase other services. Although it may be beneficial to devise a generalized strategic action plan (Kizer, 1987), it will be more profitable to develop strategies and tactics that are unique to each chosen

market segment (Gerson, 1988; McCaffrey, 1983; *Optimal Health*, 1987b). This does require some extra effort, but the long-term benefits far outweigh the initial energy expenditure.

√ Market Segments

Market segments refer to portions of the total market that are categorized according to a similar characteristic or series of traits. The segments are usually broken down into eight categories. Each one allows the advertising and sales program to be geared toward a specific objective, making it more effective. Sometimes each market segment requires its own individual marketing approach or differentiation of services. In other instances, however, the program must reach a combination of markets, and therefore several objectives, simultaneously. This can prove very difficult at times for anyone in the health/fitness industry. The best way to prevent unnecessary problems such as overextending the company's resources is to focus on one characteristic of a market. Then there will be a better match between the target market and the services provided.

The following are characteristics that are used to identify types of markets:

- *Size*—The size of the health/fitness market is based on either the total volume of dollar sales (billions) or the number of potential consumers (millions). The market can be broken down into smaller, more manageable groups by considering the geographical location of the service thrust. In a club setting, this refers to the membership radius, which is usually no more than 10 or 15 miles from the site. In a corporate fitness setting, this refers to those employees who should be reached by a specific aspect of the program.

- *Geographic location*—Consumers reside in a local, county, state, regional, or national marketplace. Programs must be determined according to the geographic location of consumers. It is usually best to start small, as with marketing the health/fitness facility to local businesses, and then expand to other areas.
- *Demographics*—Potential clients can be identified by age, sex, race, income, education, marital status, religion, occupation, or leisure behaviors. These constitute some of the demographic characteristics that must be considered when targeting a market for fitness services. They cannot be neglected when developing the marketing plan because the demographics of a market will influence the purchasing behaviors. A fitness club in a blue-collar neighborhood cannot charge the same $1,000 a year for memberships as a city club would charge. The demographics just would not support the club or the pricing schedule.
- *Sociopsychological needs (Psychographics)*—It is possible, and often desirable, to develop and sell a program or service according to the emotional aspects of the consumer. What are the needs, wants, and desires that can be satisfied through these programs or services and that will entice the customer to join the health/fitness facility or purchase available programs?
- *Purchaser/user characteristics*—Be careful to identify the characteristics of both the purchaser and the user of services. They may not be the same person, as would be the case if a company contracted with an outside agency to provide employee fitness classes. Get to know the purchaser, the user, and how to best satisfy what each needs and wants.
- *Purchaser influences*—People, places, and things influence an individual in his or her purchase of health/fitness services. Identify what or who these influences are and direct the marketing and sales approach accordingly.
- *Service usage*—Determine whether clients can use the services at the times they are offered or whether the schedule must be arranged to accommodate the user. Is the providing facility capable of adapting its schedule for services to that of the client, or is there no flexibility? When answering these questions, be aware that convenience and flexibility of scheduling could be a major reason for a customer to purchase health/fitness services. Any type of facility that provides exercise classes, either to the public, private members, or employees, must be able to offer these classes at convenient times for the participants. Participants will prefer to exercise somewhere else, even if it is not all that convenient, rather than change their schedule to accommodate the closest facility.
- *How purchased*—Health/fitness services are purchased either on impulse, as when someone joins a local health club, or with tremendous analysis and forethought, as when a company purchases health/fitness services and programs. In both instances, cost is often the deciding factor. Keep this in mind during the development of products and in the determination of program price structures. Health/fitness services must be priced competitively, not at an extreme, because most purchasers are influenced by their available income. For example, a stress management program that is geared to blue-collar workers cannot be sold for the same price as one geared toward executives, especially if the participants must pay for the program themselves. Anyone who prices programs must be aware of who is paying for them—the company or the individual.

These characteristics help determine individual market types, but they are never truly separate. There is an interrelationship among all eight that becomes increasingly evident during further analysis and more definitive market segmentation. Although it was previously stated that some health/fitness providers, especially newcomers, have difficulty developing and offering programs to satisfy two, three, or four market segments simultaneously, these capabilities must eventually be developed in order to succeed. It is very rare that a market segment can be defined simply according to size, without influence from geography or how services are purchased and used. There will always be other characteristics that impact upon a chosen market segment. Health/fitness service providers must also consider other competing factors for the consumer's dollar, such as cars, houses, clothes, and so forth. These factors are often overlooked when segmenting a market according to possible influences on the purchaser. This is but one example, but it clearly illustrates the need to identify *all* appropriate influences on the market segment that must be accounted for in health/fitness marketing plans.

Marketing Services

Once the target markets have been determined, the exact population to be serviced must be selected. The target population consists of a homogeneous group of consumers who possess similar characteristics and wish to purchase fitness services. Such characteristics may include businesses and corporations with under 50 employees, over 100 employees, over $1 million dollars in revenue, or any other set of distinguishing qualities. Regardless of the choice of potential consumers, the only way to establish and enhance a position in the industry is to be able to provide the health/fitness services that the target market wants.

Three possible services can be provided: activity, facilities, and consultation. Activity refers to providing a company or an organization with exercise classes and health promotion programs. Sometimes the provider chooses the classes, programs, and their presentation times, whereas in other instances, the client dictates exactly what is to be done. In either case, the satisfaction of the participants determines whether the contract is maintained and/or renewed. Therefore, make the classes and programs interesting, fun, and at a level the participants can handle readily. The same principles apply if the activity is a health promotion class such as weight control or stress management.

The second provider service is a facility. Many YMCAs and health clubs work in conjunction with businesses to offer facilities and exercise equipment to corporate employees. It would be ideal always to have a facility to offer to clients. Unfortunately, this is usually not the case. If a facility is not directly available, then the health/fitness provider must work as a liaison between a facility and a client to bring them together.

The third approach to providing fitness services to the target market is to be a consultant. Consultants operate in many areas, including facility design, program development, staff development, training, and club management. Decide on your area(s) of expertise and pursue that path as a consultant. There are several good resources available on how to develop a consulting business (Connor & Davidson, 1985; Johnson, 1982). They all recommend one basic tenet: Do not spread yourself too thin with too many jobs, especially if they force you to overstep the boundaries of your capabilities. People will pay for information and knowledge only if they believe they cannot get it anywhere else, especially from inside their company. They will also pay if they believe your information is superior to another consultant's in helping them satisfy a need and achieve their goals. Your consulting efforts must be directed toward these ends. A good idea, especially for a new consultant, is to specialize in one area of health/fitness services that coincides with the needs of the target market.

For example, if you have decided to consult as an exercise program developer, and you have chosen health care (hospital) centers as the target markets, you may want to specialize in developing exercise programs for the elderly. This is a new market, and one that is virtually untapped. Geriatric exercise programs would definitely satisfy the needs of the elderly and the health care center that is contracting the services. Additionally, a niche for your fitness services will also have been created within a specific target market.

Marketing Mix

The next step in the marketing program is to increase the size of that niche. This is done through the development of the marketing mix. The marketing mix consists of the four Ps of marketing: product (or service), price, place (distribution channel), and promotion. The product is the health/fitness program that has the potential to satisfy specific needs of the consumer. The price is the value of the service that is agreed upon between the client and the provider during the exchange process. The place refers to the facility where the exchange occurs. In a more technical sense, the place is the distribution channel through which the health/fitness services flow from provider to consumer. Last, promotion consists of the communications that inform consumers of the existence of products and services and their need-satisfying capabilities.

The four Ps of the marketing mix process are completely synergistic, with the total effect being greater than the sum of the individual parts (Assael, 1985; Murphy & Enis, 1985; Reibstein, 1985). No one component can ever truly stand alone. This is emphasized very well, with specific reference to health promotion and fitness, by Opatz (1985) and Chenoweth (1987). Also, everything in the marketing mix focuses on consumers and positioning the product to satisfy their needs (Pfeiffer, 1986). Thus the major purpose of marketing is to satisfy the consumer, whereas the primary purpose of selling is to satisfy the seller. Therefore, all four facets of the marketing mix must be considered in the development of marketing strategies so that sales will naturally follow. The simplest marketing strategy to increase sales is to identify the target population, identify its need, and then fulfill it (marketing mix). The following example should serve as a guideline.

The *product* is the service of providing an aerobic exercise class. This service has been targeted to local corporations with 25-50 employees. The class will be offered two times per week for an hour each time. You must now determine the *price*. First, be aware of what your competitors are doing. Then, decide if a guaranteed flat rate per class or a per-person fee for each class would be better for you. Next, determine the payment policy. Will the company or the individual participants pay in full by cash or check, or will they receive an extended line of credit? Once everything is amenable to both parties, the payment terms can be agreed upon. Next, you have to provide a *place* for the activity to occur. Do you have your own center, will you lease space, or does the client have space? The place for service provision is essential because it is the only way the product can be delivered.

Last, but certainly not least, is the *promotion* of the service or program. How will the potential client be informed that you offer these employee fitness classes? Are you going to advertise, have sales representatives call, or do personal selling? You must determine how contact with clients will be made and maintained so that the sales process can be completed.

This example gives a brief overview of the proper development of a marketing mix and marketing strategy. A listing of a variety of other marketing techniques and strategies is provided in Table 10.1. There are times when extensive planning in these areas will prove very beneficial. However, there are also times when too much analysis will lead to paralysis. Do not become so bogged down in the technicalities of the planning process that you neglect to act. Situations may arise when the program or service offering must be decided upon quickly, be developed as a quality product in a short period of time, be offered to clients, have a price agreed upon, and be provided and then adapted when necessary. The action orientation at times leads to the development of a better marketing mix and strategy than a long, drawn out planning process. The motto of "Do it, try it, fix it" works well in certain situations. In either case, the marketing strategy must be put into action. The methods to do this are advertising, public relations, and product sales.

BASIC PROMOTIONAL TECHNIQUES

The marketing plan has now been completed. It is time to go out and actively market the fitness services. The four basic techniques are advertising, public relations, personal selling,

Table 10.1 Marketing Techniques

1. Marketing audit.
   - Analyze competition, distributors, suppliers, customers
   - Develop objectives for the company
   - Determine available strategies to meet the objectives
   - List the tools management will need to reach those objectives
2. Identify where the marketing authority is placed within the organization.
3. Creative versus traditional notions—try the creative approach.
4. Work out a plan of attack as if you were a chief competitor trying to destroy your company. Identify the strengths, isolate and use the weaknesses.
5. Use reprints of your work as distribution material.
6. If you sell a product, try to get the dealer/manufacturer to work with you on your marketing program.
7. Meet the public. Be visible. Tell them about your products and services but do not use overkill. Never tell them more than they want to know, and never promise more than you can deliver.
8. Test-market your product, program, or service.
   - Test it internally
   - Determine its reliability
   - Budget expenses and distribution costs so test results can be checked against targets
   - Establish clear goals and basic rules for the test
   - Prepare for reactions from your competitors
   - Never sell the product for your competitor— sell yourself first
9. Make sure the market position assumed for your product, program, or service is the correct one.
10. Include a new product in your budget and long-range planning only after it has been properly tested.

and sales promotions. Each technique offers several approaches to achieving company goals (*Optimal Health*, 1986). Choose the one best suited to the health/fitness services being offered.

Advertising

Advertising is a form of publicity defined as the paid presentation of information about a health/fitness company's services in an impersonal way—there is no direct person-to-person contact. Advertising is usually done through newspapers, radio, television, magazines, fliers, forms, brochures, direct mail pieces, and displays. All of these methods present the message, but there is no way to measure their impact or effect. For example, let's assume that a health/fitness company decides to use newspaper advertising as well as to mail company brochures to potential clients. Even if the health/fitness company were to ask each respondent to identify what caused him or her to call or write for more information, the newspaper ad or the brochure, the company still cannot accurately determine the impact of that particular brand of advertising. This is because it is impossible to control all the extraneous variables that may have also influenced the client's decision to obtain more information.

The advertising of a health/fitness facility can be direct-action oriented or indirect-action oriented. Direct-action advertising encourages the consumer to take immediate advantage of offered services. This is seen in ads with statements such as "Call now" or in letters inviting people to call or to respond by return mail. Direct-action advertising is also used in club membership sales when the membership drive is in its final days of offering a given discount.

Indirect-action advertising creates a long-range awareness about health/fitness services

and, you hope, long-range demand. This type of advertising informs potential consumers that your services are available if they are interested in pursuing them. For example, if you have a corporate exercise program developed and ready for implementation, you may want to advertise it indirectly by teaching specialized aerobic classes. This tells potential clients that their company employees can be mainstreamed into the program whenever they are ready. Another example is for the health/fitness company to display maintenance ads in some form of advertising medium. Maintenance ads are ongoing advertisements whose primary purpose is to keep the public informed about the existence of the company and the services it has to offer. Remember, though, that it is more important for the advertising program to be effective rather than slick, because slick ads do not always guarantee success (*Optimal Health*, 1987a).

Quite often, the format of the advertising program is determined by its cost. Expenses for print vary from those for radio, and both differ from those for television. The format chosen must be within the company budget. It is recommended that health/fitness providers concentrate on print advertising. It is usually less expensive than the other two, and there are more available options. Newspapers, magazines, fliers, brochures, and letters are all forms of print advertising. Each has its own associated costs. Whichever is chosen, health/fitness facilities can be marketed to a specific, and possibly more qualified, audience through print than through radio or television.

The choice of the advertising medium and the total advertising program is also influenced by company objectives and the consumer market. What sales goals must be achieved? How many consumers must be contacted to reach the sales goals? How many memberships must be sold for the club to break even or make a profit? How many contractual health promotion programs must the hospital provide to local corporations to justify the existence of its health promotion department? Finally, what method of advertising will best inform clients of your facility and its services?

Cost can be a major influencing factor in the determination of the advertising campaign, but it should never be the sole overriding factor. Company objectives and consumer target markets must always be considered when choosing the advertising medium and program. Even though print will most often be the method of choice, the beneficial effects of radio and television and the size of the audience they can reach cannot be negated. Sometimes, it is wise to use less print and supplement that with a radio spot. In any case, choose advertising placements carefully so the facility can inform the appropriate public of its services.

The following list of advertising techniques should prove helpful to anyone involved in a health/fitness business.

- Position your product so the consumer identifies it with a name.
- Budget advertising according to how much is necessary to reach a sales objective. Do not use percentage of sales—advertising is supposed to produce sales, not vice versa.
- Present consumers with your competitor's ads first and listen to their opinions. You will learn about the strengths and weaknesses of your own product.
- Begin the headline with "Which . . . ?" (It is almost impossible to write a bad headline beginning with "which.")
- Put the information you are trying to convey in the headline. Then, write the rest of the ad so it is closely tied to the headline.

- Write ads so they are directed toward your major customers, then close the ad with a phrase or a slogan they will remember.
- Keep print size for ads down and supplement with a radio spot to expand your audience.
- Tell people what they want to hear, but use moderation in making any claims about your product.
- Be ready to change your ads as the audience or the media tool changes.
- Evaluate your advertising program periodically. Advertising should be thought of as a campaign, a series of ads, not just a one-time occurrence. Redesign or even discard your current campaign based on results (i.e., product sales).

The advertising program should serve another purpose in addition to informing consumers of available health/fitness services. The campaign should also help to cultivate and promote a positive company image. The creation of the image, the subsequent promotion of it beyond advertising, and the maintenance of that image are known as public relations.

Public Relations

Public relations is as important as advertising in creating consumer awareness of a health/fitness facility. In fact, many people confuse public relations with advertising, but they are two distinct techniques. Advertising is the use of media that is paid for by someone, whereas public relations is not paid for in measured dollars. Public relations does cost, however, in terms of personnel wages, planning time, and program development. There are also costs for supplies, travel, and other business-related expenses. The key is to realize that, although it is imperative to try to acquire free publicity, the public relations program must be included in the company budget in terms of time and money.

The public relations program must coincide with the company's objectives. The image that was decided upon before the basic marketing plan was completed is partially created through the advertising campaign; however, the greater portion of it comes from publicity. This publicity leads to either a positive or a negative image. Somebody once said that any kind of publicity, whether good or bad, is beneficial because the consumer at least remembers the company's name. Do not adhere to this philosophy. Always try to be viewed in the best possible light by potential clients.

There are several ways to create a positive public image. Whereas the advertising program concentrates on demographics and statistical data for the purchase of media time and space, the public relations campaign focuses on editors, publishers, reporters, station managers, and news commentators. Thus public relations can also be viewed as community relations. Get to know all the people in the community who can possibly help your health/fitness business and develop a healthy relationship with them. Telephone them personally, mail them letters and brochures, set up business meetings, or arrange to meet them at social and athletic events. Then, when there is something important to say, or something that your company can or will do, these people can be contacted. They, in turn, will inform the public through their respective channels.

Here is an example. Your company wants to make contact with some local businesses to provide them with employee exercise programs. However, it is not feasible to visit each potential client and teach an exercise class. Therefore, your facility volunteers its services in the form of an exercise demonstration for a local, well-known charity. The charity and the event will probably get media coverage, and you can personally contact and invite

other prospective clients. This gives everyone involved a very positive image of your organization as one that is charitable, community minded, and service oriented. Not only that, but there will be numerous other potential clients who will see, hear, or read about the demonstration and the services you can offer either at your facility or at a corporate site.

There are also other methods that can be used to create a positive public image and gain free publicity, such as a calendar of events in the newspaper, public service announcements (PSA) on radio and television, and news releases to local media. There are still more techniques that can be used, but these require the assistance of an outside public relations firm. The methods that have been mentioned are sufficient to provide the publicity needed to develop a name in the field and in the community.

Networking is one other method of public relations to strongly consider. Get out and meet as many people as possible. Go to professional meetings and conventions. Attend chamber of commerce meetings. Be seen by people and see people. Give them your business card. Telephone them just to say hello and keep in touch. It doesn't matter whether these people are potential clients, because they know two friends who know two friends, and somewhere down the line, a client will develop. That client may come from a very unexpected source, but the only way for this to happen is to keep all networking channels open. Word-of-mouth publicity is often more beneficial and creates more clients for a facility than all the advertising and deliberate public relations efforts combined. This fact is borne out by the statistic that most health clubs receive 70%-75% of their new members through internal member referrals. This type of publicity (public or community relations) could never be purchased, nor could a price value be placed on it.

Remember that advertising and public relations, no matter what their nature, are two different methods for achieving similar goals: to build a good company image and to promote business through increased sales. The value of a good advertising and public relations program is seen in the results. These include reduced selling costs with expanded sales efforts, increased consumer awareness about health/fitness services, establishment of your company as the prime source for health/fitness services, establishment of community goodwill, a respected reputation, stimulation of customer inquiries and prospective buyers for your services, and development of an ever-expanding client list. The only way to achieve these results is to use advertising and public relations techniques properly to keep the facility's name and image constantly in front of the consumer.

One final point must always be considered. Advertising and public relations are somewhat mechanical, impersonal means of informing people of the availability of your fitness services. It is up to you and the people of your organization to maintain and build upon whatever business the campaigns have created. The best way to do this is to provide excellent service to customers. Always put them first, and the word will get around that yours is a customer-oriented health/fitness company. This improves the company image dramatically and brings many more clients. After all, a positive image and a good reputation are the greatest assets any company can have when dealing with customers; and customer service creates that image and reputation better than anything else. The following list summarizes 10 ways to build that desired image and reputation.

1. Newspapers: display and classified sections
2. Magazines: general consumer, trade, association, local, and society publications
3. Telephone directories: yellow pages, specialty directories
4. Direct mail: letters, cards, leaflets, catalogs
5. Radio and television: live or prerecorded messages
6. Outdoor displays: billboards, posters, signs, car cards, handbills
7. Specialty items: calendars, pens, pencils, key chains, and other premiums or remembrance items
8. Exhibits and shows: regional and national trade shows, local civic exhibits, airport terminal displays, traveling road shows
9. Participation by articulate people as speakers at business or technical conferences or as panel members at seminars
10. Networking

THE SALES PROCESS

Everything that has been done up to this point—the business plan, marketing program, and advertising and public relations campaigns—has prepared you to offer health/fitness services to customers. Now those services must be sold. This can be the most difficult part of the entire marketing process. However, it is as important, and perhaps more vital, than anything that has come before.

There are two approaches to selling a health/fitness facility. The first is personal sales, through which you or a company representative makes contact with potential clients. The second is sales promotions, which involve a number of techniques to acquaint people with available services. Each is discussed in some detail.

Personal Sales

Personal selling involves making contact with prospective customers through direct mail, such as a letter, brochure, or flier. A letter is preferable, and it should be addressed to a specific person, usually the personnel director, president, or owner. Call this person by name rather than title. It is very easy to find out the name of this person. Simply telephone the company, ask who would receive the information to be sent, and then write a letter to that person. You should only send a form (generic) letter if you cannot send a personal letter. Whatever is done, though, make sure the letter (material) introduces you, the facility, and your services. This direct mail technique will pave the way for a future telephone sales approach.

All correspondence should be followed with a telephone call to the contact person. Although it is possible to make contacts and even sales through cold calls, it is much better to introduce yourself by mail first. Then, when you do call, the person has an idea of who you are and what you are trying to sell. You should also refresh his or her memory very quickly at the beginning of the conversation:

"Hello Mr./Ms. _____. I am _____ from the XYZ Fitness Company. I sent you a letter describing the health/fitness services we can offer you and your employees. I would like to discuss this with you further."

The conversation can go from there. Either you will continue talking about the services, or you will schedule an appointment to make a formal presentation. There is also the possibility that the client is not interested at this time. If this happens, thank the contact person, keep the information on file, and send another letter in 3-6 months. Things change rapidly, and you have to remind people that the services are still available.

Let us take a more positive approach and assume that an appointment is scheduled. Be very professional in your appearance, approach, and presentation. Remember, you are the product packaging. During the interview, try to get the contact person to talk about himself or herself and his or her needs, then gear the presentation toward satisfying those needs. Keep the presentation short, no longer than 15 minutes; otherwise, you will lose your audience. Sell the services and benefits, which are continuous, rather than just the programs, products, or features, which are finite. This enhances the possibility of making the sale.

It is rare that a contract to provide fitness services is signed after the initial presentation. More often than not, clients will want some time to think about the material (make sure you give them something) and compare your offer of services and prices with other providers. This is a natural course of events, and it may take weeks, even months, before a response is forthcoming. You must be patient. However, immediately follow up the interview with a thank-you letter that reminds him or her about hour services and summarizes how you can help the client.

There will be times when no word is received from a client to whom a presentation has been made. Feel free to contact that person by telephone to ask about the status of the offer; be prepared for a yes, no, maybe, or a request for another presentation. Sometimes presentations must be made two or three times to make the sale. However, unless you receive a definite no and the person is not at all interested, persistence usually results in a sale. It is also possible that this contact will lead to a network of other potential clients. Whether it is a referred client or new client, the entire procedure must be followed again. It takes time and effort to sell health/fitness services, but the outcomes are usually worthwhile.

One other method of personal selling is public speaking. If you speak to clubs, business and professional organizations, chambers of commerce, charities, and social groups, the possibility of meeting new clients and making more sales is increased. It is not always necessary to get paid for these speeches, especially when you are just beginning in the health/fitness industry. The opportunity to distribute business cards and other information to a captive audience is often more than adequate compensation for giving a speech. In fact, this method has been used very successfully by many facility managers to generate new memberships for their clubs.

Sales Promotions

Once several sales have been made and a client base has been established, it may be time to engage in sales promotions. Sales promotions are sometimes used by beginning companies to develop clientele, but the promotions can be costly in terms of time, money, and image. Although the promotions usually work, new companies run the risk of creating a cheaper product/service image in the minds of the public. The key factors in preventing this negative impact are the nature of the promotion and how it is presented to the public.

Several types of sales promotions can be used when marketing health/fitness services and facilities, including free samples of services, such as a complimentary exercise class or health promotion lecture; discounts on prices for the services or club memberships; contests; and giveaways, such as a free exercise class. The sales promotion techniques are designed to increase future business. They can be used in the advertising campaign, in conjunction with any of the personal selling methods, or as individual public awareness campaigns. The manner in which they are used depends on the goals to be achieved, such as the total number and types of sales that are desired.

Closing the Sale

Selling health/fitness services is not complete unless the sale is actually closed. This means that all the terms of the sale have been agreed upon, there is a written contract or letter of agreement stipulating all the features of the sale and the responsibilities of all parties involved, and this contract is signed by both parties. Closing the sale involves four basic steps:

1. Determining a delivery plan for the fitness services
2. Developing the contract including obligations of each party
3. Developing a schedule for the payment of services
4. Delivering the services

When these steps have been completed, a client has been secured.

After the fitness services have been agreed upon, it is up to the provider and the client to develop a delivery plan for those services. The plan must be applicable to exercise classes, health promotion programs, evaluations, screening, and any other type of service to be provided. There should be both a written and a graphic representation of the plan that includes specific service delivery dates. The project completion schedule, which was described earlier, can be used here to map out the delivery plan. Try to adhere to the dates as closely as possible, because prompt service results in returning clients and contract renewals.

When all parties involved have agreed on the delivery dates for fitness services, a written contract or letter of agreement is signed. The contract details everything that will be provided in the way of fitness services. The contract also details the client's obligations. These written statements can be drawn up in a simple letter of intent or a more formal legal agreement. However the contract is written, make sure everything is specified, including the payment terms.

The contract must be explicit about the method and terms of payment. If payment is to be monthly, state that in the contract. The client will pay according to the terms of the contract. Be aware, though, that the client may want to negotiate the payment terms before signing the contract. Be flexible during the negotiations and the contract signing. Do not sell yourself short or provide the services at an inexpensive price. You should receive appropriate payment for the services in a time frame that is acceptable to both parties. It is not wise to lose a sale because of a few dollars' difference either way, nor is it wise to give the facility or services away to secure the contract. The important thing is to sign a contract with which both parties are comfortable and whose terms can be met.

It may appear that the sale is closed once the contract is signed; however, that is not completely true. The services must now be delivered as promised. Remember that the product is you, your services, and your programs. A defective product cannot be exchanged for a new one. Therefore, everything must be done right the first time. Memberships can be dropped and usage rates can decline if service is poor in a club setting. This affects the signing of a subsequent or renewal contract. Treat the clients properly, and they will treat you the same way. Furthermore, they will probably refer new clients, especially if they are happy with the programs and services that were provided.

Providing Long-Term Service

Signing a contract means a service account has been acquired. The provision of health/fitness programs and services to this client determines contract renewals and new customer referrals. It also helps create a public awareness for your company, which is the key to any marketing program. Often the client's view of you, your company or facility, and the manner in which services are provided are the deciding factors in his or her signing a contract.

You can facilitate this decision by making sure the service provisions are continuous during the term of the contract. The following are strategies that may help in the delivery of these services:

- Develop a program that is hard for others to imitate
- Achieve the lowest cost position relative to competition
- Differentiate services from competition by market segment
- Develop a dedicated staff
- Develop innovative services
- Enhance value-added services
- Broaden the market base through service proliferation
- Specialize within a given market segment
- Package and present services according to the market segment
- Provide customer-oriented services

These service-delivery strategies are quite generic, and they would probably apply to any business. That makes them all the more effective for the health/fitness industry. In addition to these operations strategies, the company must possess the resources to provide long-term services, assuming several contract renewals or extensions. Nothing can hurt an image more than inability to provide continuous and long-term service to a client.

SUMMARY

This chapter has reviewed some of the methods necessary to market health/fitness facilities, programs, and services. There are eight preliminary questions that must be answered prior to developing and writing the actual marketing plan. Once these questions have been answered to your satisfaction, they should be used as the basis for a more in-depth analysis of the marketing program. The marketing program consists of several activities that precede implementation of the plan and several that serve as the active part of the plan. The precursors include a market analysis, a strategic analysis, the identification of market segments according to specified criteria, the identification of particular health/fitness services that will be offered to selected market segments, and the development of the market mix. The market mix contains the product or service you are going to provide, its price structures, how it will be distributed to consumers, and the types of promotions that will be used to cause consumers to make a purchase.

The market mix is the key to an effective marketing program, but it must be activated through a variety of promotional techniques. These include advertising, either through print or electronic media, public relations, personal sales, and sales promotions, which usually refer to discount programs or giveaways (e.g., 2 years for the price of 1 in a health club membership). When these activities motivate a customer to buy your health/fitness service or program, then you must be able to provide long-term and follow-up service. Quite often, the treatment someone receives after making a purchase determines whether or not he or she will make another purchase from you in the future. This is best exemplified with health club memberships. If someone joins your facility and then receives little or no attention from the staff, there is a very good chance he or she will not renew his or her membership. However, if the staff is attentive and caring, the person will feel special and will probably not only renew, but bring a few friends in to join as well.

This overview of marketing health/fitness facilities, programs, and services is meant as a guide. More extensive treatment of the methods for developing and implementing a marketing program is provided in *Marketing Health/Fitness Services* (Gerson, 1989). An important point to remember is that marketing is a relatively new field as it relates to the fitness industry. Do not be afraid to seek help from your colleagues who have more experience or ask for assistance from professional marketers in other fields, and apply their knowledge and teachings to your business. It is really not as difficult as it first may appear, because all professionals in the health/fitness industry are really marketing themselves or their services all the time.

11 Day-to-Day Operations

The management of a health/fitness facility has evolved into a highly complex and demanding position. The days when a fitness director or a club owner needed only to open the doors and allow members to use the facility are gone. Today's fitness managers are no different from managers of any business; they must have the ability to plan and organize, establish policies and procedures, and stand up and support their policies. The success of any health/fitness facility is directly proportional to how well the day-to-day operational activities are organized and managed.

This chapter discusses the operational areas considered essential to any health/fitness endeavor. The general focus is a generic setting, encompassing operational issues that can be adapted to a commercial, corporate, clinical, or community setting. Specifically, the chapter discusses the following topics:

- Policies and procedures
- Business office management
- Maintenance management
- Swimming pool/whirlpool maintenance
- Safety procedures
- Pro shop operations
- Massage
- Nursery
- Locker desk procedures
- Food and beverage services

A recent study of reasons people join health clubs (Game Plan, Inc., 1985) discovered that individuals who belong to health/fitness facilities are more educated, have higher incomes, and are younger than the national average. They are more demanding when choosing a fitness center and have a higher awareness of the importance of physical fitness. This study concluded that the biggest reason members decide to leave a facility is the club's management and atmosphere. If members viewed a facility as being mismanaged and not providing an atmosphere conducive to exercise, then over 90% of them considered not renewing their memberships.

This study underlines the fact that the daily operations of a health/fitness facility must be well organized not only for management, but for members as well. You must give careful thought to the development of every policy and procedure while never forgetting to provide the kind of personal service that consumers are looking for in their health/fitness pursuits.

POLICIES AND PROCEDURES

Management priorities of health/fitness facilities vary from setting to setting. In a commercial facility, where the for-profit aspect plays such an important role, sales, membership quotas, and membership marketing are the key issues. As in any business, the bottom line is the success or failure indicator. In a corporate or community setting, where the corporation or federal government financially subsidizes these facilities, program justification is the most closely monitored area. The emphasis is placed on documenting participant results through exercise record logs, periodic fitness assessments, and activity programming. Management evaluates the continued efforts to show the cost-effectiveness, cost benefits, and participant support of the program.

These differences in management priorities play a significant role when initial policies and procedures are established. The overall management structure, financial goals, and program justification are prioritized according to each program's setting. Each setting is evaluated according to the initial facility concept, short- and long-term goals, and overall objectives before determining the degree of importance placed on all policies and procedures. For example, a commercial facility that is open 18 hours a day, accommodates both children and adults, and provides a wide range of activity programs needs more specific and comprehensive policies than a small in-house corporate facility.

House Rules

During the early stages of organizing a facility, management establishes a governing set of rules and policies, or house rules, which are prepared in writing for the members' use. The house rules state management's policies on a variety of operational topics and are used primarily as a guide to answer new members' questions, while providing a uniform and consistent approach to each policy.

The problems associated with house rules are not in their preparation, but in their actual enforcement. Occasionally, participants will disagree with the policies established and argue against them. Despite these feelings, it is the responsibility of every employee to uphold each policy once it has been established by management. It must be understood that these rules are not only for the safety of the participants, but for the prevention of potential liability problems that could result if not communicated to everyone involved. To assist in circumventing this problem, many fitness facilities have asked members to aid in policy-making decisions. Membership advisory boards have been used frequently in both community and commercial settings. This group of individuals can be used as a sounding board for all rules that could be objectionable to participants. It is generally recognized that, although the board's input is very important, the ultimate decision on any policy must come from the management or staff

Topics discussed in the house rules should focus on potential problem areas as they relate to crowd control, facility security, safety, and individual usage. Some examples of these topics are mentioned below:

- Membership cards
- Hours of operation
- Guests
- Parking
- Children
- Lost and found
- Racquetball court reservations
- Tennis court reservations
- Pool rules
- Types of memberships

Here is an example of the XYZ Fitness Center house rules:

House Rules for the XYZ Fitness Center

House rules have been established to ensure maximum enjoyment and usage of the XYZ Fitness Center. As members, your constant cooperation is expected and appreciated.

MEMBERSHIP CARDS—Membership cards must be presented at the locker desk upon arrival, regardless of locker room usage. A towel and a key to a day locker will be issued in exchange for the card. Lost keys or lost membership cards will be replaced at a $3 charge to members.

GUESTS—Upon arrival, members must check their guests in at the locker desk. A fee of $5 is charged for each guest. Guests unaccompanied by a member will not be admitted. A guest is limited to 3 visits a year.

CHILDREN'S HOURS—On Saturdays during the hours of 9 a.m. to 2 p.m. and 6 p.m. to 9:30 p.m., only children who are members who are 17 years and under may use the facility. Children 14 years and under must be under their parents' strict supervision at all times and are not allowed in the weight room or cardiovascular room.

WHIRLPOOL AND SWIMMING POOL—Showers are required before entering the whirlpool or swimming pool. A shower is located outside by the swimming pool.

NO BLACK-SOLES SHOES—No black-soled shoes are allowed on the gym floor. Court shoes are recommended.

DRIVE CAUTIOUSLY—Upon entering the XYZ Fitness Center grounds, be aware of people on the tracks crossing the driveways. Those on the tracks have the right-of-way.

PARKING—Members should park on the north and east sides of the Fitness Center building.

LOST AND FOUND—Lost articles are kept at the locker desk. The XYZ Fitness Center is not responsible for lost items.

MESSAGES—Members are paged to the phone in case of emergency. Phone messages are posted by the locker desk.

NO SMOKING—Smoking is not permitted in the XYZ Fitness Center facility.

RACQUETBALL REGULATIONS
- Court reservations may be made by any member in person or by telephone at the locker desk within 24 hours of requested playing time.
- Name and membership number of the member making court reservations must be submitted.
- Court reservations begin at 5 a.m. and end at 8:30 p.m. Courts 1 and 2 are reserved on the hour and Courts 3 and 4 on the half hour. Courts are reserved for one hour only.
- Players with reservations must check in at the locker desk for confirmation. Two players must

(Cont.)

House Rules (Continued)

be on the playing court within 10 minutes after the scheduled time or the court will be declared open and eligible for rescheduling.
- Prime time hours are from 4:30 to 7:30 p.m., Monday through Friday. Courts are reserved for members only. A member and approved guest may reserve a court at any other time Monday through Friday.
- Children may use the courts on an availability basis only on Saturdays during the children's hours. No reservations may be made by children.
- Black-soled shoes are not allowed on the courts.
- Protective eyewear is recommended for racquetball/handball.

TENNIS REGULATIONS

- Court reservations may be made by any member in person or by telephone at the locker desk within 24 hours of requested playing time.
- Name and membership number of the member making court reservations must be submitted.
- Court reservations begin at 5:00 a.m. and end at 8:30 p.m. and are reserved for 1 hour for singles or 1-1/2 hours for doubles.

Membership Requirements

Another area that should be addressed while the governing policies are being formulated is the requirements for membership. Every facility has different prerequisites for membership. Some have age restrictions, others require medical clearance tests (stress test, field assessment, or complete physical), and many have no requirements. Regardless of what requirements you decide upon, you should base your decision on the answers to the following questions:

- What is practical for the facility?
- Which requirements represent prudence in the eyes of the insurance companies?
- Could a percentage of the membership be symptomatic, and is it necessary to determine who these people are (ACSM, 1980)?
- What will be used to determine exercise prescription protocols?

Most often membership requirements are established to obtain the target clientele iden-

tified by management, help aid in program safety, and improve the service to the members. Although specific membership prerequisites have not been used much in the past, facilities opening today that claim individualized exercise prescription and a medically supervised component will undoubtedly lead to the need for premembership screening.

Release Forms

As the legal issues associated with operating a health/fitness facility become more complex, every step should be taken to reduce the potential risk of legal action. Initially, the best way to address the legal issue is to make everyone associated with the program aware of the risks and dangers. This procedure is often accomplished through a written informed consent. Informed consent is a voluntary agreement to undergo a particular activity or procedure. For the informed consent to be valid, the participant must

- be legally capable to consent (full age, mentally competent),
- know and understand the risks and dangers involved, and
- voluntarily give his or her consent (Herbert & Herbert, 1984).

The informed consent should notify all participants of the risks and dangers of exercise, as well as any medical or fitness tests given as part of the exercise program, and discuss facility regulations regarding injuries. An opportunity for questions and answers should be encouraged. Include room on the consent form to make notes for questions or special concerns arising from the explanation (Patton et al., 1986). Most informed consent forms are accompanied by a membership application. The informed consent form also needs to be signed by the participants before they enter the program. The following is an example of an informal consent form.

Informed Consent Form—XYZ Fitness Center

The facilities and activity programs offered by the XYZ Fitness Center have been designed and established to provide the optimum level of beneficial exercise and enjoyment without compromising the health or safety of the members or guests who use the facilities or participate in its activities. Because of the nature of the program made available at the XYZ Fitness Center and the equipment that is an integral part of many of these activities, there is an inherent risk of injury that characterizes any exercise activity resulting in a practical limitation placed on the Fitness Center in its efforts to prevent injuries to participants, whether actively participating in exercises, using the equipment, or taking advantage of the various other facilities at the Center. The Center would enlist your assistance in assuring that the facilities and the equipment are used in a proper manner so that those inherent risks that exist under the control of the Fitness Center as well as those outside the control of the Center and partially within the control of each individual participant are minimized by the participant's thoughtful and cautious use of both the equipment and the facilities in general.

In consideration of the above factors, the undersigned participant acknowledges the existence of risks in connection with these activities, assumes such risks, and agrees to accept the responsibility for any injuries sustained by him or her in the course of his or her use of the facilities and/or its equipment. More specifically, the participant acknowledges and accepts responsibility for injuries arising out of those activities that involve risks in one or more of the following general areas:

(a) The use of exercise equipment.
(b) Participation in the unsupervised activities that are made available at the Fitness Center, in the swimming pool, on the running track, in the gym, and in other individual or group exercise activities.
(c) Possible injuries or medical disorders arising out of the participant's exercising at the facilities, such as heart attack, stroke, heat stress, or other injuries that arise out of individual or group sporting activites, such as sprains, broken bones, torn muscles, torn ligaments, and the like.

(Cont.)

Informed Consent Form (Continued)

(d) Accidents that occur within the facilities provided by the Fitness Center, such as the locker rooms, steam room, dressing rooms, and showers.

The participant further acknowledges the existence of and need for certain rules concerning the use of the equipment, facilities, and other procedures related to activities at the Center. He or she agrees to abide by those rules and to make every individual effort to assure that the equipment and facilities are kept in a safe and usable condition.

Those participants and guests who bring their children to the Center only during specified times further agree to accept full responsibility for the safety and well-being of their children and agree to maintain control and discipline over their children while they are at the Center.

Having read the preceding, the participant acknowledges his or her understanding of those risks set forth herein and knowingly agrees to accept full responsibility for his or her own exposure to such risks.

This the _____ day of _____, 19_____.   _____
                                                                                    Participant

---

Hours of Operation

The hours of operation for a health/fitness facility should be determined during the early planning stages. Most commercial and community settings, which have freestanding facilities, dictate their own hours of operation. These facilities have found that the peak hours (6 a.m. to 9 a.m., 11 a.m. to 1 p.m., and 4 p.m. to 7 p.m.) are the times when members use the facility most often. Consequently, it is not uncommon for clubs to operate from 6 a.m. to 9 or 10 p.m., 7 days a week. Variations of these hours are occasionally seen. Some facilities open later on Sundays, whereas others follow the tradition established by country clubs and close on Mondays.

In a corporate setting, hours of operation are determined by management. Because many companies offer fitness programs as a benefit to the employee, management will usually agree upon one of the following policies:

- Employees can use the fitness center before work, after work, or during their lunch hours.
- Employees can use the fitness center during working hours, if the time is made up.
- Employees are allowed flextime during the day to exercise at prescheduled times. Flextime is a concept that allows employees to exercise in preassigned time periods; it is viewed as an employee benefit.
- Employees may use the fitness center at any time.

It is in management's best interest to make a fitness setting available to and convenient for its participants. Closing a facility for no reason, or not adhering to posted opening and closing time schedules, eventually effects member adherence. Every effort should be made to provide participants with as much use of the facility as possible. Some commercial clubs in large metropolitan cities have started staying open 24 hours to accommodate variances in work shifts. Occasional holiday closings are acceptable if members have been notified ahead of time of the house rules or with written notices placed strategically around the facility. However, many facilities have found holidays to be excellent times for providing special programs (e.g., a New Year's Day celebration).

Guest Procedures

An important policy that is often overlooked is the procedure established for guests. Many programs have seen the benefits of allowing guests a trial workout in their facility. In a commercial fitness setting, friends and colleagues of participants make up 48% of the people who join these facilities. Friends are considered the single most important factor in obtaining potential participants (Game Plan, Inc., 1985).

It is good business to welcome guests into your facility on a limited basis. Therefore, the next step is to establish a policy that allows facility usage, but does not sacrifice crowd control or change membership requirements. It is not uncommon for facilities to place a maximum number of guest visits per year on an individual, to allow guests only during certain times of the day, or to ask that a member be present for a guest to use the facilities. Restrictions are recommended if the estimated number of guests threatens to disrupt the atmosphere of the members.

In the commercial club business, it has been estimated that between 12% and 20% of the membership will use the facility per day. This number sometimes results in a maximum load for some facilities and causes a concern among members as to why guests are even allowed to use the facility. However, once this figure is determined, management can decide whether restrictions should be placed upon guest usage.

A guest fee is suggested to cover a per-day operational expense. Consideration should be given to facility and equipment costs, utilities, towels, locker rental, and any other amenities provided. In a commercial setting guest fees range from $5 to $10 per visit. A corporate setting varies from company to company. Some companies do not allow guests, whereas others charge a nominal fee of $3-$5 per visit. The community setting allows for a reduced fee similar to that of the corporations. Periodic increases in guest fees should be reviewed regularly as facility expenses continue to escalate.

BUSINESS OFFICE MANAGEMENT

The business office is the nerve center of almost every business. No matter how small a business office is, the principal activities of any business are generally coordinated through this area. In health/fitness centers the business office placement varies from setting to setting. For example, some business offices are situated in an open atmosphere where participants have easy access, others are behind closed doors for added privacy, and still others are combined with the locker desk. The decision of business office placement is not arbitrary and will depend on whether it is more appropriate for your setting to have a public or a private office. The following issues should help you decide which is best:

- The efficiency of coping with the volume of paperwork
- Telephone usage
- Daily mail distribution

- Security for financial and participant records
- Member accessibility

The layout of a business office should be designed around the specific responsibilities that are performed in that area. A typical mistake in the design phase of the facility is the lack of preplanning associated with office space. No reasoning or planning enters into the design of the layout, and no attention is paid to the need for efficiency or the fact that the office is often the place where potential members have their first contact with the business and formulate their initial impressions.

As with most other aspects of a health/ fitness facility, the specific business office responsibilities will vary among corporate, commercial, clinical, and community settings. In general, however, there are certain similarities that are associated with establishing any business office arrangement. Examples of some common business office responsibilities in the health/fitness field are listed in Figure 11.1.

Once the responsibilities have been determined, it is much easier to determine how to equip the office. Any equipment purchased should be bought to fulfill a specific purpose, and every item purchased should help speed up the process of making records easier to find, fill out, or understand. A well-equipped office will promote greater accuracy, improve neatness, and provide protection for the handling of cash, mail, and other security-related office details. Specifically, it is best to purchase office equipment with the following guidelines in mind:

- Before buying new office furniture, check into renting. Renting is not uncommon in today's business offices. Investigate the possibility of renting such items as photocopying machines, typewriters, and identification machines.

- Always maintain a look of uniformity with office equipment. Don't buy equipment that is a different standard or color from already-existing equipment.
- Always consider the space that is available for office use. Take into consideration layout limitations, noise, lighting, and other conditions that could cause problems.
- Once you purchase a piece of equipment or furniture, keep a record showing the manufacturer, serial number, model, cost, and date of purchase. This record will be useful when maintenance is needed. Also record dates of repairs and maintenance costs as they occur.
- Look seriously into a maintenance contract. Periodic cleaning and repairs can be made with little or no extra cost. If a company does not stand by its equipment with a maintenance contract, inquire about quality control and how specific problems will be handled. Often maintenance contracts can be purchased from sources other than the retailer.

Record Keeping/Filing System

A key ingredient to the success of a business office is the record-keeping system. Accurate books and records are essential for planning and making management decisions. In the health/fitness market there are generally three areas where good records must be kept: finances, participant/member information, and personnel. Each of these records should be designed with a filing system that uses the most efficient method of locating documents. The following ideas will help develop a good record-keeping system:

1. Spend time preparing an overall file plan and stick to it. Allot a specific place in the files to each folder. If you use

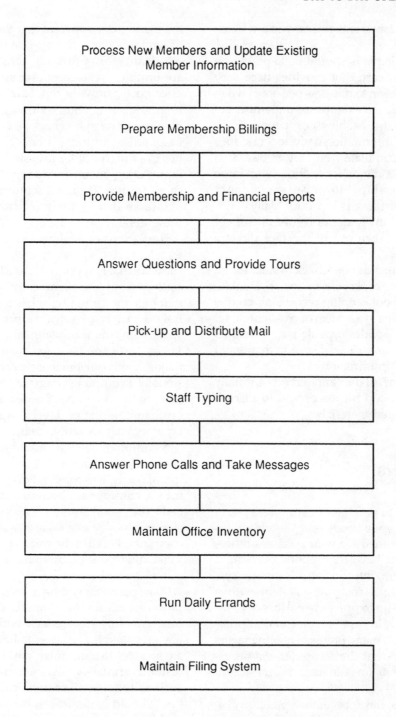

Figure 11.1. Typical business office responsibilities in the health/fitness field.

proper labels and guides, you can locate material more easily. All matters relating to participants should be kept on one account card that provides necessary information to business personnel when needed. An example of a member account card is shown on page 271.

2. File all information daily so work does not accumulate from day to day. It is not uncommon for facilities with large memberships to misplace account cards if filing is not done daily.

3. Return any folder or record document that is taken out of the files directly after use.

4. Develop a double-check system for all records, especially financial. Double-entry bookkeeping records all credits and debts in a system of cross-checking. Many facilities provide both a manual and a computerized system to prevent loss of information.

5. Examine all files and records annually to clean up file space and to discard unwanted materials.

Computers

The decision to purchase a computer system depends on your needs and the objectives you have outlined for your business office. Basically, you have the options of using a manual system, introducing a computer system, or using a computer system with a manual back-up to prevent total loss of participant records in case of a mechanical problem. However, many fitness center managers have realized that the computer is a necessary ingredient for adequate business efficiency.

Computers have become a necessity in many business offices today. It is becoming more and more apparent that the advantages of having a computer system outweigh the disadvantages. Currently, business offices are finding that a computer system will reduce costs, provide rapid data processing, improve accuracy and controls, and avoid the high cost of outside service bureaus. The business offices in today's health/fitness facilities use the computer to assist with financial information, membership records, and clerical assistance. Figure 11.2 indicates the various tasks that a computer can perform in these areas.

The various capabilities of a computer system depend to a great extent on the available software that is appropriate to a health/fitness setting. Software is the computer program that tells the computer what to do. There is now a variety of software programs made specifically for the health/fitness industry. These software packages will handle the majority of your business needs, but occasionally a computer program will need to be tailored to fit a specific demand. Always evaluate the cost of developing such a program against its cost-benefit.

A computer system should be selected in terms of both your present and your expected future needs. If expansion is in the foreseeable future, consider a system that is easily modified to increased tasks and capabilities. Expansion may not be as simple as adding another computer, because the software for one computer might not be compatible with a computer of another make.

Make sure that you have an uninterrupted power supply for the computer system. Many problems that have arisen with computers have resulted from power failures that cause a computer to shut down and lose data as a result. Fortunately, advances in technology, such as the new fiber-optic communication line, should begin to resolve power-related problems.

Member Account Card

(FRONT)

	MR. ☐ MISS ☐ MRS ☐	MEMBERSHIP NUMBER
LAST FIRST MIDDLE INITIAL		BIRTHDATE
HOME ADDRESS MAIL TO ☐		HOME PHONE
ZIP		
BUSINESS ADDRESS MAIL TO ☐		BUSINESS PHONE
ZIP		
BILLING INSTRUCTIONS:		POSITION

RENEWAL DATE	DATE PAID	AMOUNT	YEAR	TYPE MEMBERSHIP	COMMENT:

(BACK)

RENEWAL DATE	DATE PAID	AMOUNT	YEAR	TYPE MEMBERSHIP	COMMENT:

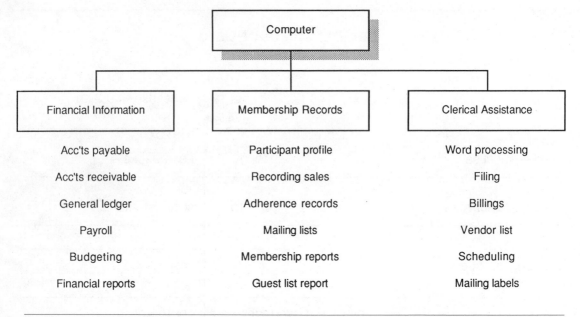

Figure 11.2. Various tasks a computer can perform.

Designing Forms

The stationery, documents, applications, and other forms for the business should be designed to simplify the activities of the business office. Clarity is the key ingredient to good forms. To help save money, make a list of all the forms and other printed materials that will be needed to operate the business office successfully. A partial list of such materials would include the following:

- Membership applications
- Facility brochures
- Stationery/envelopes
- Health/fitness consultation forms
- Member/financial information forms
- Billing statements
- Business cards
- Cash vouchers
- Employment applications
- Purchase order forms

Any printed instructions on the forms should be straightforward and leave no question of procedure and purpose. Determine size specifications for easy filing. Provide preset address positioning so that window envelopes may be used. Remember to leave space for coding or numbering, which will also aid in filing.

Finally, design, or hire a professional to design, a logo that depicts the mission of the facility. This logo is used as a letterhead and placed on many of the business forms. A professional advertising agency or printing company can help with every stage of this process, from early design concept to the final art work. This procedure is not cheap, but the cost should be weighed against the positive message portrayed to the consumer and its effect on your business.

MAINTENANCE MANAGEMENT

Facility maintenance is one of the biggest problems that faces a manager, director, or owner of any health/fitness facility. Today's participants of corporate, community, commercial, and clinical settings demand that every aspect of a facility be well maintained and that all equipment be operational. Any facility not actively following a preestablished maintenance schedule is in danger of violating city and state safety and health regulations and is opening the doors for potential legal action.

Herbert and Herbert (1984) state that a potential area in which fitness professionals encounter legal issues of negligence and liability is facility and equipment maintenance. Specific areas in which issues of liability and negligence occur are

- floor surfaces (workout rooms and locker areas),
- outside grounds (entryways free of snow and ice),
- jogging trails (lights, terrain, traffic concerns),
- general facility (electrical, water temperatures, posted instructions on sauna use), and
- exercise equipment (bikes, rowers, treadmills, weight room).

There is nothing special about providing a quality maintenance program. A good maintenance plan and a hardworking maintenance crew are the two key ingredients. Successful facilities follow an inspection procedure that adheres to a definite schedule, which reflects every maintenance task that is performed daily. Before you develop a maintenance schedule, make a list of all the facility's maintenance needs. Consider every phase of the physical plant with special attention to the areas that participants come in contact with daily. This checklist should specify every room that requires daily maintenance needs, while also noting outdoor maintenance responsibilities. Here is an example of a maintenance checklist for a multirecreational facility.

Maintenance Checklist for the XYZ Health Club

Facilities

Locker rooms
_____ Whirlpool
_____ Steam room
_____ Sauna
_____ Showers
_____ Sinks
_____ Commodes/urinals
_____ Towels
_____ Soap
_____ Locker appearance

Racquetball courts
_____ Floors
_____ Walls
_____ Lights
_____ Gallery section

Tennis courts
_____ Ball machine
_____ Windscreens
_____ Tennis nets
_____ Court surface

(Cont.)

Maintenance Checklist (Continued)

Cardiovascular room

_____ Stationary cycles
_____ Treadmills
_____ Room appearance

Swimming pool

_____ Daily chemical check
_____ Tile
_____ Mechanical equipment
_____ Cleaning schedule

Weight training room

_____ Nautilus
_____ Universal Gym
_____ Exercise mats
_____ Dumbbells
_____ Free weights
_____ Other _____

Locker desk

_____ Reservation booklets
_____ Employee bulletin board
_____ Washers and dryers
_____ Bags and pins
_____ Desk appearance

Storage lockers

_____ Appearance of lockers
_____ Names on lockers
_____ File system
_____ Terminated member locker
        cleaned out

You can now prepare a detailed, daily responsibility schedule based on this checklist. This schedule should depict each specific duty and the expected time frame in which the task should be completed. When constructing this form, you should consider both daytime and nighttime maintenance, peak usage versus light usage hours, and available personnel. An added benefit of a daily responsibility schedule is that it can be used as an evaluation tool to assure that all work is being accomplished and performed to facility standards. Many of the tasks that are listed will change as a facility becomes more experienced in handling the maintenance needs. The following is an example of a daily maintenance responsibility schedule.

A Daily Maintenance Responsibility Checklist

Daytime Maintenance Checklist

_____ Inspect and clean the locker room every 20 minutes or as needed, depending upon traffic.

_____ Wash, dry, and fold the towels.

_____ Test the whirlpool every 2 hours and record the results.

_____ Police the outside grounds and sweep the entrance.

_____ Clean the glass in the front foyer between 1:00 and 2:00 p.m.

_____ Vacuum the Nautilus center during quiet time in the afternoon.

_____ Wipe down and clean all cold air returns in locker rooms, foyer, and lounge.

_____ Mix up 10 gallons of body soap.

_____ Check trash containers and empty and change them as needed.

_____ Vacuum lint filters in clothes dryers.

_____ Record any special projects carried out.

_____ Sign and date checklist.

_____ Return checklist to Operation Manager's mailbox at end of shift.

Evening Maintenance Checklist

_____ Check locker rooms every 20 minutes or more as needed, depending upon traffic. Be sure to check the following:

____ sinks   ____ lockers (should be closed)
____ mirrors   ____ trash (should be picked up)
____ counters   ____ floors
____ toiletries supply   ____ paper towels
____ hair dryers

_____ Check wet rooms, steam, and sauna every 20 minutes:
____ report to supervisor if facility is not operational
____ spray and wipe down toilets, urinals, etc.
____ remove hair and soap from drains
____ fill shampoo and soap containers

_____ Clean towels regularly during the evening:
____ remove soiled towels from the front desk
____ wash and dry all towels (12 towels maximum per washer load; 24 towels maximum per dryer load)
____ fold towels and return them to front desk
____ clean lint filters in washer once a day

_____ Check whirlpool every 2 hours:
____ check chlorine level, pH, and temperature
____ adjust settings as needed and record results
____ check Spa Pure level and mix more if needed
____ add water as needed to keep proper level
____ clean out skimmer basket
____ clean out hair filter in circulating pump
____ cover pool and turn off lights
____ bleed off air and make sure valves are properly adjusted

(Cont.)

Daily Maintenance Checklist (Continued)

_____ Perform court maintenance once each night:
   _____ sweep out all courts
   _____ wash all windows, inside and out
   _____ clean out goodie boxes
   _____ remove all garbage

_____ Do a complete tour of the club three times each night, looking for problems and making sure lights are out in unused areas.

_____ On Monday, Wednesday, and Friday, blow off steam generator, add cleaner, and start generator up again.

_____ Record any special projects carried out.

_____ Sign and date checklist.

_____ Return checklist to Operation Manager's mailbox at end of shift.

Late Evening Maintenance Checklist

Foyer/Main Lobby/Court Hallway duties:

_____ Vacuum all carpeted areas, moving all furniture, game machines, plants, etc.

_____ Wipe down all sills, counters, tables, chairs (including chrome), and couches with disinfectant.

_____ Clean water fountains with creme cleanser.

_____ Clean all glass in entranceway, both sets of doors (inside and out).

_____ Change all trash bags and clean and disinfect tops (both sides). Replace with new trash liners.

_____ Mop and disinfect linoleum flooring.

Shower/Wet Room duties

_____ Scrub, sanitize, and deodorize all toilets and urinals.

_____ Scrub, sanitize, and deodorize shower walls (top to bottom) and floors.

_____ Clean, sanitize, and deodorize steam baths. (Do not scrub grout joints.)

_____ Scrub, sanitize, and deodorize all tile on walls.

_____ Clean, sanitize, and deodorize bathroom partitions.

_____ Scrub metal shower drains one time per week with steel wool.

Locker Room duties:

_____ Open, wipe out, and spray-disinfect all lockers (top and bottom). Wipe tops of lockers with Dust Control.

_____ Scrub, sanitize, and deodorize all sink basins and Formica cabinets.

_____ Spray and wipe all Formica with dust control.

_____ Clean all mirrors, hair dryers, paper towel dispensers, and soap dispensers.

_____ Wipe down scales.

_____ Clean, sanitize, and deodorize sauna bath wood seats and tile floor.

_____ Wipe and clean TV sets (front and back).

_____ Scrub red flooring with stiff broom and disinfectant solution.

_____ Roll up red flooring, wash entire concrete floor with disinfectant, and replace flooring.

_____ Wipe down all locker bases with Dust Control.

_____ Vacuum carpet in locker room.

The maintenance personnel options differ with each facility setting. Corporate fitness facilities are generally housed within the physical plant of the company, so they are cared for by the maintenance personnel of the company. Although this procedure is the most practical, it still has pitfalls that continually plague corporate fitness directors. The cleaning standards of an office building and a fitness facility are quite different. A fitness center that is being used regularly has continued maintenance needs. Periodic cleaning by a maintenance crew that is also responsible for the daily cleaning of a office building is inefficient. Consider establishing a schedule that satisfies the maintenance needs of the complex and recontract with an outside service, if necessary, to achieve necessary standards.

Community and commercial settings have a number of options available for maintenance service. They include the following:

1. The facility enters into a contract arrangement with an outside cleaning service. If you choose this option, agree to sign a 1-year contract with the cleaning service. Conditions of the contract should include services provided, fees, bonding information, personnel requirements, termination of contract, and equipment provided. Most cleaning services have their own contracts that can be revised to satisfy both parties.

2. The facility hires its own maintenance personnel. This option requires a job description of the available position, employment prerequisites, salary and benefits, and a reference check. Other items to consider are equipment procurement, employee uniforms, and supervision.

3. The facility uses a combination of Options 1 and 2. For example, you hire the daytime cleaning crew and contract for the nighttime cleaning. This option is preferred by the majority of commercial and community fitness centers.

Although many clubs hire maintenance personnel, smaller fitness facilities might find that financial limitations require fitness leaders or locker staff to assist with maintenance responsibilities. This is not the preferred method, but if supervised and scheduled properly, it can accomplish the necessary housecleaning goals.

Hiring a full-time operation supervisor is an option to consider. Maintaining a fitness facility can be a full-time position. The need for constant maintenance supervision, handling special projects (e.g., facility renovations, heating/air-conditioning or electrical/mechanical problems), and preventive maintenance are issues that concern every facility. The financial savings of hiring a maintenance supervisor can be significant, especially when you consider the high cost of service calls. Some fitness centers have actually covered the annual salary of the operation supervisor from savings associated with not calling service firms. If you are unable to hire a full-time supervisor, consider appointing a staff person to oversee the maintenance division.

According to a 1984 survey (IRSA, 1984), the average multipurpose club with an indoor pool spent 7.1% of its total revenues ($91,035) on repairs and maintenance. Other multipurpose clubs invested 6.7% ($56,620). For tennis clubs, the figure was 6.3% ($30,788), and for racquetball clubs, 6.6% ($31,781). Average hourly wages for maintenance personnel ranged from $4 to $5 per hour.

An issue of maintenance and general repairs that needs to be addressed early on in

---

A Work Order Form

REQ. NO.	UNIT NO.		
TODAY'S DATE	PHONE NO.		ASSIGNED TO

WE WERE HERE TODAY TO SERVICE YOUR REQUEST

WE WERE UNABLE TO REPAIR THE PROBLEM FULLY ☐   WE WERE ABLE TO REPAIR YOUR SERVICE REQUEST ☐

WE HAD TO ORDER A PART   ☐

WE HAD TO CALL AN OUTSIDE CONTRACTOR   ☐   TIME STARTED _____

OTHER: ☐   TIME COMPLETED _____

THE WORK SHOULD BE COMPLETED BY: _____

REMARKS: _____

_____

_____

_____

SIGNED: _____

OFFICE COPY

the process is how all maintenance requests will be handled. The suggested method is a work order system, which accounts for each needed repair by reporting it to a designated individual who prepares a work order request form. This form is then forwarded to the necessary maintenance person who performs the work. Accountability of the tasks completed is the key aspect of this system. You can monitor time to complete the job, materials used, and who was responsible for the work. Copies of work orders can be periodically reviewed to evaluate work output. Page 278 gives an example of a work order form.

Ordering maintenance supplies or equipment should be accomplished through a purchase order form. A purchase order describes what specific supplies need to be ordered, the estimated cost, a purchase order number, the vendor being used, and who is ordering the supplies, and provides a space for an approved signature from management. Copies of the form are given to the person authorizing the purchase, the vendor, and the business office for filing. As monthly checks are written, a copy of the purchase order accompanies each check showing that the purchase was authorized and approved. The purchase order system ensures that nothing is bought unless management approves. An example of a purchase order form is on page 280.

Finally, a good preventive maintenance program should be instigated. Preventive maintenance is a future-oriented approach that allows a facility to save money, avoid down-time, and maintain equipment efficiency. Typically, health/fitness centers only react to maintenance problems as they occur. This approach is called maintenance through crisis. Everyone haphazardly scrambles to fix the problem and, in the process, sacrifices time and money and places additional stress on the staff.

The organized manager has an annual preventive maintenance plan that requires doing periodic inspections of specified equipment and replacing parts that deteriorate over time. Clearly, the object is not to wait until a problem arises, but to investigate at designated times during the year and replace, tighten, or adjust any areas that are potential problems.

SWIMMING POOL/WHIRLPOOL MAINTENANCE

The use of swimming pools and whirlpools is growing at a phenomenal rate (Athletic Institute and American Alliance for Health, Physical Education, Recreation and Dance, 1983). The increased interest in swimming as an excellent mode for physical fitness and the therapeutic and relaxing effect derived from a whirlpool are both contributing factors to the influx in participant use. As a result, added attention needs to be given to the preventive and day-to-day maintenance of these areas.

If a swimming pool or whirlpool is left unattended or not cleaned regularly, the managers or owners face the risk of an inspection by the local health department. Complaints can be registered by participants of a health/fitness facility if the standards of the swimming pool or whirlpool are not maintained. Health department officials also make unannounced checks of these areas and file violation warnings if maintenance is deficient. If the violation warnings are not corrected within the allotted time period, the officials order the whirlpool or swimming pool to be closed. To prevent this chain of events, consult your local health department for the standards that will be measured during an inspection.

Members of health/fitness centers are increasingly cautious about the quality of spa

Purchase Order Form

Date _____

SHOW THIS NO.
ON ALL PAPERS
AND PACKAGES

VENDOR:

_____ Purchase Order No. _____

_____ Vendor Invoice No. _____

_____

_____

ITEM NO.	DESCRIPTION	QUANTITY & UNIT	UNIT PRICE	PRICE

PLEASE SEND TO: PLEASE INVOICE (IF DIFFERENT FROM ADDRESS)

_____   _____

_____   _____

_____   _____

_____   _____

Purchaser _____

and pool water. The incidents of lawsuits over contracting skin and organ infections are increasing. Some of the more common infections or diseases include ear infections, salmonella, conjunctivitis, Legionnaires' disease, pseudomonas, folliculitis, and urinary-tract infections (Patton, 1986). No health/fitness facility wants to risk the possibility of being closed down by the health department or having a suit filed against it. A well-designed maintenance program is the only solution to avoiding these problems.

General day-to-day care for both a whirlpool and a swimming pool includes cleaning all tile or plaster water scum lines, checking pool chemicals, cleaning all skimmer baskets, checking water temperature, and monitoring water pressure gauges. These duties should be performed daily, if not twice a day, depending upon the level of usage.

Proper preventive maintenance measures for a whirlpool and swimming pool include regrouting and replacing loose tile, annually draining and acid-washing plaster areas, replacing filter ingredients, checking heater systems, having an extra pump in case the existing pump malfunctions, replacing gauges and valves, and checking the tightness of ladders and handrails.

In addition to the day-to-day maintenance and preventive measures, a list of additional maintenance tips for both a whirlpool and a swimming pool is provided on page 282.

The proper maintenance of whirlpools and swimming pools encompasses a wider range of care than most people realize. For this reason the educational sessions that are sponsored by city health departments, equipment manufacturers, or commercial spa/pool companies are recommended. In some cities it is now a requirement that anyone operating or managing pools or spas must annually register for the city-sponsored pool school. Any facility not participating in this meeting risks closure of its swimming pool or whirlpool by the city health department.

SAFETY PROCEDURES

Each health/fitness facility creates its own liabilities when the program is implemented. Those sponsoring health/fitness programs have to become overly conscious of potential problem areas. Our society suffers from a "sue syndrome," and injuries that occur in health/fitness programs are becoming part of the "injury industry." Avoiding lawsuits requires paying close attention to many aspects of the fitness setting operations. Previous lawsuits have shown that legal liability can be influenced by these five factors:

- *Ignorance of the law*-simply not knowing that something was illegal or contrary to the law.
- *Ignoring the law*-doing something that is contrary to the law.
- *Failure to act*-knowing that something should be done, but not doing it for one reason or another.
- *Failure to warn*-not making everyone sufficiently aware of real dangers that exist in a given situation.
- *Expense*-failing to budget or spend money to further the safety objectives (Ross, 1985).

Minimizing the risk of litigation depends entirely upon the preventive safety measures that are introduced into a health/fitness setting. Pertinent safety features include conducting daily inspections and maintenance of equipment and facilities, developing an emergency procedure plan, providing qualified personnel, and having a protective insurance policy.

The environment for the health/fitness program must be free from inherent dangers or

Common Maintenance Tips for XYZ Swimming Pool and Whirlpool

General Tips:

1. Place signs in strategic areas that cover the following topics:
   - Length of time in the whirlpool
   - Lifeguard hours
   - Medical restrictions for whirlpool use
   - Shower before using whirlpool or swimming pool
   - Scheduled cleaning times
   - Local emergency telephone numbers

2. Have staff become familiar with all phases of whirlpool and swimming pool operations. Provide meetings to explain equipment use, reinforce information with laminated checklists placed strategically around equipment to aid in backwashing, lighting of pilot light for heater, adding water, and obtaining prime in case water pressure is lost.

3. Daily checks for water balance and disinfectant levels. To test the water balance adequately, a quality testing kit should be purchased. The kit should provide testing measures for acid or base level (pH and chlorine), total alkalinity (TA), and the total dissolved solids (TDS). Accepted values for the following chemical factors are
   - pH = 7.2–7.8
   - Chlorine = 3–5 parts per million (ppm)
   - TDS = 1,200 ppm
   - TA = 80–150 ppm

   A chlorinator system is recommended to introduce the desired level of chlorine. Once a week the water should be shocked by increasing the free residual chlorine level to 10–15 ppm. This procedure will prevent the growth of algae and pollutants.

4. Maintain appropriate water temperatures:
   - Whirlpool—102–106 degrees Fahrenheit
   - Swimming pool—78–82 degrees Fahrenheit

   A strategically placed thermometer is recommended so temperatures can be taken daily.

5. Never mix chemicals or store muriatic acid, soda ash, or chlorine in the same areas. Chemicals should always be added to water, but water should never be added to chemicals.

6. The water in a whirlpool should be changed two or three times per week, depending upon the number of people using it.

7. Provide a filtering system that gives a proper turnover rate. Every bit of water should be filtered within the following time frames:
   - Whirlpool—30–45 minutes
   - Swimming pool—six daily water exchanges

defects, appropriate for the planned activity, and equipped for that activity. A daily facility inspection should be performed following the "Daily Maintenance Responsibility Checklist" (see earlier section on "Maintenance Management"). Environmental factors such as temperature and humidity should be monitored. For outdoor areas, warning flags or other devices should be used to inform participants of exact weather conditions.

Equipment must always be in good working order. Staff members should inspect and maintain equipment and facilities on a regular basis. An added responsibility should also include instructing participants in the proper use of the equipment. Accident report forms should be completed by staff as soon as possible after an accident or injury to document the circumstances and the first aid/emergency procedures used. Page 284 shows a sample injury report form.

Written policies and guidelines for emergency situations should be established to handle any medically related problem. A good emergency plan should include the code used to alert the staff, the location of the problem, staff assessment of the problem, first aid equipment responsibility, and the call for emergency help. This plan should be distributed to all staff members and posted by the locker desk phones. Staff members calling for emergency help should be instructed to give their name, location of the facility, a call-back number, where the emergency occurred on the facility, and a preliminary assessment of the situation. Examples of such program guidelines are available from the ACSM (1980).

An emergency plan is only as good as the staff members who participate in it. Preparing the staff for emergency situations is a responsibility that should not be overlooked. Periodic, unannounced, mock emergency sessions should be performed to evaluate staff respon-

siveness and whether the emergency plan was correctly activated. All staff members should at least have their CPR certification and preferably the instructor certification so that on-site CPR training can be given to members as well as staff. This is an excellent method for keeping CPR procedures current with all staff.

Another component of an emergency plan is to establish a first aid station where the necessary medical equipment is located. Contact the American Red Cross for details of what medical supplies to include in the first aid kit. At least one staff person should be given the responsibility of coordinating and maintaining all medical supplies.

Providing a qualified staff should be the top priority of any health/fitness program. Ideally, the staff members should be certified by the ACSM or another professional organization. Personnel should be mature, responsible individuals who are prudent in carrying out their duties and assignments. If an unqualified staff member is involved in the injury of an individual, a number of claims could be brought against the fitness center and that staff member. The claims against personnel frequently include the following:

1. Failure to monitor an exercise test properly.
2. Failure to instruct on how to use exercise equipment or perform activities properly.
3. Failure to evaluate participants capabilities and identify limits that would contraindicate certain exercises.
4. Failure to prescribe proper exercise intensity according to metabolic or cardiovascular demand.
5. Failure to supervise activities properly or advise on proper restrictions or modifications during unsupervised workouts (Herbert & Herbert, 1984).

A Member Injury Report
for the XYZ Health Club

Name of Injured Member _____

Membership # _____

Address _____ Telephone #: Business _____ Home _____

What time of the day did the accident occur? _____

Location of accident _____

_____

Describe fully how accident occurred, and state what actions were taken by staff. _____

_____

_____

_____

_____

_____

_____

Was the injured member taken to a hospital or emergency room?   Yes _____   No _____

If so, give name and address of hospital. _____

_____

_____

Describe the injury in detail and indicate the part(s) of body affected. _____

_____

_____

_____

_____

_____

Signed by _____

Date _____

Another preventive safety measure is to review all insurance policies on an annual basis. Determining how much and what type of insurance an organization should provide depends on the approach of the health/fitness program. Insurance protection is much better in a supervised fitness program with well-qualified staff. Protection is less favorable in an unsupervised recreation program. Owners and managers are now finding that insurance companies may not cover instances of gross negligence, nor will they pay court damages that exceed the coverage. For this reason an annual meeting that reviews coverage amounts, actual covered areas, and recent appraisals of land and building costs is recommended. Suggested minimal insurance for health/fitness centers includes:

- Liability
- Workmen's compensation
- Fire insurance
- Car insurance (company car)
- Business interruption

Finally, safety reviews should be performed in every health/fitness center. There are various ways to conduct periodic safety reviews, depending on facility needs and goals. The easiest way is to appoint a committee that inspects all equipment and facilities and then lists the areas of potential litigation. Another way is to bring in an outside consultant experienced in the fitness area, such as a safety engineer, insurance representative, or physical educator. Although this method is more expensive than using inside staff, it does provide independent, disinterested objectivity and accountability (Ross, 1985).

Many health/fitness practitioners believe that most injuries are preventable and many lawsuits are avoidable if safety issues are addressed regularly. Unfortunately, as long as consumer litigation is on the rise, all health/fitness facilities will be considered targets.

PRO SHOP OPERATIONS

Any health/fitness facility that wants to start a pro shop does so for two reasons: to provide a service to the members and to return a profit or break even financially. A pro shop is the retail merchandising of consumer goods as it relates to the activities of the facility. It is a separate business and should be treated as one. A fundamental part of managing a pro shop is a well-thought-out, carefully determined plan, which takes into account

- location,
- management,
- inventory procedures,
- pricing of merchandise, and
- advertising.

This plan should be developed along the same lines as a business plan for starting a new business.

Most pro shops are located near the main entrance of a facility, so that locker desk personnel are available to sell and keep an eye on merchandise and participants can see the merchandise every time they enter the facility. Some facilities build separate rooms with storage areas close to the locker desk area, although this is a more expensive undertaking. However, the extra benefits of improved security, additional storage space, and walls for displays are all worth contemplating when deciding in which direction to go.

Attention should be given to the visual appearance of the pro shop. The color scheme should coordinate with the color scheme of the facility. Track lighting should be used so that the lights can be adjusted easily as displays change.

The two ways to operate a pro shop are leasing the pro shop from an outside source and operating the pro shop as a division of the health/fitness facility. The lease arrangement reduces the burden of investing money in inventory, inventory depletion, separate bookkeeping records, maintenance upkeep, and tax reports. The negatives associated with a leased operation are the loss of control over this area of the facility and reduced potential of profit. If profit is the purpose of the shop, then an owner-operated pro shop is better. However, if providing a pro shop as a service to the members and having an allocated amount paid for the space is sufficient, then a leased operation is preferred. The IRSA (1984) industry data survey reported that 79% of tennis, racquetball, and multirecreation facilities completely owned and operated their own pro shop.

A lease arrangement requires that both parties mutually agree on a written contract. Some conditions of the contract should include the following:

- Description of leased space
- Terms—length of lease
- Rental fee
- Payment of utilities
- Repairs and maintenance
- Advertising
- Insurance
- Termination of lease
- Employees
- Stock and manner of sales

An attorney prepares the contract, and both parties finalize the transaction by signing it.

The range of merchandise varies from a small line of convenient articles to a full line of merchandise and assorted sporting goods. The former would consist of toilet articles, racquetball/tennis balls, gloves, sweatbands, swimming goggles, and other essential items. A full line of merchandise would include various makes of sportswear (shirts, shorts, warm-ups, tights, etc.). In determining which direction to go, consider the concept of the facility, the number of participants, the income level of the participants, and the competition.

Merchandise can be purchased from specific manufacturers and wholesalers. A direct purchase from the manufacturer usually yields the lowest purchase price, whereas higher prices come from the wholesaler. A combination of sales representatives, catalogs, and trade shows provides the best selection of merchandise. When negotiating with vendors, make sure that the merchandise is of good quality and that order requests can meet preestablished time deadlines.

Payment for a merchandise order is done by prepayment, cash on delivery (COD), or credit. To protect the cash flow of many pro shops, many facilities establish a line of credit, which varies from manufacturer to wholesaler, depending upon the length of time as a customer, the volume, and the past billing history.

To maintain the level of merchandise in inventory, you need to determine when to reorder. The reorder determination, or the level of stock at which a reorder is necessary, is influenced by projected sales and the time necessary for delivery. A problem that faces pro shop owners today is the reorder time for small volume merchandise. Items that are sold out for extended periods of time will eventually become a negative factor. A good communication line with the manufacturer or wholesaler can prevent sporadic supply lines.

Establishing merchandise pricing is another problem area for pro shop operators. Attempting to provide a markup percentage that covers all operational expenses plus a built-in profit is the primary cause for this problem. Owners often make the mistake of not considering both the initial markup, which covers the operational expenses plus a profit, and the maintained markup, which covers the hidden costs that also need to be taken into account when determining the price. Maintained markup refers to the figure arrived at after taking into account reduction, mark-downs, employee discounts, and damaged or soiled merchandise (IRSA, 1984). Both mark-ups are essential in determining the final price. The average price markups for pro shops range from 30% to 100%.

A successful pro shop should have an inventory that turns over two to three times a year and a profit margin between 25% and 30%, depending upon the size of the pro shop, merchandising techniques, sales staff, product variety, and pricing (Winemer, 1984).

The hours of operations for pro shops generally parallel those of the fitness facility. The personnel on duty at the locker desk can also be trained to sell retail merchandise. This approach allows a pro shop to remain open unless the facility itself closes.

A promotion and advertising plan is a necessity if a pro shop is to be successful. A determination must first be made as to whether the pro shop can cater to the general public or confine sales to members and guests. If the general public is the target population, then the traditional advertising methods should be used. If the pro shop sales are restricted to members and guests only, then the bulk of the advertising must be done on the facility. All sales areas must be designed to lure members and guests, and displays should be changed regularly. Various sales promotions range from having monthly sales; using the staff as models for selected attire; and providing gift certificates, discount coupons, two-for-one offers, and holiday specials.

Separate financial records will help you determine if the turnover of inventory and profit margins are being attained. These records account for total sales, direct cost of sales, income (before direct expenses), sales per individual, and income per individual. Finally, the direct and indirect expenses of the shop should be carefully reviewed. This gives you an accurate and realistic determination of the pro shop's status.

MASSAGE

Massage has recently become a popular amenity in many health/fitness centers. Although massage has been slow to catch on in this country, the practice has become indispensable to many athletes and executives. The current belief is that massage does more than just reduce tension and muscle soreness; it also allows athletes to work out harder and longer without suffering the ill-effects of overtraining. To fulfill the increased needs for massage, a growing number of trained massage therapists are entering the health/fitness market.

Currently, over 15 states have regulations governing the licensing or registration of massage therapists. The standards of training are maintained by the American Massage and Therapy Association (AMTA), which is the national organization for massage therapists. Massage therapists cannot diagnose or prescribe treatment, but they can provide therapeutic services prescribed by physicians.

The qualifications for a massage therapist follow these three options:

1. *School-trained*—a combination of educational credentials, personal references, and previous job experiences.
2. *Apprentice-trained*—individuals who demonstrate a competence by a test of their knowledge or skills from the interview, or the showing of state certification, licensing, or registration.
3. *Self-trained*—individuals who have attended seminars and practiced extensively. Their skills can also be judged by the same criteria as #2.

A massage therapist who is a member of the AMTA must have passed a written and a practical competency test. Along with this membership comes a $1 million malpractice and liability insurance policy to cover any litigation that could arise.

Within the AMTA are formal titles designated for massage personnel that cannot be used by another association:

MsT—*Massage Therapist*—an individual who has passed a written and practical test in massage that is administered by members or representatives of the AMTA.

RMT—*Registered Massage Therapist*—after 3 years, an MsT is eligible to take the more advanced RMT test.

CI—*Certified Instructor*—After being an RMT for 2 years, the individual is qualified to take the CI test.

Experience is the best qualification to look for when hiring a massage therapist. A prospective employee should be able to demonstrate his or her skills to a staff person who is experienced in receiving massage. Pay special attention to how the therapist directs and cares for the client and shows concern for modesty by using proper draping.

The two most popular forms of massage in health/fitness centers are swedish massage and shiatzu. Swedish massage is the most popular form of massage in America. The techniques include stroking and compression movements that increase circulation and mobility. Shiatzu is one of the most popular massage techniques in Japan. In Japanese, *shiatzu* means finger pressure. Shiatzu includes applying pressure with the ball of the thumb to one of the body's pressure points, relieving muscle tension and increasing circulation.

Various management options are available to any establishment wanting to start a massage division. Some facilities prefer a percentage arrangement, according to which the massage therapists are hired by management and given a percentage of the generated fees. Percentages vary from 40% to 90% of the funds going to the therapists. This arrangement allows the facility to collect a small percentage to cover basic operational expenses. Another option is to enter into a contractual arrangement with an outside massage service. This service pays a monthly fee for renting the space and keeps all funds generated. The equipment is provided by the establishment, whereas the daily operational expenses are paid for by the service. The final option is to hire a massage therapist as a full-time employee of the facility. The massage therapist is paid an annual salary, is supervised by management, and submits all daily massage fees. This method is preferred by community settings, because it ensures the massage therapist a steady income.

Forms of payment range from cash, check, and credit card to a predesigned billing arrangement. Credit vouchers or tickets can be sold as gift certificates to help promote the service. Insurance forms are also used for third-party payment if the massage was prescribed by a physician. The fees charged for a massage vary from $25 to $60 per hour, depending upon the area of the country, the facility setting, whether it is an urban or a rural setting, the class of clientele, and the therapist's expertise. Treatments are also given in half-hour increments, with fees ranging from $10 to $40.

The massage area should receive the normal custodial cleaning, with special attention given to the floors around the massage table, doorknobs, and handrails. These areas should be sterilized as part of a daily cleaning schedule. Linens should be changed after each client, including pillow cases and any draping material. The table surface should be cleaned with alcohol and the linens stored in a closed container until they can be transported for cleaning. Finally, therapists must wash their hands following each treatment. Alcohol can be used if water is not easily available. These sanitation rules are established to prevent the transferrance of any skin infection or disease from one client to another.

NURSERY

Many fitness center managers who currently manage nurseries state that they are rarely profitable (they often end up costing money to operate), and they are considered one big headache to operate. But they quickly add that having a nursery means the difference between an individual's joining their club or a competitive club (Heckelman, 1987). In today's market a nursery is a necessary ingredient for providing a full-service health/fitness facility.

The operation of an on-site child care facility has become a complicated matter. Recent litigation of child care centers has caused federal and local government agencies to reevaluate licensing standards for all child care facilities. The confusion that exists with health/fitness centers that have nurseries is the distinction between a complete day-care center and a nursery or drop-in care center.

The complaint among club owners is that the type of care offered in a health/fitness facility is different from that which is offered by a full-time day-care facility. The parents of the children are actually on the premises and available in case of an emergency. The length of time that a child is left at a health/fitness facility averages between 1 and 2 hours, compared to the 8–10 hours a child spends at a full-time nursery.

As a result, a wide variation of child care regulations exists from state to state. Before you include a nursery in your plans, contact city or state officials for clarification of the code requirements. For example, some states require ratios for the number of square feet per child and a child-to-staff ratio depending upon the age of the child. Costly mistakes can be prevented by following this approach. As an example of the differences that exist between states regarding day-care licensing, Table 11.1 compares and contrasts the regulations of New York and Texas.

Table 11.1   A Comparison of Day-Care Licensing Between New York State and Texas

New York	Texas
Day-care of children shall mean care provided for 3 or more children	Day-care of children shall mean care provided for 12 or more children.
Such care shall be for more than 0 and less than 24 hours per day.	Such care shall be for 3 hours less than 24 hours per day.
No child shall be accepted for care unless the child has received a medical examination by a physician.	No child shall be accepted for care unless the child has immunization shots.
One sanitary toilet and one sanitary washbasin for every group of 15 children.	One sanitary toilet and one washbasin for every 25 children.
Readily accessible outdoor play space shall be provided.	The center must have at least 80 square feet of outdoor space for each child.
A room temperature of at least 68 degrees Fahrenheit must be maintained.	No provision for this requirement.
In a center with less than 45 enrolled children, a full-time staff person shall possess (a) an associate of arts in a child-related area or 2 years of college, and (b) 1 year of related supervisory experience.	In a center with less than 35 enrolled children, a full-time staff person shall possess (a) a high school diploma, and (b) 2 years of related supervisory experience.

The staffing of a child care area depends upon whether the facility must meet licensing standards. The staff requirements of a drop-in care center are established by city or state personnel. Prerequisites for employment include age, education, and experience. Other options for hiring include using services such as the American Nanny Program, which is a training program for child care professionals. However, the most widely used child care employees are young mothers who have their own children and want to supplement their incomes.

Those individuals who apply for the nursery position must be carefully screened and interviewed; have all references checked; and show competency, good judgment, and self-control in working with children. Some health/fitness center directors even ask for character references so they can obtain further insight into how this individual handles him- or herself around children.

The peak hours of health/fitness centers dictate the nursery's hours of operation. Facilities that have a constant flow of participants leave the nursery open 10–12 hours a day. If the participant usage is sporadic, a split schedule is used based on the high-volume hours. To accommodate the long hours of some nursery operations, management dictates shifts that last approximately 3–4 hours to limit the stress of child care. Other clubs restrict the number of children that can be allowed at one time and limit the age requirement to children no younger than 6 months. A maximum time limit for child care is also recommended to prevent parents from taking advantage of the service offered.

Fees for nursery care range from a free service to $1–$3 per hour per child. The fees are generally adjusted to a minimum level because the nursery is offered as a benefit to the patrons. The average hourly rate for nursery attendants ranges from $4 to $5 per hour, depending upon the size and location of the club.

Nurseries built in health/fitness centers are currently constructed in rooms of 500–800 square feet and placed away from fitness-related areas. A bathroom is built into the room, or an existing bathroom close to the nursery is made available for the children's use. Some fitness centers even have nurseries with access to the outside for outdoor play. Everything in the nursery should be up to professional safety standards, including covered electrical sockets, daily maintenance requirements, and toys that are safe for children's use. A one-way mirror or observational window is an additional item that parents like having so that they can periodically monitor their children.

Despite the difficulties that nurseries are experiencing, their popularity is high among members of health/fitness facilities. Over 86% of all tennis clubs, racquetball clubs, and multi-recreation centers polled in the IRSA (1984) industry survey had nurseries or baby-sitting facilities. The increasing number of members with infants and children and the ongoing need to attract new members make nurseries a necessity for today's health/fitness centers.

LOCKER DESK PROCEDURES

The front desk of a corporate, commercial, or community health/fitness facility is the first point of contact for individuals entering the facility. The front desk reflects the overall management and organizational atmosphere, and is typically located in the midst of a stimulating environment for the participants' workout area. Many owners and operators are convinced that the front desk is the backbone for every successful health/fitness facility.

The quality of a properly managed front desk depends entirely upon the staff and how each responsibility is carried out. Management looks for individuals who possess an open and friendly personality, a natural service attitude, and a personal commitment to the fitness field. By choosing individuals with these traits, an organization also obtains salespeople for the program. Hiring locker desk personnel must follow a predetermined interview process. Each potential staff member should complete an application form that provides past work experience, educational history, and a personality profile. After this individual is interviewed, a complete check of all references should then be performed.

Once the appropriate individuals are hired, the training phase begins. This phase is the most important part of the front desk operation. Time should be spent in educating the new employee about locker desk procedures, explaining the specific job responsibilities, and reinforcing management's position on such areas as greeting members, using the PA system, observing the dress code, and following court reservation procedures. The essential tools of a good locker desk attendant should be presented during this phase of training.

A common mistake of fitness center managers is to overload the front desk with responsibilities. These additional responsibilities prevent attendants from properly servicing the participants. Locker desk personnel should primarily be concerned with providing personalized service, controlling member check-in, and answering the phone. Additional locker desk responsibilities include the following:

- Laundry
- Lost and found
- Racquetball/tennis court reservations
- Pro shop sales
- Special events
- Equipment check-out
- Maintenance

Customer service is the area that should be stressed. If any of these additional responsibilities prohibit personnel from servicing

members immediately and efficiently, then a reduction in responsibilities or an increase in personnel should be considered.

The number of employees at the front desk is determined by the volume of people participating during the peak hours. One attendant can operate the front desk during slow periods in the day. An additional two to three attendants are necessary as the numbers increase. This arrangement often calls for a split work schedule or an overlapping schedule.

Member and guest check-in procedures are a major concern of management. Numerous identification (ID) check-in systems are being used with varying degrees of success. The most common systems include the pictured ID card, the magnetic strip or bar code ID for computers, and the plastic-laminated ID card. Each identification card provides basic information that identifies the individual and indicates whether the membership is current or expired.

If guests are allowed in the facility, a separate identification card should be prepared for them. The guest card should require the following information:

- Name
- Address
- Date
- Sponsoring member
- Approved signature
- Paid or complementary status
- Identification number

Numbering guest cards allows management to verify the guest usage with the actual guest fees collected. This method also alerts the locker desk attendants that management is closely monitoring the guest income.

Once the system of identification is decided upon, a check-in procedure should be written out and explained to all locker desk attendants. Here are some examples of member and guest check-in policies for the XYZ Fitness Center.

Member and Guest Check-In Procedures
for XYZ Fitness Center

Membership Cards:

1. Members are to present a card each time they use the facility. In exchange for their card give them a key to the locker room, one or two towels, and a laundry bag. Make sure the picture on the card matches the person who gives it to you!

2. Check the date on the card and, if it has expired, keep it and insert it into the guest fee money bag.

3. If member has no card, check the file for it; if it's not there, inform the member that he or she must fill out a blue card. The member can forget his or her card three times. From then on the member must pay $5 each time he or she forgets the card.

4. Do not allow members to leave their cards consistently at the desk. Try to make sure they pick cards up before they leave.

5. If a member has lost his or her card, send that person to the business office for a new one.

6. Members who leave without turning in their keys will be dealt with by the professional staff. Their cards will be turned in to the business office and members must go there to get the card back.

7. If members lose their key they must pay a $3 fee before their card is returned.

Guest Policy:

1. All guests will pay a $5 guest fee. They must be accompanied by a member when they check in.

2. Guest cards are to be issued and placed in the key slot. When the key is turned back in, place the guest card into the money bag. Please fill the card in completely! If you cannot read the names/numbers, ask the guest to rewrite their card legibly.

3. Minimum age for a guest is 18.

4. A guest is limited to using the facility a maximum of three times per year. While the guest fills out the card, check for his or her name on the computer printout of three or more visits.

5. Any staff member must pay for his or her guests and follow all guest policies above.

An efficient phone answering and paging policy can effectively portray a professional image of the organization. It is management's responsibility first to provide a quality phone system. The system should provide updated features that allow locker attendants to transfer calls easily to other staff members, numerous lines so a busy signal is never heard, and

Phone and Paging Procedures
for XYZ Fitness Center

Phone Procedures and Paging:

1. Always answer the phone politely and professionally, such as, "Hello, this is the XYZ Fitness Center, may I help you?"

    Extension 000 is to be used

    a) to contact other offices.
    b) before and after business office hours.

2. The phone number 000-0000 is for racquetball and tennis court reservations.

3. When paging with the PA system, remember:
    a) Never page during an exercise class. The only exception would be for an extreme emergency.
    b) Repeat the message twice.
    c) Messages for members are to be posted near the locker desk on the message board. When paging the member say, "Joe Johnson, you have a message at the locker desk; Joe Johnson, you have a message at the locker desk." Tack the message on the board and make sure to print the message so it can be read.

4. Do not use the phones at the locker desk to make personal calls.

---

an automatic call-back to prevent excess holding time. Procedures should be established for answering the phone and greeting the caller. Policies pertaining to making court reservations and taking messages need to be listed and monitored. The following list provides some examples of phone and paging procedures.

A racquetball and tennis court reservation policy is another area that management needs to develop. Prior to implementing the policy, management decides on a uniform reservation form for both tennis and racquetball. The two most popular reservation forms are printed reservation booklets or computer software packages. The method chosen is only as good

as the procedures followed by the staff. An example of racquetball and tennis court reservation procedures is shown on page 294.

FOOD AND BEVERAGE SERVICE

Operating a food and beverage service in a health/fitness setting is a challenging business. The types of food and beverage services available are so varied that no two facilities follow the same operational format. Managers have found that tastes and trends differ with geographic areas, ethnic groups, and metropolitan

---

Racquetball and Tennis Court Reservation Procedures for XYZ Fitness Center

Racquetball and Tennis Court Reservations:

1. Print when making the reservations and place your initials beside the reservation.
2. Print the last names of the players who wish to play during the designated times in the reservation book.
3. Be familiar with the program brochure regarding tennis and racquetball regulations.
4. Staff may use the courts on an availability basis only.
5. Check the courts each hour to make sure players have checked in and turn out lights on courts not being used.

---

populations. The inconsistencies of the food and beverage business often cause health/fitness owners to be reluctant to enter this market.

Although there are inherent risks involved in providing a food and beverage service, history has shown that this area ranks third in total revenues for a multipurpose fitness center. According to the IRSA (1984) industry data survey, food and beverage revenues accounted for 8.5% of sales at multipurpose clubs with indoor pools and 9.8% of sales at other multipurpose clubs.

The success of any business must start with a plan. In the food and beverage business this plan should address

- the basic philosophy of operation,
- overall design concepts,
- management options,
- operational functions, and
- problem areas.

Each issue should be addressed thoroughly, keeping in mind that the customers want quality, convenience, value, and exclusivity.

Deciding upon a basic philosophy consists first of answering a number of questions. For example, what kind of food service do I want? Do I want to maximize profits or am I more interested in providing a service to the participants? Will alcohol be served? Will breakfast, lunch, and dinner be served? Will the menu selection provide an assortment or will there be a restricted menu? The answers to these questions will dictate the operational structure and management guidelines you require.

Basically, there are two kinds of food and beverage operations: the traditional sit-down restaurant and the fast-food restaurant. These options are further broken down into the services that the majority of health/fitness centers provide:

- juice bar,
- vending machines,
- restaurant, and
- cocktail lounge/restaurant

Your decision on the option that is most suitable will depend on

- participant volume,
- space availability,
- type of clientele and income levels,
- competition, and
- labor issues.

After determining the type of food and beverage service to provide, management's alternatives will need to be discussed. The options include owner-operated, lease arrangement, and seeking the guidance of a consulting team. Currently, the majority of health/ fitness facilities are staffing and operating their own food and beverage services. The total management control and the opportunity of increased profits make this option most appealing. The second option, a lease arrangement, reduces the financial risk while relieving the facility of operational responsibilities. The third option involves consulting firms that assist in organizing issues related to managing a food and beverage service.

Pricing the food and beverage selections depends on the actual food cost, comparing pricing of similar facilities, and what the clientele can afford. An average markup of 100% is used for food items, whereas beverages are priced according to market value. Depending upon the type of food and beverage operation, food costs should range from 25% to 45% of sales; alcohol and other beverages should be between 25% and 35%. A successful restaurant in a health/fitness facility can break even or reflect a profit as high as 10%–15% annually.

On the average, inventory should turn over one to two times per month. Any periodic fluctuations in inventory can result in a lack of control. Control manuals, ordering books, item counts, and personal observation are methods available to help control inventory. An inventory system should be organized and implemented to determine overall food usage and the types of food used the most and to double-check inventory depletion against cash receipts.

Before you get into the food and beverage business, you should understand the possible pitfalls associated with it. These pitfalls can only be prevented through education and experience in the restaurant business. An awareness of these areas can guide managers away from costly mistakes. Common pitfalls include the following:

- *Food costs out-of-line:* Price food according to value to avoid reducing revenues.
- *Insufficient purchasing procedures:* Prices for food are negotiable. Work toward a purchasing power position.
- *Excessive labor costs:* Organize staff schedules to maximize labor output.
- *Attempting to satisfy everyone's needs:* The old adage that you can't please everyone all the time is especially true in the food and beverage service.
- *Exotic menu selection:* Stick to an average menu selection that pleases the masses.
- *Improper facility design:* Plan ahead for such things as crowd flow, volume increases, kitchen design, and food preparation areas.

The essential ingredient for a successful food and beverage operation is volume. When you put a restaurant in a health/fitness facility the volume will naturally be less than that of restaurants in shopping malls or on heavily travelled thoroughfares. Architects of health club restaurants design them to accommodate 35% of the daily volume of the center. This figure provides an estimated number for owners and operators to use when comparing actual versus expected portions.

SUMMARY

This chapter outlined specific operational issues that can be adapted to a commercial, corporate, or community program. The specific topics mentioned (policies and procedures, business office management, maintenance management, swimming pool/whirlpool maintenance, safety procedures, pro shop operations, massage, nursery, locker desk procedures, and food and beverage service) were designed to show the variety of organizational procedures that must be established prior to opening any health/fitness facility. Staff philosophy, daily responsibility lists, attention to detail, and communication must all be considered when addressing the topic areas mentioned in this chapter. It is recommended that an operational manual stating the necessary procedures to be followed by your staff be prepared. This approach will insure a consistent level of management by all personnel involved.

CHAPTER 12

Documentation

Documentation in a health/fitness facility simply means keeping records of all aspects of the operation. Careful record keeping is sometimes overlooked, and this can lead to problems when operational reports are required by management, owners, administrators, and so forth. Learning to document thoroughly helps a manager improve the program's operational efficiency, effectiveness, and profitability. In fact, careful record keeping sometimes reveals many aspects of a program that may not be commonly known.

As explained in chapter 8, documentation is needed for the evaluation of performance and procedures used within a health/fitness program. In this age of accountability, the health/fitness manager must be able to state objectives for the program and show its operational efficiency and accomplishments.

In developing the overall documentation plan for the health/fitness center, the manager should determine specific items within three major areas that need to be tabulated: membership, staff, and operational departments. The manager should then determine who will tabulate the data within each of those three areas. Due dates for data reports should be estimated so that final results can be analyzed. The results of this documentation/evaluation procedure are used, of course, to help set plans for the future.

In this chapter we examine the key items that need to be tabulated in the three areas. Then we explore how computer systems can aid in the comprehensive documentation of a program. Finally, we illustrate how a program can be documented through a cost-benefit analysis and how this might impact an organization's bottom line.

MEMBERSHIP DOCUMENTATION

Perhaps the most important documentation that takes place within a health/fitness program pertains to the member/participant/patient. Details of collecting demographic, health screening, testing, and exercise information on the participants have been described in chapter 8. Basically, the information should include the following:

- Name, sex, age, height, weight
- Marital status, children
- Address, telephone (home and office)
- Membership contracts, program registration
- Health screen information, needs and interests
- Medical clearance records
- Fitness test results, fitness goals
- Exercise records, club usage
- Services purchased, amenities desired
- Injury reports

A well-organized filing system is needed to supplement any computer records kept on participants. In addition to computer records of account balances, addresses, and membership status, items that might be kept in files include registration or membership contracts, signed informed consent forms, fitness test results, medical examination records, and health risk appraisal results. These records are important from insurance and liability standpoints. For example, should a participant incur an injury, records in the file can show that the person was informed of the program risks and the recommended exercise prescription. This helps document the safe policies and procedures of the health/fitness center and may avert a possible lawsuit stemming from the injury incident. However, you can never guarantee that such documentation will protect you. It is simply one step you can take to sway things in your favor.

STAFF DOCUMENTATION

Next in order of documentation importance is the evaluation of program personnel. This has been described in chapter 7 and involves the collection of information about the staff. Generally, the personnel evaluation involves the following:

- Job knowledge, training, and experience
- Willingness to accept responsibility
- Planning and organization of work
- Quality and quantity of work
- Cost consciousness and control
- Relationships with others
- Leadership qualities
- Initiative and resourcefulness
- Originality and creativeness
- Soundness of judgment
- Dependability
- Personal appearance, speech, and habits
- Attendance and punctuality

- Support for organization goals and policies
- Career objectives

DEPARTMENT DOCUMENTATION

This type of documentation involves the various operations within a health/fitness facility. The exercise and health promotion programs, of course, are the major operations to evaluate, but other departments in a health/fitness facility might also include maintenance, laundry, food and beverage, pro shop, and so forth.

For a health/fitness program in a corporate setting, a high priority for documenting operational departments might involve a cost-benefit analysis. This is explored later in this chapter. In this case, activity levels could be documented by recording participant exercise days or calories expended and related to medical costs and absenteeism rates incurred by the employees. The costs of the program (budget analysis) could then be compared to potential savings in medical claims and sick time to determine the cost-benefit ratio.

A high priority in the community and clinical settings may be to document participation rates in various programs such as exercise classes, weight control classes, stress management programs, and smoking cessation courses to determine the success of those programs. The highest priority in the commercial setting is profitability; therefore, operating costs are closely monitored in this setting to determine program charges and minimum registration rates.

Although the priorities of documentation in the various health/fitness settings may be different, there is some overlap of application. For instance, there may be as much concern about profitability in the community and clinical settings as there is in the commercial setting. Therefore, operating costs in community and clinical programs are also tracked carefully to determine program offerings and fee structures. In addition, operating costs are documented carefully in the corporate setting because companies are concerned about operating a cost-efficient health/fitness program. Although there may not be program fees for employees in corporate health/fitness programs and there may be no concern about profitability, there still is concern about cost containment.

Next we will discuss the value of the computer and its inherent use for documenting the operations and programs of a health/fitness facility.

COMPUTER SYSTEMS

In this age of high technology, the computer is becoming increasingly accessible to health/fitness facilities for documenting operations and programs. In fact, health club owners and managers of health/fitness facilities are being inundated with computer options including micros, PCs, ATs, XTs, supermicros, multi-users, minis, mainframes, modems, scanners, dot matrix printers, ink-jet printers, laser printers, and color monitors. The software for these computer systems is even more extensive, with options ranging from health risk screening and fitness testing to club management. Reductions in the cost of hardware and improvements in the efficiency and application of the software have almost made the computer a necessity for a successful operation. The computer is now becoming a very practical tool that can save time, help managers make decisions, and control operations.

For these reasons, many computer software companies have been formed to meet the needs and interests of the health/fitness field. Software systems are now available for documenting the following:

- Health screening procedures
- Fitness test results
- Medical reports
- Exercise prescriptions
- Nutrition evaluations
- Diet plans
- Educational reports
- Check-in control
- Activity participation rates
- Exercise log records
- Tournament schedules
- Equipment utilization
- Inventory
- Traffic flow
- Membership status
- Accounting procedures
- Club management
- Research

A myriad of health risk appraisals (HRAs) are available on the software market to aid in the screening of participants. Patton et al. (1986) listed 56 different health risk appraisal instruments, 36 of which are computer scored. These HRAs may be useful for documenting levels of health risk and as educational motivators for encouraging lifestyle changes to reduce disease risk.

Computerized report systems for fitness testing are also available to show strengths and weaknesses in a participant's cardiovascular, body composition, flexibility, and strength fitness profile. The computer can also be used to show progress over time in these fitness parameters as an individual participates in a prescribed health/fitness program. In this situation, the computer facilitates the counseling process as a motivational tool to encourage participants to change lifestyles and improve fitness.

Software systems are now available for retrieving medical reports from physicians and merging those reports with health risk appraisals and fitness test results for the purpose of writing an exercise prescription. This system is used in those health/fitness centers that work closely with physicians and hospital wellness centers in evaluating participants before exercise prescriptions are written and activity programs are initiated.

Exercise prescription software is also available and becoming very popular because it individualizes the exercise program to the participant based on fitness test results and saves a considerable amount of time for the health/fitness staff member. Exercise prescription software is available for programs of stretching, walking, jogging, swimming, outdoor cycling, stationary cycling, rowing, cross-country skiing, rope jumping, bench stepping, calisthenics, and weight training.

Exercise equipment is also being computerized to provide individual exercise prescriptions. For example, on some stationary cycle ergometers, the computer comes to life when the participant starts pedaling. A preprogrammed workout is selected in which the computer automatically regulates the cycle's resistance simulating a warm-up, a steady climbing workout, a rolling hills regimen, a constant workload program, and a cooldown. All of this is conducted by the computer while the participant watches color television or listens to FM stereo radio or a tape.

The computer records and stores the work, compares the individual's progress over time, and sets goals for the participant. It monitors the calories burned, the distance traveled, and the average heart rate response. Some exercise devices monitor the participant's heart rate during the work and regulate the workload to keep the heart rate at a preset target rate.

Strength training equipment is also being manufactured with computer-assisted monitoring for the participant. Strength levels are tested individually and stored by the computer for future reference. Training resistances are then selected by the computer, and the participant follows the recommended circuit. The computer compares the individual's progress over time and sets new goals.

Computerized exercise devices are designed to challenge, motivate, and entertain participants. This strategy saves documentation time for health/fitness staff members, keeps the participant interest high, and helps ensure a recurring participation rate in the health/fitness facility's programs.

An extensive array of computer software is now available for analysis of nutrition levels. The programs are designed to calculate the nutrient content of typical meals and red-flag areas of deficiency. The programs are also designed to generate diet and menu plans based on selected calorie levels or areas of special interest.

Educational report software is available for summarizing test results from health risk appraisals, medical and fitness evaluations, and exercise progress reports. Recommendations are made for improving health and fitness by modifying lifestyle behavior and following programs of regular exercise, good nutrition, stress management, smoking abstinence, and avoiding other substance abuse.

Some health/fitness centers now use the computer for check-in control at the entrance to the facility. Membership card readers verify a member's status and allow entry to the facility. The card reader is part of a computer system that can be programmed to flag delinquent dues payments and therefore reject a member's card and entry to the facility until the account is balanced.

The member's card can also be used to enter a computer program designed to record exercise workouts and track participation rates in various programs. The computer is thus used to determine equipment utilization and traffic flow throughout the health/fitness facility. It can also be used to schedule special events such as tournaments and keep track of results in an accurate and efficient way.

Only a few years ago pencils and ledgers were used for accounting and budgeting procedures and the typewriter for word processing, management reports, mailing lists, and membership maintenance. Now the computer and a handy letter-quality printer are used for these management tasks. The electronic funds transfer (EFT) system allows a club to deduct dues automatically from a member's checking account or credit card account, simplifying bookkeeping and billing procedures.

Membership accounting software can also accommodate different charge rates for different types of memberships and special charge accounts. The software program stores membership data such as birthdays, anniversaries, and special interests, as well as business and home addresses.

And last, computers are used for research in health and fitness programs. It would be an enormous task to attempt researching medical costs, absenteeism, turnover, exercise patterns, fitness levels, and health risks without the aid of a computer. Data base software programs are available to manage the voluminous amount of data required to analyze such concepts as the cost-benefit ratio and generate management reports.

To illustrate how documentation of an operational program might be conducted in a corporate setting, we will now present a cost-benefit example.

COST-BENEFIT DOCUMENTATION

Cost-benefit analyses are probably most appropriate in the corporate setting, but the information on the cost-benefit ratio of health/fitness programs can be used by the community, clinical, and commercial settings to sell their programs to the corporate setting. The costs of a health/fitness facility and program are obvious and easy to document, as illustrated in chapter 13. Those costs generally include the following:

- Facility
- Construction
- Amortization
- Rent
- Utilities
- Maintenance
- Equipment
- New purchases
- Maintenance
- Supplies
- Testing
- Educational
- Exercise/sports
- Office
- Staff
- Salaries
- Fringe benefits
- Miscellaneous
- Special events
- Awards
- Publications and dues
- Printing
- Travel
- Insurance
- Advertising and promotion

The benefits of an employee health/fitness program are not always as obvious as the costs, and some benefits may be difficult and sometimes impossible to document. Even so, many corporations view an employee health/fitness program very positively as a fringe benefit for employees, a recruiter of employees, an advertisement of the company, an upgrading of corporate image (Shephard,

1986), a saver of money, and increaser of profits (Gettman, 1986).

The American Heart Association (1984) lists several benefits of health/fitness programs, some of which are beneficial directly to companies and some directly to the participants. Those benefits of having fit employees may include the following:

- Reduced health care costs
- Lower absenteeism
- Lower turnover
- Higher morale
- Lower risk of developing cardiovascular disease
- Lower risk of incurring injuries during work or recreation
- Faster recovery time from injury or illness
- Increased energy and stamina
- Increased mental alertness
- Increased self-confidence and self-esteem
- Less tension and anxiety
- Increased productivity

Some of these benefits from implementing health/fitness programs have been documented. Benefits such as medical costs, absenteeism, turnover, activity participation, injury rate, disease risk, stamina, self-confidence, and anxiety levels can be documented and analyzed by scientific methods. Although the process can be quite extensive and time-consuming to obtain accurate records for scientific analysis, these benefits are considered tangible and measurable.

Other benefits such as productivity, morale, and mental alertness may be difficult, if not impossible, to document. Nevertheless, these benefits are often considered as real benefits, and even if they can't be documented, employee fitness programs are still offered in an attempt to achieve these outcomes.

In the corporate setting, cost-benefit documentation has been reviewed extensively by Shephard (1986). He states that the published information on cost-benefit ratios is primarily on white-collar employment. These published studies generally show favorable cost-benefit ratios. It is quite possible that studies showing unfavorable cost-benefit ratios have not yet been published.

Program Costs

As mentioned previously in this chapter and illustrated in chapter 13, program and facility costs are easy to document. In the corporate setting, the cost for exercise programs ranges from less than $50 to more than $600 per employee per year (see Table 12.1). These costs entail expenses for developing and maintaining in-house facilities and programs as well as expenses for using outside resources that are available in the community.

Table 12.1 Approximate Costs for Exercise Program Resources

Resources $0-$10 per month per employee

1. Self-help exercise programs
2. Walk, jog, cycle routes
3. Parks and recreation facilities
4. Public schools and college/university facilities
5. Community agency programs (social service/ health)

Resources $10-$50 per month per employee

1. Public school and college/university health and fitness programs
2. YMCA facilities and programs
3. Medical facilities and programs
4. Contract exercise instructors

(Cont.)

Table 12.1 (Continued)

Resources more than $50 per month per employee

1. Private health and fitness facilities
2. Dance/exercise studios
3. Commercial health clubs
4. In-house exercise programs

Note. From *Heart at Work: Exercise Program Coordinator's Guide* (p. 6) by the American Heart Association, 1984, Dallas, TX: Author. Copyright 1984 by the AHA. Reprinted by permission.

Gettman (1986) reported costs of $494 and $485 per employee-year spent by a petroleum company in 1982 and 1983, respectively, for an employee health/fitness program. An illustration of calculating these costs per employee-year from the documented budget costs of a corporate health/fitness program appears in Table 12.2. Those budget costs were compared to the potential savings per employee-year from having reduced absenteeism and medical costs associated with exercising employees. This analysis is discussed later in the "Program Benefits" section.

Table 12.2   Sample Corporate Health/Fitness Program Line-Item Budget Costs

Item	1982 cost ($)	1983 cost ($)
Staff salaries and fringe	108,788	113,140
Facility utilities and maintenance	89,204	86,007
Equipment purchases	9,868	465
Supplies	9,682	9,246
Miscellaneous:		
Health club memberships	98,840	89,820
Key employee medical exams	18,052	14,427
Special events	7,7891	3,088
Awards	10,617	5,531
Travel	10,378	4,222
Juice bar services	9,764	10,176
Data entry	5,525	2,315
Printing	2,594	1,668
Publications and dues	2,473	1,972
Service and repairs	756	818
TOTAL	384,332	342,895
Cost per employee-year	494	485

Shephard (1986) has also provided estimated costs of providing employee fitness facilities based on the anticipated number of participants (Table 12.3). His cost range of $100 to $350 is fairly narrow compared to the estimate from the American Heart Association. As Shephard noted in Table 12.3, Fielding (1982) reported that some companies spend as much as $1,000 per employee-year.

Shephard has also estimated that even in the simplest form of a home-based exercise program, the cost for extra clothing and food is approximately $300 per year. If an individual owned a health club membership in a commercial enterprise, joined a community- or clinically-based program, or participated in a company fitness program, this cost for extra clothing and food would exist along with the price for the club membership, community, or clinical program, or company program. In addition, travel expenses to and from the health/fitness center would have to be considered as an extra cost.

As the costs of health/fitness facilities and programs escalate with the increasing extensiveness of this endeavor in this country, the concept of cost sharing between the employee and the employer is also escalating in popularity. The cost-sharing idea not only reduces the program costs for both the individual and the company, but also promotes commitment on the part of the employee to participate in the program in which he or she has invested.

The concept of determining a cost-benefit ratio by comparing the costs of a health/fitness program to the benefits is explained in the next section.

Program Benefits

An excellent summary of the potential economic impact of employee fitness programs is provided by Shephard (1986) in Table 12.4. In analyzing the program benefits, Shephard includes such things as worker satisfaction,

Table 12.3 Estimated Costs of Providing Employee Fitness Facilities

Anticipated number of participants	Recommended facility	Cost per participant-year (in U.S. $)
5-50	minimal facility, testing, and exercise prescription only	100-350
75-250	150-300 m² facility with part- or full-time supervisor	250-350[a]
400-850	600-1,200 m² facility with full-time supervisor	200-350[a]

Note. From *Fitness and Health in Industry* (p. 243) by R.J. Shephard, 1986, New York: Karger. Copyright 1986 by Karger. Reprinted by permission.

[a]Some U.S. companies quote costs as high as $500-$1,000 per participant-year (Fielding, 1982). Much depends on (a) charges levied by a company for space occupancy, (b) size and luxury of the facility, (c) level of program supervision, and (d) efficiency of utilization.

Table 12.4 Potential Economic Impact of Employee Fitness/Lifestyle Program, Expressed in 1982 U.S. Dollars Per Worker-Year

Source	Economic impact ($)
Worker satisfaction	may be large (unknown)
Productivity	116
Absenteeism	30
Turnover	230
Health care costs	233
Injuries	40
Lifestyle	
Changes of appraised age	36[a]
Costs of cardiovascular illness	32
Cigarette- and alcohol-related diseases	32
Geriatric impact	35
	784

Note. From *Fitness and Health in Industry* (p. 255) by R.J. Shephard, 1986, New York: Karger. Copyright 1986 by Karger. Reprinted by permission.

[a]This figure assumes the lower age persists into retirement.

increased productivity, reduction of absenteeism and turnover, improvement of health, reduction of injuries, favorable changes of lifestyle, and enhanced geriatric prospects.

His total of $784 per worker-year represents an estimate of overall savings relative to costs of operating a fitness facility used by 20% of employees. As Shephard noted, this estimate is subject to considerable uncertainty. The estimate pertains to white-collar workers, and it is not known if it is applicable to blue-collar workers. Also, it is not known how long the benefits last or how much the benefits are attributable to the "halo" effect rather than exercise alone. For example, Manuso (1983) reported that reduced health care costs and more effective work could also be achieved by just using biofeedback.

Even if the intangible fringe benefits of enhanced recruitment and improved corporate image are overlooked, employee fitness/lifestyle programs seem well justified on a cost-benefit scale (Shephard, 1986). The fiscal gains from worker satisfaction are well recognized but not estimated in Table 12.4 because they are difficult to quantify. As an illustration of recognizing the benefits of worker satisfaction, Shephard noted that the Ford Motor Plant in Oakville, Ontario, reported a dramatic drop in the number of cars returned for warranty repairs following the implementation of a program designed to enhance the quality of working life for the employees. Shephard concluded that the satisfied worker has a better perception of health and is not likely to disrupt company productivity by smoking or alcohol/drug abuse.

The productivity benefit of $116 per worker-year in Table 12.4 was derived from an assumption that 20% of employees participate in an exercise/lifestyle program and the overall benefit would be 0.8% of payroll ($14,500 annual salary × 0.8% = $116 per worker-year). Gettman (1986) reported higher estimates of increased productivity represented by lower absenteeism rates in active versus sedentary employees in a petroleum company. The difference in sick time (and thus work time) between the two groups was 0.6% in 1982 and 1.1% in 1983. The average salary in the petroleum company was also higher ($27,000 in 1982 and $30,000 in 1983) than Shephard's value resulting in higher estimates of productivity benefits ($162 in 1982 and $330 per employee-year in 1983 for the petroleum company). In addition, the percentage of active participants in the petroleum company was higher than Shephard's estimate (58% active employees in 1982 and 63% active in 1983 for the petroleum company).

Shephard's estimate that 20% of employees become high adherents to an exercise/lifestyle program resulting in a $30 per worker-year benefit for reduced absenteeism is modest when compared to other studies on absenteeism. In the petroleum company study by Gettman (1986), the difference in sick time between active and sedentary employees represented $156 per employee-year in 1982 and $303 per employee-year in 1983.

The $230 turnover savings estimated by Shephard was based on a 13.5% turnover rate reduction among high adherents to an exercise program in a life insurance company measured over a 10-month period. At this particular company, the average cost of hiring and training a new employee was estimated to be $7,090. Assuming a 20% participation rate,

Shephard calculated the $230 per worker-year value as $7,090 × .135 × .20 × 1.2 = $230. Gettman (1986) has confirmed that companies can save substantial money from reduced turnover by having active employees. In his study, the turnover rate was lower among active employees; only 14% of all active employees resigned or were terminated during 1983 compared to the 41% of all sedentary employees who resigned or were terminated during 1983.

The $233 per worker-year savings in health care costs in Table 12.4 were based on an estimate of a $171 reduction in hospital costs plus a $62 reduction in physician fees from less use of the health care system after introduction of an employee fitness/lifestyle program (Shephard, 1986). Using a different analysis approach, Gettman (1986) found a similar medical cost savings value ($217 per employee-year) in the difference between medical claims filed by active versus sedentary employees.

Shephard (1986) also suggests that $40 per worker-year can be saved through containment of injuries during leisure hours resulting from enhanced physical fitness. This was calculated using Pravosudov's (1978) assumption that a fitness/lifestyle program could reduce the cost of recreation injuries by at least 50% and that there would be a reduction in absenteeism associated with the reduction in injury rate resulting in sick time savings.

In addition to the favorable economic impact shown for productivity, absenteeism, turnover, health care costs, and injuries, Shephard (1986) also provides a lengthy discussion on the assumptions underlying the positive economic impact estimates appearing in Table 12.4 from lifestyle changes including health risk appraisal studies, costs of cardiovascular disease, tobacco- and alcohol-related diseases, and the geriatric impact.

The $784 savings total estimated from all the benefits listed by Shephard seems reasonable. Gettman (1986) calculated a potential savings of $520 per employee-year by having active employees from just two documentable lifestyle factors—absenteeism and medical cost. Gettman (1986) has shown that even if the intangible benefits of an exercise program are overlooked, an employee fitness program recovered 107% of its operating budget (i.e., it paid for itself) from the savings in absenteeism and medical costs by having employees who exercise.

A Cost-Benefit Scenario

Perhaps the ultimate documentation goal in a corporate setting is calculating the cost-benefit ratio. Based on the combined information from Gettman (1986) and Shephard (1986), such a documentation procedure is presented in Table 12.5. When the estimated benefits for turnover, injuries, age, cardiovascular ill-

Table 12.5 A Cost-Benefit Scenario for a Corporate Health/Fitness Program

Cost item	1983 cost ($)	Benefit item	1983 benefit ($)
Salaries	113,140	Productivity[a]	233,310
Utilities and maintenance	86,007	Absenteeism[a]	214,221
Equipment purchases	465	Turnover[b]	162,610
Supplies	9,246	Health care costs[a]	153,419
Miscellaneous:		Injuries[b]	28,280
Health club memberships	89,820	Lifestyle	
Key employee medical exams	14,427	Appraised age[b]	25,452
Special events	3,088	Cardiovascular health[b]	22,624
Awards	5,531	Cigarette and alcohol disease[b]	22,624
Travel	4,222	Geriatric impact[b]	24,745
Juice bar services	10,176		
Data entry	2,315		
Printing	1,668		
Publications and dues	1,972		
Service and repairs	818		
Total	342,895	Total	887,285
Cost per employee-year	485	Benefit per employee-year	1,255

[a]Calculated values for 707 total employees.

[b]Shephard estimations (see Table 12.4) for 707 employees.

ness, tobacco- and alcohol-related diseases, and the geriatric impact provided by Shephard are added to the calculated benefits for productivity, absenteeism, and health care costs, the benefit per employee-year soars to a value of $1,255. This is a cost-benefit ratio of 1:2.5.

Based on this information, it would be appropriate to conclude that the tangible (measurable) benefits of an employee fitness program added to the intangible (undocumentable) benefits more than justify the investment in the program. This conclusion could apply to programs that use in-house facilities as well as programs that use outside resources. In fact, the outside providers would be wise to use the available cost-benefit data in selling services to corporate clients. The costs of an outside provider can be analyzed in the same way as costs for an in-house program, and the benefits can be treated similarly. The end result is the same—fitness/lifestyle programs seem well justified on a cost-benefit scale. All of this information is possible because careful records were kept on participants and documentation procedures were used to analyze real data.

MANAGEMENT REPORTS

Documentation of a health/fitness program makes good business sense. Management decisions about particular programs are usually made based on a mixture of intuition, emotion, facts, figures, and calculations or estimations of the program's effectiveness. Management reports typically include membership demographics, program participation rates, and budget information. Documenting participation rates and costs of programs helps to determine which programs are offered. The ideal management report probably includes a calculated cost-benefit ratio.

SUMMARY

The documentation principles outlined in this chapter will help determine the effectiveness, operational efficiency, or profitability of a health/fitness program. Careful record keeping can not be overemphasized. In developing the documentation plan for the health/fitness facility, the manager should determine specific items that need to be tabulated within three major areas: membership, staff, and operational departments.

Although the priorities of documentation differ among the corporate, community, clinical, and commercial settings, there is some overlap of application. Operational costs are important items documented in all settings.

Documenting a cost-benefit ratio seems most appropriate for the corporate setting, but the community, clinical, and commercial settings would be wise to help companies conduct such documentation to show program effectiveness.

CHAPTER 13

Financial Considerations

A sound understanding of financial management is a prerequisite for operating a business effectively. Traditionally, health/fitness managers have not been trained in the business and financial aspect of operating a facility; instead, their training has placed more emphasis on the knowledge of the fitness area (Povermo, 1984). Unfortunately, poor financial management has contributed to the wave of bankruptcies now seen in the commercial fitness market (Kilburg & Stischek, 1985). Successful fitness center managers have found that the financial management methods used in a small business are easily applied to budgeting a health/fitness program.

Providing a well-structured financial plan is as important as hiring a good staff, providing quality programs, and designing a first-class facility. The financial strategy must include all possible fiscal considerations, not in a loosely structured fashion, but in a comprehensive and concise plan. The goal of this chapter is to introduce the necessary ingredients in developing basic financial planning. The issues presented can be applied to a community, corporate, or commercial health/fitness setting. We will discuss how to establish bookkeeping/accounting procedures; prepare a budget; and keep track of revenues, expenses, financial statements, insurance, and taxes.

An assortment of accounting terms is used throughout this discussion. To assist your reading of this chapter, a list of accounting definitions is presented in the appendix to this chapter.

ESTABLISHING BOOKKEEPING/ ACCOUNTING PROCEDURES

Prior to establishing an accounting system, you would benefit from the expertise of an experienced accountant. The accountant's role is not only to help establish the books but also to balance the books periodically and advise you on tax-saving measures. The accountant also answers your financial questions and provides guidelines as the business grows.

The purpose of developing a good bookkeeping system is not only to satisfy the government tax law requirements, but more importantly to obtain the necessary information to operate the business. The books are the only source of complete information that a business can use. Only with a good bookkeeping and accounting system can a manager/

owner evaluate the business and make changes and plans for the future.

The key to establishing any bookkeeping system is accountability. The books must account for every penny coming into and going out of the business. To achieve this system, there must be a series of checks and balances so all funds can be checked and rechecked. A single-entry bookkeeping system is common in small health/fitness centers (gross revenues of $500,000 or less). This type of bookkeeping system tracks all funds in a single-ledger arrangement. A system of this type is best for a small business because it keeps paperwork and financial calculations to a minimum, while providing the basic information to manage the business and to prepare tax returns.

There are two disadvantages to a single-entry bookkeeping system. First, although income and expense figures are recorded, a complete record of inventory, equipment, outstanding loans, or other assets and liabilities is not available. Second, there is no built-in double-check system for financial accuracy. Often these disadvantages can be offset by keeping additional asset records and inventory reports, but the lack of a double-check system for financial transactions is an important issue to consider when establishing a bookkeeping system.

As more multimillion dollar health/fitness facilities are built, the accounting complexities of operating these facilities also increase. A single-entry bookkeeping system lacks the complete set of financial information required to deal with the complexities. An alternative is a double-entry system that provides cross-checks and automatically balances the books. Every transaction requires two separate entries: a *debit* or a *credit*. Total debits must equal total credits for the books to be in balance.

It is not uncommon for some health/fitness programs to combine specific features of both a single- and a double-entry system. For example, adding assets, liabilities, and equipment records to an already-established single-entry system is a way to integrate both systems. Double-entry bookkeeping is highly complex and should be managed by a skilled professional. A double-entry system is only recommended when all other methods prove to be inefficient.

Whatever system is adopted, daily records should itemize all membership sales and other revenues. Expenditures should be classified by heading (e.g., maintenance, utilities, equipment, etc.). A daily ledger should account for all income and expense items. Samples of an income ledger and an expenditure ledger are shown on page 311.

Record keeping is of little value unless the results are closely analyzed and compared to the organization's objectives. To operate a health/fitness facility properly, accurate records must be kept for (a) fulfilling legal requirements, such as filing income taxes; (b) safeguarding assets, such as evaluating profits/losses; and (c) planning and controlling operations, such as marketing programs (Epperson, 1977). Financial information should at least be kept for membership records, accounts payable, payroll, bank statements/cash receipts, and tax records. As a result of maintaining these records, you have the option of generating a variety of management reports. Figure 13.1 is a list of reports that can be developed from bookkeeping records.

The next step in establishing a bookkeeping system is opening a business checking account. Visit a variety of banks and determine the internal requirements of each. For example, what will the bank charges be, what is the minimum amount that must remain in an account before a service charge is assessed, and what additional services can be provided that other banks cannot (free printing of checks, easy deposit capabilities, or an initial line of credit)? Take the time to find a banker who will work with you and is willing to accommodate your needs.

Sample Income Ledger

1	2	3	4	5	6	7
DATE	SALES PERIOD	TAXABLE SALES	SALES TAX	NON-TAXABLE SALES		TOTAL SALES
1	Mart Lease			750 00		750 00
2	Coke Money			60 00		60 00
3	Men's Income (Dues)	11 190 00	685 39			11 875 39
4	Women's Income (Dues)	5 000 00	306 25			5 306 25
5	Guest Fees			100 00		100 00
6	Kit Locker Fees (ladies)	250 00	15 31			265 31
7	Racquetball Tourney			150 00		150 00
8	Kit Locker Fees (ladies)	50 00	3 06			53 06
9	One month membership	100 00	6 13			106 13
10						
11						
12						
13						
14						
15						
16						
17						
18						
19						
20						
21						
22						
23						
24						
25						
26						
27						
28						
29						
30						
31						
	Totals for month	16 590 00	1 016 14	1 060 00		18 666 05

Sample Expenditure Ledger

DATE	CHECK NO.	PAYEE	TOTAL	1 MDSE. & MATLS.	2 SUPPLIES, POSTAGE, ETC.	3 LABOR NON-EMPL.	4 EMPLOYEE PAYROLL	5 ADVERTISING	6 RENT	7 UTILITIES	8 TAXES & LICENCES	9	10 MISC.	11 NON-DEDUCT.
1/2	737	Smith Electric	2819	2819										
1/3	738	U.S. Postmaster	3200	3200										
1/4	739	Jones Hardware	1950	1100									850	
1/5	740	Electric Company	14812							14812				
1/5	741	Johnson Holding Company	100000						100000					
1/6	742	Smith Electric	1238	1238										
1/7	743	Acme Paper	15200		15200									
1/8	744	Telephone Company	2863							2863				
1/9	745	City of Dallas (Triathlon)	52200					52200						

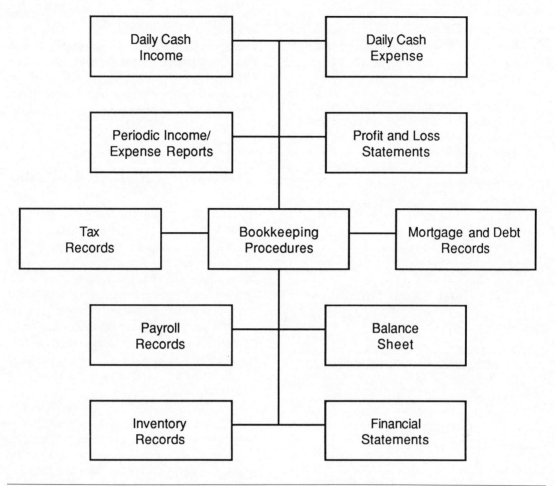

Figure 13.1. Reports that can be generated from bookkeeping records.

Certain business rules should be observed when handling cash transactions:

- Keep your personal cash separate from cash generated by the business.
- Use a bank account for your business funds and deposit all cash receipts in the account on a daily basis.
- Record all incoming cash—the amounts, along with their sources and dates.
- Pay all business bills by check. Never make a disbursement out of daily cash receipts.

- Make a disbursement only when you have received a supplier's invoice, receipt, or paid-out voucher dated and signed by the person who gets the check.
- Keep a check on all daily cash receipts and disbursements (Lasser, 1983).

Another system that needs to be established is a petty-cash fund. Not all expenditures are paid for by check. Cash is needed to pay for such things as postage, delivery charges, entertainment expenses, car fares, and minor maintenance items. You start a petty-cash fund by writing a check of a predetermined amount to ''Petty cash'' and placing the funds in a cash box. The distribution of funds should be organized according to a strict accounting procedure:

- Establish a maximum amount that can be used for cash disbursements. Any expenditures above this amount must be paid for by check.
- Develop a petty-cash slip or voucher that is used by any staff member requesting cash. This voucher must state what the cash is for and the cost of the item and have an approval signature. A typed petty cash slip looks like this:

Petty Cash Slip

No. _____ Amount $_____

RECEIVED OF PETTY CASH

For _____

Charge to _____

_____

_____ _____
Approved by   Received by

- When cash is given out, always replace it with a petty-cash slip so the amount of cash plus the vouchers always equals the check amount that was originally drawn.
- Once petty cash becomes low, write another check to petty cash to restore the fund to its original amount.

Simplicity is the key to organizing a good bookkeeping/accounting system. Adopt a system that is easily integrated into the business, provides quick daily use application, and is understood and periodically analyzed.

Be wary of the claims of highly technical accounting packages. These systems are oftentimes only understood by the people who sell them. It is important for the manager, who is ultimately responsible for the financial success of an operation, to have a clear understanding of all phases of the accounting process.

BUDGET PREPARATION

It is not uncommon for some health/fitness centers to attempt to operate a facility without a budget, hoping that memory or luck will work out the financial situation. Typically, this style of management has caused facilities to encounter early cash flow problems without realizing they exist. A health/fitness facility that doesn't have financial projections or monthly comparisons is operating by crisis management. As a result, when financial problems occur, it is often too late to respond to the situation.

Budgeting for any business involves projecting the amount of money that will be spent during a 1-year period and allocating the money among various operational components. Planning and controlling a budget are important for ensuring the cost-effectiveness of all phases of the business. A budget also enables management to evaluate the importance of various programs, while determining the overall financial status of the organization.

Planning a budget involves estimating increases or decreases in the cost of facility operations and the initial cost of developing new programs. All costs should be included when planning the budget. Nonprojected expenses, which usually consist of equipment expenditures, facility renovations, and additional staffing needs, are often overlooked. The biggest problem facing health/fitness managers and owners is paying for capital expenditures that are not allocated in the annual budget. Avoiding this problem requires additional time and preplanning in the preparation of the budget. Periodic planning meetings should be held to determine specific issues that will affect the budget during the year and the potential costs involved. Once the plan is adopted it must be strictly adhered to throughout the year to be effective.

In a corporate setting, the full cost of a health/fitness program is clearly stated in an annual budget that is presented for management's approval. It may be difficult to justify the full costs of a health/fitness program because many of the benefits are intangible and the return on investment might be slower than expected. However, it is important to know the complete costs associated with a program to understand its role and significance within the organization.

Individuals experienced in developing budgets have found that an annual budget evolves from a number of sub-budgets, which provide detailed breakdowns and projections of various categories that account for a large percentage of the total budget. For example, to determine annual revenues, separate budgets should be prepared for membership sales and for operational or other income (guest fees, locker rental, towel fees, court costs, etc.). The combined totals of these sub-budgets provide the total revenue projections. To determine yearly expenses, separate budgets should be prepared for programs, maintenance, and capital expenditures. Once staffing and debt service (or rent) are included, these five categories represent the greatest percentage of the total expenses for many health/fitness facilities.

Additional financial forecasts should also be prepared for pro shops, restaurants, massage services, tanning booths, and so forth. Detailed projections should be prepared as part of the overall annual budget. These totals are estimated monthly for an entire fiscal year.

The steps in preparing a budget are as follows:

1. Prepare yearly goals.
2. Collect data.
3. List projected capital expenditures.
4. Determine profit margin.
5. Determine if it's realistic.

Prepare Yearly Goals

A budget is a tool for dealing with the future; therefore, it's imperative that yearly goals are prepared to help turn expectations into reality. Establish the goals that must be accomplished to have a successful year. For example, in a community or commercial setting, an increase in profits as a result of increased member projections could be a desired goal. In a corporate fitness program, a reduction in health care costs might be a yearly goal. Meetings should be organized to discuss potential goals with both staff and upper management. Strive to obtain as much input from all sectors of the business prior to preparing the budget.

Collect Data

A listing of all revenues and expenses should be broken down into line items on a worksheet that provides columns for past year totals and estimated projections for the current year. Past financial records are the greatest forecasting tool available to health/fitness owners and managers. The most difficult time to develop a budget occurs during the first year of operation when past records are not available for comparison. To account for this, spend time consulting with people in the health/fitness field or an accountant to obtain the necessary budgetary information. Remember that gathering financial figures without accurate information planning is guesswork and thus is not recommended. An example of a budget worksheet is provided in Table 13.1.

Table 13.1 Budget Work Sheet

Costs	Current month			Year-to-date			Costs	This period			Year-to-date		
	budget	actual	variance	budget	actual	variance		This year	Last year	Variance	This year	Last year	Variance
Revenues							Revenues						
Initiation fees							Initiation fees						
Dues							Dues						
Court fees							Court fees						
Guest fees							Guest fees						
Activity fees							Activity fees						
Other							Other						
Total revenues							Total revenues						
Operating expenses							Operating expenses						
Advertising/promotion							Advertising/promotion						
Maintenance/repairs							Maintenance/repairs						
Supplies							Supplies						
Printing/postage							Printing/postage						
Program expenses							Program expenses						
Rent							Rent						
Utilities/telephone							Utilities/telephone						
Payroll/fringe benefits							Payroll/fringe benefits						
Professional fees							Professional fees						
Management fees							Management fees						
Total operating expenses							Total operating expenses						
Net operating income							Net operating income						
Other expenses							Other expenses						
Insurance							Insurance						
Real estate taxes							Real estate taxes						
Interest/debt service							Interest/debt service						
Depreciation							Depreciation						
Total expenses							Total expenses						
Net income before income taxes							Net income before income taxes						

List Capital Expenditures

The planning of a realistic budget depends on the ability to determine projected capital expenditures. The costs associated with purchasing such items as exercise or maintenance equipment can easily deplete working capital. The desire for facility renovations is another area that should be planned for years in advance. An organization should be sure it is financially capable of meeting long-term investments in equipment or renovations. Finally, each year's budget should take into account the settlement of a long-term debt, not merely the payment of interest.

Determine Profit Margin

Before a budget is finalized, the anticipated profit margin is determined. Management usually makes this projection based upon a predetermined percent return on investment, a return on the services provided, or simply a net profit increase over the previous year. Also included in the profit margin is an amount for state and federal taxes. The larger the profit margin, the larger the amount that will have to be added to account for taxes. The ultimate objective in the community and commercial setting is to make a profit; only through careful budget analysis can this objective be accomplished.

Is It Realistic?

In the final analysis the budget must be realistic. Despite the fact that the financial numbers look feasible on paper, those involved must ask themselves whether the projections can be achieved. To reduce the guesswork involved, a close analysis should be made by comparing the projections with industry data surveys and seeking the approval of an accountant. A budget can only be useful if it is functional. When actual costs continually deviate from the budget, confidence is lost and the budget no longer serves its purpose.

The completed budget is then implemented and monitored throughout the fiscal year. The measuring criteria for comparing actual data to the budget varies from setting to setting. Monthly or quarterly monitoring is sufficient for most health/fitness programs. However, you will encounter seasonal or once-a-year expenses that are difficult to compare to a normal monthly budget. Reporting is the validation process that goes into budgeting. Collecting actual information and comparing it to the initial budget is still the theory of success for any business.

Financial variations from the budget are closely monitored, as any deviation from projections signals potential problems. For example, if a club's revenues were below budget for a particular month, whereas payroll expenses for the same month exceeded the budget, an investigation should be made to determine whether the financial plan was incorrect, the operations were poorly managed, or there were inaccuracies in the accounting system. Close monitoring of the budget can also reveal positive aspects, such as the savings made in a particular program area.

For a budget to be an effective operational tool, any employee who is responsible for meeting budget criteria should be included in the preparation process. A manager shouldn't criticize employees for not meeting financial goals if they didn't participate in the original planning stage. Once all employees agree upon the budget, they feel a part of the plan and will be instrumental in helping meet the established goals. An important aspect of preparing an annual budget is to get personnel to follow the same plan and realize management's projections for the year.

REVENUES

Membership fees account for 60%-70% of the commercial and community settings' total revenues. For this reason special consideration should be given to establishing a membership fee structure that is realistic and easily understood by the consumer.

The facilities and services provided have a dollar value associated with them. The amount that an individual will pay usually depends on how interested he or she is in becoming a member, how much he or she perceives membership in a facility to be worth, how the membership fee structure is arranged, and what services and facilities are available when compared to other nearby clubs.

All too often membership fee structures are not taken seriously. Past experience has shown that incorrect membership rates have caused significant financial consequences. If fees are set abnormally high, the prospective member perceives that the facility is simply overpriced for what it offers. In addition, a membership fee structure that is too high can be out of the financial reach of the target population. If rates are set too low, a prospective member may question the quality of the facility. Insufficient rates can also lead to cash flow problems.

Another consideration when establishing a membership fee structure is offering a segmented fee structure. A common practice for many commercial and community settings is to charge separately for court costs, aerobic/conditioning classes, storage lockers, laundry, and program activities. However, too many additional charges are viewed as nickel and diming the member. Often this style of charging results in high member turnover and sporadic cash flow problems. Another consequence of this type of membership structure is that it confuses the prospective member by offering too many choices. When faced with too many decisions, an individual usually choose the least expensive membership or simply opts not to join.

The value of a membership offered must balance with the fees requested. It is better to offer one or two memberships that can be adapted to meet the financial needs, than to have a menu of fees. The simpler the fee structure, the easier it is for management and the consumer to support the membership requirements.

Michael Chaet (1985) identifies three basic membership fee options currently being offered by health/fitness facilities: renewable term membership, annual membership plus court or usage fees, and initiation fee and monthly dues.

Renewable Term Membership

Memberships are sold for a predetermined amount of time, usually a 3-month, 6-month, 1-year, 2-year, or lifetime membership. The fee for this membership is paid before the individual is able to use the facility.

This type of membership is usually offered by facilities that have an affluent clientele, an exclusive facility, or a reputation for being prestigious.

Positive Attributes

- Club gets money up front.
- It is convenient for some members to pay once a year.
- There is no financial penalty for using club often.
- Front desk operations are simplified.
- Club can control closing for holidays.

Negative Attributes

- Renewing memberships at the end of term is a serious problem.
- Potential exists for very high membership loss.
- Short-term members (up to 6 months) tend to disappear quickly. You must pursue them constantly.
- Because of aforementioned reasons, organization must be highly sales oriented.
- Cash flow revenues are highly dependent on sales.
- It is hard to get a reading on nonusers.
- Rates cannot be changed during term of membership.
- Seasonal cash flow problems may develop.
- If contract is financed, collections may pose a problem.
- Legal problems in the enforcement of contracts may arise.

Annual Membership Plus Court or Usage Fees

An annual membership is similar to a term membership; both are established for a predetermined period of time. However, annual memberships are usually a lot lower in price than term memberships. The court-fee system is dependent upon court fees and other usage fees to generate revenues. Therefore, the object is to get as many members as possible to buy memberships, so that the courts and other paying areas and programs are in constant use. The major drawback of this system is that almost all income is dependent upon usage, as opposed to paying a one-time membership fee for all facilities.

Positive Attributes

- It is easy to sell large numbers of memberships if annual fee is low.

- It may allow you to be unique in the market.
- In some small, single-purpose clubs, this system may provide for members' needs better than other systems.

Negative Attributes

- It may cause very serious renewal problems.
- Revenues drop as interest in facility drops.
- Racquetball is not a stable-usage sport like handball or tennis.
- There are serious seasonal fluctuations.
- You make money only if club is used; you may not be receiving enough privilege-of-use money.
- There is a continual need to sell the same people on both memberships and usage.
- It's a very sales-sensitive system.

Review "Term Membership" section for other negatives.

The Initiation Fee and Monthly Dues System

The most widely used membership fee structure is the initiation fee and monthly dues system. The initiation fee is basically a financial commitment that individuals make to themselves. The philosophy behind an initiation fee is that by paying up front, each individual is investing in the exclusive right to be a member of a particular facility. Monthly dues represent a preestablished fee for the use of the facility and the services offered. This system differs from the term or annual membership in that each month members must decide to continue or terminate their membership.

Positive Attributes

- There is a membership base due to low turnover.

- There are fewer resignations due to convenience of payment system.
- There is a stable, predictable cash flow.
- There is flexibility of club programming.
- It is easy to track members.
- There is no financial penalty for using the club.
- The customer becomes a member and thus belongs to the club.
- It reduces the nickel-and-dime syndrome.
- Rate changes are reflected by size of membership base.
- There is less need to resell each year.
- It is easily marketed and sold.
- Initiation fee may be manipulated as a marketing tool.
- It may result in substantial increase in revenues.
- Fewer different people use the club.
- There is less of a need to sell retail court times.
- It provides simple handling procedures at front desk.
- There are reduced seasonal cash flow problems.
- There is more control of facilities for repairs or closing for holidays.
- It allows for predictable staffing of club.

Negative Attributes

- Members may be more demanding.
- Court reservation systems must distribute the courts on a more equitable basis.
- You must overcome initiation fee objections.
- You may have to become very service oriented to maintain members.
- Large cash influx seasons cease to exist.
- Increased and different bookkeeping and accounting are needed.
- You may exclude the occasional racquetball player from membership.
- If you bill, receivables may be a problem.

Other revenue sources, which comprise the remaining 10%-40% of the total income, include activity programs, member amenities, and other income. Examples of revenue sources from activities include

- Racquet sports
- Special events
- Dance/exercise
- Swimming/whirlpool
- Private instruction
- Cardiac rehabilitation

Examples from amenities include

- Pro shop
- Massage
- Food/beverage
- Tanning booth
- Nursery
- Travel agency
- Beauty salon

Examples from other sources would include
- Guest fees
- Storage lockers
- Vending machines
- Interest income
- Affiliate services

In the commercial health/fitness setting, club operators are now using revenue per square foot as an indicator of how the consumer is responding to what a club has to offer. By dividing the total revenues into the total square footage, club owners can determine whether members are making use of the facilities. An industry average for clubs without tennis courts is $30 per square foot, which is considered good performance, $35 per square foot, which is considered excellent, and $40, which is considered outstanding (McCarthy, 1984).

A continuing problem for health/fitness settings that obtain revenues from membership fees and initiation fees is the actual collection of these funds. Typically, bills are mailed out prior to a member's anniversary date (i.e., monthly, quarterly, biannually, or annually). Cash flow problems result when the time that passes between sending the bills and receiving payment is extensive.

As a means to improve this situation, health/fitness center managers have developed pricing strategies that involve alternative methods of obtaining payment. The objective is to make payment as easy and efficient as possible. Two new forms of billing that have improved on procedures are electronic funds transfer and credit card billing.

Electronic Funds Transfer and Credit Card Billing

Both of these involve an arrangement entered into through a local banker that allows monthly membership fees to be drawn either through an electronic funds transfer or on a credit card. Members authorize a predetermined membership fee deduction through their checking account or credit card company that is automatically withdrawn on an established date. There are several advantages to these two billing systems:

- Monthly payments are instantaneous.
- They are cost-effective when compared to traditional billing practices.
- They help increase membership adherence.
- They eliminate paper exchange.
- No fee is assessed for dropping a member.

As with the other methods of billing, there are negative attributes. The initial membership charge could range from 25 cents to 50

cents per member. In addition, there is a merchant fee charged by credit card companies. Finally, they do not account for the miscellaneous costs that could be charged for new members and the collection of past due accounts.

The difficulty that all new health/fitness owners and managers face is determining what membership fee structure best suits their philosophies and financial goals. There is no easy answer to this question. After all, no two fitness centers are alike. In 1980, 21% of club revenues came from membership dues, 67% came from court fees, and 12% came from other sources. Today, these figures have almost completely reversed. For the industry as a whole, membership dues account for 60% of total club revenue, and court fees account for less than 25% (Chaet, 1985).

Each of the billing systems has advantages and disadvantages. The one that you choose will depend on the characteristics and needs of your particular facility. You can, however, use the following guidelines in your decision-making process.

- Determine what your competitors are doing and what their fee structures are.
- Develop an understanding of the target population and use demographic data to determine what the market can financially handle.
- Analyze what your facility has to offer. Is it a full-service facility? If so, what are the membership rates for similar facilities?
- Establish a break-even point, which provides a bottom line that must be met to cover all fixed operational expenses.
- Project the membership capacity of your facility. A general rule of thumb is to estimate 10-15 square feet per member.
- Determine a profit margin that you would like to achieve at the end of the fiscal year.

EXPENSES

Learning to control the expenses of a health/fitness facility should be the goal of every owner/manager. To date, there is no comprehensive method for completely controlling the expenses of any business. However, there are industry standards and management procedures that provide a gauge for expense controls.

A financial profile comparing the most profitable commercial fitness centers with less successful operations indicates that the top clubs are marginally superior to the other clubs in every expense category. The difference between the more profitable clubs and the less successful operations was not the fact that they paid less debt service or payroll, but that they managed their expenses better (McCarthy, 1986).

Here is a checklist of items that will aid in overall expense control:

Expense Control Reminders

General management

- Know your expenses: Involve yourself personally in expense control, perhaps by signing the checks.
- Compare your expenses to the industry averages and flag any category that appears to be outside the normal range.
- Use a chart of accounts designed for the industry that you're in and tailor it to fit your particular setting.
- Examine large expense items to determine what they represent.
- Realize that a computer is an essential tool for expense management.
- Obtain competitive bids from vendors for all goods and services.
- If in a for-profit environment, maintain a level of security that ensures all funds are being collected.
- Keep informed about possible cost increases, such as postal rate changes or utility rate increases, and plan ahead to handle the additional expenses.
- Evaluate all costs at regular intervals throughout the budget period.
- Communicate the expense objectives to staff and vendors.
- Obtain prompt monthly financial statements comparing actual to budget projections.

Facility management

- Make sure facility is properly insulated.
- Create a double door or vestibule area to reduce energy loss at the major entrance.
- Keep spare parts available to avoid equipment down-time.
- Install light switches that allow users to turn on only the lighting that is needed instead of having large groups of light fixtures controlled by a single switch.

- Keep cleaning and maintenance supplies out of sight to cut down on unnecessary or unauthorized use.
- Monitor thermostat settings: lowering heating levels by a degree reduces energy use by 3%; raising cooling levels by a degree results in a 5% savings.
- Install ceiling fans to circulate warm air back into the room.
- Examine utility rate schedule and use to make sure billing fees are correct.
- Insulate hot water pipes.
- Cover an outdoor pool when not in use to reduce evaporation and heat loss.
- Protect an outdoor pool from wind (a mild breeze of 7 mph can raise energy use by 400%).

Insurance

- Reduce liability claims by setting up a good accident prevention program that identifies and controls potential hazards.
- Establish safety rules for all activities and publicize them to staff and members.
- Inspect the facility regularly for unsafe conditions.
- Consider reducing premiums by investigating self-insurance or increasing deductibles.
- Review insurance coverage to eliminate nonessential policies.

Note. From ''Profitable Clubs and How They Do It'' by J. McCarthy, 1986, March, *Athletic Business*. Copyright 1986 by *Athletic Business*. Adapted by permission.

To control expenses, it is important to categorize them so they can be assimilated and broken down for better clarification. As an example, the checklist provides the primary operational expenses in a commercial health/fitness setting. The model divides them into fixed or operating expenses and provides acceptable ranges for both types. As mentioned in chapter 3, fixed expenses are incurred whether or not an individual uses a fitness facility; they are not dependent upon the volume of a business. In contrast, operating expenses are dependent upon volume and the magnitude of various operational aspects (size of facility, size of staff, hours of operation, programs, etc.). As Table 13.2 indicates, any expense falling outside the acceptable range should be reviewed closely.

In Table 13.2, the total expenses in a commercial setting are 40% fixed and 60% operating. The major expenses that need close monitoring are payroll, debt service, utilities/maintenance, and depreciation; combined, these equal 68% of all expenses. An acceptable profit is 11% and should be included in the annual fixed expenses budget. Depreciable expenses should be listed as *real expenses*, because health/fitness centers undergo more deterioration and repairs than other facilities.

Depreciable expenses are assets that cannot be fully deducted as a business expense the year they are purchased. Each year, a portion of the cost of the asset can be deducted. Generally, these assets are called *fixed, operating,* or *depreciable assets*. Examples of depreciable assets include

- maintenance tools and equipment,
- fitness equipment,

Table 13.2 An Expense Model for Club Management[a]

Expenses	Range (%)	Average (%)
Fixed:		
Debt service	12-16	14
Real estate taxes	2- 4	3
Insurance	2- 4	3
Depreciation	8-10	9
Profit		11
Total, fixed		40
Operating:		
Payroll	28-32	30
Utilities	7- 9	8
Repairs/maintenance	6- 8	7
Marketing	4- 6	5
Administrative equipment and supplies	2- 4	3
Club equipment/supplies	2- 4	3
Professional fees	2- 4	3
Other	0- 2	1
Total, operating		60

[a]Model developed by Clay Hammer, former consultant to the National Tennis Association, and Alan G. Schwartz, president of Tennis Corporation of America.

- clerical equipment (typewriters, computers),
- furniture and fixtures, and
- major repairs that increase the value or extend the life of an asset.

Depreciation rules change from year to year. As a result, the rule that was in effect when an asset was purchased is the rule that is used to determine the tax write-off period. At this point, it's a good idea to seek the assistance of an accountant to compute depreciation from year to year.

One way to control expenses on a daily basis is to use a purchase order system for all expenditures. Individuals responsible for business expenses must be aware of estimated costs before they order operational items (e.g., supplies, equipment, etc.). Therefore, all staff members responsible for purchasing are required to complete a purchase order form, which provides basic information (projected cost, vendor, date ordered, expected date to receive, and signature of staff person responsible) that can be reviewed and accepted or rejected by management. This system prevents personnel from ordering items not previously approved and also allows managers to compare budgeted areas to actual monies spent.

FINANCIAL STATEMENTS

Periodic financial statements are prepared to determine the financial position of a fitness center. Financial statements allow managers to compare budgetary items to what is actually being spent, while monitoring profits and losses. Oftentimes, cash balances and the day-to-day cash income and outgo are used to determine profit and loss, but in actuality these are poor indicators of a health/fitness facility's financial status. Cash flow provides a misleading picture of how a business is doing.

The two most important financial statements are the balance sheet and the profit-and-loss statement. The difference between the two is best explained by comparing the balance sheet to a still picture and the profit-and-loss statement to a moving picture. The balance sheet presents a financial picture of the business assets, liabilities, and ownership position (e.g., equity, capital stock, or surplus) on a given date. The profit-and-loss statement measures expenses against membership revenues and other income over a specified period of time. The profit-and-loss statement reflects the net profit or loss for a business based on a predetermined time period. Both of these statements are considered essential for giving a manager/owner an updated picture of the financial position of the business and indicating whether the financial goals are being met.

A balance sheet has two sections: The first represents the assets and the second shows the liabilities and the owner's equity. A common accounting principle is that the total assets always equal the combined total of the liabilities and the owner's equity. This is the main reason why this financial statement is called a balance sheet.

The following is a glossary of terms that you will encounter in the various components of a balance sheet.

Assets include anything that a business owns that has money value. The assets of a health/fitness facility commonly include cash, land, building, notes receivable, accounts receivable, equipment, and other investments. Assets are usually classified as current or fixed.

Current assets are cash and other assets that will be converted into cash generally within a fiscal year (e.g., notes receivable, accounts receivable, and cash). If these items are not expected to be converted into cash within a year they should be treated as fixed assets.

Fixed assets are those items acquired for long-term use in the business. They include land, equipment, furniture, and buildings. These assets are typically not for resale and are recorded on the balance sheet at their cost, less depreciation.

Liabilities are the claims of creditors against the assets or debts owned by a business. Among the more common liabilities are notes payable, accounts payable, taxes, and accrued liabilities. An example of accrued liabilities is personnel wages that must be accounted for even if the accounting period does not coincide with the last day of a pay period.

The difference between current and fixed liabilities is similar to the difference between current and fixed assets. The debts that will be paid within 1 year are current liabilities, whereas those debts not due for payment in 1 year are fixed liabilities.

Equity is the assets of a health/fitness facility minus its liabilities. This equity is the investment of the owner(s) plus any profits that have been left to accumulate (or minus any losses).

If the fitness center is incorporated, a capital stock account is shown in the books that represents the paid-in value of the shares issued to the owners of the business. Undistributed profits are recorded in an earned-surplus account. If the business is a sole proprietorship or a partnership, the capital accounts appear under the name(s) of the owner(s). A sample balance sheet was shown on page 67.

Profit-and-loss statements are generally prepaid monthly from ledgers that record daily financial transactions. A profit-and-loss statement is a schedule showing income and expenses and the difference between the two. A profit-and-loss statement should provide information on not only the current period, but also a similar past period for comparison purposes. A percent column, where total income and expenses equal 100%, should also be included to help assist in providing information on efficiency trends. A sample profit-and-loss statement is shown on page 68.

The difficulty often associated with financial statements is learning to interpret the results and then applying that knowledge to the business. The financial statements provided are only as good as the person interpreting the results. A good owner/manager takes the necessary time each month to study the various trends of the figures presented. A number of indicators have been developed to help with this process. In the health/fitness industry these indicators are represented as ratios or percentages. Each indicator is used as a comparative measure to analyze the business operations. Clues are provided so that you can spot trends in the overall performance, while comparing your fitness center to a similar facility.

Common methods of interpreting financial statements consist of determining overall liquidity and profitability of an organization. Liquidity is best described as the ability to pay bills. Is there enough cash on hand, or current assets that could be turned into cash,

to pay all debts? Profitability is determining if the business is earning as much profit as it should, based on the amount of money invested. Both liquidity and profitability are standard measures of establishing how successful or unsuccessful a fitness center has become. An accountant can help you determine the specific financial ratios needed to obtain information on profitability and liquidity.

As an example of financial ratios for the commercial fitness setting, IRSA has developed industry averages for use in determining financial performance. This financial model is broken down into return ratios, expense ratios, and revenue ratios. Table 13.3 illustrates financial ratios in the commercial fitness setting.

Table 13.3 Financial Ratios for the Commercial Fitness Industry

Return ratios

1. Sales return = gross membership sales before taxes and after depreciation—it is the net return.

    6%-12% = good

    12%-18% = excellent

    18%-25% = outstanding

2. Investment return = varies from setting to setting depending upon calculation and variables used. Considered to be after-tax cash distribution on original equity investment.

    20%-25% = good

    25%-30% = excellent

    30%-40% = outstanding

Expense ratios

1. Any expense lying outside the acceptable range should be carefully analyzed.

2. Because of the nature of the club industry, depreciation should not be considered a paper expense.

3. If fixed expenses exceed 40 cents per dollar of revenue, the club may be at risk.

4. If debt service exceeds 15% of revenues, the club will not provide a reasonable return on investment; more than 25% of revenues, the club will lose money.

Revenue ratios

1. Over 5 years, the annual increase in total sales and revenue per member data will constitute a trend. Whether growth, no growth, or decline, it invites strategic response.

2. $30 in revenue per square foot = good

   $35 in revenue per square foot = excellent

   $40 in revenue per square foot = outstanding

3. One of the goals of the health/fitness industry is to move the dues-to-ancillary (other income) revenue ratio from 70:30 to 65:35 to 60:40.

Note. From ''Profitable Clubs and How They Do It'' by J. McCarthy, 1986, March, *Athletic Business*, p. 32. Copyright 1986 by *Athletic Business*. Adapted by permission.

Financial statements should be viewed not as ends in themselves, but as tools that can help answer financial questions. Methods for computing financial statements vary from facility to facility. As a result, the figures from one fitness setting differ from those of another setting. Also, financial ratios are calculated for specific dates, and unless they are prepared often, seasonal characteristics may be overlooked. The real purpose of financial statements is to obtain clues for the future, so a manager/owner can prepare for problems and opportunities that lie ahead.

INSURANCE

Every new business venture is a gamble and the health/fitness field is no exception. Even with a well-developed business plan, adequate financing, and good managerial experience,

the owner/manager realizes that there is an element of risk involved in operating a health/fitness facility. Accidents, thefts, lawsuits, and fires are only a few examples of risks that threaten not only the business, but the personal assets of the owner and the support staff.

The recommended approach to counteracting risk is to take whatever steps possible to protect the business and the personnel involved. This means adopting an insurance plan or a risk management plan that provides protection for individuals and the business against loss caused by damage to property, life, or limb in any situation. It is important that owners/managers of health/fitness facilities not only accept that there is a need for insurance but learn to live with and manage insurance properly.

Experienced managers periodically evaluate and write down all the potential problems associated with their facility, consult with a professional, and then arrange the list in order of importance as it relates to possible damage to the building. Obviously, insurance protection against a catastrophe is placed on top of the list. The following is the recommended minimal insurance that a health/fitness center should have:

- Liability insurance
- Business interruption insurance
- Workmen's compensation
- Fire insurance
- Business life insurance

Some additional insurance coverage would include crime insurance, auto/machinery coverage, liquor insurance, suntan liability, water damage, and extra expense insurance.

Liability Insurance

In the health/fitness industry, there is always the possibility that an owner/manager may become involved in legal action brought about by individuals who have been injured and seek to attribute the injury to negligence on the facility's part. This is an ever-present threat that can devastate a successful operation. Unfortunately, in recent years, courts have generally sided with the claimant rather than the defendant in such cases. Also, the amounts awarded have rapidly escalated. These actions cover not only all medical and disability expenses, but also compensation for loss of future earnings. Therefore, total coverage should be considered in those areas as well.

Today, many health/fitness facilities are faced with skyrocketing liability insurance rates. To get the best rates possible, you have to shop around for potential insurance companies. You can lower the facility's liability insurance by:

- raising total deductibles,
- reducing coverage in low-risk areas,
- sticking with one broker, and
- becoming familiar with your underwriter.

A substantial increase in liability coverage is usually accomplished by a minimal increase in premium. If in doubt as to the amount of liability insurance to have, remember that it is better to have too much coverage in this area than too little.

Workmen's Compensation

By law, a business must provide a working environment free from the possibility of accidental injury. Workmen's compensation makes employees eligible for benefits regardless of whether negligence is proven. Compliance with the laws of various states is usually accomplished by acquiring a standard form of insurance policy.

Workmen's compensation insurance provides an injured employee with medical reimbursement and replacement of lost wages. Premiums for workmen's compensation are usually based on size of payroll, type of jobs within an organization, and extent of the hazards faced in the particular business. Premiums range from as little as 1% of total payroll to 20% or more.

Fire Insurance

No business should be started without fire insurance, given that a fire could destroy an entire business. Basic fire policies protect against damage from fire or lightning; however, it is recommended that you extend coverage to include smoke, windstorm, hail, and explosions.

The premium for fire insurance is based on the location of the business, the condition and overall maintenance of the facility, the structure of the building, and preventive measures taken. The overall amount is based on the actual cash value of the facility. This amount is the total replacement cost less depreciation. For example, a piece of equipment that originally cost $3,000 could now be valued at less than $2,000.

Business Interruption Insurance

In the event that a health/fitness facility suffers a fire, the insurance policy generally covers direct losses to inventory, equipment, and building structure. However, indirect losses are also sustained; an operation might have to be closed for weeks or months after extensive fire damage. This setback means that little or no income will be coming in for some time. Yet, the salaries for key personnel, monthly utility bills, and insurance premiums will have to be paid during this time.

Business interruption insurance covers fixed expenses and profit when a business is closed or operating at less than full capacity. The error often made with business interruption insurance is in determining the deductible. Some policies are based on gross revenues, others on profits, and others are figured according to specific time periods. Another error is not fully understanding the magnitude of coverage required. A disaster can occur at any time of year, and additional coverage may be necessary to get a club through a lean season after recovering from such a disaster.

Business Life Insurance

Although some health/fitness owners/managers probably have their own life insurance policies, many believe that business life insurance is a luxury they cannot afford. However, if you are the sole owner of a particular club, business life insurance may be something you can't afford to live without.

What would happen to the business if you died or became disabled? How would your family manage? If the business must be liquidated, who will be responsible for taking care of this? Or, if there is a partnership and a partner dies, how can you protect your share of ownership? These are all questions that must be answered when entering into a health/fitness business as the sole owner or as a partner.

Business life policies protect owners and their families from financial loss due to death or serious injury. Arrangements can be made to ensure that the business continues in this event. With life insurance to provide necessary cash and a properly prepaid buy-and-sell agreement, the deceased's share of ownership is returned to the heirs and the surviving owners carry on without business interruption.

Even though insurance coverage is available to protect a business against every kind of accident or disaster, relying totally on insurance is not a good business practice. A better approach is to take steps to reduce risk. For example, you can take preventive measures to safeguard against fire or accidental injury:

- Place approved fire extinguishers in selected spots around the facility. Check them on a regular basis. Also, see that staff members know of these locations.
- Store flammable materials in proper areas.
- Install a sprinkler system. Use smoke alarms in storage areas.
- Make sure that all fire doors and exits are clearly marked.
- Keep locker desk area, aisles, and stairwells free from encumbrances.
- Keep all equipment and machines in good condition. Train employees in the proper handling of all equipment.
- Practice good housekeeping. Don't permit trash to accumulate.

TAXES

Once a commercial health/fitness facility is opened it becomes subject to taxes under all three levels of government: federal, state, and local. The tax management phase of a business must be professionally organized to meet the standards established by the government. Because of the complexities of tax law, frequent new rulings, changing regulations, and difficulties of interpretation, it is most difficult for an owner/manager to handle these areas without assistance.

The Internal Revenue Service (IRS) and/or a personal accountant can provide assistance with tax forms and record keeping. There are individuals who handle and prepare their own taxes, but managing a business is significantly more complicated than preparing a personal tax form. Every manager worries about the possibility of an IRS audit. Generally, this fear provides the incentive to keep good bookkeeping records and receipts on all bills. These are the federal taxes with which all health/fitness facilities must comply.

Federal Income Taxes

The legal form of ownership determines the tax regulations that apply to a business.

Sole Proprietorship

Legally, the individual owner and the business activity are inseparable. If a facility is based on this structure, federal tax is levied the same as if the owner were an employee. However, the owner must also submit details of the business activity for each year.

Partnership

Tax liability is assessed only for incomes of individual partners and not against the business directly. Furthermore, a report of business operations is required.

Corporation

Taxing becomes more complex for corporations. Income, as well as dividends from the corporation, must be reported. Also, a separate return must be filed by the corporation.

Social Security Taxes

The Federal Insurance Contributions Act (FICA) provides employees with coverage for old age, survivors, disability, and hospitalization. Taxes are assessed on both employer and employee. The responsibility of levying these taxes rests with the employer. Presently, the FICA tax is 7.15% of each employee's income. Furthermore, each business is required to match the total amount collected from its employees at 7.15%.

Withholding Tax

The federal government requires businesses to withhold from employees a percentage of earnings for income and social security taxes. The business, in turn, is required to return these funds to the government. This tax is the purpose for all employees' completing a W-4 form at the time of employment. The withholding tax is calculated based on the W-4 form information.

State Taxes

The list of state taxes for health/fitness facilities varies from state to state. Many states tax gross income, real estate, sales on retail goods, and membership fees when joining a club. For example, the state of Texas views commercial fitness centers as an entertainment/amusement operation and charges 6.1% on all membership fees. Additional taxes may be levied from state to state, so investigate all potential tax assessments before entering into the business.

SUMMARY

This chapter has described the major issues of financial planning that face the owner or manager of a health/fitness program. The purpose was to provide pertinent information on bookkeeping/accounting procedures, the budget, revenues, expenses, financial statements, taxes, and insurance. The general points covered pertain primarily to commercial health/fitness programs, but many of the topics mentioned could be developed for use in the community and corporate settings as well. Those responsible for managing the finances of a health/fitness facility should seek out available resources that will assist them in developing their financial management skills (e.g., workshops, seminars, and accountants).

APPENDIX

Basic Bookkeeping/Accounting Definitions

Accelerated depreciation: A method of depreciation that charges off more of the original cost of a plant asset in the earlier years than in the later years of the asset's service life. Used mainly in calculating taxable income.

Accelerated cost recovery system (ACRS): Calculations set by the government for a 5-year asset at graduated percentages.

Account payable: The amount that an entity owes to a creditor, usually a supplier, not evidenced by a promissory note.

Account receivable: An amount that is owed to an entity, usually by one of its customers, as a result of the ordinary extension of credit.

Accounting: A systematic means of providing information on the economic and business affairs of an organization.

Accounting period: The period of time over which an income statement summarizes the changes in owners' equity. Usually the official period is 1 year, but income statements are also prepared for shorter, or interim, periods.

Accrual basis: Accounting for revenues in the period in which they are earned and for expenses in the period in which they were incurred.

Acid test ratio: Ratio of monetary current assets to current liabilities.

Amortization: The process of recognizing the cost of intangible assets as expenses. Sometimes the term is used as a general term for writing off long-lived assets of all types.

Asset: An item of value owned by a business.

  Current asset: Cash and assets that are expected to be converted into cash or used up in the near future, usually within 1 year.

  Fixed asset: Property, plant, and equipment.

Audit: The process of reviewing the accounting records.

Average collection period: The average number of days that receivables are outstanding.

Average collection period ratio: The ratio obtained by multiplying receivables by days in the year and dividing by the annual credit sales. The ratio helps evaluate how current the receivables are.

Average inventory: The average of the beginning and ending inventories.

Balance sheet: A financial statement that lists the account balances on a particular date representing all of the company's assets, liabilities, and owners' equity (or partners' capital). The assets are listed on the left and the equities on the right.

Band-of-investment approach: The combination of borrowed funds plus equity contributions.

Book value: The total owners' equity divided by the number of shares of common stock outstanding. It bears little relationship to the stock's market value.

Business entity: The individual unit for which accounting records are kept, enabling the accountant to separate the events of the business enterprise from the personal financial transaction of the owner.

Capital: Owners' equity or worth.

Capital turnover: A ratio: annual sales divided by the amount of permanent capital.

Cash basis: The process of identifying and and accumulating manufacturing costs and assigning them to goods in the manufacturing process.

Chart of accounts: A list of the names and number of the accounts included in an accounting system.

Common stock: The principle source of ownership funds for most corporations. Its owners do not enjoy an special preferences, advantages, or privileges over any other stock.

Comparative analyses: Analyses based upon two or more fiscal periods (2 years of income statements, changes in financial position, or retained earnings).

Compilation: When the accountant prepares monthly, quarterly, or annual statements but offers no assurance as to whether material changes are necessary for the statements to conform to certain generally accepted accounting principles.

Cost of goods sold: The cost of merchandise sold or services performed. For merchandise, the label often used is cost of goods sold.

Current ratio: The ratio obtained by dividing the total of current assets by the total of current liabilities. Used as a means to judge a company's ability to meet short-term obligations and remain solvent in the event of adversities.

Debt capital: Capital raised by the issuance of debt securities, usually bonds.

Debt-equity ratio: The ratio of debt capital to total permanent capital. A measure of an entity's financial risk.

Debt service coverage ratio: The annual cash flow before interest and taxes divided by interest and principal debt payments. Shows that the firm can adequately meet the lender's interest and principal payment requirements.

Declining balance method: Involves applying the selected depreciation rate multiplied by some percentage greater than 100.

Deficit: Negative retained earnings.

Depreciation: The process of systematically allocating the cost of an asset to the various periods receiving the benefits from that asset so that a proper matching of revenue and expenses may be obtained.

Desired income approach: Tries to identify what an owner/manager needs to earn to take the risk of putting in a certain level of investment.

Economic life: The period over which improvements to real estate contribute to the value of the property.

Effective age: As applied to a structure, the age of a similar structure of equivalent utility, condition, and remaining life expectancy as distinct from chronological age;

the years of age indicated by the condition and utility of the structure.

Equity capital: The capital supplied by owners, who are called equity members.

Expenditure: The decrease in an asset or increase in a liability associated with the acquisition of goods or services.

Expenses: A decrease in owners' equity associated with activities of an accounting period, that is, resources used up or consumed during an accounting period.

Fixed expense: A cost element that does not vary with the volume of activity.

Operating expense: Expenses associated with operating activities.

Fee simple: Absolute ownership unencumbered by any other interest.

Financial leverage: The relationship between owners' equity and debt financing.

Financial statement: Summarization of the financial status and operating results of the business.

Gross margin: The difference between sales revenue and cost of sales.

Historical cost: The cash or cash equivalent value of the item at the time it was acquired (i.e., the market value at the time of the transaction).

Income: Assets acquired through the sale of merchandise or services.

Income statement: A statement of revenues and expenses and the difference between them for an accounting period; a flow report. It explains the changes in owners' equity associated with operations of the period.

Inventory turnover ratio: Cost of goods sold divided by the average inventory.

Investment approach: An assumption of the availability of a total set of funds that businesspeople believe they can raise, and the projected profit and return-on-investment they can expect.

Investment tax credit: A reduction in income tax liability, calculated as a percentage of the cost of newly purchased long-lived assets (with certain exceptions).

Leased fee estate: Ownership interest held by a landlord.

Leasehold estate: The right to use and occupy real estate for a stated term under certain conditions, usually conveyed by a lease.

Liability: The equity or claim of a creditor.

Current liability: Obligations that become due within a short period of time, usually 1 year.

Non-current liability: A claim that does not fall due within 1 year; similar to debt capital.

Limited partnership: A partnership with two levels of partners, one or more general partners and one or more limited partners. Limited partners are responsible only for the funds they invest; general partners are liable for all that happens in the business, including deficits.

Market value: The amount a buyer is willing to pay and a seller is willing to accept to effect a transfer of shares.

Modified cash basis: Utilizes the principles of the cash basis system but does not permit buildings and equipment to be charged off at the time of payment as these items will last for long periods of time.

Net income: The amount by which total revenues exceed total expenses for an accounting period; the bottom line.

Net loss: Negative net income.

Net profit margin: The net profits after taxes divided by sales. Shows the relative efficiency of the firm after taking into account all expenses and income taxes, but not extraordinary charges.

Overhead cost: Product costs other than direct materials and direct labor. It includes, for example, supervision, building maintenance, and power.

Owners' equity: The original capital stock plus the retained earnings.

Periodic inventory: Involves businesses actually physically counting the quantities in inventory and adjusting their accounting records to reflect this information at regular, periodic intervals.

Periodicity: Provides for the regular summing up of the firm's activity and establishes the time for regular reporting on that activity.

Perpetual method: Keeping a constant record of the quantity and cost of the various items purchased for and sold from inventory.

Preferred stock: Entitles the shareholders to specified preferential rights in regard to the distribution of earnings and assets in the event of a liquidation.

Profit center: Those services or products that generate the largest profits for a business.

Profit margin percentage: Net income expressed as a percentage of net sales.

Proprietary corporation: An unincorporated business with a single owner.

Quick ratio: See *Acid test ratio*.

Rate of return on company stock equity ratio: The net profits after taxes minus preferred stock dividend divided by net worth minus par value of preferred stock. Allows reader to judge the earning power on the shareholders' book investment.

Receivable turnover ratio: The annual credit sales divided by receivables.

Remaining economic life: The number of years remaining in the economic life of the

structure or structural component, as of the date of the appraisal.

Rental approach: Involves projecting sales volumes, gross margins, and other costs to determine feasibility of certain rental levels assuming a tenant's status.

Retained earnings: The increase in shareholders' equity that has resulted from profitable operations; net income to date minus dividends to date. It is an owners' equity item, not an asset.

Return on assets ratio: The net profits after taxes divided by total tangible assets. A measure of the return on assets by deducting any goodwill from the equation.

Return on investment (ROI): Determined by dividing the projected earnings for 1 year by the total investment required. Can mean either return on owners' investment or return on permanent capital. The meaning must be deduced from the context.

Revenue: The increase in owners' equity resulting from operations during a period of time, usually from the sale of goods or services.

Review: A financial statement conducted by an independent accountant who issues a report giving a limited degree of assurances.

S corporation: A corporation that has elected to be taxed as if it were a partnership.

Statement of change in financial position: A financial statement explaining the changes that have occurred in asset, liability, and owners' equity items in an accounting period.

Static analysis: A study of one point in time (e.g., balance sheet comparison).

Straight line method: The depreciation base is divided by the estimated life of the asset to determine the fixed amount each year.

Sum of the year's digits: The sum of the digits expresses the individual year's life expectancy of the asset. Assumes that an asset becomes less and less productive as time passes.

Trial balance: A listing of all accounts with their balances separated into two columns: debits (assets, dividends, and expenses) and credits (liabilities, capital stock, and revenues).

Working capital: The difference between current assets and current liabilities.

Note. From *Financial Management Manual* (pp. 115-120) by IRSA, 1986, Brookline, MA: IRSA. Copyright by IRSA. Reprinted by permission.

14 Trends and Issues in the Health/ Fitness Industry

Any book attempting to break new ground in a field that is experiencing explosive growth would be negligent if it did not address new trends in the profession. Such a discussion is difficult because our field is growing and changing so rapidly that anything written today will probably be out of date by the time it reaches its audience. Notwithstanding this limitation, we can identify some trends and issues in the field that help to define our current status and give direction to our actions. Certainly, new technology and inventions, as well as changing demographics and consumer interest, will have an impact on these trends. We discuss the business plan and organization first, followed by facility design considerations, program innovations, and personnel trends. The last section deals with future trends that are likely to emerge as a result of the impact of present conditions on the profession.

PROPOSALS/BUSINESS PLANS

The use of market research to determine feasibility of a program has become a recent trend.

In the corporate setting this involves a needs analysis, which includes interest surveys of employees and health care statistical analyses, as well as absenteeism studies. In the commercial sector, where competition is fierce, market research is especially critical. Large market research groups, such as Arthur Andersen and Co., have recently begun dedicating personnel for the health/fitness industry to assist the larger clients. By doing their own research, smaller businesses can also use market data without spending the fees for market research firms, which can be $15,000 or more. In addition, firms are available to assist in developing preliminary demographic data by providing instant demographic information and forecasts that are essential to conducting certain aspects of the market research. Such companies have software packages that provide sales-potential reports for selected industries that diminish the risk of failure among potential investors.

Another trend in the health/fitness field is joint ventures. The small corporate employee fitness program might choose to joint-venture with a community or commercial center to provide better overall services at lower costs. This in effect strengthens the programming opportunities for all concerned. Joint ventures between hospitals and community agencies are also becoming commonplace. The hospitals have clinical expertise that community agencies generally do not possess; and the community agencies, such as the YMCA, have fitness programming that can benefit the hospital when providing wellness services for employee and community outreach programs.

There is a clear shift in the direction of commercial business structures. Ten years ago, fewer than 10% of commercial health/fitness businesses were incorporated and franchised. The traditional approach to running the commercial fitness center was through a sole proprietorship or a partnership. Today, however, there is a definite trend toward group ownership and/or management. There are many examples of this trend including Club Corporation of America, Pritikin, and Bally. In addition, the chain fitness centers such as President's, the Court House, and Nautilus are widespread. An indirect but significant example of this trend is in the area of hotel chains opening fitness centers in their guest complexes. Similarly, large real estate groups are routinely including fitness centers in their new construction plans. Another significant example is the YMCA and its recent shift in focus of the innercity programs from traditional, holistic, and family-oriented recreation to adult-oriented health/fitness concerns. The nonprofit tax status of the YMCA has raised some serious concerns among its commercial competition for fitness consumers and will become a major issue in the future.

Business plans are no longer merely a primitive process of seeking local bank financing. Instead, business plans now entail a strategic planning process designed to maximize the potential of various investors to secure the large sums needed and to forecast prospects for success of an entrepreneurial venture.

Business plans will become increasingly complex as health/fitness continues to grow as an industry.

Corporate employee fitness proposals are also becoming more sophisticated. Patton recently prepared three separate proposals when attempting to justify a start-up program in a Fortune 500 corporation. A data-based proposal showing anticipated cost-effectiveness and cost-benefit was developed for the vice president in charge of financial affairs. A different proposal was developed for the vice president in charge of human resources that focused on personnel recruitment and retention. A final proposal was developed for the CEO that was a 1-page summary of the proposed employee fitness program. Each individual was "pitched" separately prior to the executive board meeting in which all members were involved in the decision-making process.

Hospital-based wellness proposals are probably the most complex of them all. An element of the program must be commercially oriented because most are viewed as profit centers. There is also the corporate fitness element in that employees are normally eligible users of the facility. These commercial and corporate orientations must also be blended into traditional clinical services. Cardiac rehabilitation for example is frequently imbedded in the program services of hospital wellness programs. Thus a mixture of purposes is involved in the development of the plan/proposal in the hospital setting.

The functioning professional in our field will probably have to become involved in the development of a corporate proposal or commercial business plan in the future. There is even more likelihood that existing programs will fall prey to periodic justification, especially during periods of diminishing resources. Skills in these areas will determine whether you flourish or perish in this industry.

FACILITY CONSIDERATIONS

The technology associated with the manufacturing process, programming innovations, demographic changes, and more informed and demanding consumers leads to change in existing health/fitness facilities. If you are not upgrading, or planning to upgrade, an existing facility, then you are falling behind the competition and thus creating the potential for losing members. Unless you are reading and keeping abreast of the literature on facility design and construction, you would be well advised to find a good consultant to assist you in the process of planning a new facility. You can bet that your competition is aggressively trying to get the edge on you by providing some new bells and whistles in their facility. The following discussion deals specifically with some of these facility issues.

Space Planning

Architects are space planners, but not all space planners are architects. There are advantages to the use of either or both. A definite trend in the health/fitness business is to specialize in the area of space planning/architectural design. You will be light-years ahead of your competition if you get a good designer at the outset who specializes in health/fitness facilities. For example, Donald Demars of California and Thomas Wills of Florida are space planners who specialize in health/fitness facilities. More specifically, they do not specialize in the stadium and field-house-type of athletic facility design. These individuals are distinguished by their design excellence in corporate and commercial settings rather than educational and professional athletic complexes. In fact, if you look

at their projects, you will find that Wills has focused his efforts more in the area of corporate and hospital facilities, whereas Demars has emphasized the commercial and hotel projects. Although the differences in their work are subtle, they are noticeable and important. Demars tends to be graphic in design and dazzles the commercial member/user, whereas Wills tends to be functional, parsimonious, and efficient with the user space. Both space planners are effective leaders in the broad health/fitness field, yet they flourish best in a specialized environment. It should be noted that there are many good space planners in the marketplace. These two examples were introduced merely to illustrate the degree of specialization that has occurred in recent years and to caution the potential user of space planners and architects to take care in the selection process. This trend toward specialization will undoubtedly grow if the health/fitness building boom continues, as we suspect it will, in the foreseeable future.

Facility Purpose

Until very recently there was a definite tendency toward the construction of single- and dual-purpose facilities. Racquetball centers were very popular in the early 1980s, and tennis centers preceded them. Aquatics and golf clubs predated the racquet-type clubs. Today, the typical single-purpose club is the fitness center. Yet, a clear-cut trend has been to develop a multipurpose facility that appeals to any member and his or her family. Indeed, there is a tendency to offer a holistic recreation and fitness/wellness facility to members. The racquet sport boom diluted the membership of the country club, and the fitness boom is now diluting the membership of both the racquet and the country clubs. The present trend in facility construction is a design that includes as much as possible in the way of recreation and fitness services. Most modern facilities in the corporate, commercial, and community settings have aquatic, racquet, fitness, open gym, and child care facilities as a minimum. Many new facilities will offer outdoor recreational activities, interclub leagues, and excursion/travel trips to its members. Thus, by having many services, you can appeal to the broadest segment of the target market.

Specific Facility Areas

The following may be trends in specific facility areas.

Control Desk

Contemporary locker desk design is not unlike that of the typical hotel registration desk. Because it is the user's first exposure to the facility, the current attempt is to dazzle him or her with an impressive entrance and congenial introduction to the facility. The member can log in to the facility by desk clerk recognition, membership card check, computer, or a combination of these methods.

The front desk also serves as an information center for guests regarding facility guidelines and as a marketing tool for new memberships. It is a communication center for the members where special events and announcements can be made or posted. In addition, the control desk employees screen out nonmembers, which is a very important function. The personnel are ambassadors of goodwill as well as security guards. It requires a highly skilled person to play these two roles simultaneously. The control desk is no longer just a place to pick up a locker key and towel; it is moving toward being a showcase and a communications center of the program.

Laundry Areas

The trend toward using washer-extractors in the laundry areas is growing. The washer-extractor is a heavy-duty washer capable of handling laundry loads up to 125 pounds and drying these loads at speeds up to 300 Gs. Moreover, some of the newer units have advanced programmable microprocessors that simplify operations and expand their capabilities. The net effect of this process is that each laundry load can be quite large and handled more efficiently, and the materials come out of a spin cycle damp, but not wet. This reduces the amount of drying time, and consequently, the need for as many dryers. Although washer-extractors are more expensive than traditional washing machines, they have been proven very cost-effective in that they are quite durable and require about half the total number of washers and dryers (and half the square footage) needed in a traditional laundry room. Consequently, with building and maintenance costs rising, the trend is toward smaller, more compact laundry areas with more efficient and durable equipment.

Locker Areas

There are a number of trends in the locker areas of health/fitness facilities. The most noticeable trend is an enhanced environment, which is accomplished by well-placed, indirect lighting to create a pleasant ambience. The textured surfaces of the lockers are often wood veneer or some synthetic material, replacing the ventilated metal storage locker. Carpets are now a standard in the locker area. Air exchanges in the locker area are about twice that of years past, and it is not uncommon to find systems producing seven or more air exchanges per hour in such areas.

Another change in lockers is the shrinkage of unit size and configuration. The traditional approach in most clubs has been to assign a full-length locker to each active member or to use kit lockers for storage and full lockers for day use in the club. Although this remains the standard, many new clubs are moving to the use of footware/valuables storage only in miniature lockers of about 4'' x 12'' x 18'' which permits at least 14 stacked miniatures in the space of one traditional full locker. The advantages of permanent storage space for expanded numbers of members is obvious. However, some caveats should be mentioned. For example, there is still a need for hanging space adjacent to the lockers, but there is no effective way to secure these items. Although valuables and shoes remain secure in the miniature locker, suits or other garments are left unprotected. Strangely enough, theft of shirts, trousers, and so forth does not seem to be a problem in the settings in which these miniature lockers have been installed. The second caveat is that this system can only be used in clubs where uniforms and towels are supplied.

The miniature locker system is particularly effective in the corporate or commercial setting where the member simply walks into the club with nothing in his or her hands and is supplied with everything needed to secure a decent workout and to groom before returning to work or home. There is also the added bonus of providing a permanent space to each member. This trend toward smaller lockers has yet to stand the test of time; however, there appears to be much to recommend the concept.

Shower Areas

Traditionally, men have used communal showers and women have used individual showers. Today, facilities are providing individual showers for all adult club members. Some communal showers remain in even the finest of clubs to provide a spillover shower area for unusually heavy peak usage times. The contemporary approach is to provide a small, private space next to the actual shower area that can be privated by a curtain. Clothing hooks and a seat are also provided in this dressing/drying area. Ideally, but unfortunately not very often, the water volume and temperature controls are in this same space next to the shower. This configuration permits the adjustments of volume and temperature prior to stepping into the water stream—a much more pleasant approach to bathing than the shock treatment endured in the single stall shower with the controls directly below the shower head. The lighting should be quite bright in the shower. The locker area lighting can be somewhat subdued and indirect to suggest privacy areas for dressing, but the grooming area, in contrast, must be brightly lit for members to prepare themselves for the world after the workout. Also, a railing of some sort should be placed in the shower area to assist disabled or injured users. Finally, there is a trend toward making all surfaces in the wet areas of glass, tile, stainless steel, or some other mildew- and rust-resistant material.

Grooming Areas

The grooming areas in today's facilities are no longer confined to a mirror over a sink near the toilet facilities. Instead, the contemporary grooming areas are self-contained, cosmetic areas for both men and women. The less well-lit dressing room area provides a privacy space and creates a contrast for the member as he or she enters the well-lit grooming area. There should be a laundry drop-off receptacle between the two rooms to make a clean break from the dressing to the grooming space. Conceptually, the workout is over; the preparation for the remainder of the day begins. The countertop below a mirrored wall should have hair dryers, hair spray, talcum powder, sanitized combs and hairbrushes, shaving cream, razors, after-shave lotion, deodorant, and so forth for men; and a similar array of supplies should be available for women. The idea is to provide a space where members can groom in a fashion that will not compromise appearance for work or leisure activities that follow the exercise period. This service is no longer considered a luxury; rather, it is a service that is now considered commonplace and expected.

Amenities Areas

Including amenities areas in a club such as massage, equipment rental, retail store, and food and beverage services is a vital trend that oftentimes makes the difference between a profit and a loss for the business. The country club setting has for years enjoyed a situation where these amenities generated as much revenue as dues. With 50% of their revenues coming from sources other than dues, the country club could boast of competitive membership fees when being compared to the other dues-driven club settings. The commercial fitness centers, for example, obtain 70% or more of their revenues from dues.

In the competitive world of the fitness center business, there is much data to recommend that more emphasis be placed on amenities areas and services within the club. People tend to trade up as their income rises. Likewise, they tend to trade up in the club business as they mature and become more affluent. This tendency can be forestalled by providing the same services and amenities as the more upscale competitors. Moreover, the profit margin in amenities areas such as food and beverage is routinely higher than that enjoyed by the club dues alone. A future trend will probably be joint ventures between outside vendors providing such amenities and the fitness centers offering them.

Amenities in the corporate setting must be competitive with those of the commercial fitness centers. Many upper executives are also members of other clubs and have come to expect the same or better level of amenities in their corporate fitness centers.

Computers

A discussion of trends in any business would have to include the impact and future importance of computers. The health/fitness field is no exception. Currently, all forms of computer systems are being employed to meet the computing needs of the various aspects of the health/fitness business. For instance, mainframe computers are employed to track medical surveillance data of corporate wellness members to engage in cost-effective and cost-benefit studies. These computers are also used in large corporate programs to store interactive data sets such as health care costs, absenteeism, and productivity records. The amount of data collected on each individual across years of service to a company becomes awesome and requires the capacity of large computer systems.

Minicomputers are used in numerous fitness centers to store medical and fitness evaluation data on members and then to apply commercially available software to interact with these data to assist the staff in the counseling process. The use of software programs to assist the staff in counseling members on their dietary and exercise needs is becoming commonplace, and it permits the ratio of highly trained staff to entry level staff to be smaller, thus economizing on staff expenses. The minicomputer can also be used in data base management for business applications. In fact, most of the well-known fitness- and wellness-related software companies also supply business packages in their inventory of software. Some of the business applications in the software inventories include data base management, word processing, and spread sheet and budget management. The minicomputer is widely used in commercial fitness centers and will probably continue to be used at an even greater rate in the future.

Microprocessors are used in many of the individualized equipment items such as office machines, environmental control equipment, laundry machines, exercise equipment, and security systems. Today, very little of what we do is not being influenced by the microprocessor. The age of the computer is upon us and we may as well take advantage of its capabilities.

Future developments in computer applications are almost limitless; however, some of the more prominent trends in the offing appear to be in the areas of voice recognition and voice simulation, coupled with artificial intelligence. These advancements would permit a verbal dialogue with a computer system similar to that of two individuals in conversation, yet provide the individual with the awesome capabilities of having a computer at his or her verbal command. The user-friendliness of this breakthrough in computers would greatly enhance the capabilities of our programs and their operations.

Interactive computerization is probably a safe prediction for future trends. Imagine a scenario that permits members to enter the control desk area, validate their membership, and call up their file by voice-activated computer terminals. Their cardiovascular workout could be preselected by a voice-activated unit on the exercise station of choice, and the work load could be modulated at the prescribed level and duration. These data could then be converted to calories, stored, and later called up for a member profile update. The interactions are almost limitless. Consider the corporate setting, for example, in

which both medical data are generated and cafeterias are provided. The interaction capabilities of food selection and exercise experiences together with medical status monitoring are reminiscent of Orwell's *1984*. Although the issues of free will and privacy are apparent, there is merit in the concept of facilitating a healthy lifestyle through the use of interactive computer systems. Medical surveillance to perform epidemiology studies and cost-benefit studies are further examples of justification for such technological applications.

Cardiovascular Exercise Equipment

There are several new trends in the area of cardiovascular exercise equipment. The traditional flywheel and gravity-resisted cycle ergometers, motor driven treadmills, and jump ropes remain the stalwarts of the industry. Yet the trend in this area is similar to that of other areas—diversification. We find that rowers, ski trainers, downhill ski trainers, recumbent quadripedal trainers, climbing devices, motorized stair-stepping equipment, and rebounding trampolines complement the traditional equipment. The list will undoubtedly get longer as we continue to accommodate the consumer demand for exercise equipment variety.

Within each type of equipment, it is not uncommon to find a variety of different approaches. The cycle ergometer, for example, can be purchased with different methods of work load production, monitoring, video feedback, and microprocessor capabilities. In regard to work load production, examples include the gravity-resisted Monarch bike, the electronic load-resistance bike, the wind-resisted Airdyne bike, and geared bikes that can be placed on rollers to create variable resistance. The bicycle ergometers can be purchased with no monitoring or with graduations of sophistication that will soon include monitored heart rates that can modulate work loads to accommodate a given target heart rate for a programmed period of time. Commonplace are units that have preprogrammed work loads that can produce interval, steady state, or combination training periods that are preceded by warm-up and followed by cool-down periods.

Neuromuscular Strength Equipment

Strength equipment has undergone the same growth patterns and diversification as the cardiovascular equipment. The traditional free weight equipment developed during the post-World War II period lost its popularity during the 1960s when multistation systems of rack-mounted weight plates were developed. Later, the cam-loaded units such as Nautilus, plus the hydraulic and pneumatic units of recent times, have competed for the more demanding consumer of weight training equipment. Recently there has been a resurgence in the popularity of traditional free weight units.

The present trend in most health/fitness clubs is to offer a wide variety of training modalities. It is not uncommon to find the contemporary club touting free weights, Nautilus, Hydra-Fitness, and Keiser equipment in the same complex, hoping to meet the needs and interests of the various market segments.

The anticipated trends will undoubtedly be linked to technological developments in fitness equipment. Electronics will continue to be incorporated into the product lines. Although the trends are somewhat driven by the high-tech influences, there will probably always be a place for the free weights, be-

cause it is difficult to replace the experience of overcoming a large and awesome barbell system. The dominion of the lifter over the barbell will continue to satisfy a primordial need, and free weights will be periodically resurrected amidst the ongoing technological advances.

Aquatics Facilities

A number of interesting trends are emerging in aquatics facilities, most notably the variable-level floor, which is routinely adjustable from 6 feet deep to a mere 6 inches deep. This variable depth permits a wide variety of aquatic programming for all age levels and also permits wheelchair entry without the need for a hoist. Another innovation is separated air currents over the water surface and the walking/lounging surfaces to accommodate the need for different humidities and temperatures in these areas.

Another advancement is in the materials used for pool construction. Stainless steel is becoming a popular, but expensive, option to the tiled surfaces that predominated in the past. It is not known what influence the unfounded fears of disease transmission of AIDS and herpes have had in the introduction of these materials, but the fact that stainless steel can be treated with fairly caustic solutions in the cleaning process has been mentioned by more than one club owner. The stainless steel pool is more expensive up front, but cost-effective in the long haul because of the lower cost-maintenance history.

The introduction of the miniaturized flume has enjoyed recent popularity. For those clubs whose space or budget limitations rule out a pool, the miniflume may be the answer. A serious swimmer can enter a deep, 10-foot long bathtub-type structure and turn on some adjustable water jets to prevent traveling any horizontal distance while swimming in the flume. This water treadmill is relatively inexpensive and space conserving and offers the serious swimmer a place to train in the club without an Olympic-sized pool. The appeal of this innovation has yet to stand the test of time.

Racquet Court Facilities

The popularity of racquet sports and handball has waned in recent years. However, the attempts to convert these spaces have resulted in some creative innovations. Walleyball, for example, has been developed to accommodate a team activity related to volleyball and played in the racquetball court spaces. A small free weight area is also ideal in a former racquetball court as well. The space can be arranged to ensure security as well as isolation of the serious lifters from the recreational weight trainers. The trend toward multipurpose facilities has placed the burden of change on the single-purpose club undergoing the pressures of financial survival.

This is not to suggest that the demise of court games is at hand. On the contrary, racquet games remain one of the more popular areas in our facilities. One trend worthy of mention in the handball/racquetball facility is the panel-wall system of fiber resin, which remains the most durable and maintenance free of the choices available. In addition, the trend is toward using the higher ranges of restitution (32-pounds per square inch are commercially available) to provide a solid sound and play to the game. Then, an extra layer of malamine overlay is added to the playing surface; this assures greater life expectancy and lower maintenance of the walls. Glass walls have been a recent addition to the game, especially in competition courts where spectators will be watching.

Aerobics Facilities

Aerobics classes have, by necessity, experienced some significant changes. These classes were originally taught in a multipurpose gym and scheduled between basketball games and volleyball tournaments. Today, however, the aerobics studio is a very important area in any fitness center. The sound system requirements have necessitated acoustical engineering. The floor systems have had to undergo significant changes to develop the restitution necessary to minimize impact-related injuries. Spring-loaded hardwood floors are at the moment one of the more popular surfaces, followed by heavily padded carpet surfaces that are sealed and plastic-laminate-bonded to inhibit moisture penetration beyond the pile textures. This permits regular steam cleaning and avoids the hygiene problems of accumulated perspiration in the depths of a thick carpet or its pad. Another attempt to accommodate the injury problem is the introduction of low- or no-impact aerobics classes. At any rate, the trend is definitely toward providing rhythmical exercise classes taught to upbeat contemporary music, especially for those who enjoy the creative and social dimensions to exercise. The appeal of rhythmical activities is here to stay, although the means by which it is manifested is an evolving phenomenon.

The natural size assumed by an aerobics area, coupled with the fact that many such facilities have a raised platform for better instructor visibility, provides a natural space in a facility for meetings. The sound systems can also be used for group meetings. This space can then be used for behavioral programming such as classes in nutrition, weight management, smoking cessation, low back pain management, substance-abuse control, and so forth. All that is required in such a place is a small storage area to keep stacked chairs. The trend toward multiple use of spaces, in the face of limited resources and stiff competition, is important. One must use every square foot of lease or purchase space wisely to be more cost-effective.

Gymnasium Considerations

The trend in gymnasiums is to get the most bang for the buck by using the space in as many ways as possible. A single gym floor area could, in the course of a day, be used for basketball, volleyball, badminton, tennis, and indoor soccer, as well as all the functions performed in the aerobics studio, if such an area is unavailable. Because multiuse is the trend, it is very likely that technology will permit the selective highlighting of the court lines as needed to avoid confusion. Small track lights will be imbedded in the floor surface and selectively rheostated for highlighting a given court use. Such low-wattage lights permit many or no boundaries to be highlighted on a floor surface, thus reducing confusion and improving the floor appearance.

Lighting systems are tending toward low-pressure sodium lighting because of superior performance at lower costs. The only negative feature of these systems is the unnatural gray light that emits from the structures. However, the low-pressure sodium light system is worth serious consideration.

Outdoor Facilities

Numerous outdoor facilities could be included in a discussion of trends in our industry. However, this discussion will be limited to the few areas that directly affect health/fitness programming. Perhaps one of the more recent trends is the increased use of greenbelt perimeters that serve a dual purpose of creating attractive boundary markings and providing running/biking and exercise paths. These areas are usually surfaced with an all-weather composition and have strategically placed exercise stations around the path. Frequently, planned stretching stations are included in the circuit as well. In some facilities speakers for music are mounted on lampposts to provide a pleasant background and extended nighttime programming capability. However, this is a mixed blessing, as many urban area facilities have found that outdoor areas pose security and safety problems at night. One way to alleviate this is to mount cameras strategically on the lampposts to provide participant monitoring during the crime-prone hours of the evening.

PROGRAM CONSIDERATIONS

Many new trends exist in health/fitness programming. Perhaps the most prominent is the wellness movement, or the move from exercise- and fitness-related services only toward the introduction of holistic health services. These services include nutrition, weight control, stress management, substance-abuse control, and low back pain management. Such wellness programs are usually preceded by an appraisal of health risk or health behavior. Once the net score is obtained in different assessment areas, then counseling and programming are directed toward the needs and interests of the club member. This approach is similar to the triage system in medicine, in that participants at high risk are triaged into treatments that address the most critical problems first and postpone less critical problems until later.

Special Events Programming

Special events programming is very popular at the moment, including fun runs, body building contests, group travel excursions, special population events keyed to ability and interest, and triathlons. All of these special events develop cohesion and renewed interest among members and serve as a hook for continued and new membership.

Special Population Programming

Modified programming is another means of addressing the needs of special interest groups. For instance, a power-walking group could be added for the older or overweight members, and a low-impact aerobics class could be added for the orthopedically challenged aerobics enthusiasts. Any modification that can be made in the regular programming that appeals to other member segments is worth considering. This is a trend that will probably distinguish the surviving clubs from those that struggle or perish.

Family Programming

Family involvement is an important trend in the industry. Baby-sitting and nursery services are becoming an expected service in the club industry. Special weekend time periods during which adult members can bring the entire family to the club for events exclusively scheduled for them are becoming popular.

Professional Liability

Professional liability is a growing concern in many service industries, and the health/ fitness business is no exception. Corporate fitness programs have been relatively spared from this concern to date because many are self-insured and claims are infrequent, but safe and prudent procedures are always important. The cost of liability insurance is becoming so prohibitive that many private club owners are either going out of business or are dropping their policies and risking the possibility of a devastating lawsuit.

Special Market Segment Programs

Many programs are now marketing their services in creative ways to many different market segments. For example, the one-on-one training concept is a programming twist that provides a personal exercise trainer to be scheduled for each member. Although this is an expensive service, several programs and individuals have instituted this type of program. Some creative individuals have started offering this service to home-bound and/or time-urgent individuals by having a fitness van, loaded with exercise equipment, dispatched to the home-serviced clientele.

Flextime

Flextime is another interesting concept that impacts program delivery. In corporate programs where the employee has traditionally had a standard workday and a noon hour lunch break, competition for those time periods arises among nursery services, cafeterias, employee fitness centers, and staff training and development classes. Flexible work hours could provide for an early arrival and a late departure to accommodate the needs of an extended midday break. This and other types of flexible scheduling can reduce some of the burdens of peak programming times, because employees can schedule their exercise breaks at less congested time periods.

Customer Mixes

Heterogeneous users create a programming problem in some settings such as hotels and hospitals. For instance, in a hospital-based exercise facility, at any one point in time there could be an outpatient working on a physical therapy program, a hospital employee implementing an exercise prescription resulting from the comprehensive test battery offered in the hospital-supported employee fitness program, and a corporate membership person who just came in for a workout. These mixes challenge the continuity of a program and pose a real problem for those concerned about quality exercise prescriptions and undisturbing health/fitness environments.

PERSONNEL CONSIDERATIONS

Staff members in the corporate, commercial, community, and clinical settings will be the discriminating factor for success in the future. Most facilities now have bright, shiny equipment located in well-lighted and carpeted areas, but many commercial clubs have yet to make the investment necessary to secure, train, and retain quality staff. One manager of a large commercial facility recently reported that the average employment longevity of entry level staff was 6 months. One must wonder if this is related to compensation, working conditions, ability level, academic background, or other factors that contribute to the attrition of professional staff. At any

rate, the role of the staff member in all settings is changing.

The hospital-based programs have traditionally had a professional staffing situation of haves and have-nots, where the physicians and administrators were in the former grouping and the remainder of the staff were in the latter. The introduction of the hospital-based wellness programs has resulted in an attempt, in many situations, to reassign a nurse to the wellness center. In some cases this may work quite well, especially when the individual may have another degree or some experience in a health-promotion-related field. In other cases, however, the reassigned person is a poor role model and is ill-equipped by training and experience to function in a wellness setting. Most recognized hospital programs have sought out trained and experienced professionals in the health/fitness field. Others are now realizing that the key to the success of this new profit center is qualified personnel. The health promotion specialist is usually one with an advanced degree and several years of management experience, commanding a salary exceeding that of the nursing staff. Although hospital administrators have been slow to recognize the supply/demand characteristics of this growing field, they are now attending to the situation and modifying their job descriptions and salary ranges. Ultimately, this will impact favorably the field and the clients being served.

The commercial setting is not a great deal different from the hospitals in that personnel has been traditionally viewed as the area in which cost containment is exercised. Traditional wisdom has held that any young person who is a good role model can serve effectively in the programming of health/fitness. However, the demanding consumer, who is now a much more informed consumer, is placing greater demands on the commercial staff member. Various attempts have been made to rectify this staff development problem. One of the trends has been to install computerized software packages to assess and prescribe for the staff, thus permitting computers to supplement a generally less qualified staff than would be required without the computer support. This approach has helped, but there is no substitute for the dialogue between an informed and caring staff member and the program participant. Another trend that seems to have merit is hiring one well-trained and experienced staff member at a high level whose main function is to supervise the staff development of entry level employees. This is extremely popular among clubs that have franchised or merged with other clubs and can share the expense of the staff trainer.

Certification Programs

Over two dozen certification programs for professionals now exist in our field. Some of these programs are intended to be broadly conceived and implemented. The ACSM certification programs (discussed in earlier chapters) are an example of these certifications. In addition, some certification programs are very specific in focus. The Aerobics and Fitness Association of America, for example, offers a certification for exercise instructors primarily involved with adult aerobics classes. Then, there are single facilities such as the Aerobics Center that offer different workshops culminating in certification examinations. Although the proliferation of these certification programs is not providing a uniform upgrading of the professional personnel in our field, there is clearly an attempt among organizations to develop a better trained professional. This trend, coupled with enhanced professional preparation programs in colleges, and

licensure by the states, may combine to create a much improved practicing professional in our field.

FUTURE TRENDS

A number of forces are acting on our profession that will have a definite influence on the direction our field will take in the future. These influences will be the basis for our future trends. A few of these future trends are discussed in the following paragraphs.

Geriatric Fitness Programs

The baby boomers have now turned 40 years of age, and these people represent the very core of the fitness boom. The baby boomers will be of retiring age in about 20 years, and it is very likely that their heightened health consciousness will remain intact and the geriatric programs will have to accommodate their interests. Thus there will be a real need for trained professionals and upgraded facilities for this large segment of our society.

Incorporated Fitness Programs

Both consumer sophistication and competition for those consumers have increased in the marketplace. The demands of the informed consumer are rapidly approaching the information level of many of the entry level professionals. Indeed, with the knowledge turnover rate increasing as it is, the intelligent and interested club member may have a knowledge-base edge on many staff members due to more reading resources and leisure time for avocational interests. Small sole proprietorships cannot afford the luxury of having the staff trainer that a chain operation might provide. Also, the economies of scale provided by the incorporated fitness conglomerate can provide many services unavailable to the mom-and-pop operation. Better resource management and the power of quantity buying are but a few of the advantages offered by incorporations. Merging facilities and programs has already begun. A small number have already captured a sizable portion of the market.

High-Technology Programs

The age of high technology will continue to affect our programs in many ways. In many programs the technology has already outstripped the staffing capability. Examples include the computerized card readers for logging in to the facility, the interactive computer programs available for prescription and programming, and the management software programs. When this technology is compared to the level of sophistication of, for example, the floor exercise leader, the deficit is apparrent in most situations. This deficit will get even larger unless management provides a vehicle to minimize the differential between the technology available and the services delivered by the staff.

Future Markets

There are a number of directions that our field may take in the future, but we don't think the major growth will be in traditional corporate or community programs. We believe that hospital-based facilities and programs will be particularly expansive in the future as they continue to respond to shrinking resources and changes in traditional medical practice.

Another marketplace that is particularly bright is the hotel and real estate development industry. Renters and travelers are now expecting to continue their wellness lifestyle as they move to new quarters or travel in their business. Fitness facilities in these settings are becoming an important marketing tool in such industries.

The American home will become an integral part of the wellness movement. It is conceivable that mini-fitness centers could assume equal importance with other spaces in the home such as game rooms, media rooms, and other recent innovations. When homes incorporate fitness into their construction, we will then take comfort that wellness is here to stay—one's home is a statement of who and what its owner is and wants to be.

SUMMARY

This discussion of present and future trends is the result of active reading, researching, consulting, and writing in the health/fitness field, as well as being involved with curriculum development in professional preparation programs and certification development. It is very likely that some trends have been overlooked or misread. It is very important, however, that we occasionally take the time and effort to find out where we are so that we can establish and achieve new goals.

References

Albrecht, K. (1978). *Successful management by objectives*. Englewood Cliffs, NJ: Prentice Hall.

American College of Sports Medicine. (1980). *Guidelines for graded exercise testing and exercise prescription* (2nd ed.). Philadelphia: Lea & Febiger

American College of Sports Medicine. (1986). *Guidelines for graded exercise testing and exercise prescription*. Philadelphia: Lea & Febiger.

American College of Sports Medicine. (1988). *Resource manual for guidelines for exercise testing and prescription*. Philadelphia: Lea & Febiger.

American Heart Association. (1984). *Heart at work: Exercise program*. Dallas, TX: Author.

American Hospital Association. (1982). *Planning hospital health promotion services for business and industry*. Chicago: Author.

Assael, H. (1985). *Marketing management*. Boston: Wadsworth.

Athletic Institute and American Alliance of Health, Physical Education, Recreation and Dance. (1983). *Planning facilities for athletics, physical education and recreation*. Washington, DC: The Athletic Institute.

Berg, R. (1985, October). Clubs cry foul over tax exemption. *Athletic Business*, p. 28.

Beyond babysitting: Licensed child care in the club. (1985, July). *IRSA Club Business*, p. 32.

Blake, G., & Bly, R.W. (1983). *How to promote your own business*. New York: New American Library.

Blanchard, K., & Johnson, S. (1982). *The one minute manager*. New York: Berkley Books.

Blanchard, M., & Tager, M. (1985). *Waking well*. New York: Simon & Schuster.

Breuleux, C.E. (1982). *A profile of corporate fitness directors*. Unpublished doctoral dissertation, Ohio State University, Columbus.

Bronzan, R.T. (1974). *New concepts in planning and funding athletic, physical education and recreation facilities*. Danville, CA: APER.

Brox, A. (1986, August). How to get a bank loan. *Club Industry*, p. 36.

Burstiner, I. (1977). *A comprehensive guide to starting and running your own business*. Englewood Cliffs, NJ: Prentice Hall.

Chaet, M. (1985, February). Building a solid rate structure. *Club Industry*, pp. 18-21.

Chapman, L.S. (1984). *A comprehensive look at the cost-effectiveness of wellness programs in the workplace*. Paper presented at the Association for Fitness in Business conference.

Chenoweth, D.H. (1987). *Planning health promotion at the worksite*. Indianapolis, IN: Benchmark.

Connor, R.A., & Davidson, J.P. (1985). *Marketing your consulting and professional services*. New York: Wiley.

DeMars, D. (1985, September 10). Ten commandments of profitability, pp. 38-40.

Dillman, D. (1978). *Mail and telephone surveys: The total design method*. New York: Wiley.

Drucker, P.F. (1980). *Managing in turbulent times*. New York: Harper & Row.

Epperson, A. (1977). *Private and commercial recreation: A text and reference*. New York: Wiley.

Exerflex. (1986). *How to select a safe aerobics floor*. Terstep Recreation, Junkers Sport Floors.

A feasibility checklist for additions and conversions. (1984, October). *Club Business*, pp. 25-27.

Fielding, J.E. (1982). Effectiveness of employee health improvement programs. *Journal of Occupational Medicine, 24*, 907-916.

Fitzgerald, R.W. (1982). *Design and construction of racquetball and fitness clubs*. Cambridge, MA: IRSA.

Flynn, R.B. (1985). *Planning facilities for athletics, physical education and recreation*. Reston, VA: American Alliance for Health, Physical Education, Recreation, and Dance.

Front desk management: The foundation of every club. (1985, September). *Club Business*, p. 35.

Game Plan, Inc. (1985). *Why people join* (special report). Boston: International Racquet Sports Association.

Gerson, R.F. (1985). *Marketing fitness services*. Ft. Meyers, FL: Gerson Publications.

Gerson, R.F. (1986). How to best prepare yourself for a career in corporate fitness. *Aerobics & Fitness, 4*, 58-59.

Gerson, R.F. (1989). *Marketing health/fitness services*. Champaign, IL: Human Kinetics.

Gettman, L.R. (1986). Cost/benefit analysis of a corporate fitness program. *Fitness in Business, 1*, 11-17.

Hayes, J. (1986, February/March). Locker room convenience: The key to compliance. *Corporate Fitness and Recreation*, p. 38.

Health promotion in the marketing mix. (1986, May/June). *Optimal Health*, pp. 70-71.

Heckelman, R. (1987, February). Nurseries: Who needs kids? Maybe your club does. *Club Industry*, p. 61.

Herbert, D.L., & Herbert, W.G. (1984). *Legal aspects of preventive and rehabilitative exercise programs*. Canton, OH: Professional & Executive Reports & Publications.

Herzberg, F. (1966). *Work and the nature of man*. Cleveland, OH: World.

Hunsaker, D.J. (1984, May). Pitfalls abound in natatorium design. *Athletic Business*, pp. 30-33.

Industry briefing. (1987, June). *Athletic Business*, p. 15.

Institute for Aerobics Research. (1981). *Workshops and certificate of proficiency in the management of exercise and fitness programs*. Dallas, TX: Division of Continuing Education, The Aerobics Center.

International Racquet Sports Association. (1984). *1984 Industry Data Survey*. Boston: Pannell Kerr Forster.

International Racquet Sports Association. (1984). *Pro shop management: A special report*. Boston: Author.

Jense, J., & Miklovic, N. (1985, December 20). Occupational health, wellness offerings gaining popularity among employers. *Modern Healthcare*.

Johnson, B.L. (1982). *Private consulting*. Englewood Cliffs, NJ: Prentice Hall.

Jolly, C. (1983, June/July). Locker rooms: Is there room for improvement? *Corporate Fitness & Recreation*, pp. 13-20.

Kilburg, P., & Strischek, D. (1985, December). Lending to health clubs. *IRSA Club Industry*, pp. 49-56.

Kizer, W.M. (1987). *The healthy workplace: A blueprint for corporate action*. New York: Wiley.

Kurtz, D., & Boone, L.E. (1984). *Marketing*. New York: CBS College Publishing.

Lasser, J. (1983). *How to run a small business* (5th ed.). New York: McGraw Hill.

Lauffer, R. (1986, July). Sauna and steam rebirth of the ancient baths. *Athletic Business*, p. 44.

Locke, E.A., & Latham, G.P. (1984). *Goal setting: A motivational technique that works*. Englewood Cliffs, NJ: Prentice Hall.

Locker room can be your star attraction. (1984, April). *Athletic Business*, pp. 56-60.

Locker rooms: Home away from home. (1984, October). *Fitness Industry*, pp. 34-36.

Manuso, J.S.J. (1983). The Equitable Life Assurance Society Program. *Preventive Medicine, 12*, 658-662.

Maslow, A. (1965). *Eupsychian management*. Homewood, IL: Irwin.

McCaffrey, M. (1983). *Personal marketing strategies*. Englewood Cliffs, NJ: Prentice Hall.

McCarthy, J. (1984, February). Club marketing strategies: Price trends. *Club Industry*, p. 41.

McCarthy, J. (1985, October). Challenges, opportunities in the club industry. *Athletic Business*, p. 38.

McCarthy, J. (1986, March). Profitable clubs and how they do it. *Athletic Business*, pp. 26-35.

McGregor, D. (1967). *The professional manager*. New York: McGraw Hill.

Murphy, P.E., & Enis, B.M. (1985). *Marketing*. Glenview, IL: Scott, Foresman.

Nash, M. (1985). *Making people productive*. San Francisco: Jossey-Bass.

National Health Enhancement Systems. (1987). *The heart test: A risk factor analysis*. Phoenix, AZ: Author.

The new locker room: Pampering the clientele. (1985, April). *Athletic Business*, pp. 38-41.

Opatz, J.P. (1985). *A primer of health promotion*. Washington, DC: Oryn Publications.

Patton, D. (1986, January). Hard versus soft water: Finding the perfect mean. *Club Industry*, p. 44.

Patton, R.W., Corry, J.M., Gettman, L.R., & Graf, J.S. (1986). *Implementing health/fitness programs*. Champaign, IL: Human Kinetics.

Penman, K.A. (1977). *Planning physical education and athletic facilities in schools*. New York: Wiley.

Peters, T., & Austin, N. (1985). *A passion for excellence*. New York: Random House.

Peters, T.J., & Waterman, R.H. (1982). *In search of excellence*. New York: Harper & Row.

Pfeiffer, G.J. (1986). Management aspects of fitness program development. *American Journal of Health Promotion, 1*, 10-18.

Porter, D. (1982). *Hospital architecture: Guidelines for design and renovation*. Ann Arbor, MI: Aupha Press.

Poveromo, T. (1984, May 20). Where the spas are. *Sunshine*, pp. 6-9.

Pravosudov, V.P. (1978). Effects of physical exercises on health and economic efficiency. In O. Landry (Ed.), *Physical activity and human well-being* (pp. 261-271). Miami: Symposium Specialists.

Reibstein, D.J. (1985). *Marketing*. Englewood Cliffs, NJ: Prentice Hall.

Ross, T. (1985, June). Managing risk. *Athletic Business*, p. 22.

Rubenstein, L., & Reed, L. (1985, July). Behind-the-scenes design: Preventing water leakage. *IRSA Club Business*, p. 56.

Schlant, R.C., et al. (1986). Guidelines for exercise testing: A report of the American College of Cardiology/American Heart Association Task Force on Assessment of Cardiovascular Procedures (Subcommittee on Exercise Testing). *Journal of the American College of Cardiology, 8*, 725-738.

Shephard, R.J. (1986). *Fitness and health in industry*. New York: Karger.

Slick ads don't guarantee success. (1987, May/June). *Optimal Health*, pp. 28-30.

Smith, S.A. (1984, July). Swimming pools. *Club Business*, pp. 25-26.

Sports club design: Fitting facilities to program plans. (1985, April). *Athletic Business*, pp. 22-30.

Strategic planning: A calculated bet on the future. (1987). *Optimal Health, 3,* 24-28.

Strategic planning doesn't stop with the plan. (1987, March/April). *Optimal Health,* pp. 25-28.

Tarkenton, F. (1986). *How to motivate people.* New York: Harper & Row.

Training your staff to maximize service. (1987, April). *Athletic Business.*

Udeleff, M. (1984, June/July). Locker rooms. *Corporate Fitness & Recreation,* pp. 51-54.

Vander Zwaag, H. (1984). *Sport management.* New York: Wiley.

✳ Wheatley, E.W. (1985). *Marketing professional services.* Englewood Cliffs, NJ: Prentice Hall.

Whitehead, R. (1986, July). Word pictures: A conceptual approach to facility planning. *Athletic Business,* pp. 74-79.

Wills, T. (1984). Facility design. In M. O'Donnell & T. Ainsworth (Eds.), *Health promotion in the workplace.* New York: Wiley.

Wineman, J. (1984, June). Managing a profitable pro shop. *Club Business,* p. 21.

✳ YMCA of the USA. (1987). *Health enhancement for America's work force.* Champaign, IL: Human Kinetics.

Zigler, Z. (1986). *Top performance.* Old Tappan, NJ: F.H. Revell.

Index